Principles
of Pictorial Information
Systems Design

Principles
of Pictorial Information
Systems Design

Shi-Kuo Chang
University of Pittsburgh
and
Knowledge Systems Institute

PRENTICE HALL, Englewood Cliffs, New Jersey 07632

Library of Congress Cataloging-in-Publication Data

CHANG, S.K. (SHI-KUO), (date)
  Principles of pictorial information systems design.

  Includes index.
  1. Image processing. I. Title.
TA1632.C44 1989   006   88-17867
ISBN 0-13-710195-3

Editorial/production supervision and
  interior design: *Carol L. Atkins*
Cover design: *Wanda Lubelska Design*
Manufacturing buyer: *Mary Noonan*

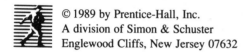 © 1989 by Prentice-Hall, Inc.
A division of Simon & Schuster
Englewood Cliffs, New Jersey 07632

Printed in the United Stated of America

10 9 8 7 6 5 4 3 2 1

ISBN 0-13-710195-3

Prentice-Hall International (UK) Limited, *London*
Prentice-Hall of Australia Pty. Limited, *Sydney*
Prentice-Hall Canada Inc., *Toronto*
Prentice-Hall Hispanoamericana, S.A., *Mexico*
Prentice-Hall of India Private Limited, *New Delhi*
Prentice-Hall of Japan, Inc., *Tokyo*
Simon & Schuster Asia Pte. Ltd., *Singapore*
Editora Prentice-Hall do Brasil, Ltda., *Rio de Janeiro*

Contents

PART I PICTURE PROCESSING AND ANALYSIS

CHAPTER 6   PICTURE ENCODING FOR PICTORIAL DATABASES   122

PART II   PICTORIAL DATABASE DESIGN

CHAPTER 7   PICTORIAL KNOWLEDGE REPRESENTATION   146

Contents

Preface

Pictures are natural means for communication between people and machines. A *pictorial information system* (PIS) is the information system that controls and manages the picture input device, picture processor, picture output device, picture storage system, and picture communication interface to provide a collection of pictorial data for easy access by a large number of users. Until recently, little attention has been paid to the management of nonalphanumeric information—such as digital pictures—which requires a large amount of storage even for pictures of moderate complexity. With the growing list of new applications in pictorial information handling, such as office automation, interactive computer-aided design, robotics, geographic data processing, cartographic and mapping applications, remote sensing of earth resources, medical data processing, medical pictorial archiving and communication systems, and so on, the problem of efficient, economic storage, and flexible retrieval and manipulation of vast amounts of pictorial information has become more important and requires careful consideration. This book is devoted to studying the principles and techniques of pictorial information system design.

The contents of the book can be divided into three parts. The first part includes the five chapters from Chapter 2 to Chapter 6, dealing with principles of picture processing and analysis. Chapter 2 gives fundamentals of picture representations and picture operations. Chapter 3 discusses picture segmentation—one of the main problems in picture processing. Picture information measures, described in Chapter 4, allow us to quantitatively measure the information contents of pictures from the viewpoint of information theory. Chapters 5 and 6 describe picture data coding techniques. Chapter 5 is dedicated to both error-tolerance coding and error-free coding for data compression, while Chapter 6 describes in detail the hypercube encoding method, which is the most effective for picture paging in pictorial database design.

The next four chapters constitute the second part. Here pictorial database design techniques are fully discussed. Recent advances in the field are included and open problems are pointed out. Chapter 7 describes pictorial knowledge representations. Chapter 8 describes zooming, data model, query processing, and picture algebra within the framework of a prototypical pictorial database management system. Chapter 9 discusses an approach for pictorial indexing and abstraction. A methodology for iconic indexing using two-dimensional strings is given in Chapter 10.

The third part, consisting of Chapters 11 and 12, is devoted to the frontiers of research in pictorial information systems design. In Chapter 11, visual languages for pictorial information systems and visually oriented human-machine interfaces are discussed. A classification and survey of various visual languages is presented. In Chapter 12, the concept of generalized icons is advanced as a unifying principle for pictorial information system design and visual language design. The theory of generalized icons is currently under active investigation, and further research is needed to fully realize its potential.

This book is the first of its kind in this increasingly important area. It is intended as a textbook for a graduate course on pictorial information system design, or as a supplementary text for a course on picture processing. It can also be used as a reference book or self-study text for professionals engaged in pictorial information system design. The book is technically oriented and contains exercises at the end of each chapter. For instructors who intend to use this book as a textbook, a solutions manual is available upon request from the publisher.

I started working on this book in early 1977. During the next ten years, many new research results and concepts were gradually incorporated into the draft. In July of 1986, I joined the Computer Science Department of the University of Pittsburgh. A temporary separation from my family led me to work even more feverishly on the draft. In the Fall of 1986, Professor Jian-Kang Wu of China Science and Technology University came to visit me. Because a car accident prevented me from going to work for nearly two months, Professor Wu took the writing project upon himself during this time to further clean up the draft. He made significant contributions to this book, for which I am very grateful. The sacrifice and understanding of my wife Judy was indispensable for the completion of this project. I am proud to devote this book to her and my two lovely daughters, Emily and Cybele.

Shi-Kuo Chang
University of Pittsburgh
and
Knowledge Systems Institute

Chapter 1

Introduction to Pictorial Information Systems

Pictures are natural means for communication between people and machines. A *pictorial information system* (PIS) is the information system that controls and manages the picture input device, picture processor, picture output device, picture storage system, and picture communication interface to provide a collection of pictorial data for easy access by a large number of users. A *pictorial database* (PDB) is a collection of sharable pictorial data encoded in various formats. The pictorial database is the core of a pictorial information system. A schematic diagram of the pictorial information system is shown in Figure 1.1.

Until recently, little attention has been paid to the management of non-alphanumeric information—such as digital pictures—which requires a large amount of storage even for pictures of average complexity. With the growing list of new applications in pictorial information handling, such as office automation, interactive computer-aided design, robotics, geographic data processing, remote sensing of earth resources, medical data processing, medical pictorial archiving and communication systems, cartographic and mapping applications and so on, the problem of efficient, economic storage and flexible retrieval and manipulation of vast amounts of pictorial information has become more important and requires careful consideration. This book is devoted to studying the principles and techniques of pictorial information system design.

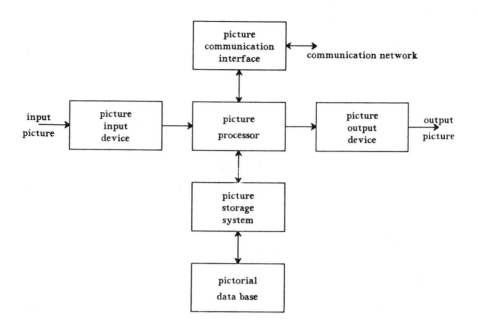

Figure 1.1 Pictorial information system.

1.1 ADVANCES IN PICTORIAL INFORMATION SYSTEMS

Advances in pictorial information system design are technology driven. New hardware devices include the following:

a. Picture Input Device. High-resolution scanners with a resolution of several hundred to a couple of thousand lines per inch are now available. Moreover, there are now many low-cost input devices, including document scanners, video cameras, digitizers, and so on which are available for mini- and microcomputers.

b. Picture Processor. Stand-alone picture processors incorporating microprocessors and array processors can be interfaced with most mini- and microcomputers. Their processing functions include pixel-by-pixel processing, spatial convolution, zoom, rotation, floating-point vector and matrix processing, smoothing, enhancement, and so on. The availability of low-cost picture processors means that many picture processing and signal processing functions previously requiring a lot of computation time can now be off-loaded to these processors and computed efficiently. Highly parallel systems can also be configured to further improve processing speed.

c. Picture Output Device. High-resolution color graphics raster displays, typically with display resolution of up to 1024 by 1024 pixels and multiple colors, offer high-quality pictorial and graphic output. High-resolution laser printers and plotters can be used to generate hard copies.

d. Picture Storage System. Video-disk technology offers the means of creating and maintaining nonerasable pictorial databases. There is also renewed interest in using microfiche for storage and retrieval of large quantities of pictures. A minicomputer stores the microfilm address and key descriptors and controls the retrieval of specific documents. Such an electronic filing system can be used to create and maintain a pictorial database.

e. Computer Communications Networks. In addition to these hardware components and systems, the recent advances in data communications, especially broadband local area networks, provide the means to interconnect many workstations for *multimedia communication,* including voice, data, and picture.

With these technological innovations, now it is possible to put together a pictorial information system, as illustrated in Figure 1.1, at a reasonable cost.

1.2 NEEDS FOR PICTORIAL INFORMATION SYSTEMS

Pictorial information systems are needed *as subsystems* for advanced information systems in many application areas, and *as stand-alone systems,* depending on the needs and practical applications. Pictorial information systems are finding applications in at least the following six broad areas.

1.2.1 Fifth Generation Computer Systems

Fifth generation computer systems are knowledge information processing systems based on innovative theories and technologies that can offer advanced functions expected to be required in the 1990s, overcoming technical restrictions inherent in conventional computers. In these systems, machine intelligence will be greatly improved, and the human-machine interface will come closer to the human system. The intelligent user interface functions include the capabilities of understanding speech, image, natural language, and so on. For many new applications, such as real-time sign language understanding, an intelligent user interface capable of picture communication and image understanding is required.

1.2.2 Office Information Systems

The ability to handle documents and forms is required for almost all office information systems. Certain fields in documents and forms, such as signature fields, photographs, special symbols, and so on, also have a natural image representation. Since documents often contain both text and graphics data, they are sometimes better treated as pictures (or document pictures). Such document pictures need to be created, encoded, edited, stored, retrieved, and transmitted. Since office information systems are distributed systems designed around local area networks, picture communications and multimedia communications are emphasized in such systems.

1.2.3 Computer-Aided Design Systems

Computer-aided design (CAD) is an increasingly important pictorial database application area. Research projects are being undertaken at many research laboratories as well as universities. Investigations on CAD/CAM (computer-aided manufacturing) database design, which is closely related to pictorial database design, have also received increasing attention.

1.2.4 Image Understanding Systems

Image understanding (IU) systems are traditionally of interest to defense-related industries. More recently, we have seen interest widen to include other industries, such as the aerospace and semiconductor industries. A combination of image understanding, knowledge base, and pictorial information handling is needed in the design of sophisticated image understanding systems. The pictorial information system is a useful tool, and an important subsystem, for such systems.

1.2.5 Computer-Integrated Manufacturing Systems

For computer vision systems in robotics and computer-aided manufacturing, a pictorial information system is also needed as a subsystem. For example, in automated very-large-scale-integrated (VLSI) chip inspection, hundreds and thousands of mask patterns need to be stored in a pattern database (which is a pictorial database), and the image observed by the electron microscope is analyzed with respect to these reference patterns for possible faults. Manufacturing automation also includes inventory control, warehouse management, parts and materials input and output, and so on. In so-called computer-integrated manufacturing systems (CIM), how to integrate many heterogeneous databases to form an integrated information repertoire becomes an important issue. Pictorial databases are useful not only because of application requirements (for example, the VLSI pattern database just cited) but can also be used as a tool in the description of other databases to be integrated (for example, in the design of CAD or CAM databases, or as a meta-database in a knowledge-based system).

1.2.6 Medical Information Systems

Medical information systems are among the fastest growing application areas which integrate local area networks, advanced workstations, and advanced image processors to provide an integrated environment serving a hospital or health care delivery institution. The concept of medical pictorial archiving and communication systems (PACS) requires the design of sophisticated pictorial information systems with flexible user interface and the ability for picture communication.

The needs for pictorial information systems are summarized in Table 1.1. In Table 1.1, the primary emphasis for each application area is indicated with an "X." It can be seen that for integrated information systems such as office information (OI) systems, CIM systems, and medical information systems, the emphasis is on flexible user interface and picture communications. For other types of information systems, the emphasis is on pictorial databases and pictorial information subsystems as design tools.

TABLE 1.1   NEEDS FOR PICTORIAL INFORMATION SYSTEMS

	Flexible User Interface	Ability for Picture Communication	Design Tools for Various Applications
Fifth Generation Computer Systems	X		X
OI Systems	X	X	
CAD Systems			X
IU Systems			X
CIM Systems	X	X	
Medical Information Systems	X	X	

1.3 REQUIREMENTS FOR PICTORIAL INFORMATION SYSTEMS

To compare the requirements of diversified pictorial information systems, we first list the major features of an (idealized) pictorial information system:

a. Picture Input. The means of capturing or digitizing an optical image, which may be originally on paper, on film, or through a camera.

b. Picture Editing. The means of changing the contents of a digitized picture, as well as interactively or automatically creating a new picture or destroying an old picture.

c. Picture Processing. The enhancement of a picture, edge detection, texture analysis, and segmentation and pattern recognition techniques, as well as algorithmic or optical means of picture transformation.

d. Picture Storage. The formatting, encoding and decoding, data structuring, and indexing of a picture for storage in a given storage medium.

e. Picture Retrieval. The retrieval of a picture from the pictorial database by indexing or by a more flexible means of retrieval using similarity measures or some type of query language.

f. Picture Output. How pictures are displayed and how hard copies are obtained; whether it is possible to obtain image montage and partial images.

g. Picture Communication. How a picture can be transmitted to computers at another location or another workstation.

The requirements of various application areas are listed in Table 1.2.

TABLE 1.2   REQUIREMENTS FOR PICTORIAL INFORMATION SYSTEMS

	Picture Input	Picture Editing	Picture Processing	Picture Storage	Picture Retrieval	Picture Output	Picture Communication
Fifth Generation Computer Systems	Maybe	—	Some	Yes	Yes	Yes	Maybe
OI Systems	Maybe	Maybe	Some	Yes	Yes	Yes	Yes
CAD Systems	Maybe	Yes	—	Yes	Yes	Yes	—
IU Systems	Yes	—	Yes	Maybe	Maybe	Yes	—
CIM Systems	Maybe	—	Some	Yes	Yes	Yes	Yes
Medical Information Systems	Yes	Maybe	Yes	Yes	Yes	Yes	Yes

1.4 ORGANIZATION OF THE BOOK

This book will cover pictorial information system design by focusing attention on the various subsystems illustrated in Figure 1.1.

The contents of the book can be divided into three parts. The first part includes the five chapters from Chapter 2 to Chapter 6, dealing with principles of picture processing and analysis. Chapter 2 gives fundamentals of picture representations and picture operations. Chapter 3 discusses picture segmentation—one of the main problems in picture processing. Picture information measures, described in Chapter 4, allow us to quantitatively measure the information contents of pictures from the viewpoint of information theory. Chapters 5 and 6 describe picture data coding techniques. Chapter 5 is dedicated to both error-tolerance coding and error-free coding for data compression, while Chapter 6 describes in detail the hypercube encoding method, which is the most effective for picture paging in pictorial database design.

The next four chapters constitute the second part. Pictorial database design techniques are fully discussed in this part. Recent advances in the field are included, and open problems are pointed out. Chapter 7 describes pictorial knowledge representations. Chapter 8 describes zooming, data model, query processing, and picture algebra within the framework of a prototypical pictorial database management system. Chapter 9 discusses an approach for pictorial indexing and abstraction. A methodology for iconic indexing using 2D strings is given in Chapter 10.

The third part, consisting of Chapter 11 and Chapter 12, is devoted to the frontiers of research in pictorial information systems design. In Chapter 11, visual languages for pictorial information systems and visually oriented human-machine interfaces are discussed. A classification and survey of various visual languages is presented. In Chapter 12, the concept of generalized icons is advanced as a unifying principle for pictorial information system design and visual language design.

Throughout this book, we emphasize the distinction between the *physical picture* and the *logical picture*. Traditional picture processing and analysis deal mainly with the processing and analysis of physical pictures. Part I of this book covers these classical approaches. Traditional database systems deal mainly with logical representation of information. Part II extends the approaches and techniques of database systems for the storage, manipulation, and retrieval of logical pictures. The final goal of pictorial information systems, however, is to effectively present both the physical picture (the visual image) and the logical picture (the underlying meaning) to the user in an integrated manner to enhance understanding. This combination of visual form (syntax) and logical meaning (semantics) leads to the concept of a *visual language*. It is therefore not surprising that visual languages have become the focus of active research in recent years. Visual languages are covered in Part III.

The combination of logical picture and physical picture also leads to the notion of *generalized icons*. Within this framework of the theory of generalized icons, we can best appreciate the relative roles played by the classical approach to picture processing and analysis, the syntactic approach to pattern recognition and picture analysis, and the more recent knowledge-based approach to image understanding. Since pictorial information systems incorporate all these aspects, we conclude this book by an exposition of the theory of generalized icons and its applications.

1.5 ACKNOWLEDGMENTS

The sources of the approaches and techniques described in various chapters are usually given in the references at the end of each chapter. In addition to these sources, three books should be mentioned specifically. Sections 2.1, 2.2, 3.3, 3.4, 7.1, 7.2.2, 7.3, and 7.4 follow closely the treatment of similar topics given by Ballard and Brown [BALLARD82]. Section 2.3 and Appendices I and II follow closely the treatment of similar topics given by Castleman [CASTLEMAN79]. Appendix III follows closely the treatment of similar topics given by [BALLARD82] and [WOS84]. In addition to this general acknowledgment, the use of any specific photograph from these books or other sources will be acknowledged individually. This author is fully responsible for any mistakes in the interpretation of these photographs.

R E F E R E N C E S

[BALLARD82] BALLARD, D. H. AND C. M. BROWN, *Computer Vision*. Englewood Cliffs, New Jersey: Prentice-Hall, Inc., 1982.

[CASTLEMAN79] CASTLEMAN, K. R., *Digital Image Processing*. Englewood Cliffs, New Jersey: Prentice-Hall, Inc., 1979.

[WOS84] WOS, L., R. OVERBEEK, E. LUSK AND J. BOYLE, *Automated Reasoning: Introduction and Applications*. Englewood Cliffs, New Jersey: Prentice-Hall, Inc., 1984.

Part I

Chapter 2

Picture Representations and Operations

This chapter introduces fundamentals of picture representations and picture operations. In Section 2.1, after introducing the discipline of picture processing, the concept of logical and physical picture representations is introduced. Section 2.2 deals with picture functions. Concepts about picture sequence and color space are also presented. Various picture operations are described in Section 2.3. Most picture processing operations are local operations, which can be performed in parallel. Line drawings constitute a kind of picture other than grey level pictures. Some brief discussion about line drawings appears in Section 2.4.

2.1 PICTURE REPRESENTATIONS

Picture processing is the discipline for the processing of digital pictures using computer-based techniques. A picture processing system can be regarded as a specialization of the pictorial information system illustrated in Figure 2.1.

A block diagram for a picture processing system is shown in Figure 2.2. An image is first digitized by an *image digitizer* (the picture input device). The digital picture is then processed by a *picture processor*. The resultant picture is displayed via an *image display* (the picture output device) for viewing by the user.

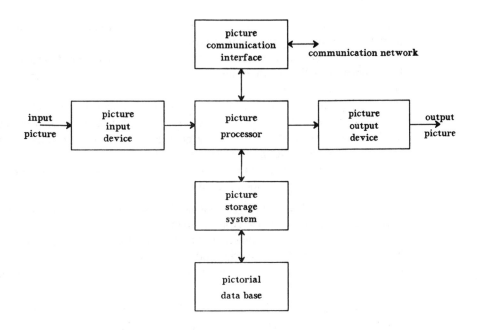

Figure 2.1 Pictorial information system.

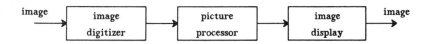

Figure 2.2 A picture processing system.

The most important topics related to picture processing include the following:

1. Digitization
2. Coding and data compression
3. Enhancement and restoration
4. Segmentation
5. Image analysis and description
6. Image understanding
7. Pictorial information management

Traditionally, picture processing usually refers to the first four topics. Computer vision includes the first six topics. Pictorial information system includes all seven topics.

The block diagram shown in Figure 2.2 is not the only type of picture processing system. If the emphasis is on image understanding, the block diagram will be different. Other types of picture processing systems, which can be regarded as variations of the block diagram illustrated in Figure 2.2, will be discussed in Chapter 3.

Our viewpoint is to emphasize the duality of representations (data structures, models) and processing (algorithms, processes).

The representation is closely related to our model for describing the images. Representation will also affect our techniques for processing the images and how we store and retrieve the images.

In what follows, we will use the terms *images* and *pictures* interchangeably. A possible distinction is that image refers to the visual data obtained from input sensory devices or generated at output display devices, whereas picture refers to all kinds of representations derivable from original visual data.

Our viewpoint in picture representations is to consider the duality of physical picture representations and logical picture representations:

1. Physical Picture Representations. Physical picture representations are directly related to the picture obtained from the picture input devices. They include the image as represented by a picture function, the segmented picture as represented by a list of line segments, and the geometric model as represented by a collection of geometric figures [MORTENSON85]. Picture processing usually deals with physical picture representations.

2. Logical Picture Representations. Logical picture representations are high-level abstracted representations, denoting the logical relationships among picture objects. Computer vision and pictorial information management usually emphasize logical picture representations.

A hierarchy of the various representations is illustrated in Figure 2.3. The physical picture representations and logical picture representations together form the picture knowledge base.

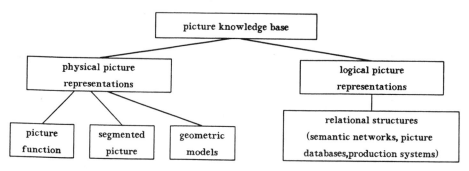

Figure 2.3 A hierarchy of picture representations. Dana H. Ballard/Christopher M. Brown, *COMPUTER VISION*, © 1982, p. 10. Reprinted by permission of Prentice-Hall, Inc., Englewood Cliffs, New Jersey.

Another way of looking at the interplay of representations and processes is to regard the various representations as forming a pyramid structure, as illustrated in Figure 2.4.

Information flow in the pyramid structure is usually from the bottom to the top layer in traditional picture processing operations. On the other hand, in computer vision and image understanding, it is often necessary to send information downward to facilitate low-level processing. For example, to detect defects on an integrated circuit (IC)

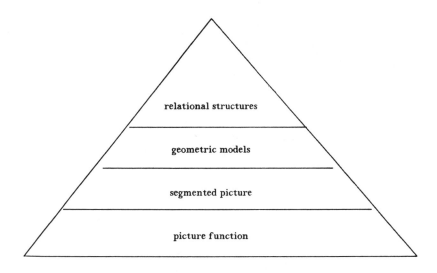

relational structures

geometric models

segmented picture

picture function

Figure 2.4   A pyramid of picture representations.

wafer, we need a model of the mask so we can identify specks and holes in the various areas. In mobile robot maneuvers, the robot must have a world model (a map), so it can recognize landmarks to estimate its own location. Such information can then be incorporated into the knowledge base or used in planning future actions. The point here is that high-level information is needed in low-level processing. We can call it model-based or knowledge-based picture processing.

In Part I of this book, we deal mainly with physical picture representations. Logical picture representations are discussed in Part II. In this chapter, we mainly discuss picture representation using picture functions. Picture segmentation is discussed in Chapter 3. Geometric models are not covered in this book, except for a brief discussion of 3D object representation in Section 6.5 of Chapter 6.

2.2 PICTURE FUNCTION

A *picture function* f(x,y) is a real-valued function of two variables, having values that are nonnegative and bounded, that is, $0 \leq f(x,y) \leq L-1$ for all (x,y). We usually assume that f is analytically well behaved.

When a picture is digitized, a *sampling process* is used to extract from the picture a discrete set of samples, and a *quantization process* is applied to these samples to obtain numbers having a discrete set of values. This is illustrated in Figure 2.5.

The resultant *digital picture function* f, or simply *digital picture,* can be represented by an array of picture elements, or *pixels*. The digital picture function f can be regarded as a mapping from $\{0,...,M-1\} \times \{0,...,N-1\}$ to $\{0,...,L-1\}$. The set, $\{0,...,L-1\}$ is called the *gray level set,* and L is the number of distinct gray levels. For example, if we use 3 bits to represent each pixel, then L is 8. If 8 bits are used, we have 256 distinct gray levels. The two integers M and N represent the size of the digital picture. An example of a digital picture is shown in Figure 2.6.

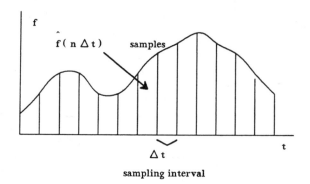

Figure 2.5 The sampling process.

0	1	0	4
1	2	3	0
1	1	1	0

f   **Figure 2.6** A digital picture.

Each point (x,y) in this rectangular grid has a *pixel value* denoted by $f(x,y)$, or a *picture element* (sometimes referred to as *pixel* or *pel*).

A *multi-spectral picture function* is represented by

$$f_f (x,y) = \left\{ f_1 (x,y), f_2 (x,y), ..., f_n (x,y) \right\} \qquad (2.1)$$

where $f_1, f_2, ..., f_n$ are picture functions.

For example, in picture processing as well as computer graphics, we often use the basic colors (red, blue, and green) to create color images. A color image can thus be represented by a multi-spectral picture function:

$$f_f (x,y) = \left\{ f_R (x,y), f_G (x,y), f_B (x,y) \right\} \qquad (2.2)$$

Each pixel $f_f (x, y)$ of this picture f_f thus is represented by (r, g, b) where r, g, b are the pixel values of the three picture functions f_R, f_G, f_B, respectively. The color pixel (r, g, b) is a point in a *color space,* as shown in Figure 2.7(a).

If the intensities r, g, b take on values between 0 and 1, the color space is in fact a *color cube.*

Another way of representing color is to use the three parameters: intensity, saturation, and hue. Intensity can be defined as the sum of r, g, and b, that is,

$$Intensity = r + g + b \qquad (2.3)$$

A constant intensity surface is a plane cutting through the color cube, as shown in Figure 2.7(b).

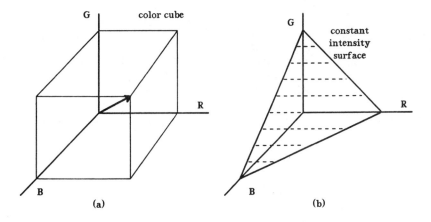

Figure 2.7 (a) The color cube; (b) constant intensity surface.

Saturation specifies how close the color is to a full color. It is defined as

$$Saturation = 1 - 3min(r,g,b)/(r+g+b) \qquad (2.4)$$

On a constant intensity plane, the saturation points occur at the three corners of a triangle with center (c,c,c), where c is one third of the intensity.

Finally, the hue is approximately proportional to the average wavelength of the color. Therefore,

$$hue = \frac{\lambda_r r + \lambda_g g + \lambda_b b}{r+g+b} \qquad (2.5)$$

where λ_r, λ_g, λ_b are the central wavelengths for red, green, and blue colors, respectively. We can rewrite (2.5) as follows:

$$(\lambda_r - hue)r + (\lambda_g - hue)g + (\lambda_b - hue)b = 0 \qquad (2.6)$$

which represents a plane cutting through the origin of the color cube.

We have seen that color images can be represented by multi-spectral picture functions. In addition to multi-spectral picture functions, we sometimes also need multiple picture functions, with multi-spectral picture function as a special case of multiple picture functions.

For example, in computer vision, we often need depth information, so we can reconstruct a three-dimensional model. If we have a range finder, we may use a range (depth) picture in addition to the ordinary gray-level picture. These two pictures considered together can be used to reconstruct a three-dimensional model.

As another example of multiple pictures, consider a pair of stereo images obtained from a binocular system. From these stereo images, we can often estimate depth information. An example for the nonconvergent binocular system is given in Figure 2.8(a).

From Figure 2.8(a), we obtain this:

$$\frac{x_1}{f} = \frac{x+d}{f+w} \qquad \frac{x_2}{f} = \frac{x-d}{f+w}$$

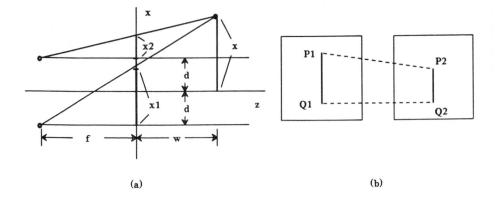

(a)   (b)

Figure 2.8 (a) Triangulation, (b) disparity. Dana H. Ballard/Christopher M. Brown, *COMPUTER VISION*, © 1982, p. 22. Reprinted by permission of Prentice-Hall, Inc., Englewood Cliffs, New Jersey.

Therefore,

$$(f + w)\ x_1 = (x + d)\ f \qquad (f + w)\ x_2 = (x - d)\ f$$

whence

$$w = -f + \frac{2df}{x_1 - x_2} \tag{2.7}$$

In other words, depth can be calculated from the disparity $(x_1 - x_2)$ of two points in the stereo image pairs. The practical difficulty lies in the identification of two matching points in the two stereo images, as illustrated in Figure 2.8(b).

Depth information as well as surface orientation can also be determined using a structured light source. The technique is also called *grid coding* [WILL71]. An example of grid coding using a laminated light source is illustrated in Figure 2.9.

The surfaces have different strips, which can be detected using edge detection operators (or matched filters).

Multi-spectral picture functions and multiple picture functions can be thought of as consisting of several picture planes, as shown in Figure 2.10.

In the hardware design of picture processors, each picture plane can be physically realized as an array of memory cells. In a raster image display, each picture plane contains one *frame* of image data. The special-purpose high-speed memory for storing the image frames is called the *frame buffer*. A monochromatic image can be created from a single frame, and a color image is created by mixing the signals from three frames, each representing red, green, and blue.

Typical picture processor operations include the following:

```
read the picture from one picture plane
write the picture into one picture plane
arithmetic operation on pictures from several picture planes
```

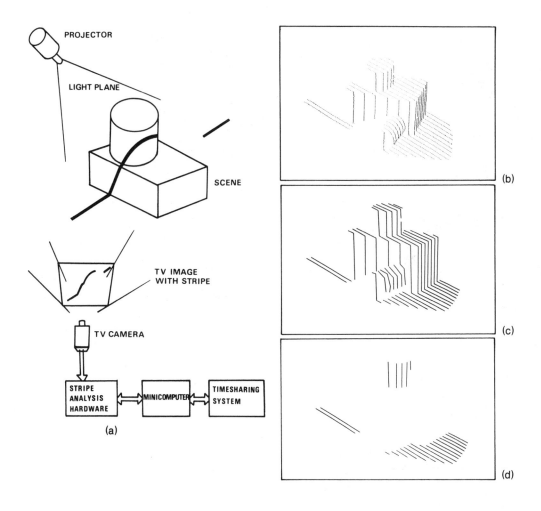

Figure 2.9. Light striping. (a) A typical arrangement, (b) raw data, (c) data segmented into strips, (d) strips segmented into surfaces. Dana H. Ballard/Christopher M. Brown, *COMPUTER VISION*, © 1982, p. 53. Reprinted by permission of Prentice-Hall, Inc., Englewood Cliffs, New Jersey.

For example, the digital pictures stored in two picture planes can be read and added pixel by pixel, and the resultant picture is written into a third picture plane. With an array of processors working simultaneously on the different local regions of the picture planes, many picture operations can be performed efficiently in parallel. Parallel operations on digital pictures depend very much on the *locality nature* of the operations to be performed. If the operations are so-called local operations (see Section 2.3), parallel processing algorithms are often applicable. We are therefore led to the concept of local operations.

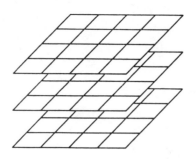

Figure 2.10. Picture planes.

2.3 PICTURE OPERATIONS

To perform picture operations, we are often interested in the neighboring points of a point in a digital picture. The *neighbor set* NS is the set of points regarded as neighbors of a point. For example, the 4-point neighbor set, NS4, is defined by

$$NS\,4(x,y) \;=\; \left\{ (x-1,y),(x+1,y),(x,y+1),(x,y-1) \right\} \tag{2.8}$$

and

$$NS\,4(2,2) \;=\; \left\{ (1,2),(3,2),(2,1),(2,3) \right\}$$

The 8-point neighbor set, NS8, is defined by

$$NS\,8(x,y) \;=\; \left\{ (x-1,y+1),(x-1,y),(x-1,y-1),(x,y+1), \right.$$

$$\left. (x,y-1),(x+1,y+1),(x+1,y),(x+1,y-1) \right\} \tag{2.9}$$

The neighbor sets just defined do not contain the original point (x,y). Sometimes, it is useful to include (x,y). We thus have

$$NS\,5(x,y) \;=\; NS\,4(x,y) \cup \left\{ (x,y) \right\}$$

and

$$NS\,9(x,y) \;=\; NS\,8(x,y) \cup \left\{ (x,y) \right\}$$

Other neighbor sets can be similarly defined.

A *picture operation* is an operation which, when applied to a picture, will transform it to another picture. Mathematically, let F denote a family of digital pictures, then a picture operation T is a mapping from F into F, or

$$T : F \to F$$

If the original picture is f_1 and the transformed picture is f_2, we will also write

$$f_2 = T(f_1)$$

A picture operation is called a *local operation* if $f_2(x,y)$ is only dependent on the value of $f_1(x,y)$ for (x,y) in $NS(x,y)$.

If $NS(x,y) = \left\{ (x,y) \right\}$, and $f_2(x,y) = T(f_1(x,y))$, then T is called a *point operation*. Point operation is a special case of local operations.

Linear local operations can be expressed by

$$f_2(x,y) = \sum_{(i,j) \text{ in } NS(i,j)} f_1(i,j) \ h(i,j) \qquad (2.10)$$

This is seen to be equivalent to the discrete cross-correlation of f_1 and h. The special picture function h is called the *local operator,* which is defined in $NS(x,y)$. If NS is represented by a small window, we can graphically illustrate h in this window by displaying its values. The local operator h is therefore sometimes called a *window operator*.

If we denote the Fourier transforms of f and h by F and H, respectively, then we have

$$\begin{array}{ccc} f * h & & F \times H \\ spatial \ \ domain & \Leftrightarrow & spatial \ \ frequency \ \ domain \end{array}$$

In other words, a linear local operation in the spatial domain is the cross-correlation of the picture function and the local operator h, which is equivalent to the multiplication of F and H in the spatial frequency domain. Therefore, a local operator can be regarded as a spatial-frequency filter. Low-pass filters will suppress high-spatial frequencies, thus blurring the image. Conversely, high-pass filters will suppress low-spatial frequencies, thus making the points of discontinuities (such as edges) more prominent.

Local operations are very useful in picture processing because they can be expressed by local operators and computed by moving the local operators in the picture plane. The following examples are some of the most commonly encountered local operations.

Example 2.1

The thresholding operation T_t transforms a picture into a *binary picture* by applying a cutoff threshold to the original picture as follows:

$$f_2(x,y) = \begin{cases} 1 & \text{if } f_1(x,y) \geq t \\ 0 & \text{otherwise} \end{cases}$$

Therefore, the following transformation in Figure 2.11 is by applying T_1, the thresholding operation with a cutoff threshold of 1.

```
121          111
100  ====>   100
210          110    Figure 2.11.   Thresholding operation.
```

Example 2.2

The averaging operation, T_{avg}, is applied to a picture to obtain a blurred picture by taking the arithmetic average of pixels belonging to a local neighbor set. For example, the 5-point averaging operation T_{avg5} is defined by

$$f_2(x,y) = \frac{1}{5} \sum_{(i,j) \ in \ NS5(x,y)} f_1(i,j)$$

If we round up or round down the numbers to the nearest integer, we have an example as shown in Figure 2.12.

```
1 1 4 4              1 2 3 4
1 1 4 4     ===>     1 2 3 4
1 1 2 2              1 1 2 3    Figure 2.12.  Averaging operation.
```

In Figure 2.12, the pixels near the edge of the picture are calculated using 3-point or 4-point neighbors. We can also surround the original picture by background pixels (0's) and use 5-point neighbors for the edge pixels.

Example 2.3

Perhaps the simplest way of recognizing patterns in an image is by *template matching*. We define a local operator h, which is our template. We then move the template around the picture f_1 and compute f_2. If we have

$$\sum_{(i,j) \ in \ NS(i,j)} f_1(i,j) \ h(i,j) \geq t \tag{2.12}$$

then there is a pattern at location (x, y). Because of noise in the picture, such a pattern recognition technique can only be applied to the simplest problems, say in OCR character recognition. More likely, we will devise many different feature templates $h_1, ..., h_n$, and the computed results form a feature vector $\{x_1, x_2, ..., x_n\}$. To classify a pattern, we can now deal only with this feature vector. This is the starting point of statistical pattern recognition.

Example 2.4

The gradient operation transforms a picture into a new picture, emphasizing edges. The classical gradient function is given by

$$\nabla f(x,y) = \frac{\partial f}{\partial x} i + \frac{\partial f}{\partial y} j \tag{2.13}$$

The magnitude of the gradient function is

$$s = [(\frac{\partial f}{\partial x})^2 + (\frac{\partial f}{\partial y})^2]^{\frac{1}{2}}$$

and the directional angle is

$$\theta = \tan^{-1} \frac{\partial f / \partial y}{\partial f / \partial x}$$

To approximate the gradient function, we can use

$$\Delta x = f(x,y) - f(x-1,y) \qquad \Delta y = f(x,y) - f(x,y-1)$$

These can be represented by two *window operators* (local operators)

$$-1 \quad 1 \qquad\qquad \begin{matrix} 1 \\ -1 \end{matrix}$$

The *strength* of an edge is the confidence level of that edge. We can use various approximations of the gradient magnitude to represent its strength:

$$s = (\Delta^2 x + \Delta^2 y)^{\frac{1}{2}}$$

or

$$s = |\Delta x| + |\Delta y|$$

or

$$s = \max(|\Delta x|, |\Delta y|) \tag{2.14}$$

and the direction of the edge is given by

$$\psi = \tan^{-1}(\Delta x / \Delta y) \tag{2.15}$$

A simplified version of the Roberts operator for edge detection is

$$f_2(x,y) = \max[|f_1(x,y) - f_1(x+1,y+1)|, |f_1(x+1,y) - f_1(x,y+1)|]$$

or approximately

$$f_2(x,y) = |f_1(x,y) - f_1(x+1,y+1)| + |f_1(x+1,y) - f_1(x,y+1)| \tag{2.16}$$

For example, assuming the picture is surrounded by 0's, we have

```
0 2 2 2          2 4 4 2
0 2 2 2  ====>   4 0 0 4
0 2 2 2          4 0 0 4
0 2 2 2          4 0 0 4
```

Figure 2.13 Edge detection using Roberts operator.

There are many gradient-derived operators. The 2-by-2 Roberts operators are

```
 0 1       1  0
-1 0       0 -1
```

Figure 2.14(a)

The 3-by-3 Prewitt operators are

```
-1 0 1      1  1  1
-1 0 1      0  0  0
-1 0 1     -1 -1 -1
```

Figure 2.14(b)

The 3-by-3 Sobel operators are

```
-1 0 1      1  2  1
-2 0 2      0  0  0
-1 0 1     -1 -2 -1
```

Figure 2.14(c)

The 3-by-3 Kirsh operators are

```
-1  0  1     1  1  1     0  1  1     1  1  0
-1  0  1     0  0  0    -1  0  1     1  0 -1
-1  0  1    -1 -1 -1    -1 -1  0     0 -1 -1
  |            -           \           /        Figure 2.14(d)
```

When we apply the four Kirsh operators, we select the one with maximum magnitude, and the direction of the edge is thus decided.

Example 2.5

The operators presented in Example 2.4 are edge detectors. Another operator, the Laplacian, usually defined as f(x,y + 1) + f(x + 1,y) + f(x - 1,y) + f(x,y - 1) − 4f(x,y), can be used to detect lines or to deblur a picture. The original form of the Laplacian operator can be written as

$$\nabla^2 f = \frac{\partial^2 f}{\partial x^2} + \frac{\partial^2 f}{\partial y^2}$$

The Laplacian operator has the nice property of being *rotation invariant*, that is, it yields the same results regardless of the orientation of the picture. To see how the discrete approximation of the Laplacian operator is derived, we consider the two differences:

$$\Delta_x f(x,y) = f(x,y) - f(x-1,y)$$

$$\Delta_y f(x,y) = f(x,y) - f(x,y-1)$$

The second-order differences are

$$\Delta_x^2 f(x,y) = \Delta_x f(x+1,y) - \Delta_x f(x,y)$$

$$= [f(x+1,y) - f(x,y)] - [f(x,y) - f(x-1,y)] = f(x+1,y) + f(x-1,y) - 2f(x,y)$$

and similarly,

$$\Delta_y^2 f(x,y) = f(x,y+1) + f(x,y-1) - 2f(x,y)$$

The Laplacian can be written as

$$\nabla^2 f(x,y)$$

$$= [f(x,y) + f(x+1,y) + f(x-1,y) + f(x,y+1) + f(x,y-1)] - 5f(x,y) \quad (2.17)$$

In other words, its effect is first to get an averaged picture and then subtract the original. The combined effect is to sharpen the boundary lines in a picture. If we subtract the Laplacian from a picture, the effect is

$$f(x,y) - \nabla^2 f(x,y) = 5f(x,y) - [f(x+1,y) + f(x-1,y) + f(x,y+1) + f(x,y-1)]$$

$$= f(x,y) + 4\left\{ f(x,y) - 0.25[f(x+1,y) + f(x-1,y) + f(x,y+1) + f(x,y-1)] \right\}$$

In other words, the original picture is enhanced by strengthening its boundaries (that is, by adding high-frequency components). The subtraction of the Laplacian from the original picture thus has a deblurring effect. The subtraction of a weighted average picture from the original picture usually will also achieve a deblurring effect. Averaging, on the other hand, will have the opposite effect of blurring the picture. However, an averaging operation can reduce noise in a picture and has a smoothing effect. Especially when we average several identical but independently obtained pictures, the noise can be significantly reduced.

Let $f_i(x,y)$ denote the stationary pictures that are contaminated by additive noise. We assume the pictures are properly registered and aligned, so that the following is true:

$$f_i(x,y) = f(x,y) + g_i(x,y) \qquad i = 1,2,...,M$$

where $g_i(x,y)$ denotes the noise. The average of M pictures is given by

$$\hat{f}(x,y) = \frac{1}{M} \sum_{i=1}^{M} f_i(x,y) = f(x,y) + \frac{1}{M} \sum_{i=1}^{M} g_i(x,y)$$

The signal-to-noise power ratio is given by

$$p(x,y) = \frac{f^2(x,y)}{E[g^2(x,y)]}$$

Therefore, the signal-to-noise power ratio for the averaged picture function is

$$\hat{p}(x,y) = \frac{f^2(x,y)}{E[(\frac{1}{M} \sum_{i=1}^{M} g_i(x,y))^2]}$$

$$= \frac{M^2 f^2(x,y)}{E[\sum_{i=1}^{M} \sum_{j=1}^{M} g_i(x,y) g_j(x,y)]}$$

$$= \frac{M^2 f^2(x,y)}{E[\sum_{i=1}^{M} g_i^2(x,y) + \sum_{j=1}^{M} \sum_{i \neq j}^{M} g_i(x,y) g_j(x,y)]}$$

To simplify the above expression, we assume that the noise functions are identical, uncorrelated, with zero mean. Therefore,

$$E[g_i(x,y) + g_j(x,y)] = E[g_i(x,y)] + E[g_j(x,y)] \qquad i \neq j$$

$$E[g_i(x,y) g_j(x,y)] = E[g_i(x,y)] E[g_j(x,y)] \qquad i \neq j$$

$$E[g_j(x,y)] = 0$$

$$E[g_i^2(x,y)] = E[g^2(x,y)] \qquad i = 1,2,...,M$$

We have

$$\hat{p}(x,y) = \frac{M^2 f^2(x,y)}{M E[g^2(x,y)]} = M \frac{f^2(x,y)}{E[g^2(x,y)]} = M p(x,y)$$

Therefore, the averaging of M pictures will increase the signal-to-noise power ratio by a factor of M for all points of the picture. Since the signal-to-noise amplitude ratio is the square root of the power ratio, the SNR will increase by a factor of the square root of M.

To reduce picture blurring, a *selective smoothing* method can also be used. In this method, a pixel is replaced by the average of its neighbors if it differs by at least t

gray levels from the average pixel value. For example, for NS8, the threshold t can be set to 3. The method just mentioned essentially attempts to classify pixels into noisy pixels and nonnoisy pixels. Only noisy pixels are smoothed, so that picture blurring can be reduced.

Picture operations that are not local operations are called *global operations*. Global operations are useful to perform nonlocal picture transformations, such as in geometric operations for barrel distortion correction, perspective distortion correction, and picture rotation. Figure 2.15 illustrates the general idea of geometric transformation. A point (x,y) in the ideal picture f is mapped to a point (x',y') in the distorted picture g, where

$$x' = T_1(x,y) \qquad\qquad (2.18\text{-}a)$$

$$y' = T_2(x,y) \qquad\qquad (2.18\text{-}b)$$

and thus $g(x',y') = g(T_1(x,y), T_2(x,y)) = f(x,y)$.

Therefore, to correct a distorted picture g and recover the ideal picture f, we must perform the inverse operation,

$$x = T_1^{-1}(x',y') \qquad\qquad (2.19\text{-}a)$$

$$y = T_2^{-1}(x',y') \qquad\qquad (2.19\text{-}b)$$

As illustrated in Figure 2.15, the mappings T_1 and T_2 can be determined if we know a few *control points*, which are matching points in f and g, respectively.

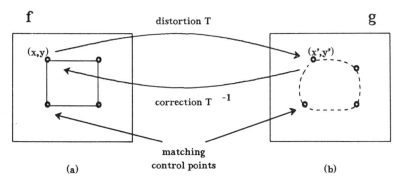

Figure 2.15 Geometric operation to transform (a) an ideal picture into (b) a distorted picture. Kenneth R. Castleman, *DIGITAL IMAGE PROCESSING*, © 1979, p. 117. Reprinted by permission of Prentice-Hall, Inc., Englewood Cliffs, New Jersey.

For barrel distortion caused by camera optics, the mappings are,

$$x' = a_1 x + b_1 y + c_1 xy + d_1 \qquad\qquad (2.20\text{-}a)$$

$$y' = a_2 x + b_2 y + c_2 xy + d_2 \qquad\qquad (2.20\text{-}b)$$

Therefore, if we know four control points, we can solve for a_1, b_1, c_1, d_1 and a_2, b_2, c_2, d_2.

For perspective distortion, the mappings are

$$x' = a_1 x + b_1 y + d_1 \qquad\qquad (2.21\text{-}a)$$

$$y' = a_2 x + b_2 y + d_2 \qquad (2.21\text{-b})$$

where three control points are needed to find the parameters. The rotation operation requires two control points to determine the four parameters.

$$x' = a_1 x + b_1 y \qquad (2.22\text{-a})$$

$$y' = a_2 x + b_2 y \qquad (2.22\text{-b})$$

If the mappings T_1 and T_2 are known, we can reconstruct f from g to remove the distortion. The *nearest neighbor reconstruction* method, or *pixel filling method*, works as follows. For each point (x,y) in f, we can find the corresponding point (x',y') in g. We can set $f(x,y)$ equal to $g(x',y')$. For digital pictures, the point (x',y') may not fall on a grid point, in which case we find the nearest neighbor (x'',y'') of (x',y') and set $f(x,y)$ equal to $g(x'',y'')$.

As an example, the mappings are

$$x' = x/2 \text{ and } y' = y/2$$

The distorted picture g is

```
1 2 3
1 2 3
1 2 3
```

The reconstruction method proceeds to construct the following table:

(x,y)	(x',y')	closest (x",y")	f(x,y)
(1,1)	(0.5,0.5)	(1,1)	1
(2,1)	(1,0.5)	(1,1)	1
(3,1)	(1.5,0.5)	(2,1)	2
..	.....	....	...

The advantage of this method is that we can reconstruct f, line by line and pixel by pixel.

A refinement of the nearest neighbor reconstruction method to the *interpolated reconstruction* method works as follows. As before, we find the point (x',y') in g corresponding to point (x,y) in f. If (x',y') is a grid point, we set $f(x,y)$ equal to $g(x',y')$. If (x',y') is not a grid point, we find the four neighbors of (x',y') and use linear interpolation to determine $g(x',y')$ and hence $f(x,y)$. Suppose the neighbor set is $\{(x_1,y_1),(x_1,y_1+1),(x_1+1,y_1),(x_1+1,y_1+1)\}$. The interpolation formulae are:

$$g(x',y_1) = g(x_1,y_1) + (x'-x_1)[g(x_1+1,y_1) - g(x_1,y_1)]$$

$$g(x',y_1+1) = g(x_1,y_1+1) + (x'-x_1)[g(x_1+1,y_1+1) - g(x_1,y_1+1)]$$

$$g(x',y') = g(x',y_1) + (y'-y_1)[g(x',y_1+1) - g(x',y_1)]$$

The interpolation scheme is illustrated in Figure 2.16.

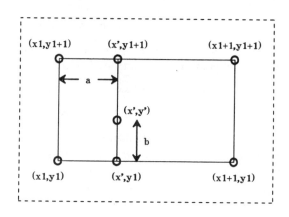

Figure 2.16 Interpolated reconstruction technique. Kenneth R. Castleman, *DIGITAL IMAGE PROCESSING*, © 1979, p. 114. Reprinted by permission of Prentice-Hall, Inc., Englewood Cliffs, New Jersey.

We let $x' - x_1$ be 'a', and $y' - y_1$ be 'b', and obtain

$$g(x',y') = (1-b)g(x',y_1) + bg(x',y_1+1)$$

$$= (1-b)[(1-a)g(x_1,y_1) + ag(x_1+1,y_1)] + b[(1-a)g(x_1,y_{1+1}) + ag(x_1+1,y_{1+1})]$$

$$= (1-a)(1-b)g(x_1,y_1) + a(1-b)g(x_1+1,y_1) + (1-a)bg(x_1,y_1+1) + abg(x_1+1,y_1+1)$$

The application of geometric operations includes distortion correction, registration of images, and map projections.

Another useful global operation is *histogramming,* which is discussed in Section II.5 of Appendix II and Section 3.4 of Chapter 3. Connectivity tests, thinning algorithms, and certain regional growing algorithms are global operations that can be implemented as *iterative local operations.*

2.4 REPRESENTATION OF LINE DRAWINGS

A digital picture is usually represented by an array of pixels. Other representations are sometimes desirable.

The line drawing represents a picture as a collection of line segments. An example is illustrated in Figure 2.17.

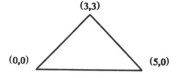

Figure 2.17 Line segment representation.

The line drawing can be represented by

$$((0,0),(3,3)) \quad ((3,3),(5,0)) \quad ((5,0),(0,0))$$

where each line segment is represented by its starting and ending points. The following representations are all equivalent:

a. Starting and ending points: $((x_1, y_1), (x_2, y_2))$

b. Starting points and increments: $((x_1, y_1), (dx,dy))$

c. Starting and ending points and slope: $((x_1, y_1), m, (x_2, y_2))$

d. Starting points, slope, and increments: $((x_1, y_1), m, (dx,dy))$

In the preceding, $dx = x_2 - x_1$, $dy = y_2 - y_1$ are the x- and y- increments, respectively, and m is the line slope.

It is also sometimes desirable to associate a gray-level code with each line segment. In vector graphics, we have commands such as

```
LINE 0,0,0
LINE 3,3,1
LINE 5,0,1
LINE 0,0,1
```

Each LINE command draws a line from the previous point to the point specified, with the last digit indicating its gray level. Thus,

```
LINE 0,0,0
```

draws a "blank" line to origin (0,0), and

```
LINE 3,3,1
```

draws a "solid" line from (0,0) to (3,3).

We can represent a polygon by

$$A = (x, y, r) \ (dx_1, dy_1) \ (dx_2, dy_2) \ \cdots \ (dx_n, dy_n) \tag{2.23}$$

where (x,y) is the initial point, r the gray level for the line segments, and dx_i, dy_i are the x- and y- increments for the line segments.

Line segment representation and polygonal representation are often used in computer graphics and in representing digitized maps.

In the representation $((x_1, y_1), m, (x_2, y_2))$, if (x_2, y_2) is always in NS—the neighbor set—then it becomes redundant, and we need only store

$$((x_1, y_1), m)$$

In chain code representation [FREEMAN74], we allow only eight directions for the slope m, so it can be encoded into 3 bits. We will describe chain coding in detail in the next subsection.

The general representation of line segments is

$$((x_1, y_1), m, (x_2, y_2))$$

although some of it might be redundant. If we use higher-order polynomials, in general the representation is

$$((x_1, y_1), (a_1, a_2, ..., a_n), (x_2, y_2)) \qquad (2.24)$$

For example, the quadratic equation of the form

$$y - y_1 = a(x - x_1)^2 + b(x - x_1)$$

will be represented by

$$((x_1, y_1), (a, b), (x_2, y_2))$$

The spline functions [AHLBERG67, BOOR78] can also be used to represent curves, such as

$$y(x) = a_3 x^3 + a_2 x^2 + a_1 x + a_0$$

Although higher-order polynomial representations of line drawings are useful in certain applications—especially in geometric modeling for computer-aided design and computer graphics—the chain code representation and the line segment representation are by far the more popular line drawing representations.

2.4.1 Chain Coding

Because the information of a region is actually contained in its boundary, the line pattern coding technique—chain coding—is capable of coding objects presented in a binary picture. The idea of chain coding is to follow line or boundary points and to code them in sequence. A well-known chain coding method is extensively described in [FREEMAN74]. The chain coding scheme can be stated as follows:

1. A link a_i is a directed straight line segment of length $(\sqrt{2})^p$ and of angle $a_i \times 45^0$ referenced to the x axis of a right-hand Cartesian coordinate system, where $a_i = 0, 1, ..., 7, p = \text{mod}(2, a_i)$.

2. A chain is an ordered sequence of links with possible interspersed signal codes:

$$A = a_1 \, a_2 \, \cdots \, a_n$$

Where the signal code is usually taken as octal digit sequence $04d_1 d_2$. For example, 0400 denotes the end of chain, 0407uv the serial number uv of the chain, 0424uvw the gray level, and 0426uvw and 0427uvw denote absolute x y coordinates of the starting point. For a closed curve in Figure 2.18, the chain code would be

0407010424001042600104270031007056423552204 00

where the starting point is the point $(1, 3)$.

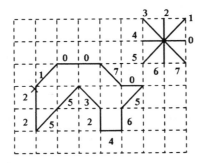

Figure 2.18 A chain-encoded closed contour.

2.4.2 Operations on Chain-Coded Objects

1. Inverse of a Chain.   The inverse of a chain is a geometric congruent of the chain and is oppositely directed.

$$(a_1 \cdots a_n)^{-1} = a_n^{-1} \cdots a_1^{-1} \tag{2.25}$$

where $a_i^{-1} = mod[8,(a_i + 4)]$

2. Length of a Chain.   The length of a chain can be easily computed as

$$L = n_e + n_o \sqrt{2} \tag{2.26}$$

where n_e and n_o are the numbers of even- and odd-valued links, respectively. The absolute coordinates of a point pointed by link a_i are

$$x_i = \sum_{j=1}^{i} a_{jx} + x_0 \tag{2.27-a}$$

$$y_i = \sum_{j=1}^{i} a_{jy} + y_0 \tag{2.27-b}$$

where a_{jx} and a_{jy} are x y components of a_j, respectively.

3. Width and Height of an Enclosed Contour   The width and the height of an enclosed contour is

$$width = \max_j x_j - \min_j x_j \tag{2.28-a}$$

$$height = \max_j y_j - \min_j y_j \tag{2.28-b}$$

4. Distance between Two Points   The distance between two points connected by a chain is

$$d = [(\sum_{i=1}^{n} a_{ix})^2 + (\sum_{i=1}^{n} a_{iy})^2]^{\frac{1}{2}} \tag{2.29}$$

Knowing the coordinates of each point on the contour, the moments of the contour can be computed. But it is difficult to calculate the geometric properties of the region enclosed by a chain-coded contour from the chain code. It is also difficult to perform scale changes.

R E F E R E N C E S

[AHLBERG67] AHLBERG, J. H., E. N. NILSON, J. L. WALSH, *The Theory of Splines and Their Applications.* New York: Academic Press, 1967.

[BALLARD82] BALLARD, D. H. AND C. M. BROWN, *Computer Vision.* Englewood Cliffs, New Jersey: Prentice-Hall, Inc., 1982.

[BOOR78] DE BOOR, C., *A Practical Guide to Splines.* New York: Springer-Verlag, 1978.

[CASTLEMAN79] CASTLEMAN, K. R. *Digital Image Processing.* Englewood Cliffs, New Jersey: Prentice-Hall, 1979.

[FREEMAN74] FREEMAN, H., "Computer Processing of Line Drawings," *ACM Computing Surveys,* Vol. 6, 1974, 57-97.

[MORTENSON85] MORTENSON, M. E., *Geometric Modelling.* New York: John Wiley & Sons, Inc., 1985.

[WILL71] WILL, P. M. AND K. S. PENNINGTON, "Grid Coding: A Preprocessing Technique for Robot and Machine Vision," *Artificial Intelligence,* Vol. 2, No. 3/4, Winter 1971, 319-329.

E X E R C I S E S

1. Prove that the Laplacian is rotation invariant.

2. Template matching is a filtering method of detecting a particular feature in an image. Provided that the appearance of this feature in the image is known accurately, one can try to detect it with an operator called a template. A popular similarity measure between a function $f(x)$ and a template $t(x)$ is the *Euclidean distance* d(x) squared, given by

$$d^2(y) = \sum_x [f(x) - t(x - y)]^2$$

By $\sum_x$ we mean $\sum_{x=-M}^{M} \sum_{x=-N}^{N}$, for some M,N, which define the size of the template. If the image at point y is an exact match for the template, then d(y)=0; otherwise, d(y)>0. Expanding the expression for $d^2(y)$, we can see that

$$d^2(y) = \sum_x [f^2(x) - 2f(x)t(x - y) + t^2(x - y)]$$

Notice that $\sum_x t^2(x - y)$ is a constant term and can be neglected. When $\sum_x f^2(x)$ is approximately constant, it, too, can be discounted, leaving what is called *Cross Correlation* between f and t:

$$R_{ft}(y) = \sum_x f(x)t(x - y)$$

This is maximized when the portion of the image "under" t is identical to t.

As an exercise, if we have a template as follows:

```
111
111
111
```

and the image with noise is:

```
11000
11100
10100
00000
00008
```

Find the aperiodic correlation array of the template and the image with noise.

3. Use the interpolation reconstruction method to reconstruct f from the distorted g given in the following example:

```
123
123
123
```

where the mappings are $x' = x + 1$ and $y' = y - 1$.

4. The original picture function f is

```
44422
44422
44422
44422
44411
```

Show the resulting picture function g after each following picture operation is performed on f:

a. Thresholding operation with threshold t equal to 3
b. Averaging operation using a 5-point neighborhood
c. Gradient operation

5. Characterize chain codes of all rectangles whose sides are horizontal and vertical.

6. Develop algorithms to find the common area(s) of
   a. Two binary pictures
   b. Two chain-coded picture objects of the form $(x, y)a_1 a_2 \cdots a_n$, where (x,y) is the starting point of the chain code representation, and a_i is the chain code from $\{0 ,.., 7\}$
   c. Two polygonal picture objects of the form

   $$(x,y) (dx_1 ,dy_1) (dx_2 ,dy_2) \cdots (dx_n ,dy_n)$$

   where (x,y) is the starting point of the polygonal representation, and (dx_i ,dy_i) is the increment in x and y direction
   In each case, illustrate your algorithm by a detailed, step-by-step example. Also, compare the computational efficiency of your three algorithms.

7. Write a program to convert chain codes into line drawings.

8. Show that chain codes representing closed curves can be characterized by (a) $n_1 + n_2 + n_3 = n_5 + n_6 + n_7$, and (b) $n_3 + n_4 + n_5 = n_7 + n_0 + n_1$, where n_i is the number of code words in the i direction.

9. Give an example of knowledge-based picture processing and show the major difference with traditional image processing.

10. Inverse the chain code of Figure 2.18, compute its chain length, and verify equations (2.28-a), (2.28-b), and (2.29).

11. Write a program to generate gray-level histogram from a picture, then use it to develop an algorithm to threshold gray-level picture locally and globally. Usually, for pictures with clear backgrounds, simple global thresholding is good enough. For pictures with complicated backgrounds, dynamic local thresholding is necessary.

12. Prove that the convolution of g_1 and g_2 in the spatial domain is equivalent to the point-wise product of G_1 and G_2 in the frequency domain

$$F(g_1 * g_2) = G_1 \times G_2$$

Chapter 3

Picture Segmentation

Consider the family F of all 1024-by-1024, 64 gray-level pictures. There are only a finite number of different pictures in F. However, the number is astronomically large, or, more precisely, $64^{1048576}$. This family of pictures, F, means different things to different people. To mathematicians, it is a finite, enumerable set. To engineers, it is an impractically large problem domain. To poets, it contains the face of every person who ever lived, who is living, or who will ever live. It also contains pictures of every alien being who is visible in the electromagnetic spectrum, including the fictitious extraterrestrial being, ET. If we exhaustively generated and catalogued all possible pictures, we would have images of all living beings. However, such a task poses immense practical difficulties. As Castleman points out, usually we must be content to develop techniques to process particular pictures or to recognize objects present in a particular picture [CASTLEMAN79]. The problem of cataloguing and indexing pictures to facilitate pictorial information retrieval is treated in Chapters 9 and 10.

A picture has a meaning. It signifies something. The association of a picture with a meaning is an *icon*. For example, a red cross signifies something to members of certain cultures, but its meaning may change for members of other cultures. The association of meaning to a picture is often application-dependent or domain-dependent.

Picture segmentation is the technique of decomposing a picture into meaningful parts to separate objects from background and to distingush among objects. The result is a segmented picture. In segmented pictures, each object is uniquely labeled. Once we have the labeled objects, we can then integrate them into a structured description of the original picture.

In picture segmentation, we try to discover either boundaries or regions or both. To do so, we will need knowledge (model) about the pictures. Depending upon the application-dependent knowledge we incorporate into the algorithms, we make different assumptions and impose various constraints to do segmentation.

For simple objects or meaningful parts of a complex object, we can apply pattern recognition techniques to classify them. Generally speaking, picture segmentation is a kind of recognition process which classifies individual pixels or a group of pixels (region or boundary) as either object categories or background. Sections 3.1 and 3.2 deal with pattern recognition techniques in picture segmentation. After briefly introducing recognition systems and template matching, we include a more detailed description of the pattern classifier.

Objects are distinguishable by the homogeneous properties of their region or abrupt changes around their boundary. Region growing, described in Section 3.4, and boundary detection, described in Section 3.3, are based on these two object properties. In this chapter, we discuss only gray-level segmentation techniques. Texture segmentation can usually be considered as segmentation with additional preprocessing by texture analysis.

3.1 PATTERN RECOGNITION IN PICTURE SEGMENTATION

A block diagram of a picture processing system to recognize simple objects is illustrated in Figure 3.1. An image is first digitized by an *image digitizer* (the picture input device). The digital picture is then processed by a *picture processor*. The output is displayed via an *image display* (the picture output device) for viewing by the user. The output for a pattern recognition system is a description of the recognized object. For example, we can display the label of the recognized object and its approximate location in the original picture.

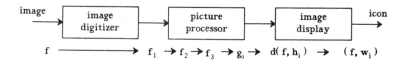

Figure 3.1 A picture processing system for simple object recognition.

In the system illustrated in Figure 3.1, an image f is first digitized and represented by picture function $f_1(x, y)$. The picture processor then performs the following:

a. Normalization

b. Thresholding

c. Classification

In normalization, we adjust the contrast, compensate for photometric nonlinearity using point operations, and perform scaling, orientation, and registration corrections. The result is picture function $f_2(x,y)$. More sophisticated normalization may also involve geometric normalization.

In thresholding, we threshold $f_2(x,y)$ to produce a binary picture $f_3(x,y)$. The threshold can be determined beforehand or adjusted dynamically.

The picture function $f_3(x,y)$ is then classified using a classifier. The classifier, for simple object recognition, can be implemented using *template matching*. In template matching, we perform point-by-point AND operations on two picture functions:

$$g_i(x,y) = f_3(x,y) \wedge h_i(x,y) \tag{3.1}$$

where h_i is the template—a binary picture function—and g_i is the resultant picture function. If two pictures f_3 and h_i match at many points, then the two picture functions f_3 and h_i can be said to be *similar*. Therefore, we can define a *similarity measure*

$$d(f_3, h_i) = black(f_3 \wedge h_i) / black(h_i) = black(g_i) / black(h_i)$$

where $black(f)$ gives the number of black pixels (1 pixel) in a binary picture f.

We can decide that the picture f contains an object of type i, if $d(f, h_i)$ is the maximum—that is, f has the best match with template h_i.

In template matching the operator is a binary picture operator. Binary picture operators perform operations on two picture functions to yield a resultant picture function

$$f'' = f \; \theta \; f' \tag{3.2}$$

where θ is the operator, such as logical AND, logical OR, logical XOR, logical NOR, logical NEGATION for binary pictures, or $+$, $-$, $*$, $/$, min, or max for gray-level pictures. Thresholding, on the other hand, is an unary picture operator. Point picture operations are also unary picture operators.

Notice also that the final decision, or classification, is dependent on the *global picture property*. For more complex pattern recognition tasks, we can extract many local picture properties, called *features*, and then perform a global classification.

The result, (f, ω_i), illustrates the concept of an *icon. The image f is labeled by the decision category ω_i. The pair (f, ω_i) makes an icon. Generally speaking, an icon is always a pair—a physical picture and a logical picture. In this case, the physical picture is f and the logical picture is ω_i.

3.2 THE PATTERN CLASSIFIER

The statistical pattern recognition approach can best be illustrated by the pattern recognition system shown in Figure 3.2.

The feature extractor extracts a *feature vector* $\vec{x} = (x_1, ..., x_n)$ from the input image. The classifier then classifies the feature vector into one of m *classes* ω_1, ω_2, ..., ω_m. The class ω_i becomes the *label* of the image f, and the icon is (f, ω_i).

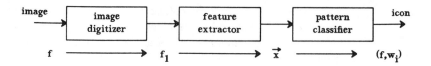

Figure 3.2 A pattern recognition system.

The problem of pattern recognition can now be formulated as a statistical decision problem to test m statistical hypotheses:

$$H_i : \vec{x} \text{ is in class } \omega_i , \quad i = 1, ..., m .$$

If the a priori probability of the occurrence of each class ω_j, is known to be $p(\omega_j)$, and the conditional probability of the occurrence of $\vec{x}$ given ω_j is known to be $p(\vec{x} / \omega_j)$, then we can use the classical *Bayesian decision rule:*

Decide $\vec{x}$ to be in class ω_i

If $p(\omega_i)p(\vec{x} / \omega_i) > p(\omega_j)p(\vec{x} / \omega_j)$ for *all* $j \neq i$

The Bayesian decision rule is known to minimize the *probability of misrecognition.*

Generally speaking, we can associate with each class ω_i a discriminant function $D_i(\vec{x})$, such that

Decide $\vec{x}$ to be in class ω_i (3.3)

if $D_i(\vec{x}) > D_j(\vec{x})$, for all $j \neq i$

For the Bayesian decision rule, the discriminant function is

$$D_i(\vec{x}) = p(\omega_i)p(\vec{x} / \omega_i) \tag{3.4}$$

The discriminant function approach allows us to specify Bayesian as well as non-Bayesian decision rules. The *decision boundary* between two classes ω_i and ω_j can be expressed by $D_i(\vec{x}) = D_j(\vec{x})$. Therefore, instead of explicitly specifying the discriminant functions, we may also choose to specify the decision boundaries.

To implement the decision rule, one should first determine the parameters of the discriminant function. This is usually done by some *learning (training)* procedure. For a given set of labeled prototypes $\{\vec{y}\}$, determine D_i, such that

For all prototypes $\vec{y}$ in class ω_i

$D_i(\vec{y}) > D_j(\vec{y})$ holds for all $j \neq i$.

Example 3.1

Suppose we have two classes of images, representing the printed characters L and T. Figure 3.3 illustrates the digital pictures of the two classes.

To extract features, we may choose the centroid (x_c, y_c) to characterize a pattern. The motivation behind this approach is the observation that the *projections* of a printed character are also its good characterizations. The projections and centroid are defined as follows:

```
2 | 11000          5 | 11111
2 | 11000          2 | 00110
3 | 11100          1 | 00100
5 | 11111          1 | 00100

  44211             11421

   (a)               (b)      Figure 3.3  Digital pictures of L and T.
```

$$f_x (x) = \int f(x,y) \, dy \tag{3.5-a}$$

$$f_y (y) = \int f(x,y) \, dx \tag{3.5-b}$$

and

$$x_c = \frac{\int x \, f_x (x) \, dx}{\int f_x (x) \, dx} \tag{3.6-a}$$

$$y_c = \frac{\int y \, f_y (y) \, dy}{\int f_y (y) \, dy} \tag{3.6-b}$$

In the discrete case, the preceding four equations become

$$f_x (x) = \sum_{y=1}^{N} f(x,y) \tag{3.7-a}$$

$$f_y (y) = \sum_{x=1}^{M} f(x,y) \tag{3.7-b}$$

$$x_c = \frac{\sum\limits_{x=1}^{M} x \, f_x (x)}{\sum\limits_{x=1}^{M} f_x (x)} \tag{3.8-a}$$

$$y_c = \frac{\sum\limits_{y=1}^{N} y \, f_y (y)}{\sum\limits_{y=1}^{N} f_y (y)} \tag{3.8-b}$$

For the image L in Figure 3.3(a), we have $(x_c, y_c) = (2.25, 2.08)$. For the image T in Figure 3.3(b), we have $(x_c, y_c) = (3.1, 3.2)$ If we plot the *sample feature vectors* $\vec{x} = (x_c, x_c)$ in a two-dimensional *feature space*, then we may observe a diagram as in Figure 3.4.

Notice in Figure 3.4 the sample points from the two classes are separable by a decision boundary which is a straight line. This is the case when the two classes are *linearly separable*.

A *linear discriminant function* $D_i (\vec{x})$ can be expressed as

$$D_i (\vec{x}) = w_{i1} x_1 + w_{i2} x_2 + \cdots + w_{in} x_n + w_{i(n+1)} = \sum_{k=1}^{n} x_k \, w_{ik} + w_{i(n+1)} \tag{3.9}$$

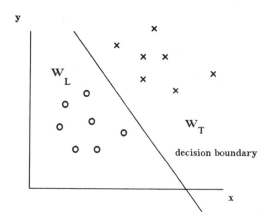

Figure 3.4 Linearly separable feature vectors.

The decision boundary between class ω_i and class ω_j is expressible as

$$D_i\ (\vec{x}) - D_j\ (\vec{x})\ =\ \sum_{k=1}^{n} x_k\ (w_{ik} - w_{jk}) + (w_{i(n+1)} - w_{j(n+1)})\ =\ 0 \qquad (3.10)$$

The preceding equation describes a straight line in two-dimensional space and a *hyperplane* in *n*-dimensional space.

For the two-class problem, the linear classifier can be realized using *threshold logic elements,* as illustrated in Figure 3.5.

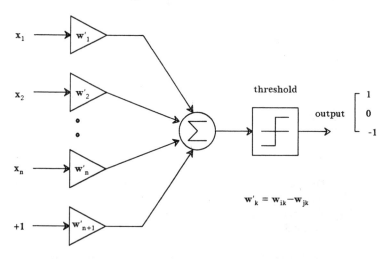

Figure 3.5. Threshold logic realization of the linear classifier.

If the two classes are linearly separable, we can use an *adaptive algorithm* to learn the parameters w_k by presenting samples with known classifications to the adaptive learning algorithm [NILSSON65]. Suppose $\vec{x}$ represents a feature vector with known classification. We first extend $\vec{x}$ to an *augmented vector* $\vec{y}$, by defining

$$\vec{y} = (x_1, x_2, ..., x_n, 1)$$

Also, let the weight vector be

$$\vec{w} = (w_1, w_2, ..., w_n, w_{n+1})$$

Let T_1 denote the training set of augmented vectors $\vec{y}$ such that the corresponding vectors $\vec{x}$ are in class ω_1. Similarly, let T_2 denote the $\vec{y}$'s whose $\vec{x}$'s are in class ω_2. If ω_1 and ω_2 are linearly separable, then there exists a vector $\vec{w}$ such that

$$\vec{y} \cdot \vec{w} > 0 \quad \text{if } \vec{y} \text{ is in } T_1$$

$$\vec{y} \cdot \vec{w} < 0 \quad \text{if } \vec{y} \text{ is in } T_2$$

Therefore, the adaptive algorithm is as follows:

STEP 1. Present each augmented vector $\vec{y}$ to the classifier.

STEP 2. If $\vec{y}$ is in T_1 and $\vec{y} \cdot \vec{w} \leq 0$, then the weight vector is updated: $\vec{w}' \leftarrow \vec{w} + a\,\vec{y}$.

STEP 3. If $\vec{y}$ is in T_2 and $\vec{y} \cdot \vec{w} \geq 0$, then the weight vector is updated: $\vec{w}' \leftarrow \vec{w} - a\,\vec{y}$.

STEP 4. If the weight vector has been updated in STEP 2 or STEP 3, go back to STEP 1.

In the preceding algorithm, the constant 'a' can be chosen as (a) a fixed positive number, such as 1, or (b) the smallest integer making the necessary correction. The choice will affect the algorithm's convergence rate. However, in either case it can be proven that the algorithm converges—that is, a weight vector $\vec{w}$ will be found after a finite number of iterations.

Two other useful classifiers are the *minimum distance classifier* and the *nearest neighbor classifier*.

In the minimum distance classifier, we decide a new feature vector to be in class ω_i, if, in the feature space, its distance to a predetermined class ω_i prototype x^i is the minimum. In case of ties, the feature vector is *rejected*. The decision rule is as follows :

Decide $\vec{x}$ to be in class ω_i

if $|\vec{x} - \vec{x}^i|$ is minimum.

The distance measure $|\vec{x} - \vec{x}^i|$ is

$$|\vec{x} - \vec{x}^i|^2 = (\vec{x} - \vec{x}^i)^t (\vec{x} - \vec{x}^i) = \vec{x}^t \vec{x} - \vec{x}^t \vec{x}_i - \vec{x} (\vec{x}_i)^t + (\vec{x}_i)^t \vec{x}_i$$

where $\vec{x}^t$ is the *transpose* of the vector $\vec{x}$. Since $\vec{x}^t \vec{x}$ is not a function of i, we can choose

$$D_i(\vec{x}) = \vec{x}^t \vec{x}_i + \vec{x}(\vec{x}_i)^t - (\vec{x}_i)^t \vec{x}_i \tag{3.11}$$

which is clearly a linear classifier.

In the minimum distance classifier, we assume each class has a predetermined prototype, which can be regarded as the most typical sample in that class. However, if we do not have such a typical prototype, how can we select a prototype? Instead of considering a single prototype, we can regard all the feature vectors in a class to be prototypes. Therefore, for the two-class problem, let R_1 and R_2 be the set of feature vectors in each class. We define a new distance measure as follows:

$$d(\vec{x}, R_i) = \min_{\vec{r} \ in \ R_i} |\vec{x} - \vec{r}| \qquad (3.12)$$

In other words, $d(\vec{x}, R_i)$ is the minimum distance to any member in the set R_i. We now decide x to be in class ω_i, if $d(\vec{x}, R_i)$ is minimum.

The nearest neighbor classifier is useful when we have classes that are not linearly separable, but each subclass of a class is linearly separable. Since now it is necessary to store all the samples, and the distance measure is also defined with respect to all the samples, the computation cost may be quite large for nearest neighbor classifiers.

As a final note, a pattern classifier can make a decision or reject a sample. A decision may be correct or wrong. Therefore, to evaluate a pattern classifier, we have three rates:

a. Recognition rate (percentage of correct decisions)

b. Misrecognition rate (percentage of incorrect decisions)

c. Rejection rate (percentage of no decisions)

3.3 BOUNDARY DETECTION

The object region can be completely specified by its boundary. Boundary detection works based on the fact that there are gray-level changes around boundary points. Because of problems such as illumination, the reflectance of object surface, the degradation of image quality due to noise in image acquisition, and so on, modeling those gray-level changes is quite difficult. Researchers have developed many edge-detection techniques based on different models. We include some in this section. Edge detection by resolution pyramid is a hierarchical method, which combines crude edge detection and sophisticated edge detection at different levels. The relaxation method makes use of contextual information by introducing consistence function and dynamically adjusting edge confidences. Contour following produces a list of boundary points. After a discussion of contour following of binary pictures, a technique for gray-level pictures using graph searching is briefly described, which invokes edge graph searching and can produce an optimal result. The Hough transform detects boundaries of known shape. It is actually a template-matching process.

3.3.1 Edge Detection by Resolution Pyramids

We discussed local operators for edge detection in Chapter 2. We now present another algorithm for edge detection, this time using the resolution pyramid. In so doing, we will better understand the hierarchical data structure commonly used in many segmentation algorithms.

An example of a three-level resolution pyramid is shown in Figure 3.6(a).

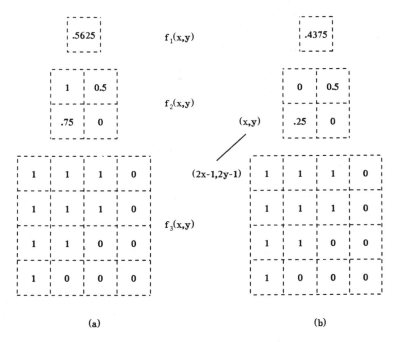

(a)

(b)

Figure 3.6 (a) Three-level resolution pyramid; (b) edge detection by picture information measure.

The lower-resolution picture is obtained from the higher-resolution picture by a consolidation or reduction process:

$$f_{i-1}(x,y) = .25(f_i(2x-1, 2y-1) + f_i(2x-1, 2y) + f_i(2x, 2y-1) + f_i(2x, 2y))$$

The enlargement process is defined by

$$f_i(x,y) = f_{i-1}(\lfloor 0.5(x+1) \rfloor, \lfloor 0.5(y+1) \rfloor)$$

The pyramid edge detection algorithm is a recursive algorithm. It starts from the highest level (lowest resolution) picture f_1 in the pyramid and expands to the next level whenever necessary. If there could be an edge, the algorithm then checks whether there really are edges. If there really are edges, it reports their locations. Otherwise, it will expand the pyramid one more level.

In the following algorithm, the parameters have the following meanings: (x,y) is the coordinate of the lower-left corner of a subpicture; i denotes the i-th level subpicture; n is the total number of levels; t_i is the i-th level threshold; and h_i is the i-th level edge detector.

```
edge-detect(x,y,i)
begin
if i> n then break;
for x'=2x-1 until 2x step 1
for y'=2y-1 until 2y step 1
        if maybe-edge(x',y',i,t_i)
        then    if sure-edge(x',y',i,t_i)
                then report-success(x',y',i)
                else edge-detect(x',y',i+1);
end


maybe-edge(x,y,i,t_i)
begin
if 1-t_i > f_i (x,y) and f_i (x,y) > t_i then return(1) else return(0)
end


sure-edge(x,y,i,t_i)
begin
/*apply i-level edge detector h_i*/
if |    ∑       h_i (u, v)f_i (u, v) | > t_i then return(1) else return(0)
    (i,j) in NS_i(x,y)
end


report-success(x,y,i)
begin
```

$$x' = 2^{n-i} x - 2^{n-i} + 1$$

$$y' = 2^{n-i} y - 2^{n-i} + 1$$

```
print("there are edges at ",i," level subpicture ",x',y')
end
```

The algorithm is invoked by the following main procedure:

```
main-procedure()
begin
if maybe-edge(1,1,1,t_1) then edge-detect(1,1,2)
end
```

In the preceding, we used a crude edge detection algorithm to find out whether there may be edges. This algorithm simply checks whether the average gray-level of the subpicture is between $1-t_i$ and t_i. A more sophisticated edge detection algorithm is used to find out whether there are sure edges. The edge detector h_i could be different from level to level. If for levels between 1 and n-k, we are never sure (because the images are of low resolution), then we simply set t_i to 1, so that the sure-edge procedure always returns 0.

An example of pyramidal edge detection is shown in Figure 3.7. For computer processing, the resolution pyramid can be stored in n separate arrays. A better way is

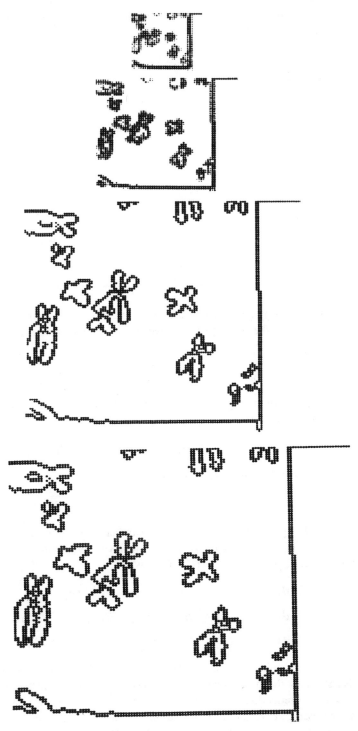

Figure 3.7 A Pyramidal edge detection (from S. Tanimoto and T. Palvidis, ''A Hierarchical Data Structure for Picture Processing,'' *Computer Graphics and Image Processing*, June, 1975, p. 104-19.

to use an *RGB pyramid*, which stores three resolution pyramids in a big picture array, as shown in Figure 3.8.

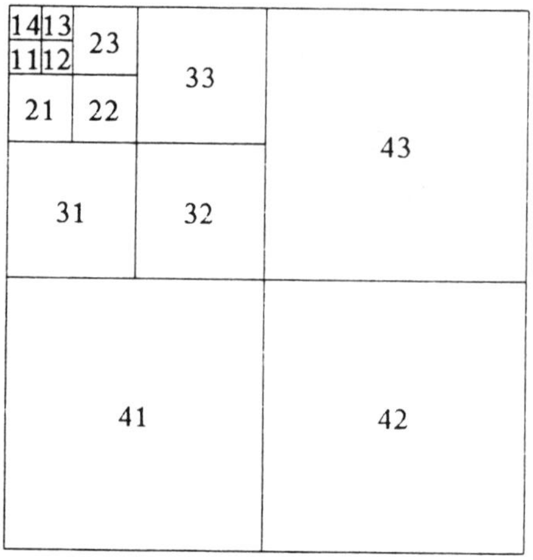

Figure 3.8 RGB pyramid.

The RGB pyramid can be used to store three color images at various resolutions. When we store the RGB pyramid, we follow a clockwise sequence to store the following subpictures:

$$f_{14} \ f_{13} \ f_{12} \ f_{11} \ f_{23} \ f_{22} \ f_{21} \ f_{33} \ f_{32} \ f_{31} \ f_{43} \ f_{42} \ f_{41}$$

where f_{14} is a "dummy picture," representing the dark pixel at the upper-left corner of a picture array. Let

$$f_{(i+1)4} = f_{i4} + f_{i3} + f_{i2} + f_{i1}$$

Let N_{ik} denote the size of f_{ik}. We also have

$$N_{(i+1)4} = N_{i4} + N_{i3} + N_{i2} + N_{i1}$$

Let $d(i_1, k_1; i_2, k_2)$ denote the distance (number of memory cells) from the i_1-th level subpicture of k_1 pyramid to the i_2-th level subpicture of k_2 pyramid, where $1 \le i_1, i_2 \le n$, and $1 \le k_1, k_2 \le 3$. We have

$$d(i, 3; i+j, 3) = 3N_i + 3N_{i+1} + 3N_{i+2} + \cdots + 3N_{i+j-1}$$

$$d(i, 2; i+j, 2) = 2N_i + 3N_{i+1} + 3N_{i+1} + \cdots + 3N_{i+j-1} + N_{i+j}$$

$$d(i, 1; i+j, 1) = N_i + 3N_{i+1} + 2N_{i+2} + \cdots + 2N_{i+j-1} + 2N_{i+j}$$

The pyramid is a data structure from the viewpoint of representation. We can also think of the processing of the subpictures in the pyramid with the objective of information reduction. From this viewpoint of processing, we have a *processing cone*. A processing cone is normally used for image reduction. From the generation viewpoint, we can enlarge smaller pictures into larger ones. This generation process is best described by the Chinese Taoist philosophical saying: "One begets Two, Two begets Three, and Three begets Everything."

As far as the development of algorithms for parallel computers is concerned, in the domain of picture processing we may often use the "pyramid machine" methodology of algorithm design that greatly simplifies such development. The highly parallel "pyramid machine" architecture supports several styles of programming for parallel machines, and it allows complicated transformations of pictures to be computed very rapidly [TANIMOTO87].

In the recursive edge detection algorithm just described, we used a crude one-pixel edge detection algorithm based on the average gray level of the subpicture. We can also use a *picture information measure.*

A measure for the amount of information contained in a picture f is based on the minimum number of pixel gray level changes to convert a picture into one with constant gray level [CHANG83]. Let $h : \{0, 1, ..., L-1\} \rightarrow N$ represent the *histogram* of f, where $h(i)$ is the number of pixels at gray level i. We define the picture information measure $PIM(f)$ as follows :

$$PIM(f) = [\sum_{i=0}^{L-1} h(i)] - \max_{i} h(i) \qquad (3.13)$$

We can also define a *normalized picture information measure* as $NPIM(f) = PIM(f) / N(f)$.

The picture information measures just introduced will be discussed in Chapter 4. They can be used to select subpictures in edge detection. For example, if $NPIM(f)$ is less than a threshold, then f need not be further decomposed. An example of using $NPIM(f)$ in hierarchical edge detection is illustrated in Figure 3.6(b). Suppose the $NPIM$ threshold is 0.1. Since $NPIM(f_1) = 0.4375 > t$, we will go to the second level. Since $NPIM(f_{11}) = 0.25$ and $NPIM(f_{22}) = 0.5$, these two subpictures need to be processed, and f_{12}, f_{21} need not be processed any further.

Both the average gray level and the pictorial information measure are examples of measures for pictorial homogeneity. A *homogeneity property* H is a function from the family of all pictures to the real line R. Depending upon the application domain, we must choose an appropriate homogeneity property for these pyramid-oriented algorithms.

3.3.2 A Relaxation Method For Edge Detection

We can improve the results of edge detection operation using a relaxation method [ZUCKER77, PRAGER80]. This method utilizes *local information* to improve the confidence of detected edges.

Crack Edge Detection

In crack edge detection, the edges are located between adjacent pixels. Let $f(x, y)$ and $f(x', y')$ be two neighboring pixels. The strength of an edge is

$$s = |f(x, y) - f(x', y')| \qquad (3.14)$$

We detect a crack edge e, if $s(e)$ is above a given threshold. The direction $g(e)$ of the crack edge e is either horizontal or vertical. An example is given in Figure 3.9.

Figure 3.9 Crack edge detection.

If the threshold is 1, the two detected crack edges have strength 2 and 3, respectively.

The Relaxation Algorithm

After the crack edges have been detected, we use a relaxation algorithm to improve the results of edge detection operation. The basic idea is to adjust the edge strength utilizing local information. For each edge, its confidence level is initially defined as its edge strength. The confidence level is then adjusted dynamically. If a weak edge (low-confidence edge) is positioned between strong edges (high-confidence edges), we should increase its strength (confidence level). Conversely, if we have an isolated weak edge, its confidence level should be further decreased. Therefore, based upon local information, the confidence level of an edge can be increased, decreased, or remain unchanged. The algorithm follows.

Edge Relaxation Algorithm.

STEP 1. Determine confidence level $C^0(e)$ for all edges e. Initially, we define

$$C^0(e) = s(e) / \max_{all\ e} s(e)$$

Let $k = 0$.

STEP 2. While there exists $C^k(e)$ which is neither 0 nor 1, do the following:

　　　　STEP 2.1. $k = k+1$.

　　　　STEP 2.2. Compute $C^k(e)$ from local information around edge e.

　　　　　　　　STEP 2.2.1. Classify the two vertices of an edge e, based on the confidence levels of surrounding edges.
　　　　　　　　STEP 2.2.2. Classify edge e, based upon its vertex types.
　　　　　　　　STEP 2.2.3. Update $C^k(e)$, based upon its edge type.

Computation of $C^k(e)$

To compute $C^k(e)$, we proceed as follows:

Vertex Classification: Each vertex of an edge can also be the vertex of three other edges. Suppose these three edges have edge confidence levels a, b, and c. With no loss of generality, we can assume that $a \geq b \geq c$. The situation is illustrated in Figure 3.10.

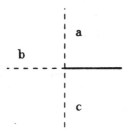

Figure 3.10 Vertex classification.

We define $m = max(a,b,c,q)$, where q is a parameter, $q > 0$. We compute vertex confidence levels as follows:

$$Conf(0) = (m-a)(m-b)(m-c) \quad (no\ edge)$$

$$Conf(1) = a\ (m-b)(m-c) \quad (one\ edge)$$

$$Conf(2) = a\ b\ (m-c) \quad (two\ edges)$$

$$Conf(3) = a\ b\ c \quad (three\ edges)$$

We determine a vertex to be of type i, if $Conf(i)$ is maximum. $Conf(i)$ represents the confidence level for a vertex to have i incident edges (other than the edge in question).

The parameter q is so chosen to force the vertex type to be 0, when the edge confidences a,b, and c are very small. As an example, if $a = 0.03$, $b = 0.02$, $c = 0.01$, and $q = 0.1$, $Conf(0)$ will be maximum, so that the vertex is of type 0. On the other hand, if $a = 1$, $b = 0.05$, $c = 0.01$, and $q = 0.1$, $Conf(1)$ will be maximum, so that the vertex is of type 1.

The edge type is determined by the pair of vertex types. Depending on the edge type, the update rule is as follows:

Type D (Decrement)	Type I (Increment)	Type U (Unchanged)
0–0	1–1	0–1
0–2	1–2	2–2
0–3	1–3	2–3
		3–3

The edge confidence updating formula is as follows:

$$C^{k+1}(e) = \begin{cases} min(1, C^k(e) + d) & \text{if } e \text{ is of type } I \\ C^k(e) & \text{if } e \text{ is of type } U \\ max(0, C^k(e) - d) & \text{if } e \text{ is of type } D \end{cases} \qquad (3.15)$$

where $d > 0$ is the selected increment or decrement. In this edge relaxation algorithm, strong edges will influence their weak neighbors to convert to strong ones, and vice versa.

The preceding relaxation algorithm may not converge. Consider the example in Figure 3.11.

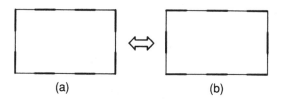

Figure 3.11 (a) Initial edge; (b) the edge after one iteration.

(a)   (b)

In Figure 3.11(a), a strong edge is denoted by double lines, and a weak non-edge is denoted by a single line. Each edge is of type $D(0-0)$, and therefore its strength should be decreased. Each non-edge is of type $I(1-1)$, and therefore its strength should be increased. If the edge strength and non-edge strength are $t + 0.5d$ and $t - 0.5d$, where t is the edge threshold, we will have the reverse situation, as shown in Figure 3.11(b). There will be no convergence in this case. In practice, we can terminate the algorithm after a fixed number of iterations.

The preceding algorithm can be regarded as a *parallel algorithm* in the sense that all edges are considered simultaneously. A *sequential algorithm* will update the edges one at a time. If we apply the sequential algorithm to the picture in Figure 3.11(a), it will converge to either a picture consisting only of strong edges or a picture consisting only of non-edges. The result of the sequential relaxation algorithm is therefore non-unique.

A practical example of the edge relaxation algorithm is illustrated in Figure 3.12. Figure 3.12(a) illustrates the digitized half-tone picture of a wrench. The initial result after applying the edge detection algorithm is shown in Figure 3.12(b). After six iterations, the improved result is shown in Figure 3.12(c).

The relaxation algorithm also motivates the use of *local context* in picture processing. The update rule can be expressed as rewriting rules in a formal grammar:

$$v0(x-1,y)e(s,x,y,0)v0(x+1,y) ::= v0(x-1,y)e(s-d,x,y,0)v0(x+1,y)$$
$$v0(x-1,y)e(s,x,y,0)v2(x+1,y) ::= v0(x-1,y)e(s-d,x,y,0)v2(x+1,y)$$
$$v0(x-1,y)e(s,x,y,0)v3(x+1,y) ::= v0(x-1,y)e(s-d,x,y,0)v3(x+1,y)$$
$$v1(x-1,y)e(s,x,y,0)v1(x+1,y) ::= v1(x-1,y)e(s+d,x,y)v1(x+1,y)$$
$$v1(x-1,y)e(s,x,y,0)v2(x+1,y) ::= v1(x-1,y)e(s+d,x,y)v2(x+1,y)$$
$$v1(x-1,y)e(s,x,y,0)v3(x+1,y) ::= v1(x-1,y)e(s+d,x,y)v3(x+1,y)$$

In the preceding, $v0(x,y)$, $v1(x,y)$, $v2(x,y)$, and $v3(x,y)$ denote vertices of type 0, 1, 2, and 3, respectively. $e(s,x,y,0)$ denotes an edge having strength s at location (x,y) with direction 0 (horizontal edge). The first rewriting rule says that if an edge $e(s,x,y,0)$ is in the context of $v0(x-1,y)$ and $v0(x+1,y)$, then it can be replaced by $e(s-d,x,y,0)$. Notice with the formal rewriting rules, we are dealing with *picture objects* (in this case, edges and vertices). Some objects have attributes, which are the characteristic parameters or the features of these objects. The preceding grammar rules deal with horizontal edge updating. Similar rules can be written for vertical edge updating.

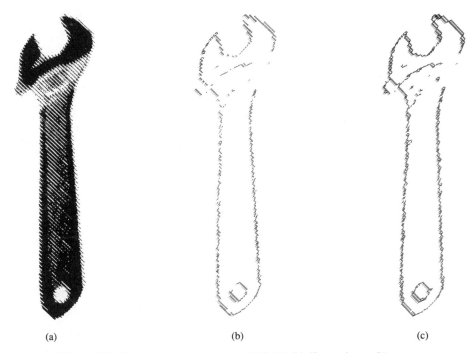

(a) (b) (c)

Figure 3.12 Example of edge relaxation. (a) Original half-tone picture; (b) initial edge detection result; (c) result improved after six iterations.

3.3.3 Contour Following

In contour following, we try to extend the boundary by tracing the boundary points. For binary pictures, the contour following algorithm is quite simple. In the following algorithm, the direction d can take on four values, as illustrated in Figure 3.13.

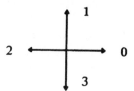

Figure 3.13 Direction code for contour.

```
contour-following(f,M,N)
begin
/*scan the picture until a 1-pixel is encountered*/
for x₀ = 1 until M
    for y₀ = 1 until N
        if f(x₀ ,y₀) = 1 then break;
/*initially S is empty, direction d is 0, (x,y) is (x₀ ,y₀) */
S = {}; d = 0; (x,y) = (x₀, y₀);
/*boundary tracing:
    turn left if a 1-pixel is encountered, and turn right otherwise*/
while (x,y) not equal to (x₀, y₀) or S is empty
    begin
    if f(x,y) = 1 then left(x,y,d) else right(x,y,d);
    S = S ∪ {(x,y)}
    end
end

left(x,y,d)
begin
    case d
    0:  y=y+1;
    1:  x=x-1;
    2:  y=y-1;
    3:  x=x+1;
    end case;
d = (d+1) mod 4
end

right(x,y,d)
begin
    case d
    0:  y=y-1;
    1:  x=x+1;
    2:  y=y+1;
    3:  x=x-1;
    end case;
d = (d+3) mod 4
end
```

An example is given in Figure 3.14.

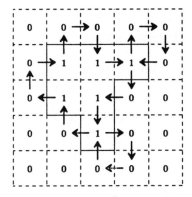

Figure 3.14   Contour following example.

The preceding contour following algorithm can be generalized to gray-level pictures. The essential idea is to try to follow the general direction of the edge. As illustrated in Figure 3.15(a), a circular scanning path can be used to trace the boundary curve [PINGLE71].

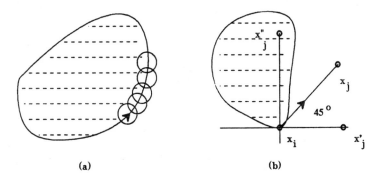

(a)   (b)

Figure 3.15.   (a) The tracing path; (b) contour following.

Suppose x_i is found. We first find x_j adjacent to x_i, along the same direction as the edge at x_i (or the direction perpendicular to the gradient at x_i). If $s(x_j) > t$, then x_j is taken as the next point on the boundary. Otherwise, we try x'_j or x_j'', depending on whether x_j is in the object or not. This technique is illustrated in Figure 3.15(b). A triangular scanning path can also be used with a possible reduction in processing time [CHANG74].

3.3.4 Graph Searching Technique for Edge Following

We can also adopt a graph searching technique to find the best contour in a picture, satisfying certain optimization criterion. This is best illustrated in Figure 3.16. The detected edges and their directions are shown in Figure 3.16(a). From Figure 3.16(a), we can construct an edge graph, as shown in Figure 3.16(b). For an edge to connect from (x_1, y_1) to (x_2, y_2), (x_2, y_2) must be one of the three possible 8-neighbors in front of this edge, and $s(x_1, y_1) > t$, $s(x_2, y_2) > t$ —that is, the edges must have enough strength.

As an example, if we start from point (2,1), there are three 8-neighbors in front of the edge at (2,1), which are (1,2), (2,2), and (3,2). But $s(1,2) = 0$ because there is no edge at that point. Consequently, we can connect (2,1) to (2,2) and (3,2) but not to (1,2).

Once the edge graph is formed, we can search for a path from a starting point (x_1, y_1) to a terminating point (x_n, y_n) or a set of terminating points, with minimum cost. The cost can be defined depending on applications, such as accumulated edge strength, total sum of curvature, closeness to a model curve, and so on. As an example, the minimum cost path from (2,1) to (3,4) is indicated by the heavy line.

Heuristic search or exhaustive search techniques can be used to find the best path.

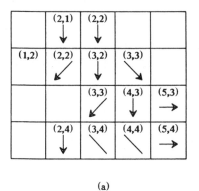 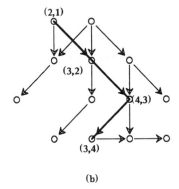

(a)   (b)

Figure 3.16 Graph representation of a gradient image (from Dana H. Ballard/Christopher M. Brown, *COMPUTER VISION*, © 1982, p. 131. Reprinted by permission of Prentice-Hall, Inc., Englewood Cliffs, New Jersey.) (a) Detected edges; (b) an edge graph.

3.3.5 Hough Transform for Boundary Detection

Suppose two points (x', y') and (x'', y'') are colinear. We have, as shown in Figure 3.17,

$$c' = m'x' + y' \tag{3.16-a}$$

$$c' = m'x'' + y'' \tag{3.16-b}$$

Now if we regard (x',y') and (x",y") as fixed, then we have equations (3.16) which describe lines in the c-m parameter space, as shown in Figure 3.17(b).

Therefore, if $(x_1, y_1), ..., (x_n, y_n)$ are n colinear points, then they should pass through a common point in the parameter space. If we quantize the parameter space into an array $A(c, m)$ and update those entries having a line passing through them, then the maxima in $A(c, m)$ corresponds to the colinear points in the picture space. The algorithm now follows.

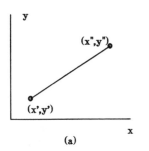

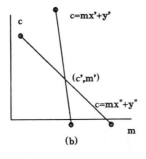

Figure 3.17 (a) Colinear points; (b) lines in c-m parameter space. (From Dana H. Ballard/Christopher M. Brown, *COMPUTER VISION*, © 1982, p. 123. Reprinted by permission of Prentice-Hall, Inc., Englewood Cliffs, New Jersey.)

The algorithm now follows.

```
Hough-transform(f,list)
begin

    initialize parameter space array A to zeros;
    initialize list of colinear points to empty;
    initialize current max to zero;

    for x = 1 until M
       for y = 1 until N
           /*if edge strength at (x,y) exceeds threshold then
                update entries in the parameter space array A */
           if s(x,y) > t then
              for c = 1 until Cmax
                 for m = 1 until Mmax
                     if c = mx + y then  begin A(c,m) = A(c,m) + 1;
                                         if A(c,m)>max then (c',m')=(c,m)
                                         end

    /*find all colinear points*/
    for x = 1 until M
       for y = 1 until N
           if |c' - m'x - y| < tolerance
               then add (x,y) to the list of colinear points;

    end
```

The Hough transform uses this parameter space to detect the most likely line passing through n points. In fact, any parametric curve (straight line, conic curve, and so on) can be detected using the Hough transform, which is relatively immune to noise and gaps in the boundary curves. For example, if the curve is a circle with fixed radius, the equation is

$$(x-a)^2 + (y-b)^2 = r^2 \qquad (3.17)$$

where the parameters are a and b. An example of tumor detection application is shown in Figure 3.18. A section of the chest film (Figure 3.18(b)) is searched for circles of radius 3 units. In Figure 3.18(c), the resultant parameter space array $A(a,b,3)$ is shown in a pictorial fashion by interpreting the array values as pixels. This process is repeated for various radii, and then a set of likely circles is chosen by setting a radius-dependent threshold for the array A contents. Figure 3.18(d) shows the locations of possible tumors for the chest film of Figure 3.18(a).

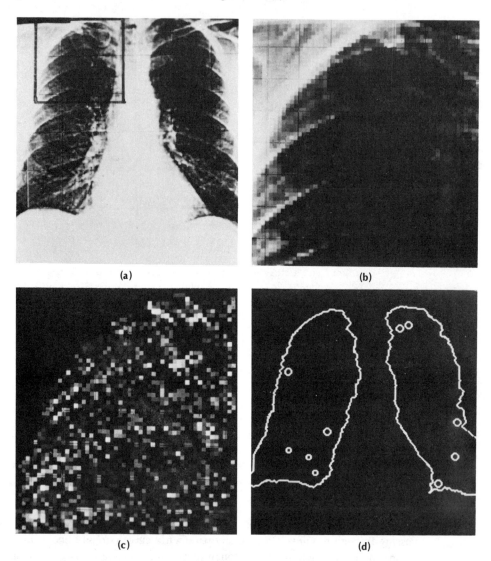

(a)

(b)

(c)

(d)

Figure 3.18 Tumor detection by using Hough transform (From Dana H. Ballard/Christopher M. Brown, *COMPUTER VISION* © 1982, p. 126. Reprinted by permission of Prentice-Hall, Inc., Englewood Cliffs, New Jersey.)

3.4 REGION GROWING TECHNIQUES

Region growing techniques make use of the gray-level homogeneous property of the object region. Thresholding supposes that the gray-level distribution of each object region is uni-modal. Therefore, the optimal threshold can be selected statistically. The primary region growing method is pixel based, starting from a single pixel and adding more points into the region if after adding those points the homogeneous predicate on the region is still true. The split-and-merge algorithm grows regions controlled by a certain data structure—for example, a pyramid data structure.

3.4.1 Thresholding

Regions are usually areas in an image occupied by picture objects. Thresholding techniques can be used when picture objects have characteristic patterns of gray levels, or characteristic textures. The general approach is as follows :

STEP 1. Perform local operations such as gradient operation, local averaging, and so on, to obtain an enhanced image.

STEP 2. Select an appropriate threshold to identify picture objects. A point (x, y) is considered to be in the object if $f(x, y)$ exceeds the threshold.

The threshold is usually determined by finding the valley between the two peaks of the histogram, as shown in Figure 3.19(a). If the histogram is not bimodal, we could attempt to decompose the picture into subpictures and find a different threshold for each subpicture. This leads to "local" histograms and "local" thresholds, as shown in Figure 3.19(b).

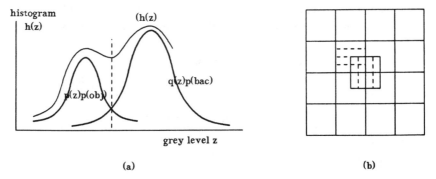

Figure 3.19 (a) Threshold selection and (b) dynamic thresholding, where the subpictures for local histogramming may overlap.

For the bimodal case, a threshold can be obtained by minimizing certain error measures. Suppose $h(z)$ is a mixture of two density functions, $p(z)$ for the object pixels and $q(z)$ for the background pixels. Object pixels occur with probability $p(obj)$, and background pixels occur with probability $p(bac)$. We have

$$h(z) = p(obj)p(z) + p(bac)q(z) \qquad (3.18)$$

Suppose t is the chosen threshold. Then the probability of misclassifying a background pixel is

$$E_1 = \int_0^t q(z)\, dz$$

and the probability of misclassifying an object pixel is

$$E_2 = \int_t^\infty p(z)\, dz$$

To minimize the error $E = E_1 \, p(bac) + E_2 \, p(obj)$, we choose t such that

$$p(t)p(obj) = q(t)p(bac)$$

If $p(t)$ and $q(t)$ are normal, we have

$$p(t) = \frac{1}{2n \, \sigma_1^2} \, e^{\frac{-(t-m_1)^2}{2\sigma_1^2}} \,, \qquad q(t) = \frac{1}{2n \, \sigma_2^2} \, e^{\frac{-(t-m_2)^2}{2\sigma_2^2}} \,,$$

We thus obtain

$$\sigma_1^2 \, (t-m_2)^2 - \sigma_2^2 \, (t-m_1)^2 = 2 \, \sigma_1^2 \, \sigma_2^2 \ln \left(\sigma_1 \, p(obj) \,/\, \sigma_2 \, p(bac) \right)$$

If $\sigma_1 = \sigma_2$ and $p(obj) = p(bac)$, we have

$$t = (m_1 + m_2) / 2$$

For arbitrary density functions, we can use the Bayesian rule. Suppose the probabilities are as defined:

p(obj,z) is the joint probability that a point belongs to an object and has gray level z

p(bac,z) is the joint probability that a point belongs to the background and has gray level z

p(obj) is the a priori probability that a point belongs to object

p(bac) is the a priori probability that a point belongs to background
$$(p(bac) = 1 - p(obj))$$

h(z) is the probability that a point has gray level z

Since

$$p(obj/z) = p(obj,z) / h(z)$$

$$p(bac/z) = p(bac,z) / h(z)$$

Therefore, $p(obj/z) > p(bac/z)$ if and only if $p(obj,z) > p(bac,z)$, or

$$p(obj) \, p(z/obj) > p(bac) p(z/bac)$$

That is,

$$p(obj) \, p(z) > (1 - p(obj)) \, q(z)$$

Therefore, if $p(obj)$, $p(z)$ and $q(z)$ are known, we can use the preceding rule to determine Z, the set of gray levels belonging to the objects.

Another technique for threshold selection is to select a threshold so that *pMN* points are thresholded into 1. In other words, it is assumed that objects occupy a fraction of $p(obj)$ of the original image; p is selected in advance. This is called the *p-tile method*.

The *neighborhood method* works as follows: Let $p(i,j)$ be the relative frequency with which points having gray level j occur in some neighborhood of points of gray level i. If there are L gray levels, $p(i,j)$ is an L-by-L symmetric matrix. For each i, $(p(i,1),...,p(i,L))$ characterizes the types of neighbors that points of gray level i have in f.

We can then measure the closeness between a gray-level pair. For example, gray levels i and j are considered close, if

$$\sum_{k=1}^{L} w_k \, p(i,k) \, p(j,k) \geq t \qquad (3.19)$$

where

$$w_k = [\sum_{k=1}^{L} p(i,k)^2 \sum_{k=1}^{L} p(j,k)^2]^{-\frac{1}{2}}$$

We can then select a set of gray levels Z as the object gray level cluster. A point (x,y) is considered to be in the object, if $f(x,y)$ is in Z.

3.4.2 Region Growing by Coloring

When we apply thresholding to find regions, the implicit homogeneity property we use is that a region is homogeneous if all pixels have gray levels below (or above) a threshold. The regions we obtain may be disconnected. A region R is connected if any two points in R are connected; otherwise R is disconnected. To find connected regions, we can apply the region growing technique.

For binary pictures, we first scan the picture to find an initial 1-pixel. We grow a region by finding all 1-pixels connected to this initial 1-pixel. When this region can grow no more, it is labeled (colored), and we find another initial 1-pixel to grow another region (using a different label). For example, the first region is labeled 1, the second region is labeled 2, and so on.

For binary pictures, the definition of connectedness depends on the neighbor set. A 1-pixel (x_1, y_1) is 8-connected to another 1-pixel (x_2, y_2) if either (x_2, y_2) is in the 8-neighbor set $NS8(x_1, y_1)$ or there exists (x', y') which is 8-connected to (x_2, y_2), and (x', y') is in the 8-neighbor set $NS8(x_1, y_1)$. We can likewise define 4-connectedness. For example, the region in Figure 3.20(a) is 8-connected but not 4-connected, whereas the region in Figure 3.20(b) is both 8-connected and 4-connected. Therefore, 4-connectedness implies 8-connectedness but not the converse. The labeled 4-connected regions of Figure 3.20(a) are shown in Figure 3.20(c).

```
0 1 0 0    0 0 1 0    0 1 0 0
1 0 1 1    1 1 1 1    2 0 3 3
1 0 0 1    0 0 1 0    2 0 0 3
1 0 0 1    0 0 1 0    2 0 0 3
  (a)        (b)        (c)
```

Figure 3.20 (a) 8-connected region; (b) 4-connected region; (c) labeled 4-connected regions.

3.4.3 Split and Merge Algorithm for Region Growing

For gray-level pictures, each region must satisfy a certain homogeneity property H. For example, we may require that the absolute gray level difference between any two points (or two neighboring points) in R must be less than a certain threshold. If we use picture information measure, we can stipulate that $NPIM(f/R)$ is less than a certain threshold, where f/R is the support picture for R (see Section 4.1).

The split-and-merge algorithm works as follows: we start from an initial collection of regions. If for any region R, $H(R)$ is false, we split R into sub-regions. If for neighboring regions $R_1, R_2, ..., R_m$, $H(R_1 \cup R_2 \cdots \cup R_m)$ is true, we merge them into one single region.

To perform region merging, suppose we maintain a neighbor-region list S_i for each region R_i. When we merge R_i and R_j into a new region, say R_k, we update the neighbor-region list as follows:

Rule 1. Merge S_i and S_j, and delete R_i, R_j from this list, to form S_k.

Rule 2. For any other S_m, rename R_i to R_k and R_j to R_k, and remove duplicate names.

If a region R_i is split into two regions R_j and R_k, we update neighbor-region list as follows:

Rule 3. For any R_m, add R_j to the list if R_j is connected to R_m; add R_k to the list if R_k is connected to R_m; and delete R_i.

The selection of initial regions is important for this algorithm. We can start with a single region R containing all pixels and use a pyramid structure to split regions. We can also start with every pixel representing a different region and try to merge them into larger regions.

3.5 DISCUSSION

The results of segmentation are usually included in a list of segmented objects:

$$R_1(x_1), R_2(x_2), ..., R_n(x_n)$$

Each object may have one (or more) of the following attributes:

a. A list of line segments or a chain code describing its boundary or contour.

b. Description of the minimum rectangular window enclosing that object, usually specified by its lower-left-corner and upper-right-corner coordinates (x_L, y_L, x_R, y_R).

c. The gray-level picture or a thresholded binary picture enclosed in this rectangular window containing that object.

d. The classification category ω_i of that object.

Attributes a through c give the physical representation of that segmented object. Attribute d is the result after applying some pattern recognition algorithm and is the logical representation of that object. Together, a through d form an *icon*, or a (physical-representation, logical-representation) pair.

Therefore, the result of segmentation and recognition is a list of icons. The segmented picture is the representation at the second level of the pyramid illustrated in Figure 2.4. The segmented picture can be used to construct geometric models. If we can discover the relations among these icons (segmented objects), we can then obtain relational structures, which are at the highest level in the pyramid of picture representations.

R E F E R E N C E S

[BALLARD82] BALLARD, D. H. AND C. M. BROWN, *Computer Vision*. Englewood Cliffs, New Jersey: Prentice-Hall, Inc., 1982.

[CASTLEMAN79] CASTLEMAN, K. R. *Digital Image Processing*. Englewood Cliffs, New Jersey: Prentice-Hall,Inc., 1979.

[CHANG74] CHANG, S. K., "A Triangular Scanning Technique for Locating Boundary Curves," in *Computer Graphics and Image Processing*, Vol. 3, 1974, 313-317.

[CHANG83] CHANG, S. K., AND C. C. YANG, "Picture Information Measures for Similarity Retrieval," *Journal of Computer Vision, Graphics and Image Processing*. Academic Press, Vol. 23, 1983, 366-375.

[NILSSON65] NILSSON, N., *Learning Machines*. McGraw-Hill, 1965.

[PINGLE71] PINGLE, K. K., AND J. M. TENENBAUM, "An Accommodating Edge Follower," in *Proceedings of the Second International Joint Conference on Artificial Intelligence*, AFIPS. London, 1971, 1-7.

[PRAGER80] PRAGER, J. M., "Extracting and Labeling Boundary Segments in Natural Scenes," *IEEE Trans. PAMI*, Vol. 2, No. 1, January 1980, 16-27.

[TANIMOTO87] TANIMOTO, S. L., "Paradigms for Pyramid Machine Algorithms," in *Pyramidal Systems for Image Processing*, (V. Cantoni and S. Levialdi, eds.), Springer-Verlag, 1987.

[ZUCKER77] ZUCKER, S. W., R. A. HUMMEL, AND A. ROSENFELD, "An Application of Relaxation Labeling to Line and Curve Enhancement," *IEEE Trans. on Computers*, Vol. 26, 1977.

E X E R C I S E S

1. Typical examples of digitized binary pictures of the letters "A," "B," and "S" are shown next. Using the techniques you have learned, develop algorithms to recognize these letters. Explain preprocessing, feature extraction, and classification algorithms clearly, and illustrate how these nine binary pictures are analyzed.

```
0011100
0100010
0100010
0111110
0100011
1000011
0000000
```

```
0001000
0110110
0100010
0111110
0100011
1000011
1100001

0011100
0100010
0000010
0111110
1100011
1000011
1000010

1111110
1000001
1000001
1111110
1000001
1000001
1111110

0011110
1110001
1100011
1111100
1000011
1000011
1111100

0000000
1111110
1000001
1111110
1000001
1000001
1111110

0011110
1110011
0110000
0011110
0000011
0000110
0111100
```

```
0011110
1100000
1110000
0011110
0000110
0000110
1111100

0011111
1110001
0110001
0011100
0000011
0000110
1111000
```

2. In an OCR system, the images are represented by 5-by-5 binary pictures. Each class of characters occurs with equal probability. The conditional probability $p(v/w)(x,y)$ is the probability of having pixel value v at (x,y) in the binary picture, given the true pixel value w in the prototype picture. We assume $p(v/w)(x,y)$ is position independent; therefore, we can write $p(v/w)$. The conditional probabilities are as follows: $P(1/1) = q, P(0/1) = 1-q, P(0/0) = p$, and $P(1/0) = 1-p$. The prototype pictures for "1" and "T" are as shown:

```
00100        11111
00100        00100
00100        00100
00100        00100
01110        00100
```

Suppose we observe

```
01110
00100
00100
00100
00110
```

Using the Bayesian decision rule, decide whether this pattern belongs to class "1" or class "T" for

    a. $p = 0.9, q = 0.9$
    b. $p = 0.9, q = 0.7$
    c. $p = 0.7, q = 0.9$

3. Derive the expression for $d(i_1, k_1; i_2, k_2)$.

4. Write programs to manage an RGB pyramid.

```
read(i,k):  read i-th level subpicture of k-th pyramid into buffer.
write(i,k): write buffer into i-th level subpicture of k-th pyramid.
reduce(i,k): reduce subpicture (i,k) and store in subpicture (i-1,k).
expand(i,k): expand subpicture (i,k) and store in subpicture (i+1,k).
clear(i,k,c): set subpicture (i,k) to constant gray level c.
```

5. Write a program to implement the edge relaxation algorithm.

6. Give explicit conditions on picture functions (or detected edges) so the relaxation algorithm will converge.

7. Write the grammar rules (rewriting rules) for vertical edge updating.

8. (x,y) and (u,v) are 4-adjacent if (u,v) is in $NS4(x,y)$. (x,y) and (u,v) are 8-adjacent if (u,v) is in $NS8(x,y)$. A binary picture is 4-connected (8-connected) if between any two 1-pixels (x_1,y_1) and (x_n,y_n) there are 1-pixels (x_2,y_2), ... , (x_{n-1},y_{n-1}) such that (x_i,y_i) is 4-adjacent (8-adjacent) to (x_{i+1},y_{i+1}). Show that the contour following algorithm described in Section 3.3.3 works for an 4-connected picture but does not work for an 8-connected picture.

9. Develop an efficient algorithm for binary picture region growing by coloring.

Chapter 4

Picture Information Measures

In pictorial information system design, we often want to measure the information content of a given picture. If the information content of a picture is low, then perhaps it should not be stored in the pictorial database. Instead, a low-resolution picture approximating the given picture should be stored. Similar considerations apply to picture communications in a pictorial information system. A picture with very little information content should not be transmitted in its original form. It should be compressed, with some distortion, into a more compact form before being transmitted. It is therefore important to have picture information measures that objectively determine the information content of pictures.

The classical information measure is the Shannon entropy. However, the Shannon entropy cannot reflect the spatial structure of pictures. In this chapter, we present a family of picture information measures based on the concept of a minimum number of gray-level changes to convert a picture into one with a desired histogram. The generalized picture information measure is theoretically related to Shannon entropy and well reflects pictorial spatial statistics. A natural extension to the Lorenz information measure makes it intuitive and meaningful. Based on these information measures, picture information measures for logical pictures can also be defined. These are referred to as structural information measures.

4.1 INTRODUCTION

Let us now start by giving several definitions for picture information measures. Given a picture function f and a point set S, f/S denotes the *restricted picture function* which is defined only for points in S—that is, $f/S(x,y) = f(x,y)$ if (x,y) is in S. f/S is called the *support picture function* or *support picture* for S. A measure for the amount of information contained in a picture f is based on the minimum number of pixel gray level changes to convert a picture into one with a constant gray level. Let $h : \{0,1,...,L-1\} \to N$ represent the *histogram* of f, where $h(i)$ is the number of pixels at gray level i. We define the *picture information measure* $PIM(f)$ as follows:

$$PIM(f) = \sum_{i=0}^{L-1} h(i) - \max_i h(i) \qquad (4.1)$$

We note that $PIM(f) = 0$ if and only if f is a constant picture (that is, $f(x,y) = $ constant for all (x,y) in $N \times N$). On the other hand, $PIM(f)$ is maximum if and only if f has a uniform histogram (that is, $h(i) = $ constant, $0 \leq i \leq L-1$). Let the total number of pixels in f be $N(f)$. f has a uniform histogram if and only if $PIM(f) = N(f)(L-1)/L$. In other words, $PIM(f)$ is minimal when f is least informative and maximal when f is most informative.

Suppose a picture point set S is divided into two disjoint subsets $S1$ and $S2$. We then have

$$PIM(f/S) \geq PIM(f/S1) + PIM(f/S2) \qquad (4.2)$$

Therefore, if we use disjoint sets Si to cover a picture f, then the sum of $PIM(f/Si)$ is always less than or equal to $PIM(f)$. We can also define a *normalized picture information measure* as $NPIM(f) = PIM(f)/N(f)$. In picture encoding (see Chapter 6), we can use PIM or $NPIM$ to decide whether a picture f should be decomposed. For example, if $NPIM(f)$ is less than a threshold, then f need not be further decomposed. On the other hand, if $NPIM(f)$ is close to maximum, and for every subpicture f/S, $NPIM(f/S)$ is close to maximum, then the picture f is almost random and also need not be further decomposed. If we define p_i as $h(i)/N(f)$, then we have

$$NPIM(f) = 1 - \max_i p_i \qquad (4.3)$$

Furthermore, if we define w_i as $N(f/Si)/N(f)$, then we can prove

$$NPIM(f/S) \geq w_1 \times NPIM(f/S1) + w_2 \times NPIM(f/S2) \qquad (4.4)$$

We can define a more general measure, PIM_k, as the minimum number of gray-level changes to convert a picture into one with k gray levels:

$$PIM_k(f) = \sum_{i=0}^{L-1} h(i) - \sum_{i \, \varepsilon \, \left\{ k \; largest \; h(i)'s \right\}} h(i) \qquad (4.5)$$

and $NPIM_k$ is accordingly defined as

$$NPIM_k(f) = 1 - \sum_{i \, \varepsilon \, \left\{ k \; largest \; p(i)'s \right\}} p(i) \qquad (4.6)$$

Based on the preceding definitions, we will theoretically derive the generalized PIM by referring to Shannon entropy and explore the properties of *PIM* (Section 4.2). We will see in Section 4.3 that *PIM* can not only characterize gray-level statistics but also the spatial statistics of the picture. Section 4.4 describes the way to make *PIM* more applicable by extension to the Lorenz information measure. Section 4.5 includes two applications: one is to apply *PIM* to the logical picture and define the structured information measure; the other is to explore *PIM* -directed picture segmentation.

4.2 PICTURE INFORMATION MEASURES AND SHANNON ENTROPY

Let us begin by giving the notation that we will use throughout this chapter. First, for any natural number, n,

$$\Gamma_n = \left\{ (p_1, ..., p_n): \sum_{i=1}^{n} p_i = 1; \quad p_i \geq 0; \quad n = 1, 2, 3, ... \right\} \tag{4.7}$$

This is the set of complete finite (n-ary) probability distributions [ACZEL75]. We often abbreviate the n-tuple as a vector:

$$\vec{p} = (p_1, ..., p_n) \tag{4.8}$$

In general, the measure can be viewed as a sequence (family) of functions $I_n : \Gamma_n \to R$ (with the various properties that we will discuss later).

The elements of Γ_n can be viewed most generally as probabilities in a space of n events. In coding theory, Γ_n represents the set of frequency distributions of symbols used in message encoding. In our context, each p_i represents the relative frequency of gray level i in a picture.

Suppose that we have a picture with gray levels $i = 1, 2, ..., n$ (to be coincident with Shannon entropy, we temporarily use this notation for the gray level) with frequencies $(p_1, p_2, ..., p_n) \varepsilon \Gamma_n$. Then there is a certain measure $I_n(\vec{p})$ for this picture (we assume that the picture is the unit square). We will at times call our measure PIM (picture information measure).

Figure 4.1 illustrates a typical case. The original picture has gray-level distribution $\vec{p}$. Now we cut the picture vertically at $x = a$. The new gray-level distributions are $\vec{q}$ (on the left) and $\vec{r}$ (on the right). Of course, we have the relation $\vec{p} = \vec{q} + \vec{r}$. On each subpicture, we normalize the gray-level vectors by dividing by area:

$$\vec{q} / a \ (on \ the \ left) \ and \ \vec{r} / (1-a) \ (on \ the \ right)$$

Thus, the *PIM* on the left is $I_n(\vec{q}/a)$, and $I_n(\vec{r}/(1-a))$ on the right. Thus, the weighted *PIM* for the cut is given by

$$I_{cut} = a I_n(\vec{q}/a) + (1-a) I_n(\vec{r}/(1-a))$$

The expression for I_{cut} can be considered the average *PIM* after one binary cut [WATANABE78, page 34]. Of course, we could perform an m-cut as follows:

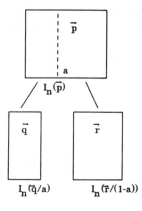

$$I_n(\bar{q}/a) \qquad I_n(\bar{r}/(1-a))$$

Figure 4.1 The computation of PIM by cutting a picture into two subpictures.

$$\vec{p} = \vec{q}_1 + \vec{q}_2 + ... + \vec{q}_m, \qquad 1 = a_1 + a_2 + \cdots + a_m$$

$$I_{cut} = \sum_{k=1}^{m} a_k I_n(\vec{q}_k / a_k) \tag{4.9}$$

As we perform successive cuts (binary or m-cuts), we produce a picture tree in which there is some information gain (decrease in average *PIM*) as we descend the tree (otherwise, why bother cutting the picture). Specifically, we insist that

$$I_{cut} \le I_{org} \quad or \quad \sum_{k=1}^{m} a_k I_n(\vec{q}_k / a_k) \le I_n\left(\sum_{k=1}^{m} \vec{q}_k\right) \tag{4.10}$$

In words, the *PIM* at any node in the tree is greater than (or equal to) the average *PIM* of its sons. We refer to this as the *concavity condition,* or *concavity inequality.*

4.2.1 The Shannon Entropy

Before investigating other measures, let us recall the standard *Shannon entropy:*

$$H_n(\vec{p}) = -\sum_{k=1}^{n} p_k \log_2 p_k \tag{4.11}$$

This entropy measure has the following properties [ACZEL75] :

1. *Symmetry.* $H_n(\vec{p}) = H_n(\sigma(\vec{p}))$ *where* σ is any permutation of n things.

2. *Normality.* $H_2(1/2, 1/2) = 1$

3. *Expansibility.* $H_n(p_1, ..., p_n)$

$$= H_{n+1}(0, p_1, ..., p_n)$$
$$= H_{n+1}(p_1, ..., p_k, 0, p_{k+1}, ..., p_n)$$
$$= H_{n+1}(p_1, ..., p_n, 0)$$

4. *Additivity.* $H_{mn} (p_1 q_1 ,..., p_1 q_n, p_2 q_1 ,..., p_m q_n) = H_m (p) + H_n (q)$

$$\text{for } \vec{p} \; \varepsilon \; \Gamma_m \quad \text{and} \quad \vec{q} \; \varepsilon \; \Gamma_n$$

5. *Strong Additivity.*

$$H_{mn} (p_1 q_{11} ,..., p_1 q_{1n}, p_2 q_{21} ,..., p_m q_{mn}) = H_m (\vec{p}) + \sum_{j=1}^{m} p_j H_n (\vec{q_j})$$

$$\text{for } \vec{p} \; \varepsilon \; \Gamma_m \quad \text{and} \quad \vec{q_j} \; \varepsilon \; \Gamma_n$$

6. *Recursivity.*

$$H_n (\vec{p}) = H_{n-1} (p_1 + p_2, p_3 ,..., p_n) + (p_1 + p_2) H_2 \left(\frac{p_1}{p_1 + p_2} , \frac{p_2}{p_1 + p_2} \right)$$

7. *Continuity.* H_n is continuous on Γ_n.

8. *Decisivity.* $H_n (1, 0, 0 ,..., 0) = 0$

9. *Maximality.*

$$H_n (\vec{p}) \leq H_n \left(\frac{1}{n}, \frac{1}{n} ,..., \frac{1}{n} \right) \quad \text{for } all \; \vec{p} \; \varepsilon \; \Gamma_n$$

10. *Concavity.*

$$\sum_{i=1}^{m} a_i H_n (\vec{p_i}) \leq H_n \left(\sum_{i=1}^{m} a_i \vec{p_i} \right) \quad \text{for } all \; \vec{p_i} \; \varepsilon \; \Gamma_n \quad \text{and} \quad \vec{a} \; \varepsilon \; \Gamma_m$$

The entropy function can be deduced up to a multiplication constant with the following axioms [FEINSTEIN58]:

1. Continuity (Property 7)
2. Symmetry (Property 1)
3. Recursivity (Property 6)

Applying normality (property 2) determines the Shannon entropy (with $\log_2$). There are other properties that can be used to axiomatize information theory [ACZEL75], but we do not consider these here.

4.2.2 Expected Properties of Picture Measures

Shannon's entropy was developed primarily for coding and transmission of information. Since our interest is in deriving information from a picture, we feel somewhat free to pick the properties that we want our *PIM* to have.

Let us now choose the properties that we consider "natural" and "essential" for picture measures.

PM1 Continuity. It is reasonable to assume that small changes in the frequencies of gray levels should create only small changes in the picture measure. (A similar property is called *stability.*)

PM2 Symmetry. This property is essential for our analysis.

PM3 Concavity. This is a natural and essential property. It gives us the concavity inequality, which guarantees that the *PIM* decreases as we descend the tree.

PM4 Maximality. See PM5.

PM5 Decisivity. PM4 and PM5 are the two "boundary values" for our picture measure. Decisivity tells us that if we have a picture with only one gray level, the *PIM* is zero. This is natural. Maximality states that the *PIM* is maximal when the gray levels are uniformly distributed. This, too, is a natural property.

PM6 Sensitivity. Recursivity is nice, but it is not an essential property. Since we assumed continuity and symmetry, if we also require recursivity, we would be back to Shannon's entropy (since these three properties are axioms for Shannon's entropy). Rather, we make a weaker requirement:

$$I_{n-1}(p_1 + p_2, p_3, ..., p_n) \le I_n(p_1, ..., p_n)$$

Stated in words, if we split a gray level (with frequency $p_1 + p_2$), the *PIM* should be at least as great. This, also, is a natural property.

PM7 Expansivity. We expect that added but unused gray levels would not affect the picture measure.

Notice that we have totally ignored Shannon properties 4 and 5 (additivity and strong additivity). These properties refer to independent events and the entropy measuring their mutual occurrences. While these appear to be important properties to classical entropy [ACZEL75], these do not seem particularly relevant to picture measures.

4.2.3 A Special Class of Measures

Before discussing general cases, let us discuss a specific class of possible picture measures. They serve as reasonable alternatives to the Shannon measure of entropy; further, they add insight into the concept of deviating from the Shannon measure.

Definition. For $\vec{p} = (p_1, p_2, ..., p_n) \varepsilon \Gamma_n$ and $a > 1$,

$$I_n^a(\vec{p}) = 1 - \sum_{i=1}^n p_i^a \qquad (4.12)$$

We claim that this class of picture measures satisfies properties *PM*1 and *PM*7.

Theorem 1. The class of measure $I_n^a : \Gamma_n \to R$ as defined for $n = 2, 3, 4, ...,$ and $a > 1$ satisfies properties *PM*1 to *PM*7.

*Proof. PM*1 and *PM*2. *Continuity* and *symmetry* are immediate from the definition.

PM3 *Concavity.* The function $f(x) = x^a$ has second derivative $f''(x) = a(a-1)x^{a-2}$. Since $a > 1$ and $0 \le x \le 1, f''(x) > 0$. Thus, $f(x) = x^a$ is a convex function; that is,

$$(\sum_{i=1}^{n} w_i \, x_i \,)^a \le \sum_{i=1}^{n} w_i \, x_i^a, \quad \text{for} \quad \sum_{i=1}^{n} w_i = 1, \ w_i \ge 0$$

Now, let $\vec{p} = \vec{q} + \vec{r}$, where $\sum_{i=1}^{n} q_i = w_1$ and $\sum_{i=1}^{n} r_i = w_2$. Thus,

$$
\begin{aligned}
I_{cut}^a &= w_1 \, I_{lft}^a + w_2 \, I_{rght}^a \\[2mm]
&= w_1 \, [1 - \sum_{i=1}^{n} (q_i / w_1)^a \,] + w_2 \, [1 - \sum_{i=1}^{n} (r_i / w_2)^a \,] \\[2mm]
&= w_1 + w_2 - \sum_{i=1}^{n} [\, w_1 \, (q_i / w_1)^a + w_2 \, (r_i / w_2)^a \,] \\[2mm]
&\le 1 - \sum_{i=1}^{n} [\, w_1 \, (q_i / w_1) + w_2 \, (r_i / w_2)]^a \quad by \quad convexity \quad of \quad x^a \\[2mm]
&= 1 - \sum_{i=1}^{n} (\, q_i + r_i)^a \\[2mm]
&= 1 - \sum_{i=1}^{n} p_i^a = I_{org}^a
\end{aligned}
$$

Of course, this result can be extended from two subpictures to any number.

PM4 *Maximality.* Let us rewrite I_n^a with a Lagrange multiplier:

$$I_n^a (\vec{p}) = 1 - \sum_{i=1}^{n} p_i^a + \lambda \, (\sum_{i=1}^{n} p_i - 1)$$

Thus, we have

$$\frac{\partial I_n^a}{\partial p_k} = -a \, p_k^{a-1} + \lambda = 0$$

which implies $p_k = \left[\dfrac{\lambda}{a} \right]^{1-a}$ for all k. Hence, $p_k = \text{constant} = 1/n$.

PM5 *Decisivity.* It is clear that $I_n^a (1,0,0,...,0) = 1 - 1^a = 0$.

PM6 *Sensitivity.*

$$
\begin{aligned}
I_n^a (p_1, p_2, ..., p_n) &= 1 - p_1^a - p_2^a - \sum_{i=3}^{n} p_i^a \\[2mm]
&= 1 - (p_1 + p_2)^a - \sum_{i=3}^{n} p_i^a + (p_1 + p_2)^a - p_1^a - p_2^a \\[2mm]
&= I_{n-1}^a (p_1 + p_2, p_3, ..., p_n) + (p_1 + p_2)^a \, I_2^a \left(\frac{p_1}{p_1 + p_2}, \frac{p_2}{p_1 + p_2} \right)
\end{aligned}
$$

Notice that the second term on the right contains $(p_1 + p_2)^a$ rather than the usual $(p_1 + p_2)$ for the Shannon entropy. Since we do not have the Shannon entropy, we do not expect recursivity to hold. However, the sensitivity inequality does hold.

PM7 *Expansivity.* If we include $p_{n+1} = 0$, this does not add to the picture measure. $\qquad\qquad\square$

We have thus established an entire class of picture measures that satisfies our required properties, $PM1$ and $PM7$. In addition to providing a specific alternative to the Shannon entropy, this development also serves as preparation for our generalization.

4.2.4 Generalized Picture Measures

We wish to find a generalization of the class of measures that we produced in I_n^a. Specifically, we seek a general class of measures that satisfies the desired picture-measure properties, $PM1$ to $PM7$.

Let us start with a sequence of functions $F_n : \Gamma_n \to R$ (which we call a *picture-function sequence, or PFS*) defined by the following properties:

PFS1. F_n is continuous on Γ_n.

PFS2. F_n is symmetric on Γ_n.

PFS3. $F_{n+k}(p_1,...,p_n,0,...,0) = F_n(p_1,...,p_n)$; that is, F_{n+k} restricted to Γ_n acts like F_n on Γ_n.

PFS4. F_n is convex; that is, for $a + b = 1; a, b > 0$; and $\vec{p}, \vec{q} \varepsilon \Gamma_n, F_n$ $(a \vec{p} + b \vec{q}) <= a F_n(\vec{p}) + b F_n(\vec{q})$.

Now we can define our generalized *picture information measure, or PIM*.

Definition. Let $F = \left\{ F_n : n = 2, 3,... \right\}$ be a PFS. We define $I_n^F : \Gamma_n \to R$ via

$$I_n^F(\vec{p}) = F_n(1,0,0,...,0) - F_n(\vec{p}) \tag{4.13}$$

to be a picture information measure (PIM).

We now claim that these PIM functions are completely characterized by properties $PM1$ to $PM7$. That is, all $PIMs$ satisfy $PM1$ to $PM7$; and conversely, any measure satisfying $PM1$ to $PM7$ defines (up to an additive constant) a unique $PFS\{F_n\}$. This statement can be proved as two separate theorems.

Theorem 2. Let $I_n^F : \Gamma_n \to R$ be a PIM defined by $PFS\{F_n\}$. Then $\{I_n^F : n = 2, 3,...\}$ satisfies $PM1$ to $PM7$.

Theorem 3. Let $\{I_n : n = 2, 3,...\}$ be a family of functions, $I_n : \Gamma_n \to R$ satisfying $PM1$ to $PM7$. Then there exists a unique (up to an additive constant) family $\{F_n : n = 2, 3,...\}$ satisfying $PFS1$ to $PFS4$ such that

$$I_n(\vec{p}) = F_n(1,0,...,0) - F_n(\vec{p}) \tag{4.14}$$

That is, I_n is a PIM. The detailed proof can be found in [SILVER86].

Thus, the seven properties $PM1$ to $PM7$, which we consider integral to picture measures, can be characterized by the four function properties $PFS1$ to $PFS4$.

We note an interesting relationship between the measure properties $PM1$ to $PM7$ and the function properties $PFS1$ to $PFS4$. Clearly, properties $PM1, PM2$, and $PM4$

correspond to *PFS* 1, *PFS* 2, and *PFS* 3 (continuity, symmetry, and concavity or convexity), respectively. *PM*7 corresponds to *PFS* 3. *PM*5 comes out of the definition. However, *PM*4 (maximality) and *PM*6 (sensitivity) come to us "free" as extra consequences of concavity and symmetry. Equivalently, we can say that *PM*4 and *PM*6 are not independent properties, but rather dependent on the other five.

The following is a trivial consequence of Theorem 3.

Corollary 1. If $f : [0, 1] \to R$ is continuous, convex, and $f(0) = 0$, then

$$F_n (p_1, p_2, ..., p_n) = \sum_{i=1}^{n} f(p_i) \tag{4.15}$$

defines a *PFS*; further,

$$I_n (\vec{p}) = f(1) - \sum_{i=1}^{n} f(p_i) \tag{4.16}$$

is a *PIM*.

4.2.5 Examples of PIM

We now provide some examples of *PIM*s as defined in the last section. (Throughout, $\sum_{i=1}^{n} p_i = 1$.)

Example 1.

$f(p) = p \, \log_2 p$, *or* $F_n (\vec{p}) = \sum_{i=1}^{n} p_i \log_2 p_i$. With the standard definition $0 \log_2 0 = 0$; this, of course, reduces to the usual Shannon entropy, $H_n (\vec{p}) = - \sum_{i=1}^{n} p_i \log_2 p_i$.

Example 2.

$f(p) = p^a$ *(for $a > 1$)*, *or* $F_n (\vec{p}) = \sum_{i=1}^{n} p_i^a$.

Since f is continuous and convex, $I_n^a (\vec{p}) = 1 - \sum_{i=1}^{n} p_i^a$ is a *PIM*. This family is the same I_n^a that we discussed in Section 4.2.3.

Example 3.

$F_n^a (\vec{p}) = [\sum_{i=1}^{n} p_n^a]^{1/a}$ for $a > 1$.

It is clear that F_n^a is continuous, symmetric, and restrictable. We now show its convexity. Let $w_1 + w_2 = 1, w_i \geq 0$, and $x, y \varepsilon \Gamma_n$. Then,

$$F_n (w_1 \vec{x} + w_2 \vec{y}) = [\sum_{i=1}^{n} (w_1 x_i + w_2 y_i)^a]^{1/a}$$

$$\leq [\sum_{i=1}^{n} (w_1 x_i)^a]^{1/a} + [\sum_{i=1}^{n} (w_2 y_i)^a]^{1/a}$$

$$= w_1 [\sum_{i=1}^{n} x_i^a]^{1/a} + w_2 [\sum_{i=1}^{n} y_i^a]^{1/a}$$

$$= w_1 F_n (\vec{x}) + w_2 F_n (\vec{y})$$

The inequality used above is Minkowski's inequality [HARDY34]. Thus,

$$M_n^a (\vec{p}) = 1 - [\sum_{i=1}^{n} p_i^a]^{1/a} \tag{4.17}$$

is a *PIM*, for $a > 1$. We can call this a *Minkowski PIM*.

Example 4.

Let us consider the Minkowski *PIM*, as just defined, as $a \to \infty$. If we let p_1 be the largest of the p_i, then we get

$$M_n^\infty (\vec{p}) = \lim_{a \to \infty} M_n^a (\vec{p}) = 1 - p_1$$

In words, this measure is the proportion of pixels that are *not* at the peak gray level. We can also arrive at M_n^∞ by defining $F_n (\vec{p}) = max(p_1, ..., p_n)$. then

$$M_n^\infty (\vec{p}) = 1 - max(p_1, ..., p_n) \tag{4.18}$$

This is perhaps the simplest (nontrivial) *PIM* available and is the same as in equation (4.3). There is a cost, however. We almost totally lose sensitivity; that is, if p_i is not maximal, then splitting $p_i = q_1 + q_2$ has *no* effect on the picture measure.

Example 5.

This is a generalization of Example 4. Specifically,

$$F_{n,k} (\vec{p}) = \sum_{i=1}^{k} p_i$$

where the p_i have been reordered $p_1 \geq p_2 \geq \cdots \geq p_n$. In other words, $F_{n,k} (\vec{p})$ is the sum of the frequencies of the top k gray levels. Thus we have

$$I_{n,k} (\vec{p}) = 1 - \sum_{i=1}^{k} p_i \tag{4.19}$$

The measure is the proportion of the $n-k$ lowest gray levels. We note that $I_{n,k}$ is the normalized picture information measure $NPIM_k$ defined in Equation (4.6). As a special case,

$$M_n^\infty (\vec{p}) = I_{n,1} (\vec{p})$$

Also, we have $I_{n,1} \geq I_{n,2} \geq \cdots \geq I_{n,n} = 0$. Like M_n^∞, this measure suffers in that only the splitting of the top gray levels affects $I_{n,k}$. We have demonstrated, by Example 4 and Example 5, that *NPIM* and $NPIM_k$ are two special cases of generalized *PIM* $I_n^F (\vec{p})$.

Example 6.

Let $k_1 \geq k_2 \geq \cdots$ be a descending sequence of positive numbers such that $\sum_{j=1}^{\infty} k_j < \infty$ (that is, (k_j) converges). Now we define

$$F_n (p) = \sum_{i=1}^{n} k_i p_i$$

where the p_i have been reordered $p_1 \geq p_2 \geq \cdots \geq p_n$. We claim that F_n is convex. Suppose $\vec{p} = a\ \vec{x} + b\ \vec{y}$; then

$$F_n\ (\vec{p})\ =\ \sum_{i=1}^{n} k_i\ p_i$$

$$=\ \sum_{i=1}^{n} k_i\ (ax_i + by_i)$$

$$\leq\ a \sum_{i=1}^{n} k_i\ x_{\sigma\,(i)} + b \sum_{i=1}^{n} k_i\ y_{\tau\,(i)}$$

$$=\ aF_n\ (\vec{x}) + bF_n\ (\vec{y})$$

where σ and τ are the permutations that reorder $\vec{x}$ and $\vec{y}$, largest component to smallest. The inequality used is a known theorem [HARDY34] that $\sum \alpha \beta$ is greatest if (α) and (β) are monotonic in the same sense. Therefore, F_n is convex. Thus, the measure

$$K_n\ (\vec{p})\ =\ 1 - \sum_{i=1}^{n} k_i\ p_i \qquad (4.20)$$

is a *PIM* if (k_i) and (p_i) are monotonic decreasing sequences. This class of measures subsumes Example 5. Specifically,

$$I_{n,m}\ (\vec{p})\ =\ K_n\ (\vec{p})$$

for the sequence

$$k_i\ =\ \begin{cases} 1 & i\ =\ 1, 2\,,..., m \\ 0 & i\ =\ m+1\,,..., n \end{cases}$$

If we choose a sequence such as $k_i\ =\ 1/\,2^i$, we get

$$K_n\ (\vec{p})\ =\ 1 - \sum_{i=1}^{n} p_i\ /\ 2^i \qquad (4.21)$$

where $p_1 \geq p_2 \geq \cdots \geq p_n$. Unlike $I_{n,m}$, this measure remains sensitive to all changes in gray-level proportion.

Example 7.

This is a negative example. Consider

$$F_{n,k}\ (\vec{p})\ =\ \max_{1 \leq i \leq n-k+1}\ (p_i + p_{i+1} + ... + p_{i+k-1})$$

Stated in words, this forms a window of width k moving along, searching for the largest proportion of k consecutive gray levels. This seems like a very reasonable measure. However, it is *not* symmetric in p_i (since consecutivity is involved). Thus,

$$I_{n,k}\ =\ 1 - \max\ (p_i + p_{i+1} + ... + p_{i+k-1}) \qquad (4.22)$$

is *not* a *PIM*. For instance, for $I_{5,2}$ (5-tuples; 2-window)

$$I_{5,2}(.2, .2, .2, .2, .2)\ =\ .6$$

$$I_{5,2}(.35, 0, .3, 0, .35)\ =\ .65$$

Hence, $I_{5,2}(.2, .2, .2, .2, .2)$ is *not* maximal and is not an acceptable *PIM*.

4.3 STRICTLY CONCAVE PICTURE INFORMATION MEASURES AND PICTURE STATISTICS

It seems, from what we have discussed so far, that the *PIM* is based on picture gray level statistics. In this section we demonstrate that the *PIM* is also related to the spatial statistics of pictures. We now investigate the circumstances under which the picture shows absolutely no decrease in measure as we descend the tree. That is, for all partitioning of the tree, the picture information remains constant. Let us define two terms.

Definition. A function $F: \Gamma_n \to R$ is *strictly convex* if $a + b = 1 \, (a > 0$ and $b > 0)$ and $\vec{x} \neq \vec{y}$ imply that

$$F(a \, \vec{x} + b \, \vec{y}) < aF(\vec{x}) + b \, F(\vec{y}) \qquad (4.23)$$

Figure 4.2 illustrates this definition.

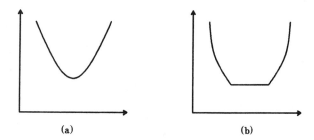

(a)   (b)

Figure 4.2 (a) Strictly convex; (b) convex but not strictly convex.

If a PFS is strictly convex, we say that its corresponding *PIM* is *strictly concave*. Examples 1, 2, and 3 of the last section are strictly concave *PIM*s. However, Examples 4 and 5 are not. In Example 6, the *PIM* is strictly concave if and only if all $k_i > 0$.

Definition. A gray-level distribution $\vec{p}$ is *homogeneous* if for all $\vec{q}$ and $\vec{r}$ such that $\vec{p} = \vec{q} + \vec{r}$ (for any partition of the picture)

$$\vec{q} = a \, \vec{p} \qquad \text{and} \qquad \vec{r} = b \, \vec{p}$$

where $a = \sum_i q_i$ and $b = \sum_i r_i$. In other words, a distribution is homogeneous if all subpictures have the same gray-level proportion as the original page.

Figure 4.3 is an attempt to illustrate a homogeneous distribution. Suppose that the black-to-white proportion is (0.2, 0.8). Since any subpicture will also have the black-to-white proportion (0.2, 0.8), we say that distribution is homogeneous.

Theorem 4. Let F_n be a PFS that is strictly convex. Also, let I_n be the *PIM* generated by F_n. Then a necessary and sufficient condition that $I_{cut} = I_{orig}$ for all cuts is that $\vec{p}$ is homogeneous.

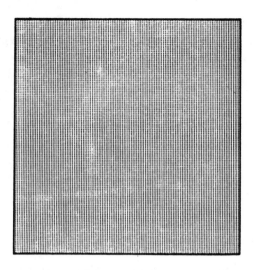

Figure 4.3 A picture with homogeneous gray-level distribution.

Proof. (Sufficient) Suppose $\vec{p}$ is homogeneous; then for any cut $\vec{p} = \vec{q} + \vec{r}$, we have $\vec{q} = a\ \vec{p}$ and $\vec{r} = b\ \vec{p}$. Thus,

$$
\begin{aligned}
I_{cut} &= aI_n\ (\vec{q}\ /\ a\ ) + b\ I_n\ (\vec{r}\ /b\ ) \\
&= aI_n\ (\vec{p}) + bI_n\ (\vec{p}) \\
&= I_n\ (\vec{p})\ =\ I_{org}
\end{aligned}
$$

(Necessary) Suppose that p is not homogeneous. Then there exists a $a\ \vec{q} \neq a\ \vec{p}$, with $\vec{p} = \vec{q} + \vec{r}$ and $q_i < ap_i$ for some i.

Then, $r_i\ =\ p_i - q_i > p_i - ap_i\ =\ (1-a)p_i\ =\ bp_i$.

Thus, $r_i\ /b > p_i > q_i\ /a$, which implies $\vec{r}\ /b \neq \vec{q}\ /a$. Now, $[\vec{1}\ =\ (1,0\ ,...,\ 0)]$

$$
\begin{aligned}
I_{cut} &= aI_n\ (\vec{q}\ /a) + bI_n\ (\vec{r}\ 'b\ ) \\
&= a\,[F_n\ (\vec{1}) - F_n\ (\vec{q}/a)] + b\,[F_n\ (\vec{1}) - F_n\ (\vec{r}\ /b\ )] \\
&= F_n\ (\vec{1}) - [aF_n\ (\vec{q}/a) + bF_n\ (\vec{r}\ /b\ )] \\
&< F_n\ (\vec{1}) - F_n\ (\vec{p}) \qquad \textit{since } \vec{q}/a \neq \vec{r}\ /b \\
&= I_{org} \qquad\qquad\qquad\qquad\qquad\qquad\qquad \square
\end{aligned}
$$

Definition. A gray-level distribution is *random* if $\vec{p}\ =\ (1/n, 1/n\ ,...,\ 1/n)$.

The ideas of homogeneous and random distributions should not be confused. They are independent of each other. Figure 4.3 shows a homogeneous distribution that is not random.

Theorem 5. Let F_n be strictly convex and I_n the *PIM* it generates. Then $I_n\ (\vec{p})$ is maximal if and only if $\vec{p}$ is random.

Proof. (Sufficient) This follows from Theorem 2.

(Necessary) Suppose that $\vec{p} \neq (1/n, 1/n, ..., 1/n)$; that is, $\vec{p}$ is not random. Let $\vec{q}_i = \sigma_i (\vec{p})$ for a permutation σ_i. Since $\vec{p}$ is not random, there is an i such that $\vec{q}_i \neq \vec{p}$. Recall that

$$\sum_i \frac{1}{n!} \vec{q}_i = (1/n, ..., 1/n) \text{ and}$$

$$F_n (\vec{p}) = \sum_i \frac{1}{n!} F_n (\vec{q}_i)$$

$$> F_n (\sum_i \frac{1}{n!} \vec{q}_i) \quad [\text{ since } \vec{p} \neq \vec{q} \text{ for } some \text{ } i \text{ }]$$

$$= F_n (1/n, ..., 1/n)$$

Thus, $F_n (\vec{p})$ is not minimal, and $I_n (\vec{p})$ is not maximal. □

Definition. A gray-level distribution that is both homogeneous and random is called *chaotic*. That is, the picture has distribution $\vec{p} = (1/n, ..., 1/n)$ and any sub-picture of area a has distribution $\vec{q} = (a/n, ..., a/n)$.

Theorem 6. Let F_n be strictly convex and I_n the *PIM* that it generates. Then I_n has a constant maximal value for all cuts if and only if $\vec{p}$ is chaotic.

Proof. This is an obvious consequence of theorems 4 and 5 and the definition of a chaotic distribution. □

4.4 LORENZ INFORMATION MEASURE

Having discussed the theoretical aspects of *PIM*, we are now ready to turn to its applications. We shall see in this section, *NPIM* can be extended to the *Lorenz information measure*, which has an intuitive and meaningful interpretation and is easy to compute.

Let us start from the normalized picture information measure $NPIM_k$ defined in equation (4.6). It can be seen that $NPIM_k (f)$ is 1 minus the sum of the first k terms in the sequence $p_1, p_2, ..., p_n$, which is equal to the sum of the last $n - k$ terms in the sequence. In particular, $NPIM (f)$ or $NPIM_1(f)$ is the sum of the last $n - 1$ terms in the sequence $p_1, p_2, ..., p_n$. The following inequalities hold:

$$0 = NPIM_n (f) \leq NPIM_{n-1} (f) \leq \cdots \leq NPIM_1 (f) \leq NPIM_0 (f) = 1 \quad (4.23)$$

If we define s_k to be $NPIM_{n-k} (f)$, we have

$$s_0 = 0$$

$$s_n = 1$$

$$s_k = \sum_{i=0}^{k-1} p_i$$

By plotting the points $(k/n, s_k)$, $k = 0, 1, 2, ..., n$, we obtain a piecewise linear curve, as illustrated in Figure 4.4, which is called the Lorenz curve [MARSH79]. We note that this curve represents the information contents of a picture. To find out the value of $NPIM_k$, we simply check the point $((n-k)/n, s_{n-k})$ on the Lorenz curve.

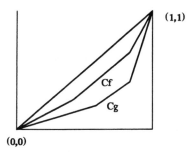

(1,1)

Cf

Cg

(0,0)

Figure 4.4 Lorenz curve.

If the gray levels of the pixels are uniformly distributed, then the curve becomes a straight line from (0,0) to (1,1). Otherwise, the curve will be a convex piecewise linear curve under this straight line. In Figure 4.4, curve C_f for picture f is always above curve C_g for picture g. That is to say, $NPIM_k(f) \geq NPIM_k(g)$ for every k or picture f is more informative than picture g. Another way of describing this relationship is that picture g is less complex than picture f. In other words, "as the bow is bent, concentration increases," and the corresponding picture is less complex and consequently less informative. Using the concept of majorants, if $C_f > C_g$, then f is more informative than g.

The Lorenz curve derived from the picture information measures $NPIM_k$ is called the *Lorenz information curve*. It can be seen that once the histogram h is given, the Lorenz information curve is completely specified. Conversely, if the Lorenz information curve is given, we know the histogram in its permutation equivalent class.

The *Lorenz information measure* $LIM(p_1, ..., p_n)$ is defined as the area under the Lorenz information curve. Clearly, $0 \leq LIM(p_1, ..., p_n) \leq 0.5$. For any probability vector $(p_1, ..., p_n)$, $LIM(p_1, ..., p_n)$ can be computed by first ordering the p_i's, then calculating the area under the piecewise linear curve. Since $LIM(p_1, ..., p_n)$ can be expressed as the sum of $f(p_i)$, and $f(p_i)$ is continuous convex function in p_i, $LIM(p_1, ..., p_n)$ is also an information measure. Intuitively, the Lorenz information measure is the weighted sum of the $NPIM_k$'s, so that LIM can be regarded as a global measure of information content.

4.5 APPLICATION OF PICTURE INFORMATION MEASURES (PIM)

As mentioned in the introduction, the *PIM* has many applications to pictorial information systems. We discuss two of them in this section. One is the structured information measure—a *PIM* of the logical picture. The other is *PIM*-guided picture segmentation.

4.5.1 Structured Information Measure

Since the Lorenz information curve is always normalized, we can plot such curves for pictures having different sizes and gray-level sets and compare them. As illustrated in Figure 4.5, two Lorenz information curves may intersect at points $A_0 = (0,0)$, $A_1, A_2,..., A_m = (1,1)$. We can define a similarity measure between f and g, $d(f,g)$, as the summation of the polygonal areas enclosed by the two curves C_f and C_g. Clearly, $0 \le d(f,g) \le 0.5$. If $d(f,g)$ is below a preset threshold t, the two pictures can be considered *informationally similar* in the sense of having similar Lorenz information curves.

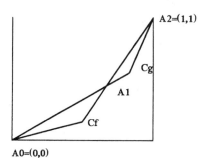

A2=(1,1)

Cg

A1

Cf

A0=(0,0)

Figure 4.5 Illustration of similarity measure defined by the area between c_f and c_g.

It should also be noted that this approach can be generalized to handle not only physical pictures defined by a picture function f, but also logical pictures consisting of logical objects and relational objects [CHANG82a]. Suppose there are N objects in the logical picture, and these objects are classified into n different types: $T_1, T_2,..., T_n$. We can define $h : \{ 1, 2,..., n \} \rightarrow N$ to be the *logical histogram*, where $h(i)$ is the number of objects having type T_i. The Lorenz information curve for logical pictures can then be computed.

As an example, consider a picture containing five objects. Suppose the picture object set is $V = \{v_1(A), v_2(A), v_3(B), v_4(B), v_5(B)\}$. The relational object set is $R = \{r_1(X, v_1, v_2), r_2(Y, v_1, v_2), r_3(X, v_1, v_3), r_4(Y, v_1, v_5), r_5(X, v_2, v_4)\}$. The picture objects and relational objects are illustrated in Figure 4.6. Objects v_1 and v_2 are of the same type A, and v_3, v_4, v_5 of the same type B. Relations r_1, r_3, r_5 are of the same type X, and r_2, r_4 of the same type Y. We can define the *structural information measure SIM* as the weighted sum of three parts:

S1. *Object information measure OIM* $= IM(a_1,..., a_n)$ where a_i is the probability of occurrence for objects of type T_i.

S2. *Intraset information measure IIM*$(i) = IM(b_{i1},..., b_{ik})$ where b_{ij} is the probability of occurrence for relations of type R_j in the object set of type T_i.

S3. *Interset information measure TIM*$(i,j) = IM(c_{ij1},..., c_{ijk})$ where c_{ijk} is the probability of occurrence for relations of type r_k between object sets T_i and T_j.

The structural information measure SIM is defined as

$$SIM = w_0\, OIM + \sum_{i=1}^{L} w_i\, IIM(i) + \sum_{i=1}^{L}\sum_{j=1}^{L} u_{ij}\, TIM(i,j) \qquad (4.24)$$

Picture Information Measures   Chap. 4

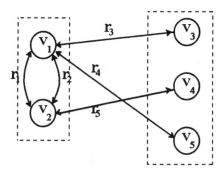

Figure 4.6 Logical picture with objects and relations.

where w_0, w_i, u_{ij} are nonnegative weights. For example, if there are n types of objects, we can set w_0 to 1, w_i to $1/n$, and u_{ij} to $2/(n(n-1))$.

In $S1$, $S2$, and $S3$, we can use any information measure IM. If we use LIM as the information measure, we have $OIM = LIM(0.4, 0.6) = 0.45$, $IIM(A) = LIM(0.5, 0.5) = 0.5$, $IIM(B) = LIM(0) = 0$, and $TIM(A, B) = LIM(1/3, 2/3) = 0.4167$. Therefore, $SIM = 0.45 + 0.5 \times 0.5 + 0.5 \times 0 + 1 \times 0.4167 = 1.1167$. If the summation of w_i is 1 and the summation of u_{ij} is 1, it is clear that $0 \le SIM \le 1.5$.

Since the structured information measure is defined with respect to a given object set V and relational object set R, we should write $SIM(V, R)$ to indicate SIM is always calculated for given V and R. Therefore, SIM can be calculated for any subpicture of a logical picture or any subpicture of a physical picture by changing V and R.

To define similar pictures, we can use a combination of the following criteria: (1) their physical (and/or logical) histograms are similar, (2) their Lorenz information curves are similar, (3) their Lorenz information measures are similar, and (4) their structured information measures are similar.

The picture information measure just introduced is based on the minimal number of gray-level changes to convert a picture to one having a desirable histogram. In the case of PIM_1, the desirable histogram consists of a peak at a single (arbitrary) gray level. For PIM_k, the desirable histogram consists of k peaks at k (arbitrary) gray levels. For similarity measurement, the exact shape of the desirable histogram can also be specified, and the algorithms for optimal histogram matching for both the $L1$ norm [CHANG78] and the Ln norm [CHANG80] have been developed. As suggested in [CHANG80], we can also use the computed minimal number of mismatches to measure the similarity between two pictures or subpictures.

4.5.2 PIM-Directed Picture Segmentation

PIM-directed measures can be applied to picture segmentation. Hsieh and Chang have researched this technique and got some very promising experimental results [HSIEH84].

The PIM-directed picture segmentation technique consists of three phases: (1) thresholding by characteristic features, (2) region growing by the PIM-directed relaxation algorithm, and (3) boundary smoothing and extraction of the most informative pixels by a measure of NPIM. In what follows, we explain the algorithm in detail by an example of a SEASAT image.

PHASE 1. THRESHOLDING BY CHARACTERISTIC FEATURES

Step 1. Choose a window size 5×5 and calculate the local gray level standard deviation (SD) for each window. This value is considered the SD value of the central pixel of this window.

Step 2. Compute the SD histogram of the picture. Find a valley between the two largest peaks of the histogram. The SD value of this valley is then chosen as the threshold T_{sd}.

Step 3. Convert the picture into binary form using the threshold T_{sd}. Because the *PIM*-directed region growing is applied in the next phase, the thresholding result will not affect the final result too much.

PHASE 2. PIM-DIRECTED REGION GROWING

Step 4. Choose a window size and a NPIM threshold T; they are 3×3 and 0.20, respectively, in this example.

Step 5. Move the window in the raster scanning manner from the top-left corner. At each location calculate the *NPIM* for the window. Change the SD value of the pixels, which are different from the SD value of dominant pixels, to the dominant SD value if their *NPIM* is not greater than threshold T. Record the result of this process as G_1.

Step 6. Repeat step 5 with the starting point at each of the other three corners of the picture, and record the results as G_2, G_3, G_4, respectively.

Step 7. Merge the four results G_1, G_2, G_3, and G_4 as follows: For all the pixels of the picture, so long as there is a corresponding SD value which is less than T_{sd} in any of the four picture records G_1, G_2, G_3, and G_4, the pixel is marked as background; it is marked as object otherwise.

PHASE 3. PIM-DIRECTED BOUNDARY FORMATION

Step 8. Divide the whole picture into fixed-sized pages with a chosen window size and select a *NPIM* threshold T again.

Step 9. Calculate *NPIM* for all pages of the picture. For each page of the picture, if its *NPIM* is greater than T and if any of its four neighboring pages has a *NPIM* below T, this page then contains boundary pixels. Mark those boundary pixels inside this page.

In the preceding algorithm, updating is carried out sequentially. Parallel updating is also possible and gives similar results. The number of iterations in parallel updating is controlled manually. Figure 4.7 shows processing results for all three phases. Figure 4.7(a) is an original SEASAT image, and the image after thresholding is shown in Figure 4.7(b). It can be seen from the figure that thresholding alone is insufficient for the segmentation of this picture. By using PIM-directed region

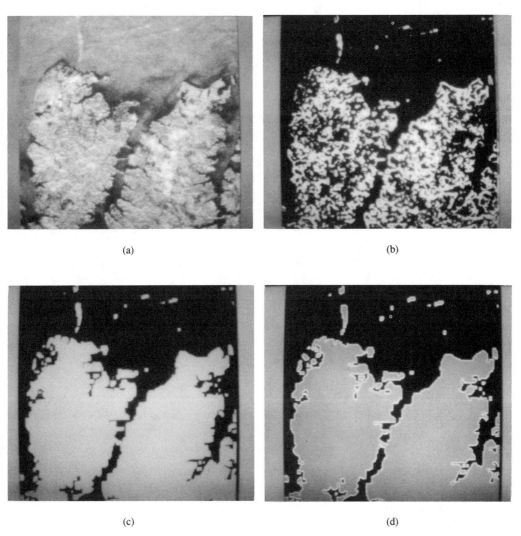

(a)   (b)

(c)   (d)

Figure 4.7 (a) Original SEASAT picture; (b) after thresholding; (c) after region growing using *PIM*-directed relaxation; and (d) the final result.

growing, a more satisfactory result is obtained (see Figure 4.7(c)). Further improvement is possible by applying phase 3. The final result is shown in Figure 4.7(d).

A similar technique has been successfully applied to parcel post address label detection, which demonstrates the advantages of this approach.

R E F E R E N C E S

[ACZEL75] Aczel and Daroczy, *On Measures of Information and Their Characterizations.* New York: Academic Press, 1975.

[CHANG78] CHANG, S. K., AND Y. WONG, "Optimal Histogram Matching by Monotone Gray Level Transformation," *Communications of the ACM* , Vol. 22, No. 10, ACM, October 1978, 835-840.

[CHANG79] CHANG, S. K., J. REUSS, AND B. H. MCCORMICK, "Design of Considerations of Pictorial Database System," *Proceedings of National Computer Conference,* AFIPS, Vol. 48, 1979, 147-156.

[CHANG80] CHANG, S. K., AND Y. WONG, "Ln Norm Optimal Histogram Matching and Application to Similarity Retrieval," *Journal of Computer Graphics and Image Processing,* Vol. 13, 1980, 361-371.

[CHANG82a] CHANG, S. K., "A Methodology for Picture Indexing and Encoding," in *Picture Engineering,* (T. Kunii and K. S. Fu, Eds.), Springer Verlag, 1982, 33-53.

[CHANG82b] CHANG, S. K., AND C. C. YANG, "Picture Encoding Techniques for a Pictorial Database," *Technical Report,* Naval Research Laboratory, 1982.

[DATE77] DATE, C. J., *An Introduction to Database Systems,* Second Edition. Reading: Addison Wesley, 1977.

[FEINSTEIN58] FEINSTEIN, A., *Foundations of Information Theory.* New York: McGraw-Hill, 1958.

[GONZALEZ78] GONZALEZ, R. C., ET AL., "A Measure of Scene Content," CH1318-5 /78 /0000-0385500.75, IEEE 1978, 385-389.

[HARALICK73] HARALICK, R., K. SHANMUGAN, AND I. DINSTEIN, "Textural Features for Image Classification," *IEEE Transactions on Systems, Man, and Cybernetics,* SMC-3, 1973, 610-621.

[HARALICK79] HARALICK, R., "Statistical and Structural Approaches to Textures," *Proceedings of IEEE,* 1979, 786-804.

[HARDY34] HARDY AND LITTLEWOOD, *Inequalities.* Cambridge: Cambridge Press, 1934.

[HSIEH84] HSIEH, CHENG-YUAN, "Picture Information Measure Directed Algorithms for Image Encoding and Segmentation," Masters dissertation, Illinois Institute of Technology, Dec. 1984.

[INGELS71] INGELS, F., *Information and Coding Theory.* Scranton: Intext Education Publishers, 1971.

[LIU81] LIU, S. H., AND S. K. CHANG, "Picture Covering by 2-D AH Encoding," *Proceedings of IEEE Workshop on Computer Architecture for Pattern Analysis and Image Database Management,* Hot Springs, Virginia, November 11-13, 1981, 76-87.

[MARSHALL79] MARSHALL, A. W., AND I. OLKIN, *Inequalities: Theory of Majorization and Its Applications.* Academic Press, 1979.

[NILSSON80] NILSSON, N., *Principles of Artificial Intelligence.* Palo Alto: Tioga Publishing, 1980.

[REUSS80] REUSS, J., S. K. CHANG, B. H. MCCORMICK, "Picture Paging for Efficient Image Processing," in *Pictorial Information Systems,* (S. K. Chang and K. S. Fu, Eds.), Springer-Verlag, 1980, 228-256.

[SILVER86] SILVER, H., AND S. K. CHANG, "Picture Information Measures," *Policy and Information,* Vol.10, No.1, June 1986, 1-16.

[THOMAS72] THOMAS, G., *Calculus and Analytic Geometry,* Fourth edition. Reading: Addison-Wesley, 1972.

[WATANABE78] WATANABE, S., *Knowing and Guessing.* New York: John Wiley, 1978.

E X E R C I S E S

1. Give an intuitive meaning for the $\log_2$ in the Shannon entropy measure.

2. Calculate the *PIM* and *NPIM* for the following picture of 4 gray levels:

0	0	0	1
0	0	1	1
1	2	2	2
1	2	3	3

3. What is the maximum weighted *PIM* for the previous picture which can be produced by one vertical or horizontal binary cut?

4. Prove that $NPIM(f) = 1 - \max_i p_i$.

5. Show that $H_n(\vec{p}) \leq \log_2 n$.

6. Define a normalized edge detection operator based on the entropy measure of the following 3×3 window, where a_i is the gray level of the pixel.

a_1	a_2	a_3
a_8	a_0	a_4
a_7	a_6	a_5

7. Consider the thresholding of an image using *PIM*. Describe a heuristic method to accomplish this. When will the "best" results be obtained?

Chapter 5

Pictorial
Data
Compression

In the schematic diagram (see Figure 1.1, p. 2) of the pictorial information system, a picture communication interface is included. With this communication interface, pictures can be transmitted from one location to another via a communication network. Since the transmission of pictorial data means transmissions of millions of bytes even for a small number of digitized pictures, the motivation to compress pictorial data is indeed very strong.

In addition to applications in picture data transmission such as digital TV and facsimile systems, pictorial data compression also has a very close relationship to picture analysis, pattern recognition, and knowledge-based systems. Indeed, feature extraction and description can also be considered as means of data compression. They compress picture data into feature vector or symbolic description, which well reflect the characteristics of the objects present in the picture for the purpose of recognition or interpretation. In various pictorial information systems, the encoding of pictures is not only to save storage space, but also to facilitate efficient retrieval.

5.1 INTRODUCTION

The research of pictorial data compression dates back to the early 1920s, when there was an effort to transmit digital pictures over the Bartlane cable picture transmission systems between New York and London. Pictures were coded in five distinct brightness levels. The transmission time was reduced from more than one week to less than three hours [MCFARLANE72].

From the 60s, as a result of progress in computer technology, the field of digital pictorial data compression has experienced vigorous growth. It attracted the most attention during the 70s. During that time, research interests were concentrated on some fundamental problems, such as image fidelity, statistical picture models, predictive coding, optimal transforms for transform coding, and so on.

From the late 70s until now there remains a constant interest in pictorial data compression. Some new compression methods—for example, block truncation, vector quantization, synthetic high systems, and motion-compensated techniques—have been proposed. Concepts of picture processing and pattern recognition have been incorporated into pictorial data compression and more sophisticated coding schemes have been invented. More and more research is conducted to investigate methods for object-oriented binary picture coding with applications to pictorial information systems and computer vision systems.

Data compression of gray-level pictures and binary pictures can be quite different. Encoding of gray-level pictures is generally represented by the block diagram in Figure 5.1, which is part of the "picture communication interface" box of Figure 1.1. The original picture data are spatially correlated. Much redundancy exists. The mapping process maps pictorial data into coefficients which are much less correlated. In other words, the coefficients are in a more compact form. The mechanism and form of mapping for different compression methods can be totally different. For example, the mapping of predictive coding (DCPM) is predictor. Transform coding uses orthogonal transforms as mapping. The quantizer quantizes the coefficients into a smaller number of possible values which are suitable for coding. The coder assigns code words to the output of the quantizer. There are extensive discussions about coder design techniques in information theory. We will not, therefore, discuss this topic here in this chapter. From a methodological point of view, gray-level picture data compression methods are distinguished by the approaches of mapping and quantization. Sections 5.2–5.7 are devoted to gray-level picture data compression. After a brief discussion of picture data models, two basic approaches—DPCM and transform coding—are dealt with in some detail. New approaches, such as vector quantization (VQ), the synthetic-high method, and motion-compensated coding, are also introduced later.

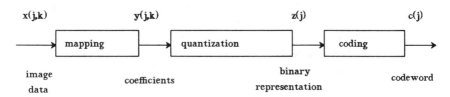

Figure 5.1 Block diagram of gray-level picture encoding.

It is well known that facsimile is one of the important applications of binary picture data compression. On the other hand, binary picture data compression is most applicable to pictorial databases, which is the kernel module for pictorial information systems, office automation systems, CAD systems, computer vision systems, and so on. Section 5.8 discusses binary picture data compression techniques. Object-oriented run-length coding is also included in Section 5.8.

5.2 BASIC CONCEPTS

Before discussing techniques for gray-level picture data compression, we introduce in this section three basic concepts: image fidelity, mathematical models of picture data, and optimal quantization.

5.2.1 Image Fidelity

For the error-tolerance compression system discussed in this subsection, image fidelity is an important measure for the performance of a compression system. Commonly used objective image fidelity measures are mean-square-error (MSE) between the input picture and the output picture and the MSE signal-to-noise ratio of the output picture.

Let $f(j,k)$ denote a digital picture with $j,k = 0,1,...,N-1$; the output picture of a compression system is denoted by $g(j,k)$. The MSE between $f(j,k)$ and $g(j,k)$ is then defined as

$$MSE = \frac{1}{N^2} \sum_{j=0}^{N-1} \sum_{k=0}^{N-1} \left[g(j,k) - f(j,k) \right]^2 \tag{5.1}$$

The MSE signal-to-noise ratio of the output picture is defined as

$$SNR = \frac{\displaystyle\sum_{j=0}^{N-1} \sum_{k=0}^{N-1} \left[g(j,k) \right]^2}{\displaystyle\sum_{j=0}^{N-1} \sum_{k=0}^{N-1} \left[g(j,k) - f(j,k) \right]^2} \tag{5.2}$$

The objective measures are easy to compute and therefore are often used for compression system design and tuning. The objective image fidelity measure MSE and SNR are picture-independent. They sometimes do not reflect the actual visual quality of a picture. Quite often, the output picture of a compression system with the same MSE appears to have different visual qualities due to the characteristics of the human visual system. Images are viewed by people. The subjective measure is therefore a picture's final judgment. The subjective measure of a picture can be evaluated by a number of people by showing them a picture and averaging their evaluations. To evaluate the performance of a compression system, one may present the input and output pictures to a number of observers to evaluate the differences.

5.2.2 Picture Models

Mathematically modeling pictures is a fundamental problem for picture data compression. The Gaussian-Markov field model has proved a good candidate in the sense of feasibility and effectiveness. Assume a picture is a sample picture from a two-dimensional discrete homogeneous Gaussian-Markov field as described in [DELP79a],

$$f(j,k) = \sum_{m=0}^{a} \sum_{n=0}^{b} \theta_{mn} f(j-m,k-n) + u(j,k) \quad m = n \neq 0 \tag{5.3}$$

where

$$E\left[u(j,k)f(j-m,k-n)\right] = 0 \quad 0 \leq m \leq a, 0 \leq n \leq b, m = n \neq 0$$

$$E\left[u(j,k)u(j,k)\right] = \sigma^2 \, \delta_{jl} \, \delta_{kl}$$

The preceding two conditions state that $u(j,k)$ is a zero mean independent Gaussian field noise. In Equation (5.3), θ is called the regression coefficient. Figure 5.2 shows the region of summation.

(0,0)   (N-1,0)

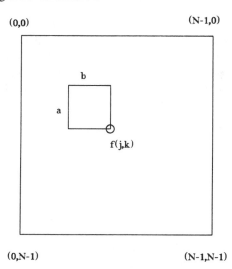

(0,N-1)   (N-1,N-1)

Figure 5.2 Region of summation for Gaussain-Markov field model.

A special case of the Gaussian-Markov field model with a and b equal to 1 is usually called a first-order Gaussian-Markov field.

$$f(j,k) = \theta_1 f(j-1,k) + \theta_2 f(j-1,k-1) + \theta_3 f(j,k-1) + u(j,k) \tag{5.4}$$

Equation (5.4) says that the gray level of pixel (j,k) is spatially related to its neighbor pixels $(j-1,k)$, $(j-1,k-1)$, and $(j,k-1)$. The degree of this gray-level dependence is described by the coefficients θ's. For a given picture one can fit this model to the picture data, solve for parameters θ_1, θ_2, and θ_3 and noise variance σ^2. Using this model, Delp showed well-fitting results to several natural pictures and good DPCM coding results.

In the model defined by Equation (5.3), the gray level of a pixel is related only to its upper and left neighbors. Extending the dependence to its other neighbor pixels is an obvious generalization.

It is worth noting that the Gaussian-Markov model defined by Equations (5.3) and (5.4) is actually a low-pass filter model. This model, therefore, will reflect low frequency and random characteristics of picture data. Consequently, the compression methods based on this model will work well as far as low frequency signals are concerned. Special techniques are needed to compensate for the high frequency performance of the system.

5.2.3 Optimal Quantization

Quantization is the representation of input data by a limited number of discrete values (usually integers). The detailed discussion is in Appendix II. For the convenience of later discussion, we quote the conclusion of optimal quantization as follows [MAX60]:

$$x_{i+1} = \frac{1}{2}(y_i + y_{i+1}) \qquad (5.5)$$

$$\int_{x_i}^{x_{i+1}} (x - y_i)\, p(x)\, dx = 0 \qquad (5.6)$$

For a given distribution density function of input data and the number of output digital values (word length), one can obtain a set of optimal quantization thresholds x_1, x_2,..., x_{N+1} by solving equations (5.5) and (5.6) using the iterative technique. However, the optimization here is subject to the valid distribution density function and in the sense of mean-square-error. If the density function does not fit the actual input data, the quantization error will not be guaranteed to be minimum.

5.3 PREDICTIVE CODING

5.3.1 Basic Concepts

From the picture model defined in equation (5.4) we note that the gray level of a pixel can be estimated from that of its neighbor pixels if parameters θ_1, θ_2, and θ_3 are known. Following this idea, the predictive coding system is constructed. Figure 5.3 shows the block diagram of basic DPCM system.

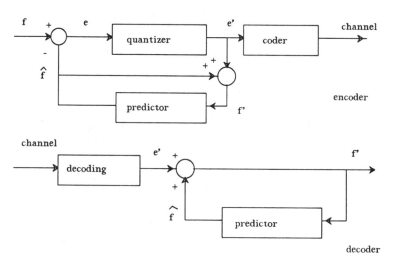

Figure 5.3 Block diagram of basic DPCM system.

Pictorial Data Compression   Chap. 5

We can drop the noise term and rewrite equation (5.4) as

$$f(j,k) = \theta_1 f(j-1,k) + \theta_2 f(j-1,k-1) + \theta_2 f(j,k-1) \qquad (5.7)$$

where θ_1, θ_2, and θ_3 can be estimated from a set of sample picture data. Based on this formula,the predictor estimates the gray level of the current pixel from that of the previous three neighbor pixels. The estimation is compared with the actual value to produce an estimation error. The predictor and comparator here work together as a mapping device in Figure 5.1. The device maps original picture data into error data. The error data are much less correlated and have a smaller dynamic range. It therefore requires fewer bits for its quantization. The encoder codes the quantized data for transmission or storage.

On the receiver side, data are first decoded and then added to the estimated data to construct the original picture. The predictor on the receiver side is a duplication of that on the transmitter side.

The basic predictive coding system in Figure 5.3 is based on the Gaussian-Markov model. In practice, picture data quite often violate this model. Large prediction errors occur when an abrupt edge, for example, is encountered. This will increase the dynamic range of prediction error and leads to large distortion.

Fortunately, the development of picture processing and pattern recognition provides us with many effective techniques for picture texture detection and classification. Based on these techniques, adaptive picture coding systems can be designed. For different types of textures, the system adaptively selects the corresponding predictor or quantizer. This yields the concepts of adaptive prediction and adaptive quantization, which are described in the following paragraphs.

5.3.2 Adaptive Quantization

The idea of adaptive quantization is to use several different quantizers, each of which fits with a certain type of picture texture. The design of adaptive quantization DPCM systems involves two basic problems: one is to detect and classify picture texture, the other is to design a set of quantizers fitting with the corresponding set of textures with minimum error.

The design of better adaptive quantization DPCM systems needs a thorough understanding of texture analysis and edge detection techniques in the picture processing field. However, there has been research investigating possible texture activity functions for quantizer control [SCHAFER81]. Schafer proposed a texture activity function as follows:

$$A_{MD} = \underset{i,j \in DN}{MAX} |d_{ij}| \qquad (5.8)$$

where $d_{ij} = f'_j - f'_i$

$$A_{WD} = \underset{i,j \in DN}{MAX} \left\{ |\delta_i| + \frac{1}{4} \left(\delta_i + |\delta_j|\right) \left[1 - sign\left[e_0\right]\right] \right\} \qquad (5.9)$$

where $\delta_i = f'_i - f_0$. The sign function is defined as

$$sign\ (e_0) = \begin{cases} 1 & e_0 > T \\ 0 & |e_0| \le T \\ -1 & e_0 < -T \end{cases}$$

DN denotes a neighborhood, which is a set of neighbor pixels of the current pixel f_0 and $e_0 = f_0 - \dfrac{1}{5} \sum\limits_{i \in DN} f_i$. The structure of the neighborhood of f_0 is shown in Figure 5.4.

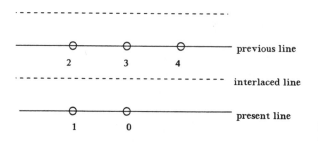

previous line

interlaced line

present line

Figure 5.4 Neighbor structures for texture classification.

The final texture activity function A_{MWD} is calculated by

$$A_{MWD} = MAX \left\{ A_{MD}, A_{WD} \right\} \tag{5.10}$$

It is obvious that A_{MD} describes the maximum difference among neighbor pixels, while A_{WD} describes the maximum difference between the current pixel and its neighbor pixels. The texture activity function A_{MWD} reflects the possible maximum gray-level changes occurring within the neighborhood of the current pixel.

The texture activity function A_{MWD} is then used as a control parameter to adaptively select L separate quantizers according to

$$Q = \begin{cases} Q_1 & A_{MWD} < a_2 \\ Q_2 & a_2 \le A_{MWD} \le a_3 \\ \vdots \\ Q_L & a_L \le A_{MWD} \end{cases} \tag{5.11}$$

The threshold set $a_2, a_3, ..., a_L$ is chosen empirically. It depends on the characteristics of the picture it deals with and on the method of designing quantizers.

We know, from Section 5.2.3, that a quantizer is specified by two parameters: one is the output word length, the other is the distribution density function of the input data. If Gaussian distribution is assumed for all cases, the mean and deviation are two parameters that specify the distribution function. However, because of the presence of textures in pictures, real-world pictures tend to violate the Gaussian-Markov model. The statistical distribution function of the prediction error based on this model cannot be simply considered Gaussian. Intuitively, we can consider it as a composite of several Gaussian distributions, each specified by its own mean and deviation and each corresponding to one type of texture. For example, picture areas with low activity measures have low deviations for prediction error, while areas with abrupt edges tend to have large deviations. One should keep in mind that human eyes are very sensitive to edges. Special attention should be paid to preserve edge information. To improve the fidelity of predictive coded pictures, two possible methods can be used to design adaptive quantizers.

One possible way is to design a set of quantizers $Q_1, Q_2, ..., Q_c$ with the same output word length. For each quantizer Q_i, the mean or deviation is different from that of others. The quantization thresholds of quantizers then turn out to be quite different from each other. Table 5.1 is an example of the thresholds of an adaptive quantization DPCM system. One can see from the table that the larger the texture activity measure, the larger the quantization steps.

TABLE 5.1. THRESHOLDS OF AN ADAPTIVE QUANTIZER

Thresholds	Texture Activity Measure
0, 3, 8, 15, 24, 25	$A_{MWD} < 15$
0, 7, 14, 23, 34, 47	$15 \leq A_{MWD} < 35$
0, 11, 22, 35, 48, 65	$35 \leq A_{MWD} < 100$
0, 15, 30, 45, 64, 85	$100 \leq A_{MWD}$

Alternatively, we can design a set of quantizers with different output word lengths. More bits are assigned to the more active picture area, fewer bits to the less active area. This scheme emphasizes active picture textures, which are more important to the human visual system.

Using adaptive quantization, the bit rate can be further reduced by about 0.5 to 1 bits per pixel compared to ordinary DPCM coding schemes.

5.3.3 Adaptive Prediction

Adaptive quantization uses a fixed predictor, allows variation of dynamic ranges of prediction errors, and adaptively quantizes the prediction errors. On the other hand, adaptive prediction tries to keep prediction errors low by adapting the prediction to the local picture textures. One fixed quantizer can be used in this case because of the low prediction error rate. Adaptive prediction and the motion-compensated estimation (to be described in Section 5.7.1) are based on the same mechanism: trying to reduce the bit rate by keeping the prediction error rate as low as possible.

Control of adaptive prediction is more complicated than that of adaptive quantization, where one needs only to care about the prediction error rate. Here, for adaptive prediction, one should understand in what circumstances a certain amount of prediction error is produced and then carefully design texture models by adjusting prediction parameter θ's to keep the prediction error rate as low as possible. As mentioned before, the gray level of the current pixel is predicted by the weighted sum of its neighbor pixels. These weights θ's are determined by a certain picture model. So far we have used the Gaussian-Markov model. To reduce prediction error, an additional picture local texture model should be designed to fit the actual picture texture. The basic procedures for adaptive prediction are first to detect and classify local textures and then to design a predictor to fit the detected texture. There have been some papers reporting research on adaptive prediction based on edge detection. Here we review the work by Zhang [ZHANG82]. Zhang classifies the textures of the neighborhood depicted in Figure 5.5 into four classes, characterized by

$$
\hat{f}_0 = \begin{cases} h_1 & \textit{flat area} \\ h_2 & \textit{horizontal contour} \\ h_3 & \textit{straight line other than horizontal} \\ h_4 & \textit{texture} \end{cases}
$$

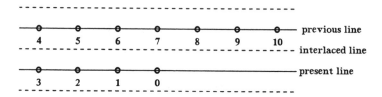

Figure 5.5   Prediction and edge detection structure.

The corresponding four predictors are defined by the following equations:

$$
h_1 = \frac{5}{8} f_1' + \frac{1}{8} (f_6' + f_7' + f_8') \tag{5.12-a}
$$

$$
h_2 = \frac{3}{4} f_1' + \frac{1}{4} f_7' \tag{5.12-b}
$$

$$
h_3 = \frac{1}{4} f_{k-1}' + \frac{1}{2} f_k' + f_{k+1}' \qquad k \in \left\{ 6,7,8,9 \right\} \tag{5.12-c}
$$

$$
h_4 = \frac{1}{5} (f_5' + f_6' + f_7' + f_8' + f_9') \tag{5.12-d}
$$

The rules to identify the texture type of the neighborhood are as follows (the gray-level range is assumed to be 256):

1. The neighborhood is said to be flat if

$$
MAX \left\{ |d_{12}|, |d_{15}|, |d_{16}|, |d_{17}| \right\} < 20 \tag{5.13}
$$

The corresponding prediction Equation (5.12-a) is an ordinary one except there is more weight on the left pixel.

2. A horizontal edge is assumed if

$$
MAX \left\{ |d_{12}|, |d_{23}| \right\} < MIN \left\{ |d_{15}|, |d_{16}|, |d_{17}|, |d_{18}| \right\} \tag{5.14}
$$

Equation (5.14) implies that there is not much gray-level change in the current line, but a considerable change occurs in the vertical direction. Vertical change represents the horizontal edge. The prediction of f_0 in this case very much depends on its left pixel. This is reflected in Equation (5.12-b).

3. The edge direction other than horizontal is identified by

$$MIN \left\{ | d_{1,k-1} | \right\} < 51 \quad k = 6, 7, 8, 9 \tag{5.15-a}$$

$$sign \ (d_{12}) \ sign \ (d_{k-1,k-2}) = 1 \tag{5.15-b}$$

The preceding two equations state the conditions of a non-horizontal edge existence as follows: (a) there is not much gray-level change in the vertical direction, (b) at the location of the detected edge, the signs of gray-level changes of two neighboring lines must be identical. On the other hand, to avoid the noise influence, the sign function is set to zero for small argument values—say less than 7.

As usual, more weights are put on neighbor pixels having fewer differences referring to the current pixel. In the Equation (5.12-c), k is the subscript in $MIN \left\{ | d_{1,k-1} | \right\}$.

4. Texture is identified by rapid gray-level change, which is detected by

$$sign \ (d_{12}) \ sign \ (d_{k,k-1}) = -1 \quad k = 6, 7 \tag{5.16-a}$$

$$sign \ (d_{k-1,k-2}) \neq sign \ (d_{k,k-1}) = sign \ (d_{k+1,k}) \tag{5.16-b}$$

The first equation is to verify that the directions of gray-level change on two adjacent lines are not the same. The second equation further assumes that even on the same line, the directions of gray-level change are different. The corresponding prediction in Equation (5.12-d) is simply the average of 5 pixels.

Using the adaptive prediction just described, very promising results were obtained [ZHANG82].

5.3.4 Remarks on Predictive Coding

Because of the mechanism of predictive coding, the system error and channel error are cumulative to reconstructed pictures. When an error occurs, one can get rid of it only by reinitializing the prediction; otherwise the error will be effective until the beginning of the next line.

Predictive coding has the advantage of being easy to implement in real TV transmission time. There has been comprehensive research conducted in this area. Most showed good results with 2 bits per pixel. Further research is being done on time-varying picture coding.

5.4 TRANSFORM CODING

Transform coding uses the transform as a mapping tool to map original picture data into transform coefficients. Unlike DPCM coding, which maps picture data pixel by pixel, transform coding usually performs a 2-D transform on picture data blocks. We then assign a different number of bits to quantize each transform coefficient by using a bit allocation matrix. Some small coefficients can even be discarded. Because the transform coefficients are nearly uncorrelated, the quantization error and channel error will be distributed to all pixels within the picture block through inverse transform, appearing as additive random noise. Transforms used for transform coding are capable of compacting the energy of the picture block into a few transform coefficients; more than half of all the coefficients have very small amplitudes and can be discarded before quantization. This results in a high data compression ratio.

In the following paragraphs we first briefly review the cosine transform—the one most suitable for data compression—then discuss the adaptive transform coding method using the texture analysis technique.

5.4.1 Cosine Transform

Although there are many transforms which can be used for transform coding—for example, the Fourier transform, the Hadamard transform, the Haar transform, the Slant transform, and so on—we choose to discuss the cosine transform because it is known to be approximately optimal when the mean-square-error criterion and the Gaussian-Markov field model are assumed. The two-dimensional forward and inverse cosine transform is defined as

$$F(u,v) = \frac{4\,c(u)\,c(v)}{N^2} \sum_{j=0}^{N-1}\sum_{k=0}^{N-1} f(j,k) \cos\frac{(2j+1)u\,\pi}{2N} \cos\frac{(2k+1)v\,\pi}{2N} \quad (5.17\text{-a})$$

$$f(j,k) = \sum_{u=0}^{N-1}\sum_{v=0}^{N-1} c(u)\,c(v)\,F(u,v) \cos\frac{(2j+1)u\,\pi}{2N} \cos\frac{(2k+1)v\,\pi}{2N} \quad (5.17\text{-b})$$

where

$$c(u), c(v) = \begin{cases} \sqrt{2}/2 & u,v = 0 \\ 1 & u,v = 1,2,...,N-1 \\ 0 & otherwise \end{cases}$$

It is well known that the Karhunen-Loeve (K-L) transform—the optimal transform—is defined by the eigenvectors of the covariance matrix of the data to be transformed. If the first-order Markov sequence model of the source data is assumed, its covariance matrix will have the form of a Toepliz matrix as follows :

$$\begin{bmatrix} 1 & \rho & \cdot & \cdot & \rho^{M-1} \\ \rho & 1 & & & \rho^{M-2} \\ \cdot & & & & \cdot \\ \cdot & & & & \cdot \\ \cdot & & & & \cdot \\ \rho^{M-1} & \rho^{M-2} & \cdot & \cdot & 1 \end{bmatrix} \qquad 0 < \rho < 1$$

It is shown that the plot of the eigenvector of a Toepliz matrix for $\rho = 0.9$ and the plot of one-dimensional cosine transform basis functions have a very close resemblance. Recall that we assume a Gaussian-Markov picture data model for picture coding. Based on this model, the cosine transform is the best approximation of a K-L transform. The K-L transform has no fast algorithms. A fast cosine transform is even faster than a fast Fourier transform. Figure 5.6 shows several curves representing the variances of transform coefficients of different transforms. Apparently, the K-L transform and the cosine transform are the best as far as the capability of compacting "energy" is concerned.

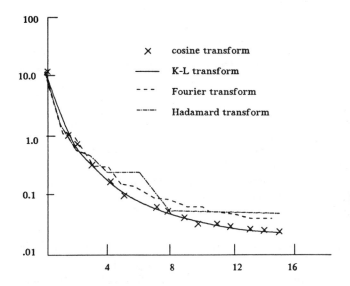

Figure 5.6 Variances of transform coefficients, $M = 16$, $\rho = 0.95$.

When the cosine transform is used for transform coding, an input picture is first divided into subpictures (picture blocks); the block size is usually taken to be 16×16 or 8×8. After transformation on these picture blocks, a certain bit allocation matrix is designed to indicate the number of bits assigned to pixels in the block for their quantization. The bit allocation matrix is stored both on the transmitter side and the receiver side. According to the bit allocation matrix, the receiver can separate the coding data for pixels and insert zeros in place of discarded pixels. The final reconstructed picture is obtained by performing inverse cosine transforms on blocks and combining blocks.

5.4.2 Adaptive Cosine Transform Coding

The transform is a fixed mapping tool in a picture coding system and no adaptive procedures can be made upon it. Therefore, adaptive transform coding implies adaptive quantization only. Since picture data are transformed block by block, adaptive quantization is also implemented blockwise by switching between a set of bit allocation matrices.

An adaptive transform coding system was proposed by Wu and Burge by introducing a texture analysis technique [WU82]. A more sophisticated method is in [WU86]. A block diagram of Wu and Burge's scheme is in Figure 5.7. An input picture is divided into picture blocks, each with 16×16 pixels, and the cosine transform is carried out on each block. In the transform domain the blocks are classified into several classes, then normalized and quantized by using the corresponding normalization matrices and bit allocation matrices, respectively. These two matrices, once determined, are common to all pictures the system is to deal with and are stored in both the encoder and decoder. Bookkeeping information is inserted in front of each block to indicate the class to which the block belongs.

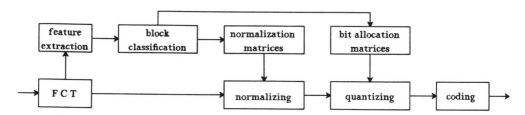

Figure 5.7 Block diagram of an adaptive transform coding system.

Blocks in the same class are quantized with the same bit allocation matrix. To minimize the quantization distortion, the differences between the blocks assigned to the same class must be minimized. In other words, inner-class differences should be reduced as far as possible. The problem of block classification can be dealt with by pattern recognition techniques in the cosine transform domain. The design procedure may include investigation of transform patterns, determination of class categories, design of texture measures which can characterize each class, and finding of the decision functions by training procedures.

Picture textures are well reflected in their cosine transforms. The cosine transform texture patterns can be characterized by directionality, frequency, and number of texture activities.

The texture activity measure mathematically described as "AC" energy is

$$MACE(p,q) = \sum_{u=0}^{p} \sum_{v=0}^{p} F^2(u,v) - \sum_{u=0}^{q} \sum_{v=0}^{q} F^2(u,v) \qquad (5.18)$$

where $q < p$. For computational simplicity, Equation (5.18) can be rewritten as

$$MACE'(p,q) = \sum_{u=0}^{p} \sum_{v=0}^{p} |F(u,v)| - \sum_{u=0}^{q} \sum_{v=0}^{q} |F(u,v)| \qquad (5.19)$$

The texture direction measure DIR is defined as the weighted average of angles of each transform component with respect to the u coordinate:

$$DIR = \frac{\displaystyle\sum_{u=0}^{M} \sum_{v=0}^{M} \tan^{-1}\left(\frac{u}{v}\right) |F(u,v)|}{\displaystyle\sum_{u=0}^{M} \sum_{v=0}^{M} |F(u,v)|} \qquad (5.20)$$

The range of DIR is 0 to $\frac{\pi}{2}$. For example, the cosine transform pattern of a picture block with vertical strips appears as a line next to the u axis; its DIR is close to zero.

The frequency measure is characterized by the slope of the cosine transform spectrum. Two frequency bands is specified. The average amplitude within the two specified frequency bands are computed. The ratio of them is defined as the measure.

$$
FIN = \frac{\int_{\rho_1}^{\rho_2} d\rho \int_{0}^{\frac{\pi}{2}} F(\rho,\theta)\, d\theta \; / \; \int_{\rho_1}^{\rho_2} d\rho \int_{0}^{\frac{\pi}{2}} d\theta}{\int_{\rho_3}^{\rho_4} d\rho \int_{0}^{\frac{\pi}{2}} F(\rho,\theta)\, d\theta \; / \; \int_{\rho_3}^{\rho_4} d\rho \int_{0}^{\frac{\pi}{2}} d\theta} \tag{5.21}
$$

Based on the preceding texture measures, a simple classifier is designed to classify transform patterns into 10 classes. Classes 1 to 4 are nondirectional and non-high-frequency patterns, each having different texture activities. Classes 5 and 6 are patterns with horizontal directionality. Classes 7 and 8 are patterns with vertical directionality. Classes 9 and 10 are high-frequency patterns. There are bit allocation matrices, each associated to one class. Bit allocation matrices are designed by training procedures. Figure 5.8 contains two bit allocation matrices corresponding to classes 3 and 6, respectively.

TABLE 5.2. DECISION FUNCTION OF CLASSIFIER

Class 1	$MACE < m\,11$	$d\,1 < DIR < d\,2$	
Class 2	$m\,11 \le MACE < m\,12$	$d\,1 < DIR < d\,2$	
Class 3	$m\,12 \le MACE < m\,13$	$d\,1 < DIR < d\,2$	FIN > f1
Class 4	$m\,13 \le MACE$	$d\,1 < DIR < d\,2$	FIN > f1
Class 5	$MACE < m\,21$	$DIR \le d\,1$	
Class 6	$m\,21 \le MACE$	$DIR \le d\,1$	
Class 7	$MACE < m\,21$	$d\,2 \le DIR$	
Class 8	$m\,21 \le MACE$	$d\,2 \le DIR$	
Class 9	$m\,12 \le MACE < m\,13$	$d\,1 < DIR < d\,2$	FIN > f1
Class 10	$m\,13 \le MACE$	$d\,1 < DIR < d\,2$	FIN > f1

Good results were reported in [WU82] for a house picture using 0.26 bits per pixel. Figure 5.9 is an example.

5.5 SYNTHETIC HIGH CODING SYSTEMS

It is well known that in audio systems two or more than two channel amplifiers are used to gain sound fidelity. The same principle applies to picture coding systems. A block diagram of a synthetic high picture coding system is shown in Figure 5.10.

```
8654332211000000        8655444444333322
6543322110000000        4443332221110000
5443322110000000        2221110000000000
4332221100000000        0000000000000000
3332221100000000        0000000000000000
3332211000000000        0000000000000000
3222110000000000        0000000000000000
2221110000000000        0000000000000000
2211000000000000        0000000000000000
1110000000000000        0000000000000000
0000000000000000        0000000000000000
0000000000000000        0000000000000000
0000000000000000        0000000000000000
0000000000000000        0000000000000000
```

(a) 0.719 bpp   (b) 0.398 bpp

Figure 5.8   Examples of bit allocation matrices.

(a)

(b)

Figure 5.9   An example of adaptive cosine transform coding. (a) Original house picture, 8bpp; (b) compressed with 0.26bpp, mean-square-error is 0.626.

An original picture is decomposed into two components by low-pass filter and high-pass filter. The low-pass component gives the general view of the picture without sharp gray-level changes. The high-pass filter component contains information about edges and detailed textures. In this section, three synthetic high coding methods are described: block truncation coding, the Laplasian pyramid method, and the contour-texture approach.

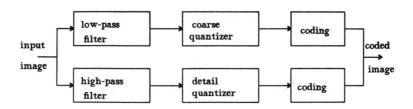

Figure 5.10   Block diagram of synthetic high coding system.

The principle of synthetic high coding coincides well with the properties of human visual system. It permits a considerable amount of redundancy reduction and shows promise for further research interests.

5.5.1 Block Truncation Coding

Block truncation coding [DELP79b,HEALY81] divides an entire picture of N by N into blocks of M by M. The block size M is usually 4. The block truncation coding can be considered a synthetic high system. The low-pass component is a picture block with a constant gray level—the mean of the original pictorial data within the block. A bit plane indicating a pixel gray level above or below the mean can be considered a high-frequency component. To quantize picture blocks, mean and variance are first computed.

$$m = \frac{1}{M \times M} \sum_{j=1}^{M} \sum_{k=1}^{M} f(j,k) \tag{5.22}$$

$$\sigma^2 = \frac{1}{M \times M} \sum_{j=1}^{M} \sum_{k=1}^{M} f^2(j,k) - m^2 \tag{5.23}$$

Mean m is the average brightness of the block; variance σ represents the texture activities. Mean and variance vary from block to block. One bit for each pixel is used to indicate whether the gray level is above or below the mean. The 1's and 0's mean something different in reconstructing the original picture. They are specified by

$$Y_0 = m - \sigma \sqrt{q/p} \tag{5.24}$$

$$Y_1 = m + \sigma \sqrt{q/p} \tag{5.25}$$

where q and p are the number of pixels above and below the sample mean, respectively. Pixels coded with 1's are set to Y_1, and others are set to Y_0.

The advantage of block truncation coding is its simplicity. Good results can be obtained with 1 to 2 bits per pixel. For example, if the block size is 4 by 4, 8 bits are used to quantize mean and variance and 16 bits for the 4×4 bit plane. The total bit rate is 2 bits per pixel.

5.5.2 Laplasian Pyramid Method

The Laplasian pyramid method intelligently uses the pyramid data structure in pictorial data compression. Starting from an original picture $f_0(j,k)$ of size $N \times N$, a low-pass filter, which is actually a local averaging, is used to compute the low-pass component $f_1(j,k)$. The high-pass component $g_0(j,k)$ at level 0 is then obtained by

$$g_0(j,k) = f_0(j,k) - f_1(j,k) \tag{5.26}$$

Since f_1 is a low-pass component, it may be encoded at a reduced sample rate. If we reduce f_1 by a sample interval of 2, a picture f_1 with a smaller size of $\frac{N}{2} \times \frac{N}{2}$ is obtained. An iteration procedure is performed on f_1 to get a picture pyramid $f_0, f_1, \cdots$ and an error pyramid $g_0, g_1, \cdots$. Suppose a 5×5 average window is used; a filtering process to construct a higher-level picture is defined by

$$f_l(j,k) = \sum_{m=-2}^{2} \sum_{n=-2}^{2} w(m,n) f_{l-1}(2j+m, 2k+n) \tag{5.27}$$

where $w(m,n)$ is a weighting function.

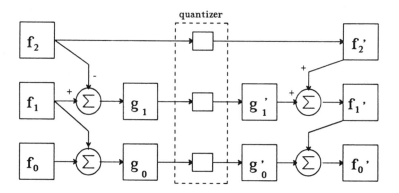

Figure 5.11 Block diagram of a 3-level Laplasian pyramid picture coding scheme.

Figure 5.11 shows a block diagram of a 3-level Laplasian pyramid picture coding scheme. The original picture f_0 here is decomposed into two high frequency components g_0, g_1 and a low-pass component f_2. We code f_2, g_0 and g_1 instead of f_0. Notice that f_2 has low resolution and requires fewer bits for its coding. Error pictures g_0 and g_1 contain information about rapid edges and fine textures usually appearing within a small portion of the picture area. Therefore, most pixels having error data close to zero can be neglected. This reduces the bit rate a great deal. Good results were reported for a head-and-shoulder picture with a bit rate of 1.58 and 0.73 bits per pixel.

The Laplasian pyramid coding scheme particularly suits progressive picture transmission, which is required in pictorial information systems. For progressive picture transmission, the picture pyramid is organized and transmitted from top to bottom. On the receiver side, coarse picture data are first received and reconstructed. The observer can view the picture from coarse to fine. A person may terminate transmission as soon as he or she sees the contents of the picture are of no interest. This saves a lot of transmission time, for one may find a picture of interest only after several tries.

5.5.3 Contour-Texture Scheme

Both block truncation coding and the Laplasian pyramid method code a picture in terms of square picture blocks. In practice, a square block does not fit the actual picture texture. Large coding errors may result if there are abrupt edges and flat areas within one block. The contour-texture scheme assumes that pictures consist of objects, the areas of which have a homogeneous property. In the contour-texture scheme, the high-frequency components are contours of detected object regions, while low-frequency components are contexts of the regions. The contour-texture scheme consists of three processing steps [KOCHER82]: picture segmentation by region growing, contour coding, and texture coding.

Region growing is a technique of picture segmentation which is operated on the original picture to identify object regions. Because of fine structures and noise existence, the segmentation process may result in too many small regions which increase the system complexity and make it impractical. Therefore, preprocessing, using an edge preserving smooth operation, is intended to reduce the local granularity of the original picture without affecting its significant contours. Region growing operations are performed on a preprocessed picture. Regions enclosed by contours are expected.

There are many techniques available for region growing and contour coding, which are described well in picture processing text books—for example [ROSENFELD83]. Contours can be encoded either by a sequence of approximated line and circle segments or by a sequence of contour points without approximation.

Texture coding here means coding of textures within object regions, which appear as object surfaces. As matter of fact, there is not much texture left after preprocessing and segmentation because of the homogeneous property of the object region. Coding object surfaces then can be achieved by fitting 2-D polynomials to regions. The parameters of polynomials are coded.

To reconstruct the original picture, a contour picture is first obtained from coded contour data. Surfaces represented by polynomials are then added to a contour picture to get the final results. The results usually can preserve object shapes well, but the natural appearance of the original picture is lost in most cases: the object surface is too smooth. Sometimes, artificial "salt-and-pepper" noises are added to make the reconstructed picture more natural.

The data compression ratio of the contour-texture scheme can reach as high as 50 for the "camera man" test picture. Of course there are still difficulties facing this technique. In fact, a segmentation method does not exist which is effective with a variety of pictures and which can generate a limited number of object regions suitable to the coding scheme. The difficulties are partially due to the nature of pictures. Some pictures inherently have fine textures with rapid gray level changes which cannot be filtered out by preprocessing.

5.6 VECTOR QUANTIZATION

5.6.1 Basic Concepts of VQ

It has been seen that the performance of pictorial data compression depends highly on the way of quantization. Vector (block) quantization is an interesting quantization technique which utilizies some well-established methodologies in the field of pattern recognition and database theory.

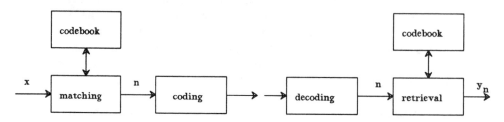

Figure 5.12   Block diagram of vector (block) quantization.

Figure 5.12 shows a block diagram of a vector (block) quantization coding system. Vector quantization is related to scalar quantization in Section 2.1.3, which quantizes data samples individually. When scalar quantization is used, one should invoke the mapping process to make use of data correlation to achieve data compression. Vector quantization combines the two processes, decorrelation and quantization, into a single matching (retrieving in decoder side) process.

We assume that we are dealing with a p-dimensional vector $\vec{x} = \{ x_1, x_2, ..., x_p \}$ and that each element in vector $\vec{x}$ is in digital form and represented by L digits. There are M possible vectors in a vector set X. The subscripts denote the sequential number of elements in a vector. Superscripts denote the vector membership number in a set of vectors.

Suppose we plot all these vectors in a p-dimensional pattern space and use the pattern recognition method to partition the space into N subspaces, each corresponding to a class. For each class of vectors, a prototype vector $\vec{y}$ is found such that the average distance from $\vec{y}$ to all vectors within this class is minimum. Obviously, the dimension of $\vec{y}$ is the same as $\vec{x}$. Now we take the set of prototypes $Y = \{ \vec{y}^1, \vec{y}^2, ..., \vec{y}^N \}$ as the codebook and store it on both the encoder side and decoder side. On the encoder side, for each input vector $\vec{x}$, the matching module finds the best match between $\vec{x}$ and $\vec{y}^n$, which is output class number n. On the decoder side, the class number n is used to retrieve $\vec{y}^n$, which is then thought of as the representative of $\vec{x}$ to reconstruct the original picture. Intuitively, if $N \ll M$, vector quantization can achieve a very high data compression ratio. The design of a vector quantization system now is focused on the problems such as the following: for a given error rate, find the minimum number of prototypes N (bit rate is $\log_2 N$); or for a given prototype number N, find the best set of prototypes with the minimum error rate. This codebook design problem can be solved by a "training procedure" in pattern recognition. Fortunately, there are some methods available. Among them, the K-mean clustering algorithm now is most frequently used in VQ. It can be summarized as follows :

Input: a set of input vector X, expected number of classes N.

Output: N prototype set Y.

    Step 1. Randomly choose N initial prototypes from X.

    Step 2. For each input vector $\vec{x}$, assign $\vec{x}$ to class n if $\vec{x}$ is closest to $\vec{y}^n$.

    Step 3. Update Y by taking $\vec{y}^n$ as the centroid of class n.

    Step 4. Check the changes of Y in this iteration; if it is under a threshold ε, stop and output Y; otherwise go back to step 2.

The *K*-mean algorithm does not require any knowledge of source data statistics. It assumes the same deviation and a different mean for classes. If the data violates the assumption, of course, the *K*-mean algorithm will not give good results.

The matching process in Figure 5.12 can be modeled as a minimum distance classifier :

$$output \;\; n \,, \;\; if \;\; d(\vec{x}, \vec{y}^n) < d(\vec{x}, \vec{y}^m) \;\;\; for \;\; all \;\; m \neq n, \;\; m = 1, 2, ..., N$$

In practice, if the dimension of a vector is considerably large, N may be too large to complete the decision-making procedure just described with a reasonable computation cost. The techniques of indexing and retrieval in information systems should then be invoked.

Chang and his students studied vector-quantization on a set of test pictures. A compression ratio of around 10 was obtained without noticeable distortion [WANG85] (see Figure 5.13).

5.6.2 Edge-Oriented VQ Picture Coding

Ramamurthi and Gersho proposed an edge-oriented VQ picture coding scheme [RAMAMURTHI84]. The vector (block) dimension was taken to be 16 (4 × 4). For edge/shade classification, two sets of gradient tables are formed, each for the horizontal (x) and vertical (y) directions. Let

$$h_{jk} \;\; = \;\; |f(j, k+1) - f(j, k)| \tag{5.28}$$

$$s_{jk} \;\; = \;\; sign \; [f(j, k+1) - f(j, k)] \tag{5.29}$$

$$m_{jk} \;\; = \;\; [f(j, k+1) + f(j, k)] / 2 \tag{5.30}$$

The element of the y-table (matrix), y_{jk} is

$$y_{jk} \;\; = \;\; \begin{cases} s_{jk} & if \;\; h_{jk} > T_e \, m_{jk} \\ 0 & otherwise \end{cases}$$

where T_e is an edge detection threshold (a typical value for T_e is 0.2). The x-table can be similarly computed for the pair of pixels $f(j+1, k)$ and $f(j, k)$. At the same time, two counters are maintained for the x and y directions. The counter is incremented if $h_{jk} > T_s \, m_{jk}$, where T_s is another threshold and a typical value is 0.025.

Using the preceding measures, input vectors are preclassified. A vector is deemed to be a shade vector if both counters are separated by less than a threshold

(a)   (b)

Figure 5.13   (a) Original picture; (b) compressed version using VQ 0.8 bits per pixel.

(2 out of 16). A vector is an edge vector if there are more than a minimum number (say 2) of +1's and -1's in either table. Otherwise it is a mid-range vector. Edge vectors are further classified into 28 classes using these gradient tables. Each class has its different edge orientation and location.

Each class of vectors has its own sub-codebook, which is designed using training procedures. For a typical picture, about 70% to 80% of its vectors are mid-range classes. The matching complexity should be reduced for this class. This can be done by simplifying the distance measure MSE of two vectors. A discrete cosine transform is performed on two vectors. The distance measures of these two vectors is then defined as the differences of a few low frequency components. This truncation does not affect the result due to the distance-preserving property of the cosine transform. In the encoder, the six low frequency components were stored in the codebook. An input vector is first classified, then transformed in real time, and a reduced complexity matching yields the optimum code vector. The decoder, of course, uses the original spatial domain codebook for reconstruction of the original picture.

Using the preceding technique, Ramamurthi built codebooks for 0.7 bpp (bit per pixel) and 0.8 bpp. Both worked well for head-and-shoulder pictures.

5.7 PICTURE SEQUENCE CODING

So far we have discussed data compression techniques for still pictures or individual picture frames. Attention has been focused on finding the schemes which can make the best use of the spatial correlation properties of pictorial data to facilitate a high data compression ratio, or, in other words, to reduce the data rate of transmission.

A large proportion of the pictures in the real world exist as picture sequences. For instance, TV pictures are time varying picture sequences, and Landsat MSS pictures and color pictures are spectrum varying picture sequences. In addition to the two spatial coordinates, picture sequence is considered a third coordinate. The third coordinate is most likely time or spectrum. There also exist data correlations in the third coordinate. This section is devoted to describing techniques for picture sequence coding.

In principle, techniques for spatial data compression—with certain extensions— are applicable to picture sequence coding. 3-D DPCM, 3-D transform, and transform/DPCM hybrid coding methods belong to this type. In what follows, instead of this type of coding technique, we discuss techniques peculiar to picture sequences: motion-compensated estimation for TV pictures and color picture coding.

5.7.1 Motion Compensated TV Picture Coding

Because of the requirement of real time transmission of TV pictures, predictive coding is often preferable. Motion compensated TV picture coding is an adaptive coding in the time domain and is based on the following coding strategies:

1. Segment each frame into two parts. One is background, the contents of which are the same as the previous frame, and the other is a moving part, which has changed from the previous frame.

2. Two types of moving area information are transmitted: (a) addresses specifying the location of the pixels of the moving area and (b) information to update the gray level of moving area pixels, which is a motion-compensated prediction error in the case we are dealing with.

3. Use the frame buffer to match the coder bit rate to the constant channel rate. Since the motion in TV scenes occurs randomly and in bursts, the amount of information about moving area will be time dependent. This makes the coder bit rate time varying.

It is clear that to reduce the bit rate one should develop a good motion-compensated prediction method. There has been a lot of research conducted for motion estimation [HUANG83]. Because TV pictures must be transmitted in real time, only relatively simple methods can be considered. In what follows, we first discuss recursive displacement estimation and describe a motion-compensated prediction picture data coding system based on it; then displacement estimation by block matching is briefly introduced.

Recursive Displacement Estimation. The recursive displacement estimation method was proposed by Netraveli and Robbins [NETRAVALI79]. The algorithm iterates on a pixel-by-pixel (or on a small block of pixels) basis, revising their displacement estimate at every moving area pixel by the following update formula:

$$\hat{D}^i = \hat{D}^{i-1} + U^i \qquad (5.31)$$

where $\hat{D}^i$ is a displacement estimate of the ith iteration. U^i is an update of $\hat{D}^{i-1}$ to $\hat{D}^i$. In other words, U^i is an estimate of $D - \hat{D}^{i-1}$. Let x represent spatial location and let $f(x, t - \tau)$ and $f(x,t)$ be the gray levels of the two successive frames at the location x and time t. We are now able to define displaced frame difference $DFD(x, \hat{D}^{i-1})$ as

$$DFD(x, \hat{D}^{i-1}) = f(x,t) - f(x - \hat{D}^{i-1}, t - \tau) \qquad (5.32)$$

Since displacement estimate $\hat{D}^{i-1}$ can take the value of a fraction, the evaluation of the preceding formula should use the interpolation process in the discrete 2-D spatial space. As defined, DFD will converge to zero as $\hat{D}^i$ converges to the actual displacement D. This can be achieved by recursive estimation. Assume the prediction of a pixel at location x_a has a displacement of $\hat{D}^{i-1}$ and a gray level of $f(x_a - \hat{D}^{i-1}, t - \tau)$, and the prediction error is $DFD(x_a, \hat{D}^{i-1})$; then in the next iteration the displacement estimate $\hat{D}^i$ produces estimate error $DFD(x_a, \hat{D}^i)$, and $|DFD(x_a, \hat{D}^i)| \le |DFD(x_a, \hat{D}^{i-1})|$. The iteration formula can take the following form:

$$\hat{D}^i = \hat{D}^{i-1} - \frac{\varepsilon}{2} \nabla_D [DFD(x_a, \hat{D}^{i-1})]^2$$

$$= \hat{D}^{i-1} - \varepsilon DFD(x_a, \hat{D}^{i-1}) \nabla_D DFD(x_a, \hat{D}^{i-1}) \qquad (5.33)$$

where ε is a small positive constant, and ∇_D is the gradient with respect to displacement D. From Equation (5.32) we have

$$\nabla_D [DFD(x_a, \hat{D}^{i-1})] = \nabla f(x_a - \hat{D}^{i-1}, t - \tau) \qquad (5.34)$$

New ∇ is the gradient with respect to x. This gives us

$$\hat{D}^i = \hat{D}^{i-1} - \varepsilon DFD(x_a, \hat{D}^{i-1}) \nabla f(x_a - \hat{D}^{i-1}, t - \tau) \qquad (5.35)$$

We notice, from this equation, that the update term to the old estimation $\hat{D}^{i-1}$ is a vector quantity. It is parallel to the direction of the spatial gradient of the picture gray level. Its amplitude is proportional to the motion-compensated prediction error.

The iteration defined by Equation (5.35) can be implemented without much difficulty. Knowing $\hat{D}^{i-1}$, $f(x_a, t)$, and $f(x_a, t-\tau)$, $f(x_a - \hat{D}^{i-1}, t-\tau)$ is estimated by interpolation. Linear interpolation is usually used for its simplicity.

The constant ε was chosen to be 1/1024 in [NETRAVALI79]. A large ε yields a quick convergence but a noisy estimation, whereas a small ε allows convergence to a finer value of displacement.

Several recursive algorithms have been proposed since Netravali and Robbin. For example, Cafforie and Rocca proposed an extended version of their former recursive algorithm [CAFFORIE83].

Based on their recursive algorithm Netravali and Robbin constructed a motion-compensated TV picture coding system. A simplified block diagram of a motion-compensated coder is shown in Figure 5.14. The outer loop produces prediction error by subtracting motion-compensated prediction from the current input TV field. The motion-compensated prediction is computed first by a displacement estimator depicted at an inner right location and then by a motion-compensated prediction on the left side.

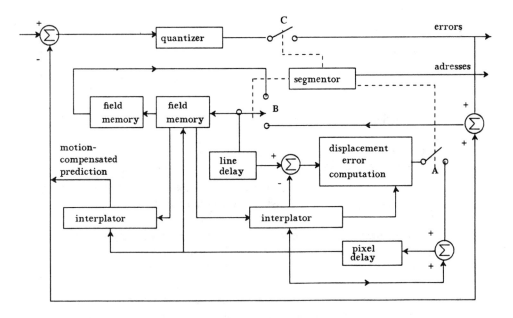

Figure 5.14 Block diagram of motion-compensated coder.

Based on the frame difference, the segmentor controls the displacement estimator through switch A and the motion-compensated predictor through switch B to let them work only in the moving area. The transmission of prediction error is also controlled by the segmentor through switch C. Moving area classification is performed using the following formula:

1. $|FDIF(x)| > T_2$ or
2. $|FDIF(x)| > T_1$ and
   $|FDIF|$ at $a, b, c, or\ d > T_1$ and
   $|FDIF|$ at $A, B, C, or\ D > T_1$

The configuration of pixels in the preceding formula is depicted in Figure 5.15, where FDIF is an abbreviation of frame difference, T_1 and T_2 are two thresholds, and $T_2 \geq T_1$. The typical values of T_1 and T_2 are 1 and 3 for the gray-level scale of 0 to 255, respectively.

As mentioned earlier in this section, the moving area is further classified into a compensable region, where motion-compensated prediction is accurate enough so that no update information needs to be transmitted, and the uncompensable region, where

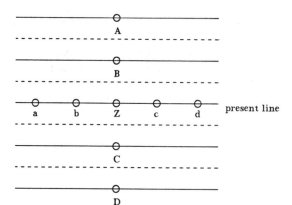

Figure 5.15 Pixel configuration used in the moving area segmentor.

the prediction error should be transmitted. The classification rule is as follows :

1. A pixel in a moving area is classified to be uncompensable if its amplitude of the motion-compensated prediction error is greater than 3 out of 255.

2. Between uncompensable pixels, compensable pixels having run lengths less than or equal to 3 are also classified as uncompensable pixels.

Quantization of prediction error is a straightforward process. Coding of moving area addresses should be carefully designed to reduce overhead information. Run-length coding of addresses was used in [NETRAVALI79].

By the motion-compensated prediction technique just described, Netravali and Robbins obtained a 30% to 50% improvement for pictures of a speaking person and a 22% improvement for pictures of complex and rapid moving objects, compared with the coding without motion-compensated prediction.

Displacement Estimation by Block Matching. Block matching is a well-known technique in digital picture processing. For displacement estimation purposes, a picture block of size $M \times M$ with the center at current pixel (j, k) is taken from frame i. The picture block is then moved around in the previous frame $i - 1$; the correlations are computed between the block and its covered region in the previous frame $i - 1$. The correlation peak is found as the right displacement. For the sake of simplicity, the mean of the absolute frame difference MAD is proposed instead of the correlation.

$$MAD(j,k) = \frac{1}{M^2} \sum_{m=1}^{M} \sum_{n=1}^{M} \left[f_i(m,n) - f_{i-1}(m+j, n+k) \right] \qquad (5.36)$$

Several searching algorithms have been proposed to reduce the number of steps to reach the matching point. The 2-D logarithmic search procedure is one of them and is proposed by J.R. Jain and A.K. Jain [JAIN81]. The procedure can be demonstrated well by Figure 5.16. It is assumed that the matching criterion, MAD, increases monotonically as the search moves away from the right point. In each searching step, five points are checked as shown in Figure 5.16. The search step distance is reduced if the minimum MAD is in the center point or at the boundary of the searching area.

Otherwise, the point with the minimum MAD will be taken as the new central searching point.

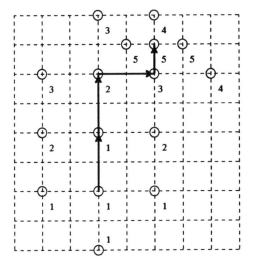

Figure 5.16 Illustration of 2-D logarithmic block searching.

5.7.2 Coding of Color Pictures

A color picture is usually represented by independent red, green, and blue pictures. If RGB pictures are coded separately, the coding error and channel error will affect the visual quality of the reconstructed color picture a great deal, due to the characteristics of human color perception. Frei and Baxter investigated the human color perception model and proposed a nonlinear transform based on it. This color perception model based on a nonlinear transform consists of three operations and is best illustrated by the block diagram in Figure 5.17.

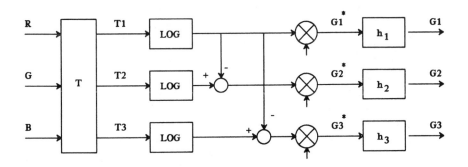

Figure 5.17 Block diagram of nonlinear transform based on the color perception model.

The first two operations are mathematically defined as

$$\begin{bmatrix} T_1 \\ T_2 \\ T_3 \end{bmatrix} = \begin{bmatrix} .299 & .587 & .144 \\ .607 & .174 & .201 \\ .0 & .066 & 1.117 \end{bmatrix} \begin{bmatrix} R \\ G \\ B \end{bmatrix} \qquad (5.37)$$

and

$$\begin{bmatrix} G_1^* \\ G_2^* \\ G_3^* \end{bmatrix} = \begin{bmatrix} 21.5 & 0 & 0 \\ -41.0 & 41.0 & 0 \\ -6.27 & 0 & 6.27 \end{bmatrix} \begin{bmatrix} \log T_1 \\ \log T_2 \\ \log T_3 \end{bmatrix} \qquad (5.38)$$

Three band-pass filters—the third operation—are plotted in Figure 5.18. The simulation results show that the distortion computed with this model coincides well with subjective measures produced by a group of observers. With the same random noise added to RGB pictures and transformed G_1, G_2, and G_3, the color picture reconstructed from G_1, G_2, G_3 appears to have a smaller chromatic error and the errors are more uniformly distributed with respect to spatial frequency. Therefore, its distortion is much lower than the color picture reconstructed from RGB pictures.

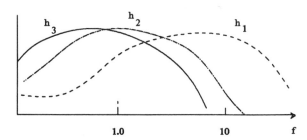

Figure 5.18 Band-pass filter functions of the color perception model.

Pseudo-Color Coding.   An alternative coding method for color pictures is based on pattern recognition techniques. Colors of a color picture represented by an RGB primary color picture can be plotted as points in RGB color space. For a particular picture—either analog or digital—its colors in color space usually appear as clusters. If a cluster is represented by one color—say, the centroid of the cluster—and all representative colors are labeled with color codes, a color picture then can be coded by a picture of the color code and a color codebook which contains the color definition of each color code (the coordinates of each representative color in color space). To display the coded pictures, one only needs to load the color code picture into a display buffer and the color codebook into a color look-up table. As a matter of fact, the principle of this color coding scheme has been used in color textile printing and color publication printing for quite a long time.

   An example of such a color coding scheme was proposed by Wu [WU86]. Its block diagram is in Figure 5.19. Each pixel in the original color picture is viewed as a pattern vector, $[f_r, f_g, f_b]$. To derive the knowledge of color clusters, the distribution of the original color picture in RGB space is first computed and then converted into a uniform color space. An unsupervised learning algorithm is performed to find color clusters and their distribution parameters—namely, means and populations. With the defined clusters, the original picture data are classified pixel by pixel by using a nearest-neighbor classifier, considering the cluster population to get the final output. Using the color coding scheme just introduced, Wu was able to code color pictures using about 16 colors without noticeable distortion.

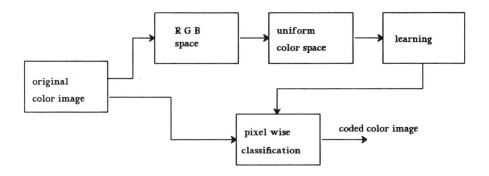

Figure 5.19 Block diagram of pseudo-color coding scheme.

5.8 BINARY PICTURE CODING

Examples of binary pictures include documents, checks, weather maps, engineering drawings, geographic maps, newspaper pages, and so on. A thorough review of coding techniques of binary pictures can be found in [HUANG77]. In this section we shall review two main coding techniques for binary pictures: white block skipping (WBS) coding and run-length coding.

5.8.1 White Block Skipping (WBS) Coding

Let us suppose from now on that the background of a binary picture is coded as '0' or white, picture objects as '1' or black. In most cases, there are many more white pixels in a binary picture than black. Intuitively, skipping white will significantly reduce the bit rate. Skipping white can be achieved both one-dimensionally and two-dimensionally.

The one-dimensional WBS coding method simply divides picture lines into N-pixel segments. The one-bit code word '0' is used for white segments containing only white pixels. Segments with at least one black pixel are coded by an $(N + 1)$-bit code word, with the first bit being '1' and the remaining N bits being the same as the original data. For example, if the original data are 00001011 and the segment size $N = 4$ is chosen, the one-dimensional WBS code of the data is 011011.

The bit rate of the one-dimensional WBS coding method is

$$bpp = (1 - p_w + \frac{1}{N}) \quad bit/pixel \tag{5.39}$$

where p_w is the probability of a white segment. For a given set of pictures, p_w can be measured experimentally. N is the length of the segment. Obviously N depends on the resolution of the pictures. Many experimental results have shown that an N value of around 10 is quite suitable for a wide range of pictures.

Two-dimensional WBS coding is exactly an extension of one-dimensional WBS coding. Instead of a one-dimensional segment, picture block size $M \times M$ is used. Again we use a one-bit codeword '0' for the white block, and an $(M^2 + 1)$-bit codeword for blocks containing at least one black pixel. Because of the two-dimensional correlation property of pictures, two-dimensional WBS coding is naturally superior to one-dimensional WBS coding.

The WBS coding method just introduced has a fixed structure despite the local texture changes. A more efficient adaptive WBS coding method using a hierarchical block size was proposed by DeCoulon and Johnsen [DECOULON76]. Suppose the coding method starts from a block size $M \times M$—say, $M = 16$; if the whole block is white, a one-bit code word '0' is assigned. Otherwise we prefix with a '1' and divide the block into four 8×8 subblocks. For each subblock, we repeat the same coding process until the block size is reduced to 2×2.

5.8.2 Run-Length Coding

As indicated by the name, run-length coding codes the gray-level run-lengths rather than the gray level itself. For binary pictures the gray-level information is implicitly included in the run-length; we then need only to declare the gray level at the beginning of a line, if necessary.

For example, a run-length code of 24,2,68,2,33 represents a binary picture line; the line length is 128 pixels; after 24 white pixels there are two black pixels followed by 68 white, 2 black, and 33 white pixels.

The dynamic range of a run-length number can be quite large. For a picture 1024 by 1024 the run-length can take the value of 1 to 1024. Therefore, it is not efficient to code run-lengths with code words of a fixed length. Let $\{1, 2, ..., N\}$ be the set of values the run-length takes, where N is picture line length. A set of probabilities $\{p_1, p_2, ..., p_N\}$ is associated with the run-length value set and can be measured experimentally over a set of pictures. Based on the set of probabilities, one can design a set of variable length codes which use short length codes for the most frequently occurring numbers to achieve efficiency. The Hoffman code is one of most efficient codes of variable length, but it is complicated to implement. In what follows we describe two classes of suboptimum codes, linear codes, and logarithmic codes, which are particularly suitable for binary picture coding.

Linear Codes. For description convenience, let us define a message set $\{m_k\}$, a probability set $\{p_k\}$, and a set $\{b_k\}$, $k = 1, 2, ..., N$, where p_k is a probability associated with message m_k, b_k is the number of bits in the code word for m_k. In the above, b_k of linear codes is proportional to k. Laemmel codes, one from the class of linear codes, is suitable for run-length coding of line drawings and is described by an example as follows.

Laemmel code is usually denoted by L_N, where N is the code block size. Let

$$k = q\,(2^N - 1) + r \qquad\qquad (5.40)$$

where

$$q = 0, 1, 2, ... \quad \text{and} \quad 1 \le r \le 2^N - 1$$

then the code word for m_k consists of $(q + 1)N$ bits. The first qN bits are '0's and the last N bits are a binary representation of r. If we use L_3-code to code message m_{15}, since $15 = 2(2^3 - 1) + 1$, the code is 000000001. Similarly, L_4-code for m_{15} is

00000000. Obviously, there is an optimum N for a class of binary pictures. It is the integer nearest to $(1 + \log_2 a)$, where a is the mean of the geometrical distribution.

Logarithmic Codes.   The code word length b_k of the logarithmic codes is approximately proportional to the logarithm of k. Among logarithmic codes, Hasler codes (H_N-codes) are most suitable for run-length coding of text binary pictures. The H_N-codes are constructed as follows. All possible N-bit words, $2N$-bit words, $3N$-bit words,... are first listed; an additional bit '1' is inserted at the end of the code word, and an additional bit '0' is inserted between any two N-bit blocks. The following is the H_1-code, with the inserted bits underlined:

$$
\begin{array}{l}
0\,\underline{1} \\
1\,\underline{1} \\
0\,\underline{0}\,0\,\underline{1} \\
0\,\underline{0}\,1\,\underline{1} \\
1\,\underline{0}\,0\,\underline{1} \\
1\,\underline{0}\,1\,\underline{1} \\
0\,\underline{0}\,0\,\underline{0}\,0\,\underline{1} \\
0\,\underline{0}\,0\,\underline{0}\,1\,\underline{1}
\end{array}
$$

Huang's experimental results showed that adaptive WBS coding and run-length coding of a set of binary pictures have a more or less similar data compression ratio.

5.8.3 Object-Oriented Run-Length Coding

Coding Scheme.   Different from run-length coding technique presented in last section, object-oriented run-length coding can be considered a variation of chain coding. To display a chain-coded picture region on a raster type display screen, the boundary points should first be sorted according to the y-axis coordinate, and the points with the same y axis are sorted according to the x axis. By parity checking, the region then can be filled line by line in a raster data structure manner.

$$
\begin{array}{l}
y_1 \;,\; x_{11} \;,\; x_{12} \;,... \\
y_2 \;,\; x_{21} \;,\; x_{22} \;,... \\
\cdot \\
\cdot \\
\cdot
\end{array}
$$

To facilitate the manipulation of object regions, object-oriented run-length coding codes the region objects using the following form, which is illustrated in Figure 5.20:

$$\{\, y_1\,(x_{11},\; \ell_{11},\; x_{12},\; \ell_{12},....),\;\; y_2\,(x_{21},\; \ell_{21},\; x_{22},\; \ell_{22},....)\,,.... \,\}$$

To form a complete relational description of a region object, an object name and several object attributes can be inserted in front of this data record. Probably the maximum and minimum of x y coordinates can give a quick estimation of object position. Other geometric properties, such as area, long axis, short axis, elongation, and so on, may also be useful in some applications. One may then have

$$\{\, objname\,,\, centroid\,,\, x_{max}\,,\, x_{min}\,,\, y_{max}\,,\, y_{min}\,,\, L_{axis}\,,\, S_{axis}\,,\, y_1\,(\,x_{11}\,,\, l_{11}\,,\, x_{12}\,,\, l_{12}\,,....)\,,... \,\}$$

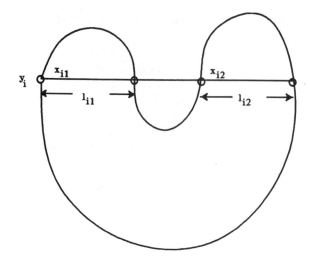

Figure 5.20 Illustration of object-oriented run-length coding.

The same coding scheme is applicable to point objects and line objects. In the case of point objects, the data record is simplified as $\{\, y(x,1)\,\}$

Operations on Run-Length Coded Objects. Let two objects be represented by

$$\{\, O_1, C_1, x^1_{max}, x^1_{min}, y^1_{max}, y^1_{min}, y^1_1\,(\, x^1_{11}, l^1_{11}, \ldots),\ldots\,\}$$
$$\{\, O_2, C_2, x^2_{max}, x^2_{min}, y^2_{max}, y^2_{min}, y^2_1\,(\, x^2_{11}, l^2_{11}, \ldots),\ldots\,\}$$

Then the union of two objects O_1 and O_2 consists of the following steps:

Step 1. If $x^1_{max} < x^2_{min}$ *or* $x^2_{max} < x^1_{min}$ or $y^1_{max} < y^2_{min}$ or $y^2_{max} < y^1_{min}$, the two objects are separated from each other, and the run-length code of union of the two objects is obtained simply by combining two run-length codes and by updating the object name and the attribute values.

Step 2. If the objects are not separable, do the following:

a. For each line y_i^1, if $y_i^1 < y^2_{min}$ or $y_i^1 > y^2_{max}$, put the data of line y_i^1 into the result record. Otherwise, find the corresponding line y_m^2 in O_2. For each run x^1_{ij}, l^1_{ij}, check to see if there is any (there can be more than one) run x^2_{mn}, l^2_{mn} such that $x^1_{ij} < x^2_{mn} \le x^1_{ij} + l^1_{ij}$ or $x^2_{mn} \le x^1_{ij} \le x^2_{mn} + l^2_{mn}$. If not, take run x^1_{ij}, l^1_{ij} from O_1 and put it into the result record. Otherwise, combine run x^1_{ij}, l^1_{ij} with all runs in O_2 which satisfy the preceding conditions and put the combination into the result record and remove all involved runs from their original places. The combination of run x^1_{ij}, l^1_{ij} and run x^2_{mn}, l^2_{mn}, x_r, l_r is

$$x_r = min\,(\, x^1_{ij}, x^2_{mn}), \qquad l_r = max\,[(\, x^1_{ij} + l^1_{ij}),\,(\, x^2_{mn} + l^2_{mn}\,)] - x_r$$

Put any runs left in y_m^2 into the result record.

For this line in the result data record, check to see if any runs overlap. Combine overlapped runs until there are none left.

Pictorial Data Compression   Chap. 5

b. Put the data left in O_2 into result record.

Step 3. Assign a new object name and compute attribute values for the result.

The intersection operation of two objects is simpler than union:

Step 1. If $x^1_{max} < x^2_{min}$ *or* $x^2_{max} < x^1_{min}$ or $y^1_{max} < y^2_{min}$ or $y^2_{max} < y^1_{min}$, the two objects are not intersected.

Step 2. For each line y_i^1 in O_1, check to see if there is a line y_m^2 such that $y_i^1 = y_m^2$. If such y_m^2 does not exist, do nothing. Otherwise do the following:

For each run x_{ij}^1, l_{ij}^1, if there is a run x_{mn}^2, l_{mn}^2 such that $x_{ij}^1 < x_{mn}^2 \le x_{ij}^1 + l_{ij}^1$, put the run x_{mn}^2, $min\,[(\,x_{ij}^1 + l_{ij}^1\,), (\,x_{mn}^2 + l_{mn}^2\,)] - x_{mn}^2$ into the result record and remove these two runs from their places.

If $x_{mn}^2 \le x_{ij}^1 \le x_{mn}^2 + l_{mn}^2$, the intersection of these two runs is x_{ij}^1, $min\,[(\,x_{ij}^1 + l_{ij}^1\,), (\,x_{mn}^2 + l_{mn}^2\,)] - x_{ij}^1$.

Step 3. Assign an object name and compute the attribute values for the result data.

The procedure to check containment of two objects is the same as the intersection operation except that each run of an object should be contained totally within that of the other object.

Computing the geometric properties of objects encoded by run-length coding is a trivial process because it involves only point operations which are fully supported by run-length coding. For example, to compute the area of an object region, one only needs to sum up all run-lengths:

$$area = \sum_i \sum_j l_{ij}$$

5.9 DISCUSSION

In this chapter, we have discussed groups of pictorial data compression techniques. Gray-level picture data compression is usually not error-free. Research has been directed toward developing techniques to reduce the data rate while keeping the error rate as low as possible. Binary picture coding is error-free. That is, no coding error is permitted. Research in picture processing, pattern recognition, coding theory, and other related research fields is adding more and more techniques to picture coding. Many interesting advances can be anticipated.

R E F E R E N C E S

[ABEL83] ABEL, D.J., AND J.L. SMITH, "A data structure and algorithm based on a linear key for a rectangle retrieval problem," CVGIP 24, 1, 1983, 1-13.

[BURT83] BURT, P.J., AND E.H. ADELSON, "The Laplasian pyramid as a compact image code," *IEEE trans. Communications,* COM-31, No. 4, 1983, 532-540.

[CAFFORIE83] CAFFORIE, C., AND F. ROSSA, "The differential method for image motion estimation," in *Image Sequence Processing and Dynamic Scene Analysis*, T.S. Huang Ed., Springer-Verlag, 1983, 104-124.

[DECOULON76] DeCOULON, F., AND O. JOHNSEN, "Adaptive block scheme for source coding of black and white facsimile," *Electronics Letters*, Vol. 12, No.3, 1976, 61-62.

[DELP79a] DELP, E.J., R.L. KASHYAP, AND O.R. MITCHELL, "Image data compression using autoregressive time series models," *Pattern Recognition* 11, 1979, 313-323.

[DELP79b] DELP, E.J. AND O.R. MITCHELL, "Image compression using block truncation coding," *IEEE trans. Communications*, COM-27, No. 9, 1979, 1335-1343.

[FREEMAN74] FREEMAN, H., "Computer processing of line-drawing images," *ACM Computing Survey* 6, 1, March 1974, 57-97.

[FREI77] FREI, W., AND B. BAXTER, "Rate-distortion coding simulation for color images," *IEEE trans. Communications*, COM-25, No. 11, 1977, 1385-1392.

[GRAY84] GRAY, R.M., "Vector quantization," *IEEE Assp Magazine*, April, 1984, 4-29.

[HEALY81] HEALY, D.J., AND O.R. MITCHELL, "Digital video bandwidth compression using block truncation coding," *IEEE trans. Communications*, COM-29, No. 12, 1981, 1809-1817.

[HUANG83] HUANG, T.S., *Image Sequence Processing and Dynamic Scene Analysis*, Springer-Verlag, 1983.

[HUANG77] HUANG, T.S., "Coding two-tone images," *IEEE trans. Communications*, COM-25, No. 11, 1977, 1406-1424.

[JIAN81] JIAN, J.R., AND A.K. JAIN, "Displacement measurement and its application in inter-frame image coding," *IEEE trans. Communications*, COM-29, 1981, 1799-1806.

[KAWAGUCHI80] KAWAGUCHI, E., T. ENDO, AND M. YOKOTA, "DF-expression of binary-valued picture and its relation to other pyramidal representations," *Proc. 5th Int. Conf. P.R.*, Miami Beach, Florida, Dec. 1980, 822-827.

[KOCHER82] KOCHER, M., AND M. KUNT, "A contour-texture approach to picture coding," *Proc. ICASSP-82*, Paris, France, May, 1982, 436-440.

[MAX60] MAX, T., "Quantizing for minimum distortion," *IRE trans. Inf. Theory*, Vol. IT-16, 1960, 7-12.

[MCFARLANE72] McFARLANE, M.D., "Digital picture fifty years ago," *PIEE 60*, No. 7, 1972.

[NETRAVALI79] NETRAVALI, A.N. AND J.D. ROBBINS, "Motion compensated television coding–part I," *Bell Syst. Tech. J.*, Vol. 58, March 1979, 631-670.

[OHSAWA83] OHSAWA, Y., AND M. SAKAUCHI, "The BD-tree – A new N-dimensional data structure with highly efficient dynamic characteristics," in *Information Processing*, R.E.A. Mason Ed., Elsevier Science Publishers, B.V. North-Holland, 1983, 539-544.

[RAMAMURTHI84] RAMAMURTHI, B., AND A. GERSHO, "Image vector quantization with a perceptually-based cell classifier," *IEEE Int. Conf. ASSP*, 1984, 32.10.1-32.10.4.

[ROSENFELD83] ROSENFELD, A., AND K. KAK, *Digital Picture Processing*, Second Edition. New York: Academic Press Inc., 1983.

[SAMET84] SAMET, H., "The quadtree and related hierarchical data structures," *Computing Survey*, Vol. 16, No.2, 1984, 187-260.

[SCHAFER81] SCHAFER, R., "DPCM coding of the chrominance signals for the transmission of color TV signals at 24 Mbit/s," *Signal Processing*, 1981.

[ZHANG82] ZHANG, C., "Ein neuer adaptiver pradiktor fur die DPCM-codierung von fernsehsignalen," *Frequenz*, Vol. 36, 1982, 161-184.

[WANG85] WANG, C.P. "Image data compression using a codebook," *Masters Dissertation*, Dec. 1985, Illinois Institute of Technology.

[WU86] Wu, J. K., "Color image coding of images," *Signal Processing,* Oct. 1986.

[WU82] Wu, J. K., AND R. E. BURGE, "Adaptive bit allocation for image compression," CGIP 19, 1982, 392-400.

[WU87] Wu, J. K., AND W. M. ZHANG, "Adaptive transform image compression by using texture analysis," *Communications China,* 1987.

E X E R C I S E S

The CCITT has a recommendation (T.4) with the aim of achieving compatibility between digital apparatus connected to general switched telephone networks. A one-dimensional coding scheme is used in which run-lengths are encoded using a modified Huffman code. The recommendation also includes a two-dimensional code, known as the modified relative element address designate (READ) code, which allows a much higher compression rate (and, of course, higher transmission efficiency). In this recommendation, binary pictures of eight documents are used as CCITT reference documents to generate the variable length code words.

The **one-dimensional coding scheme** is as follows:

- A total of 1728 pixels represent one horizontal scan line of 215 mm length.
- All data lines begin with a white run-length code word.
- Black or white run-lengths are defined by the following two types of code words: terminating code words and make-up code words. Each run-length is represented by either one terminating code word or one make-up code word followed by a terminating code word.

TERMINATING CODES:

White Run-Length	Code Word	Black Run-Length	Code Word
0	00110101	0	0000110111
1	000111	1	010
2	0111	2	11
3	1000	3	10
4	1011	4	011
5	1100	5	0011
6	1110	6	0010
7	1111	7	00011
8	10011	8	000101
9	10100	9	000100
10	00111	10	0000100
11	01000	11	0000101
12	001000	12	0000111
13	000011	13	00000100
14	110100	14	00000111
15	110101	15	000011000
16	101010	16	0000010111
17	101011	17	0000011000
18	0100111	18	0000001000
19	0001100	19	00001100111
20	0001000	20	00001101000

21	0010111	21	00001101100
22	0000011	22	00000110111
23	0000100	23	00000101000
24	0101000	24	00000010111
25	0101011	25	00000011000
26	0010011	26	000011001010
27	0100100	27	000011001011
28	0011000	28	000011001100
29	00000010	29	000011001101
30	00000011	30	000001101000
31	00011010	31	000001101001
32	00011011	32	000001101010
33	00010010	33	000001101011
34	00010011	34	000011010010
35	00010100	35	000011010011
36	00010101	36	000011010100
37	00010110	37	000011010101
38	00010111	38	000011010110
39	00101000	39	000011010111
40	00101001	40	000001101100
41	00101010	41	000001101101
42	00101011	42	000011011010
43	00101100	43	000011011011
44	00101101	44	000001010100
45	00000100	45	000001010101
46	00000101	46	000001010110
47	00001010	47	000001010111
48	00001011	48	000001100100
49	01010010	49	000001100101
50	01010011	50	000001010010
51	01010100	51	000001010011
52	01010101	52	000000100100
53	00100100	53	000000110111
54	00100101	54	000000111000
55	01011000	55	000000100111
56	01011001	56	000000101000
57	01011010	57	000001011000
58	01011011	58	000001011001
59	01001010	59	000000101011
60	01001011	60	000000101100
61	00110010	61	000001011010
62	00110011	62	000001100110
63	00110100	63	000001100111

MAKE-UP CODES:

White Run-Length	Code Word	Black Run-Length	Code Word
64	11011	64	0000001111
128	10010	128	000011001000
192	010111	192	000011001001
256	0110111	256	000001011011
320	00110110	320	000000110011
384	00110111	384	000000110100
448	01100100	448	000000110101

512	01100101	512	0000001101100
576	01101000	576	0000001101101
640	01100111	640	0000001001010
704	011001100	704	0000001001011
768	011001101	768	0000001001100
832	011010010	832	0000001001101
896	011010011	896	0000001110010
960	011010100	960	0000001110011
1024	011010101	1024	0000001110100
1088	011010110	1088	0000001110101
1152	011010111	1152	0000001110110
1216	011011000	1216	0000001110111
1280	011011001	1280	0000001010010
1344	011011010	1344	0000001010011
1408	011011011	1408	0000001010100
1472	010011000	1472	0000001010101
1536	010011001	1536	0000001011010
1600	010011010	1600	0000001011011
1664	011000	1664	0000001100100
1728	010011011	1728	0000001100101
EOL	000000000001	EOL	000000000001

The End-of-line (EOL) code follows each line of data.

1. Write a program to compress images using the preceding one-dimensional coding scheme. Using different types of pictures as input images, make a comparison of compression rates upon types of pictures. For example, choose some text documents of different fonts, some posters with big block backgrounds, some horizontal-oriented pictures, and some vertical-oriented pictures.

2. Since we already predefined that the fixed line length is 1728 pixels, in the practical encoding and decoding, EOL usually is omitted to increase the compression rate for big documents. This, of course, takes the risk of transmission error that may propagate to all the consecutive lines. Modify the preceding program by omitting the EOL. Compare the compression rates of the two programs on a big document.

TWO-DIMENSIONAL CODING SCHEME

To achieve a high compression rate, a parameter K is chosen to code $K - 1$ lines by a two-dimensional scheme. That is, we code a line by a one-dimensional scheme as described before, and then code $K - 1$ consecutive lines by a two-dimensional scheme referring to this line. The reason for limiting the value of K (2 and 4 are standard) is to prevent error propagation. But for a local picture compression application, we can ignore the communication error. So, K can be set as large as possible. In other words, only the first line of the document is coded with a one-dimensional scheme, and all the other lines are coded with a two-dimensional scheme referring to the first line.

A changing element (pixel) is defined as an element whose color (black or white) is different from that of the previous element along the same line.

- a_0

  The reference or starting changing element on the coding line. At the start of the coding line, a_0 is set on an imaginary white changing element situated just before the first element on the line. During the coding, the position of a_0 is defined by the previous coding *coding mode*.

- a_1

  The next changing element to the right of a_0 on the coding line.

- a_2

  The next changing element to the right of a_1 on the coding line.

- b_1

  The first changing element on the reference line (the line immediately above the coding line) to the right of a_0 and of opposite color to a_0.

- b_2

  The next changing element to the right of b_1 on the reference line.

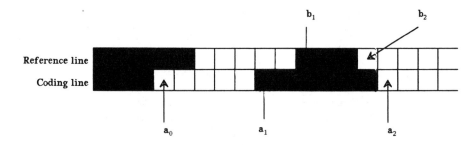

CODING MODE

One of the three coding modes is chosen according to the coding procedure and the two-dimensional code table:

Pass Mode This mode is identified when the position of b_2 lies to the left of a_1. When this mode has been coded, a_0 is set on the element of the coding line below b_2 in preparation for the next coding (that is, on a_0').

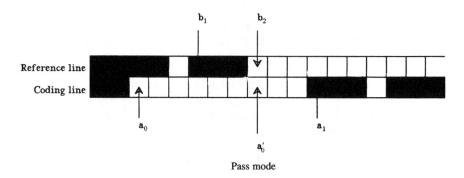

Pass mode

However, the state where b_2 occurs just above a_1, as shown next, is not considered a pass mode.

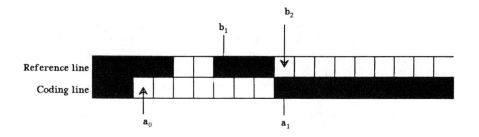

Non-pass

Vertical Mode When this mode is identified, the position of a_1 is coded relative to the position of b_1. The relative distance $a_1 b_1$ can take on one of seven values $V(0), V_R(1), V_R(2), V_R(3), V_L(1), V_L(2)$, and $V_L(3)$, each of which is represented by a separate code word. The subscripts R and L indicate that a_1 is to the right or left respectively of b_1, and the number in brackets indicates the value of the distance $a_1 b_1$. After vertical mode coding has occurred, the position of a_0 is set on a_1.

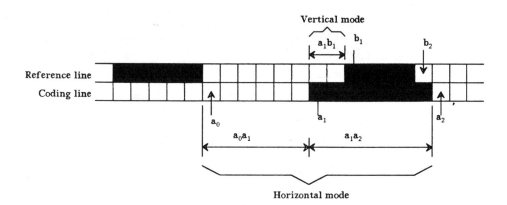

Horizontal mode

Horizontal Mode When this mode is identified, both the run-lengths $a_0 a_1$ and $a_1 a_2$ are coded using the code words $H + M(a_0 a_1) + M(a_1 a_2)$. H is the flag code word 001 taken from the two-dimensional code table. $M(a_0 a_1)$ and $M(a_1 a_2)$ are code words which represent the length and "color" of the runs $a_0 a_1$ and $a_1 a_2$ respectively and are taken from the appropriate white or black one-dimensional code tables. After a horizontal mode coding, the position of a_0 is set on a_2 as just shown.

Coding Procedure:

    Step 1.

        a. If a pass mode is identified, this is coded using the word 0001. After this processing, pixel a_0' just under b_2 is regarded as the new starting picture element a_0 for the next coding.

        b. If a pass mode is not detected, then proceed to step 2.

    Step 2.

a. Determine the absolute value of the relative distance a_1b_1.

b. If $|a_1b_1| \leq 3$, a_1b_1 is coded by the vertical mode, after which position a_1 is regarded as the new starting element a_0 for the next coding.

c. If $|a_1b_1| > 3$, following horizontal mode code 001, a_0a_1 and a_1a_2 are respectively coded by one-dimensional coding. After this processing, position a_2 is regarded as the new starting element a_0 for the next coding.

Processing the First Pixel The first pixel a_0 on each coding line is imaginarily set at a position just before the first pixel and is regarded as a white pixel. The first run-length on a line a_0a_1 is replaced by $a_0a_1 - 1$. Therefore, if the first run is black and is deemed to be coded by horizontal mode coding, then the first code word $M(a_0a_1)$ corresponding to a white run of zero length.

Processing the Last Pixel The coding of the coding line continues until the position of the imaginary changing element situated just after the last actual element has been coded. This may be coded as a_1 or a_2. Also, if b_1 and/or b_2 are not detected at any time during the coding of the line, they are positioned on the imaginary changing element situated just after the last actual pixel on the reference line.

TWO-DIMENSIONAL CODE TABLE

Mode	Elements to Be Coded	Notation	Code Word
Pass	b_1, b_2	P	0001
Horizontal	$a_0\,a_1, a_1\,a_2$	H	$001 + M(a_0a_1) + M(a_1a_2)$
Vertical	a_1 just under b_1	$a_1b_1 = 0\ V(0)$	1
	a_1 to the right of b_1	$a_1b_1 = 1\ V_R(1)$	011
		$a_1b_1 = 2\ V_R(2)$	000011
		$a_1b_1 = 3\ V_R(3)$	0000011
	a_1 to the left of b_1	$a_1b_1 = 1\ V_L(1)$	010
		$a_1b_1 = 2$	$V_L(2)$
		$a_1b_1 = 3$	$V_L(3)$

3. Give the correct two-dimensional codes for the pixels in the following coding lines, which are indicated with "•"s. Some of the lines have been provided with answers, and some are left as exercises: (3.1, 3.2, 3.3). (See the figure on p. 121.)

4. Using the same pictures that you used for one-dimensional coding, write a two-dimensional coding program and compare the compression rates on various pictures.

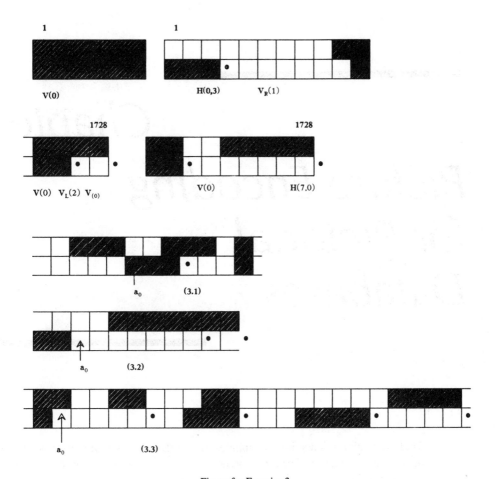

Figure for Exercise 3.

Chapter 6

Picture Encoding for Pictorial Databases

Traditional picture encoding techniques aim at data compression at an acceptable level of picture degradation. For a comprehensive survey and discussion of picture encoding techniques in general, the reader is referred to Chapter 5 and other references [PAVLIDIS77]. Advances in pictorial information system design have posed new problems in picture encoding which are somewhat different from the traditional picture encoding problems.

In pictorial database design, it is often desirable to partition a large picture into smaller pieces, sometimes called *pages* or *tiles, so that the pieces can be stored economically and retrieved* easily. The pieces of the picture are often organized hierarchically into a tree structure. The concept of hierarchy is widely used in computer graphics and picture processing, and a variety of such structures have been proposed [CHANG79, CHANG82, CHIEN80, KLINGER77, McKEOWN77, MILGRAM79, OMOLAYOLE79, SHAPIRO79, TANIMOTO76].

Another recent trend in pictorial information retrieval is the use of icons. An *icon* is a picture or a sketch referring to an object or a set of objects. The icon usually is represented by a graphical sketch or low-resolution image on the display screen. We shall call this graphical or image representation an icon-picture. Icons can be associated with a hierarchical structure to serve as indexes for interactive information retrieval. On the other hand, the construction of icon-pictures which somehow represent the original images is a research topic requiring further study.

The *picture encoding problem*, in the context of pictorial database design, can therefore be described as the partitioning of a large picture into smaller pieces, the organization of such pieces into a hierarchical structure, and the construction of icon-pictures to be associated with such a hierarchical structure to facilitate pictorial information storage and retrieval.

In this chapter, we present a methodology of picture encoding for pictorial databases. The central concept is to develop a technique called *hierarchical hypercube encoding*, which encompasses many previously proposed encoding methods. A family of pictorial information measures can then be used in the hierarchical hypercube encoding to (a) partition large picture into smaller pieces, (b) design the hierarchical structure, and (c) construct icon-pictures. The hierarchical hypercube encoding technique addresses the "structural" aspect, while the picture information measure addresses the "contents" aspect, thus forming a unified methodology.

This chapter is organized as follows. Section 6.1 gives some preliminary concepts. In Section 6.2, we discuss hypercube encoding methods, including minimal hypercube encoding, generalized hypercube encoding, arbitrary hypercube encoding, and the picture covering problem. The hypercube encoding technique generalizes tightly closed boundary encoding, run-length encoding, and picture paging techniques. The hierarchical hypercube encoding technique is also introduced. Section 6.3 deals with Picture Information Measure (PIM) directed hypercube encoding. We describe how icon-pictures can be constructed using the PIM directed hierarchical hypercube encoding technique. Section 6.4 discusses quadtree representation. 3-D object representations are briefly described in Section 6.5.

6.1 PRELIMINARIES

In this section, we present some preliminary definitions which will be used in subsequent sections. Some of them can be found in previous chapters.

Similar to the definition of the 2-D picture function f in Chapter 2, an n-dimensional picture function f can be defined as a mapping

$$f : N^n \rightarrow \{0, 1, ..., L - 1\}$$

and $f(x_1, x_2, ..., x_n)$ represents the pixel value at $(x_1, ..., x_n)$. Such higher dimensional picture functions are useful in applications such as constructive solid geometry, time-sequenced image encoding, and cluster analysis in n-dimensional feature space.

It is often convenient to extract from a picture those points with pixel values greater than or equal to a certain threshold. A *picture point set* or simply a *point set* extracted from a picture f with threshold t is defined by

$$S(f, t) = \{(x_1, x_2, ..., x_n): f(x_1, ..., x_n) \geq t\}$$

where t is the given threshold. As an example, the picture function f is

$$
y \quad
\begin{array}{|ccc}
0 & 1 & 0 \\
0 & 2 & 0 \\
1 & 0 & 1 \\
\hline
\end{array}
$$

f $\qquad\qquad\qquad\qquad$ x

and $S(f, 1) = \{ (1,1), (3,1), (2,2), (2,3) \}$.

Given a picture point set S, we are often interested in finding picture point sets H_i, so that their union contains the original S. The point sets H_i usually have some nice properties to facilitate encoding. One family of point sets useful for such encoding purposes is the family of n-dimensional hypercubes, which are point sets defined as follows:

$$H(x_{1a}, x_{1b}; x_{2a}, x_{2b}; \cdots ; x_{na}, x_{nb}) = \{ (z_1, ..., z_n): x_{ia} \le z_i \le x_{ib}, 1 \le i \le n \}$$

where x_{ia} and x_{ib} denote the minimum and maximum values of the i-th coordinate of a point $(z_1, ..., z_n)$ in the point set H.

A hypercube *covers* a point set S if every point in S is also in H. For example, $H(1,3;1,4)$ covers $S(f, 1)$. We also say that $S(f, 1)$ is covered by or contained in $H(1,3;1,4)$. An example of a 3-dimensional hypercube is given by $H(1,3;1,3;1,3)$.

Given a picture function f and a point set S, f / S denotes the *restricted picture function* which is defined only for points in S—that is, $f / S (x_1, ..., x_n) = f (x_1, ..., x_n)$, if x is in S. f / S is called the *support picture function* or *support picture* for S.

Let F denote a family of picture functions. A *picture transformation* T is any mapping from F to F. The picture $T(f)$ is the *transformed picture* of f.

6.2 HYPERCUBE ENCODING

6.2.1 Minimal Hypercube Encoding

There are many approaches to find coverings of a point set $S(f, t)$ using hypercubes. The simplest approach, called *minimal hypercube* (*MH*) *encoding,* is to find the smallest hypercube H containing $S(f, t)$. The *minimal enclosing hypercube* $H(a_1, b_1; a_2, b_2; ..., a_n, b_n)$ of a point set S is given by

$$a_j = \min \{y_j: \text{ for some } z_k, (z_1, ..., y_j, ..., z_n) \text{ is in S}\}$$
$$b_j = \max \{y_j: \text{ for some } z_k, (z_1, ..., y_j, ..., z_n) \text{ is in S}\}$$

For example, the minimal enclosing hypercube of $S(f, 1) = \{ (1,1), (3,1), (2,2), (2,3) \}$ is $H(1,3;1,3)$. In the two-dimensional case, the minimal enclosing hypercube is commonly called the *minimal enclosing rectangle* (*MER*) [FREEMAN75].

The minimal enclosing rectangle $H(1,3;1,3)$ contains many points originally not in S. Therefore the *MH* encoding technique gives only a crude approximation of S. To improve encoding accuracy, the *generalized hypercube* (*GH*) encoding will be described next.

6.2.2 Generalized Hypercube Encoding

To motivate use of the *GH* encoding technique, we consider the just-mentioned two-dimensional picture f, with picture point set $S = \{ (1,1), (3,1), (2,2), (2,3) \}$. The row point set $S_1 = \{ (1,1), (3,1) \}$ is covered by *MER* $H_1 = H(1,3;1,1)$. Similarly,

$S_2 = \{(2,2)\}$ is covered by $H_2 = H(2,2;2;2)$, and $S_3 = \{(2,3)\}$ by $H_3 = H(2,2;3,3)$. The union of H_1, H_2, and H_3 covers S.

In the two-dimensional case, the *GH* encoding technique is commonly known as the *tightly closed boundary (TCB)* encoding [MERRILL73]. In actual encoding, the *TCB* can be represented by (1; 1 3; 2 2; 2 2), where the first entry is the beginning y coordinate, and the subsequent pairs of entries represent the minimum and maximum x coordinates of picture points in rows $y, y+1, y+2$, and so on. It should be noted that if we consider column point sets, the *TCB* code will generally be different. In the preceding example, we have $H_1 = H(1,1;1,1)$, $H_2 = H(2,2;2,3)$, and $H_3 = H(3,3;1,1)$. The corresponding *TCB* code is (1; 1 1; 2 3; 1 1).

The *run-length (RL)* encoding technique is closely related to GH encoding, where we record the gray level as well as the minimum and maximum x coordinates of a continuous run of pixels having identical pixel values. Instead of recording the minimum and maximum x coordinates, a more economical way is to record the run-length (number of pixels) for each continuous run. Since in run-length encoding, the gray level for each run is recorded, we can recover the original picture from run-length codes. The hypercube encoding techniques can also be applied to icon-picture construction, if we record the average gray level of each hypercube. This will be discussed later.

We now formally describe generalized hypercube encoding [YANG78]. A GH_m encoding is the union of all *distinct* hypercubes of the form

$$H(x_1,x_1\; ; \; \cdots \; ; x_{m-1},x_{m-1}\; ;a_m,b_m\; ;..., a_n,b_n\;)$$

where $x_{ia} = x_{ib} = x_i$ for $1 \le i \le m-1$, and

$$a_j = \min\{\; y_j : \text{for } \textit{some } z_k,\; (x_1,...,x_{m-1},z_m,...,y_j,...,z_n\;) \text{ is in } S\;\}$$

$$b_j = \max\{\; y_j : \text{for } \textit{some } z_k,\; (x_1,...,x_{m-1},z_m,...,y_j,...,z_n\;) \text{ is in } S\;\}$$

When $m = 1$, we are simply using the smallest n-dimensional hypercube containing S as the *GH* code. When $m = n+1$, the original point set S is used as the *GH* code. Other intermediate values of m give *GH* codes of various levels of details. For example, if $S=\{(1,1,3),(1,1,5),(1,2,1),(1,2,4),(2,3,6)\}$, $GH_1 = H(1,2; 1,3; 1,6)$, $GH_2 = H(1,1; 1,2; 1,5) \cup H(2,2; 3,3; 6,6)$, $GH_3 = H(1,1; 1,1; 3,5) \cup H(1,1; 2,2; 1,4) \cup H(2,2; 3,3; 6,6)$, and $GH_4 = S$. In the two-dimensional case, GH_1 is *MH* encoding, GH_2 is *TCB* encoding, and GH_3 is the original point set S.

Similar to *TCB* encoding, if we permute the coordinates, the *GH* codes will generally be different. As a notational convenience, a permuted *GH* hypercube can be written as

$$GH(x_{i1},..., x_{i(m-1)};a_{im},..., a_{in}\; ;b_{im},..., b_{in})$$

where $(x_{i1},..., x_{i(m-1)})$ is the *handle vector*, $(a_{im},..., a_{in})$ is the *lower bound vector*, and $(b_{im},..., b_{in})$ is the *upper bound vector*. The index sequence $(i1,i2,..., i(m-1))$ is called the *handle sequence*.

The selection of the handle sequence uniquely determines the GH encoding. Therefore, the *GH* encoding problem is to select a handle sequence $(i1,i2,..., i(m-1))$ from $\{1,2,..., n\}$ so that the least number of *GH* encoded tuples are generated. Given m, a heuristic method of choosing the handle sequence which generates near-optimal GH_m codes is presented next:

GH Encoding Algorithm

For each index i, $1 \le i \le n$, we can compute a figure of merit K_i as follows: Let S_i be the projection of S on the i-th coordinate—that is, $S_i = \{(x_{ij}):$ for some $zk, (z1, ..., x_{ij}, ..., zn)$ in $S\}$. Let G_{ij} be the set of points in S having the same i-th coordinate value x_{ij}—that is, $G_{ij} = \{(z1, ..., x_{ij}, ..., zn): x_{ij}$ in $S_i, (z1, ..., x_{ij}, ..., zn)$ in $S\}$. Let g_{ij} be the size of G_{ij}. If g_{ij} is 1, nothing is contributed to K_i. If g_{ij} is greater than 1, the square of g_{ij} is added to K_i. The indices i are then ordered by K_i into a decreasing sequence. The handle sequence for m consists of the first m-1 terms in this index sequence.

For example, the point set S is $\{(3,1,1), (5,1,1), (1,1,2), (4,1,2), (6,2,3)\}$. We first find $S_1 = \{3,5,1,4,6\}$, $S_2 = \{1,2\}$, and $S_3 = \{1,2,3\}$. We then find $G_{11} = \{(3,1,1)\}$, $G_{12} = \{(5,1,1)\}$, $G_{13} = \{(1,1,2)\}$, $G_{14} = \{(4,1,2)\}$, $G_{15} = \{(6,2,3)\}$, and $K_1 = 0$. Similarly, $G_{21} = \{(3,1,1), (5,1,1), (1,1,2), (4,1,2)\}$, $G_{22} = \{(6,2,3)\}$, and $K_2 = 16$. Finally, $G_{31} = \{(3,1,1), (5,1,1)\}$, $G_{32} = \{(1,1,2), (4,1,2)\}$, $G_{33} = \{(6,2,3)\}$, and $K_3 = 8$. By ordering the K_i's, we obtain the handle sequence $(2,3,1)$ for $m = 4$.

The preceding heuristic algorithm was tested on random vectors with normal distributions, and the results were compared with optimal solutions [SINGH79]. To find the optimal GH_m encoding, an exhaustive search was made and the GH_m codes with minimum number of GH_m tuples were selected as the optimal GH_m encoding. Table 6.1 summarizes the results. Five-dimensional point sets are used. The number of points in S is given by N. In these experiments, the heuristic algorithm generates near-optimal results.

The technique just described is also applicable to 3-D object representation by a constructive solid geometry method where the primitives are restricted to blocks of variable sizes.

TABLE 6.1 COMPARISON OF HEURISTIC AND OPTIMAL GH ENCODING

N	GH1			GH2			GH3			GH4		
	H	O	E(%)	H	O	E(%)	H	O	E(%)	H	O	E(%)
10	8	8	0.0	10	10	0.0	10	10	0.0	10	10	0.0
20	13	13	0.0	20	19	5.26	20	20	0.0	20	20	0.0
30	10	10	0.0	29	29	0.0	30	30	0.0	30	30	0.0
40	16	16	0.0	38	38	0.0	40	40	0.0	40	40	0.0
50	21	21	0.0	49	49	0.0	50	50	0.0	50	50	0.0
60	18	18	0.0	55	55	0.0	59	59	0.0	60	60	0.0
70	18	18	0.0	64	63	1.58	70	70	0.0	70	70	0.0
80	21	21	0.0	75	75	0.0	80	79	1.26	80	80	0.0
90	26	26	0.0	84	84	0.0	90	90	0.0	90	90	0.0
100	22	22	0.0	96	92	4.35	100	100	0.0	100	100	0.0

Note: N – No. of Points; H – Heuristic; O – Optimum; E – Error

Picture Encoding for Pictorial Databases Chap. 6

The *GH* encoding technique essentially uses $(n-m+1)$-dimensional hypercubes with handles to cover the original point set S. A further generalization is to use an arbitrary collection of hypercubes to cover S. This technique is called *arbitrary hypercube (AH) encoding*. In *AH* encoding, the hypercubes may have different dimensions and different handle vectors. As an example, the picture point set $S(f,t)$, given in Section 6.1, can be covered by $AH = \{H(1,3;1,1), H(2,2;2,3)\}$.

6.2.3 Picture Covering

The *picture covering problem* can be stated as follows:

1. We are given a picture f and its associated picture point set $S(f,t)$.
2. We wish to find a collection of hypercubes, H_i, to cover $S(f,t)$. If we restrict H_i to having similar $(n-m+1)$-dimensional handle vectors, this reduces to a *GH* encoding problem. Otherwise, this is an *AH* encoding problem.
3. The objective of optimal covering is the minimization of the total number of hypercubes.

In what follows, we will describe the decomposition algorithm and the PIM-directed algorithm for *picture paging*, which is the picture covering problem for two-dimensional pictures [CHANG78b, REUSS78, LIU81]. Consider a picture where 0 denotes background pixels. We want to cover the nonbackground pixels by equal-sized rectangular pages. The decomposition algorithm first finds a *subtractor*, which is the largest rectangle that can be found containing only background pixels. An example is shown in Figure 6.1(a).

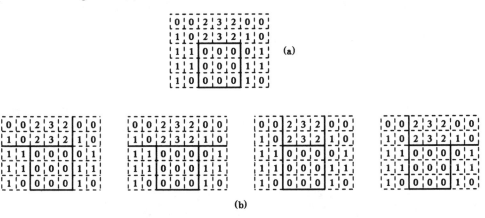

Figure 6.1 PIM-directed algorithm for picture paging.

After the removal of a subtractor, the remaining picture can be further decomposed into rectangular subpictures by extending the edges of the subtractor. The four possible cases are illustrated in Figure 6.1(b).

This decomposition procedure is applied recursively until the decomposed rectangles can all be covered by one page. The decomposition algorithm exhaustively tries all cases and selects the one with the minimal number of pages. Techniques for quickly finding the subtractor and algorithms for discarding unpromising cases to reduce the search space are described in [LIU81].

To avoid an exhaustive search of all possible cases, we can use picture information measures to select the most promising decomposition. We note from the discussion of PIM in Chapter 4, that $PIM(f) = 0$, if and only if f is a constant picture (that is, $f(x,y) = $ constant for all (x,y) in $N \times N$). On the other hand, $PIM(f)$ is maximum, if and only if f has a uniform histogram (that is, $h(i) = $ constant, $0 \le i \le L - 1$). Let the total number of pixels in f be $N(f)$. f has a uniform histogram if and only if $PIM(f) = N(f)(L-1)/L$. In other words, $PIM(f)$ is minimal when f is least informative and maximal when f is most informative.

Suppose a picture point set S is divided into two disjoint subsets $S1$ and $S2$. We have

$$PIM(f/S) \ge PIM(f/S1) + PIM(f/S2)$$

Therefore, if we use disjoint hypercubes H_i to cover a picture f, then the sum of $PIM(f/H_i)$ is always less than or equal to $PIM(f)$. In hypercube encoding, we can use the *normalized picture information measure* defined as $NPIM(f) = PIM(f)/N(f)$ to decide whether the hypercube is informative. For example, if $NPIM(f)$ is less than or equal to a threshold, that hypercube is considered non-informative and need not be further decomposed. A subtractor, as described earlier, can be regarded to be a non-informative hypercube whose NPIM is less than or equal to a threshold and whose pixels are primarily background pixels. When the threshold is 0, the subtractor consists only of background pixels with identical pixel values. In the PIM-directed decomposition algorithm, when we evaluate several decompositions, we will pick the one minimizing the sum of $PIM(f/S_i)$. Some experimental results will be described in the next section.

6.2.4 Hierarchical Hypercube Encoding

The hypercube encoding technique can be applied iteratively to create a hierarchy of hypercubes. This technique is called *hierarchical hypercube (HH) encoding*. A hierarchical hypercube encoding is a collection of arbitrary hypercube encodings $AH_1, AH_2, ..., AH_k$ satisfying the following conditions:

1. Each AH_i covers the original picture point set S.

2. AH_1 is a singleton set—that is, AH_1 consists of one hypercube covering S.

3. Each AH_{i+1} can be divided into disjoint subsets of hypercubes such that for each subset there exists a hypercube in AH_i covering that subset.

As an example, for the picture point set $S(f,1)$ of Section 6.2.1, one possible *HH* encoding has three levels: AH_1, AH_2, AH_3, where $AH_1 = \{ H(1,3;1,3) \}$, $AH_2 = \{ H(1,3;1,1), H(2,2;2,3) \}$, and $AH_3 = \{ H(1,1;1,1), \quad H(3,3;1,1), H(2,2;2,3) \}$, as shown in Figure 6.2.

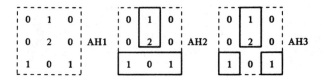

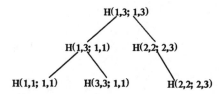

Figure 6.2 HH encoding example.

Figure 6.3 illustrates the experimental results of applying the decomposition algorithms to HH encode a SEASAT image of the Los Angeles area. The original image is shown in Figure 6.3(a). It contains 128×128 pixels with gray levels between 0 and 255. The image was smoothed using a sigma filtering technique developed in [LEE81] and then it was requantized into 64 gray levels. The nonbackground pixels occupy approximately 30% of the image. Using pages of size 10×10, the image can be covered by 169 pages. Figure 6.3(b) illustrates the result using the decomposition algorithm. One hundred and thirty-five pages are used, and the total number of nodes in the HH encoding tree is 52. Figure 6.3(c) illustrates the result using the PIM-directed decomposition algorithm with a threshold of 0. One hundred and thirty-six pages are used, and the total number of nodes in the HH encoding tree is 51. Similar experiments were then performed using the PIM-directed algorithm with different threshold values. The results are summarized in Table 6.2.

TABLE 6.2

Threshold	No. of Nodes	Number of Pages
0.10	16	3
0.05	67	55
0.04	66	90
0.03	55	107
0.02	59	116
0.01	52	130
0.00	51	136

As the threshold decreases, more and more pages are considered informative. A threshold of 0.10 will select only three pages as informative. If we are given a preset limit on the number of pages, we can also pick a threshold to select the number of pages below that preset page limit. For pictorial databases, pages (or tiles) are stored on direct-access storage devices, and the page limit represents the storage constraint.

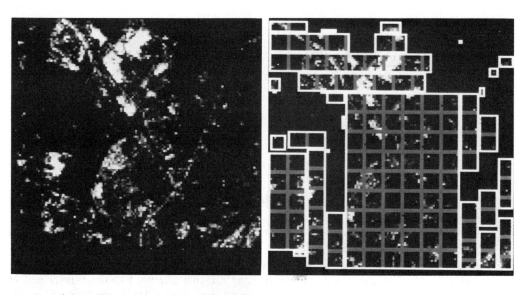

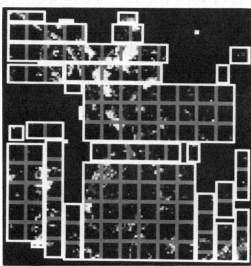

Figure 6.3 (a) original SEASAT image;
(b) result of decomposition; and (c) result
of PIM-directed decomposition.

6.3 PIM-DIRECTED HYPERCUBE ENCODING

6.3.1 Icon-Picture Construction by PIM-Directed HH Encoding

The hierarchical hypercube encoding technique described in the previous section can
be applied to icon-picture construction. An icon-picture is a low-resolution, low-bit-
per-pixel picture for visual representation of the original picture. Icon-pictures can be

used in pictorial information retrieval. Since the purpose of the icon-picture is for visual representation, distortion of the original picture can be allowed. We will first present the regular decomposition technique to construct a distortionless icon-picture. As an example, a picture is shown next:

```
3   3   7   7
3   3   7   7
3   6   6   6
0   2   6   5
```

We employ a clockwise regular decomposition scheme to decompose a picture into four equal-sized subpictures [DYER80, OLIVER83]. Whenever pixels in a subpicture have identical gray levels, we use the decomposition code 1 to indicate it is non-decomposable, and the subpicture is represented by its (average) gray level. Decomposition code 0 indicates further decomposition is necessary. Whenever we reach a 2-by-2 subpicture, if the decomposition code is still 0, we will directly encode the four pixels, because further decomposition is impossible. The preceding picture is decomposed as shown in Figure 6.4.

Figure 6.4 Picture decomposition.

The encoded representation is:

```
0;   1  7;   0  6  5  6  6;   0  6  2  0  3;   1  3
```

where the pixel values are underlined. The semicolons are for the sake of clarity and not actually required. The original picture requires 3 bits per pixel, totaling 48 bits. The encoded representation requires 5 bits for decomposition codes, and 30 bits for pixel values, totaling 35 bits.

In the preceding scheme, we can also compute a picture information measure and compare it with a threshold to decide whether further decomposition is necessary. For example, if we use an absolute threshold of 2 pixels (at most two erroneous pixels for any subpicture), the encoded representation becomes

```
0;   1  7;   1  6;   0  6  2  0  3;   1  3
```

The encoded representation now requires $5 + 3 \times 7$ or 26 bits, and 1 pixel is erroneous. Experimental results of HH encoding the SEASAT image of Figure 6.3(a) using different thresholds are summarized in Table 6.3, where the distortion is calculated as the ratio of the number of erroneous pixels over the total number of pixels.

TABLE 6.3   PIM-DIRECTED HH ENCODING OF SEASAT IMAGE

Threshold (Pixels)	Avg. No. of Bits per Pixel (Bit/Pixel)	Distortion (% Error Pixels)
35	0.172	25.921 %
25	0.226	25.854 %
10	0.579	23.425 %
5	0.932	22.229 %
3	1.120	22.100 %
2	2.149	11.401 %
1	3.373	2.832 %

After *HH* encoding, to achieve further data compression, we can use the Hoffman code to encode each pixel into a uniquely decodable variable-length bit string according to the frequency of occurrence of each gray level. The results are summarized in Table 6.4. In Table 6.4, we compare the results with the straightforward application of Hoffman encoding. In the latter case, we first find the average pixel value of a subpicture (such as a 2×2 subpicture) and then encode it using the Hoffman code. The case of a 1×1 subpicture is, of course, the direct Hoffman encoding of pixels in the original picture. The entropy of this test image is 2.0004.

TABLE 6.4   HOFFMAN ENCODING OF PIM-DIRECTED HH ENCODED SEASAT IMAGE

Threshold or Subpic Size	Avg. No. of Bits per Pixel (Bit/Pixel)	Distortion (% error pixels)
PIM thrshd 3	1.023	22.100 %
PIM thrshd 2	1.972	11.401 %
PIM thrshd 1	2.910	2.832 %
2×2 subpic	0.675	22.058 %
1×1 subpic	2.179	0.000 %

In PIM-directed *HH* encoding, the overhead for storing the decomposition codes is, in the worst case, $N(f)(1/4 + 1/16 + \cdots + 1/N(f)) \leq N(f)/3$ pixels. In other words, the worst-case coding overhead is no larger than 1/3 bit per pixel. Experimental results demonstrate that *HH* encoding is quite efficient. Further improvements are possible using a generalized PIM_k measure, as discussed in the following section.

6.3.2 PIM_k-Directed HH Encoding Technique

The picture encoding technique can be further extended with the generalized picture information measure in chapter 4. $NPIM_k$ measures the minimum number of pixel changes to convert a picture into one with only k distinct pixel values.

The encoding technique, therefore, is to test whether each subpicture can be represented using 1, 2, or 4 gray levels, or to see if further decomposition is necessary. Since there are four cases, we need two bits for the decomposition code. For each subpicture, we compute $NPIM_1$, $NPIM_2$, and $NPIM_4$. The four cases are analyzed next.

CASE 1. If $NPIM_4 > t$, then we should further decompose this subpicture, and the decomposition code is set to 00.

CASE 2. If $NPIM_4 \leq t < NPIM_2$, then the subpicture can be encoded into four distinct gray levels, and the decomposition code is set to 01.

CASE 3. If $NPIM_2 \leq t < NPIM_1$, then the subpicture can be encoded into two distinct gray levels, and the decomposition code is set to 10.

CASE 4. If $NPIM_1 \leq t$, then the subpicture can be represented by a single gray level, and the decomposition code is set to 11.

With this encoding scheme, the worst-case overhead for storing the decomposition codes is 2/3 bits per pixel. As an example, the picture is shown here:

```
3 3 7 7
3 3 7 7
3 7 3 7
7 3 7 3
```

Since $PIM_2 = 0$, in the PIM_k-directed HH encoding, we can represent the picture using two distinct pixels, by mapping pixel values 7 to 1 and 3 to 0. The code is shown here:

```
1  0  7  3  0  0  1  1  0  0  1  1  0  1  0  1  1  0  1  0
      =  =  -  -  -  -  -  -  -  -  -  -  -  -  -  -  -  -
```

where "=" marks the pixel mapping table, and "-" marks the data. The encoded representation requires 2 bits for decomposition code, 3×2 bits for pixel mapping table (assuming each pixel requires 3 bits), and 4×4 bits for data, totaling 24 bits.

If we decompose the original picture, the following code results:

```
0  0  1  1  7  0  0  7  3  7  3  0  0  7  3  7  3  1  1  3
            -        -  -  -        -        -  -  -  -
```

with a total of 40 bits.

6.4 QUADTREES

A quadtree is a hierarchical data structure providing quick data access in the sense of data retrieval. An extensive review of quadtrees and related hierarchical data structures can be found in [SAMET84]. We will only give a short treatment of quadtrees in this section.

A quadtree is based on the principle of recursive decomposition of pictures. Assume that we are only interested in digital pictures in a 2-D grid. Each decomposition produces four equal-sized quadrants. We label the quadrant white if it consists of white pixels only, black if it consists of black pixels only, gray if it consists of both black and white pixels. Further decompositions are carried out on gray blocks. Black and white blocks remain unchanged. The decomposition process is best described by a quadtree with its root representing the entire picture, the leaves representing either black or white quadrants. Figure 6.5 is an example of coding an object region by a

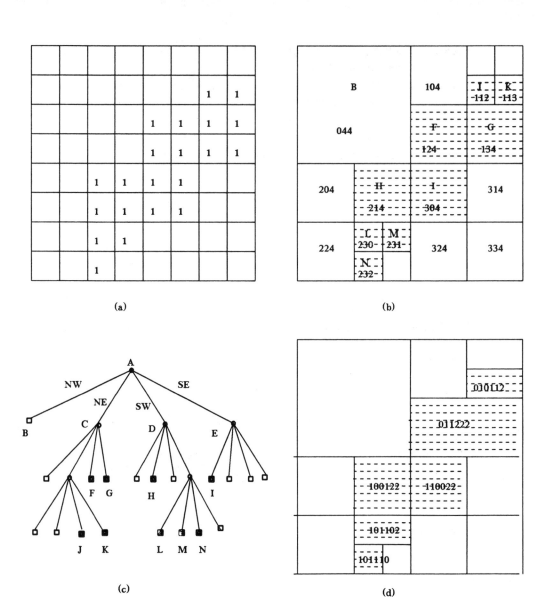

Figure 6.5 (a) An object in a binary picture; (b) quadtree decomposition of the picture in (a); (c) quadtree representation of (a); and (d) binary tree decomposition of picture in (a).

quadtree data structure, where 6.5(a) is a binary picture, the background of which is coded with 0's and the object by 1's; 6.5(b) is a decomposition of the picture in 6.5(a), whose blocks within the object region are shaded; 6.5(c) is a quadtree representation of 6.5(b); 6.5(d) is a binary tree decomposition of the picture in 6.5(a). We notice from Figure 6.5(b), that in quadtree representation the object region is now considered composed of large square blocks instead of pixels. This is why a quadtree can represent picture data in a more compact way than a raster data structure.

6.4.1 Ways of Representing Quadtrees

A natural way to represent a quadtree is to use tree structure, as shown in Figure 6.5(c). Each node of the tree is represented by a record with four pointers to its four son records and one pointer to its father record. The use of pointers facilitates tree traversal. Operations based on tree traversal can be performed without too much difficulty.

The number of nodes of a quadtree when representing a picture may be quite large—sometimes even larger than the number of pixels of the picture. Therefore, representing a quadtree using a tree structure has the disadvantage of requiring too much storage. A linear quadtree codes a collection of black leaf nodes only using location code. This is described in a number of publications—for example, [ABEL83]. Location code is a base 4 number, with code 0,1,2,3 corresponding to, for example, quadrants NW, NE, SW, and SE, respectively; code 4 denotes a "don't care," indicating no decomposition at this level. Assuming that a picture size is $2^N \times 2^N$. The location code will be N digits long. A leaf corresponding to a $2^k \times 2^k$ block will then be coded by a location code having $(N - k)$ "don't care" digits.

An object region can then be represented by a collection of location codes of picture blocks of which the object region consists. For example, the object region in Figure 6.5 is coded by a linear quadtree as

$$\{ 112, 113, 124, 134, 214, 230, 231, 232, 304 \}$$

The location codes listed correspond to blocks J, K, F, G, H, L, M, N, and I, respectively. It is interesting to note that this location list is in increment order, and the corresponding block list is a depth-first traversal of the quadtree's black nodes.

Kawaguchi and others [KAWAGUCHI80] proposed a quadtree representation using the depth-first traversal list of quadtree leaves. The list is a string consisting of symbols '(', 'B', 'W', corresponding to GRAY, BLACK, and WHITE labels. The quadtree in Figure 6.5 is coded by Kawaguchi's method as

$$(W\,(W\,(WWBBBB\,(WBW\,(BBBW\,(BWWW$$

The original picture is reconstructed from DF-expression (depth-first expression) by the fact that the degree of each terminal node is always 4 and that the traversal is in the order of NW, NE, SW, SE.

Among the three representations just introduced, linear quadtrees are the most widely used ones. They are compact. The operations based on them can be defined as algebraic algorithms. In what follows, we will describe properties of linear quadtrees and the operations on objects represented by linear quadtrees.

6.4.2 Properties of Linear Quadtrees

Suppose a block is coded by a location code

$$a_1 a_2 \cdots a_i \cdots a_N$$

where $a_1, a_2, ..., a_i \neq 4$, $a_{i+1}, ..., a_N = 4$. Then the size of the block is $2^{N-i} \times 2^{N-i}$. The coordinates of the upper left corner of the block are

$$x = \sum_{j=1}^{i} mod(2, a_j) \, 2^{N-j} + 1$$

$$y = \sum_{j=1}^{i} [a_j - mod(2, a_j)] \, 2^{N-j-1} + 1$$

We now try to develop rules to determine if two given blocks are neighbors. It is worthwhile to clarify that the concept "neighbor" here refers to direct neighbors located side by side. Suppose the location codes of two blocks are

$$a_1 \, a_2 \, \cdots \, a_i \, \cdots \, a_N$$

$$b_1 \, b_2 \, \cdots \, b_i \, \cdots \, b_N$$

Again $a_{i+1}, ..., a_N$ are supposed to be 4's, and same are $b_{j+1}, ..., b_N$. Without any loss of generality, we can assume $i \leq j$; this means block A is greater than or equal to block B. The neighbor identification operation is then as follows:

1. Compare a_k with b_k for $1 \leq k \leq i$. If $a_k - b_k = m$, $|m| < 3$, both $(a_k = 1, b_k = 2)$ and $(a_k = 2, b_k = 1)$ are not true. (The last two conditions are to guarantee direct neighbor relation; if we use 8-neighbor definition, diagonally related blocks are also considered neighbors, then these two conditions can be removed). Block A and block B are neighbors if $a_n - b_n = -m$ for $k < n \leq i$ and

    a. If $m = 1$, block B is to the west of block A. $b_{i+1}, ..., b_j$ should be either 1 or 3. For example, blocks 324 and 233 in Figure 6.5 are neighbors.

    b. If $m = -1$, block B is to the east of block A. $b_{i+1}, ..., b_j$ should be either 0 or 2. For example, blocks 044 and 104, 124 are neighbors.

    c. If $m = 2$, block B is to the north of block A. $b_{i+1}, ..., b_j$ should be either 3 or 2.

    d. If $m = -2$, block B is to the south of block A. $b_{i+1}, ..., b_j$ should be either 0 or 1. For example, 044 and 204,214 are neighbors.

6.4.3 Operations on Objects Represented by Linear Quadtrees

Operations on linear quadtrees can be performed by algebraic algorithms. We describe here mainly the set operations and connected component labeling.

Set operations on two object regions are based on containment checking between two picture blocks. Let us use the same expressions as the previous subsection for blocks A and B. Block A is contained in (or equal to) block B, if and only if $i > j$ ($i = j$) and $a_k = b_k$ for all $0 \leq k \leq j$.

The union operation on the two object regions $A = \{A_1, A_2, ...\}$ and $B = \{B_1, B_2, ...\}$ is performed by checking containment between blocks within the two object regions:

1. For each block A_i in object region A, check if there is a block B_j in object region B which contains or is equal to A_i.

   a. If this is true, place B_j into the result region and remove B_j from B, and remove A_i and any other blocks contained in B_j from A.

   b. If it is false, place A_i into the result and remove A_i from A and remove any blocks contained in A_i from B.

2. Place all blocks left in B into the result.

The intersection operation of the two object regions is essentially the same as the union operation except that smaller blocks are placed into the result region instead of larger ones. It is worth noting that spatial relationships between two blocks of two object regions represented by a linear quadtree are only "contained-in," "equal-to," and "close-to" if the binary pictures have the same size. This property of the quadtree makes the set operations simple.

Labeling of connected components in an object region requires a clear definition of connectedness on the quadtree representation. Analogous to the connectedness definition of regions in a square grid, we define a region A to be connected if for any two blocks A_1 and A_N in A there is a sequence of N blocks A_1, A_2 ,..., A_N such that

$$A_i \cap A_{i+1} = \varnothing \qquad 1 \le i < N - 1$$

$$A_i \text{ is a direct neighbor of } A_{i+1}$$

The labeling of connected components in an object region can be completed by the following algorithm.

STEP 1. Take a block from block list A of a region as an initial block of a component, and label it by L.

STEP 2. Scan the rest of the blocks in list A; for each block in A, check to see if it is a neighbor to any blocks already in a component list C. If it is true, put the block into C.

STEP 3. Repeat step 2 until no blocks can be put into C.

STEP 4. Increment L, go back to step 1.

STEP 5. Terminate the algorithm if list A is empty.

Computing the area of a region represented by a linear quadtree is a trivial process. The area of each block is simply $2^n \times 2^n$, where n is the number of 4's in the location code. The area of the blocks are then summed up to get the overall area of the region.

The moments are also computed block by block. For each block, the coordinates of each pixel can be easily calculated. The computing of moments is then a straightforward process.

6.5 THREE-DIMENSIONAL OBJECT REPRESENTATION

To represent a 3-D object, we can start from a set of *primitives, such as*

blocks	(x,y,z,Lx,Ly,Lz)
cubes	(x,y,z,L)
unit cubes	(x,y,z)
cylinders	(x,y,z,r,x',y',z')

where L's are the length of sides.

These primitives can then be combined into more complex objects using the following *set-theoretic operators:* (a) union, (b) intersection, and (c) difference; and *movement operators:* (a) translation (Dx, Dy, Dz) and (b) rotation (α, θ, γ). In the simplest case, we consider only one primitive: block; and one operator: union. Figure 6.6(a) illustrates how a 3-D object is constructed from smaller blocks, and Figure 6.6(b) illustrates the corresponding tree structure describing the 3-D object. Such a tree description is called a *CSG description* (Constructive Solid Geometry description).

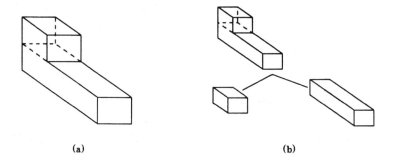

(a)   (b)

Figure 6.6 (a) A 3-D object consists of smaller blocks; (b) tree structure description of object in (a).

If all the blocks are unit cubes or cells, we are then representing a 3-D object by direct *cell decomposition.* If we have a 3-D picture function $f(x,y,z)$, then we set the 3-D pixel at (x,y,z) to 1, if $f(x,y,z)$ is in the object. An example is shown in Figure 6.7(a).

Similar to quadtree decomposition for 2-D pictures, we can use oct-tree decomposition for 3-D pictures, as illustrated in Figure 6.7(b). We start from the cube containing the 3-D object $f(x,y,z)$, where $f(x,y,z)$ is 1 if (x,y,z) is in the object. For each cube, we compute the normalized picture information measure NPIM. If NPIM is less than the threshold, we stop the splitting. Otherwise, we decompose this cube into eight subcubes and repeat the same procedure. The oct-tree decomposition procedure splits a 3-D object into constituent cubes of all sizes. This can be followed by a merge procedure to recombine some cubes into blocks, resulting in a standard split-and-merge procedure.

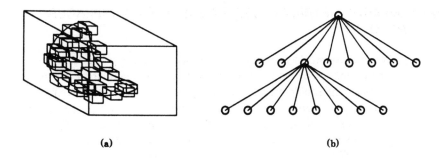

(a)   (b)

Figure 6.7   (a) A 3-D object and (b) oct-tree representation.

CSG descriptions of solid objects are useful in robotics, where it is often necessary to compute the transformation of rigid objects. Another application is in computer graphics. To display a 3-D object on a 2-D screen, we can use the technique illustrated in Figure 6.8.

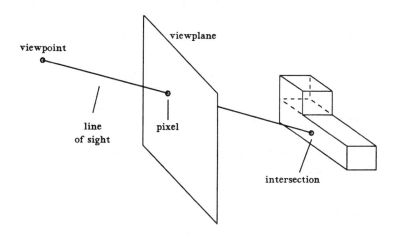

Figure 6.8   The projection of a 3-D object on a 2-D screen.

From a given viewpoint, we can calculate the intersection of the line-of-sight with (a) the view plane and (b) the object. If the line intersects the object, the corresponding pixel at the viewplane is set to the surface shading of the object at the intersection point. If the line does not intersect the object, the pixel is set to some background value. To find the point of intersection, we can use a CSG description such as the example of Figure 6.6(b), and find whether the line intersects any block in the tree description. In other words, instead of solving the original complex problem with the CSG description, we can solve a number of simpler problems to find the answer. This divide-and-conquer strategy is applicable to find whether a point is outside, on, or inside the object.

6.6 SIMILARITY RETRIEVAL USING GENERALIZED HYPERCUBE ENCODING

In similarity retrieval from a pictorial database, it is often desirable to find a set of data records (or set of pattern vectors) that are most similar to the test record (or pattern vector). The problem can be formally stated as follows: Given point set $S_1, S_2, ..., S_k$ in an n-dimensional space and a target point $P_0 = (x_1, x_2, ..., x_n)$, find S_i which is most similar to P_0 with respect to certain distance measure $d(P_i, P_j)$, where P_i, P_j are points in n-dimensional space. A straightforward approach would be to compute the shortest distance from P_0 to the points in the point set and select the nearest one. If the point set contains a large number of points, this approach may become too time consuming and impractical. Instead of using this straightforward approach, we can consider the following steps for the hypercube encoded data to attack this problem.

Let $\{y_1, ..., y_{m-1}; a_m, ..., a_n; b_m, ..., b_n\}$ represent a *GH* encoded hypercube H. To compute the distance between a point P_0 and a *GH* encoded point set S, we compute the following:

$$
\begin{aligned}
D_j &= f(x_j - y_j) & \text{if } j < m \\
D_j &= f(a_j - x_j) & \text{if } x_j < a_j \text{ and } j \geq m \\
D_j &= 0 & \text{if } a_j \leq x_j \leq b_j \text{ and } j \geq m \\
D_j &= f(x_j - b_j) & \text{if } x_j > b_j \text{ and } j \geq m
\end{aligned}
$$

and

$$
D(P_0, H) = g\left(\sum_{j=1}^{n} D_j\right)
$$

where f and g are monotone nondecreasing functions. For example, for Cartesian distance, $f(z) = z^2$, and $g(z) = z^{1/2}$. For rectilinear distance, $f(z) = |z|$ and $g(z) = z$. The distance $d(P_0, S)$ may then be defined as the smallest distance $D(P_0, H_i)$, where H_i are *GH* encoded hypercubes of S. Finally, P_0 is determined to be more similar to S_i, if $d(P_0, S_i) < d(P_0, S_j)$ for all other S_j.

6.7 DISCUSSION

We have presented a methodology of picture encoding for pictorial databases. The first application of this methodology is in pictorial database design. A number of ad hoc techniques have been combined, providing a unified conceptual framework to design and analyze pictorial data structures.

The second application is new but may gain in importance as interactive pictorial information systems become widespread. Therefore, we will discuss this new application area in more detail.

In image understanding and pictorial information retrieval, a picture is often specified by a picture function f, together with a picture object set V and a relational object set R. (V, R) can be regarded as the *logical picture* extracted from the *physical picture* f. It describes the syntactic and semantic structure of the picture.

A *picture object* v_i is represented by $v_i = \{(A_1, a_1), (A_2, a_2), ..., (A_k, a_k)\}$, where $a_1, a_2, ..., a_k$ are the attributes (for example, resolution, average gray level, size, orientation, and so on). A *picture object set* $V = \{v_1, v_2, ..., v_n\}$, is a set of picture objects. As an example, if the picture objects v_i are pixels, then $v_i = \{(type, pixel), (x, x_i), (y, y_i), (c, f(x_i, y_i))\}$, where $f(x, y)$ is the pixel value at point (x, y). As another example, if the picture objects v_i denote average pixels over a local window area, then $v_i = \{(type, picture), (x, x_i), (y, y_i), (r, r_i), (c, c_i)\}$, where r_i is the size of the window, (x_i, y_i) the location of its lower left corner, and c_i the average pixel value for the area inside the window.

Each hypercube H_i in hypercube encoding can be associated with an *icon X*, which contains information extracted from the support picture f / H_i. The icon X consists of two parts: a *logical part* X_m containing picture objects and relational objects extracted from the support picture, and a *physical part* X_i containing a transformed picture derived from f / H_i. For example, the logical part may contain information about the average gray level of the support picture f / H_i, the local histogram of f / H_i, the recognized picture objects in f / H_i, and the relationships among picture objects. The physical part may be an encoded picture derived from f / H_i. (In this chapter, we have referred to the physical part as an icon-picture.)

In actual implementation, X_m could be realized as relations in a relational database or represented by a semantic network. For large pictorial databases, we need to provide icons so that pictures can be retrieved by interactive means. The logical and physical parts can be used to design such icons. The logical part describes the contents of this icon, and the physical part gives a visual representation of this icon. The PIM-directed HH encoding technique can then be used to construct icon-pictures.

R E F E R E N C E S

[ABEL83] ABEL, D.J., AND J.L. SMITH, "A Data Structure and Algorithm Based on a Linear Key for a Rectangle Retrieval Problem," *Computer Vision, Graphics and Image Processing*, Vol. 23, 1983, 1-13.

[CHANG78a] CHANG, S.K., AND Y. WONG, "Optimal Histogram Matching by Monotone Gray Level Transformation," *Communications of the ACM*, Vol. 22, No. 10, ACM, October 1978, 835-840.

[CHANG78b] CHANG, S.K., J. REUSS, AND B.H. McCormick, "Design Considerations of a Pictorial Database System," *International Journal on Policy Analysis and Information Systems*, Vol. 1, No. 2, January 1978, 49-70.

[CHANG79] CHANG, S.K., B.S. LIN, AND R. WALSER, "A Generalized Zooming Technique for Pictorial Database Systems," *Proceedings of National Computer Conference, AFIPS*, Vol. 48, 1979, 147-156.

[CHANG80] CHANG, S.K., AND Y. WONG, "Ln Norm Optimal Histogram Matching and Application to Similarity Retrieval", *Computer Graphics and Image Processing*, Vol. 13, 1980, 361-371.

[CHANG82] CHANG, S.K., "A Methodology for Picture Indexing and Encoding," *Picture Engineering*, (Kunii and Fu, eds.), Springer Verlag, Berlin, 1982, 33-53.

[CHANG83] CHANG, S.K., AND C.C. YANG, "Picture Information Measures for Similarity Retrieval," *Computer Vision, Graphics and Image Processing*, Academic Press, Vol. 23, 1983, 366-375.

[CHANGNS79] CHANG, N. S., AND K. S. FU, "A Relational Database System for Images," TR-EE 79-28, Dept. of Electrical Engineering, Purdue University, May 1979.

[CHIEN80] CHIEN, Y. T., "Hierarchical Data Structures for Picture Storage, Retrieval and Classification," in *Pictorial Information Systems* (Chang and Fu, eds.), Springer-Verlag, West Germany, 1980, 39-74.

[DYER80] DYER, R. D., A. ROSENFELD, AND H. SAMET, "Region Representation: Boundary Codes from Quadtrees," *Communications of the ACM*, Vol. 23, 1980, 171-179.

[FREEMAN75] FREEMAN, H., AND R. SHAPIRO, "Determining the Encasing Rectangle for an Arbitrary Curve," *Communications of the ACM*, Vol.18, No. 7, ACM, July 1975, 409-413.

[KAWAGUCHI80] KAWAGUCHI, E., T. ENDO, AND M. YOKOTA, "DF-Expression of Binary-Valued Picture and Its Relation to Other Pyramidal Representations," *Proceedings of the Fifth International Conference on Pyramidal Representations*, December 1980, 822–827.

[KLINGER78] KLINGER, A., M. L. RHODE, AND V. T. TO, "Accessing Image Data," *International Journal on Policy Analysis and Information Systems*, Vol. 1, No. 2, January 1978, 171-189.

[LEE81] LEE, J. S., "A Simple Speckle Smoothing Algorithm for Synthetic Aperture Radar Images," CGIP, 1981.

[LIU81] LIU, S. H., AND S. K. CHANG, "Picture Covering by Two-Dimensional AH Encoding," *Proceedings of IEEE Workshop on Computer Architecture for Pattern Analysis and Image Database Management*, Hot Springs, Virginia, November 11-13, 1981, 76-87.

[McKEOWN77] MCKEOWN JR., D. M., AND D. J. REDDY, "A Hierarchical Symbolic Representation for Image Database," *Proceedings of IEEE Workshop on Picture Data Description and Management*, IEEE Computer Society, April 1977, 40-44.

[MERRILL73] MERRILL, R. D., "Representation of Contours and Regions for Efficient Computer Search," *Communications of the ACM*, Vol. 16, No. 2, ACM, February 1973, 69-82.

[MILGRAM79] MILGRAM, D. L., "Constructing Trees for Region Description," *Computer Graphics and Image Processing 11*, Academic Press, 1979, 88-99.

[OLIVER83] OLIVER, M. A., AND N. E. WISEMAN, "Operations on Quadtree Encoded Images," *COMPUTER Journal*, Vol. 26, No. 1, 1983, 83-91.

[OMOLAYOLE79] OMOLAYOLE, J., AND A. KLINGER, "A Hierarchical Data Structure Scheme for Storing Pictures," *Technical Report*, Computer Science Department, UCLA, 1979.

[PAVLIDIS77] PAVLIDIS, T., *Structured Pattern Recognition*. Springer Verlag, 1977.

[REUSS78] REUSS, J. L., AND S. K. CHANG, "Picture Paging for Efficient Image Processing," *Proceedings of IEEE Computer Society Conference on Pattern Recognition and Image Processing*, IEEE Computer Society, May 1978, 69-74.

[ROSENFELD76] ROSENFELD, A., AND A. C. KAK, *Digital Picture Processing*. New York: Academic Press, 1976.

[SAMET84] SAMET, H., "The quadtree and related hierarchical data structures," *Computing Survey*, Vol.16, No.2, 1984, 187-260.

[SINGH79] SINGH, K. K., S. K. CHANG, AND C. C. YANG, "A Heuristic Method For Generalized Hypercube Encoding," *Proceedings of COMPSAC 79*, Chicago, November 6-8, 1979, 531-534.

[SHAPIRO79] SHAPIRO, L. G., AND R. M. HARALICK, "A Spatial Data Structure," *Technical Report* #CS 79005-R, Dept. of Computer Science, Virginia Polytechnic Institute and State University, p. 35, August 1979.

[TANIMOTO76] TANIMOTO, S. L., "An Iconic/Symbolic Data Structuring Scheme," in *Pattern Recognition and Artificial Intelligence*, (ed. by C. H. Chen), Academic Press, 1976, 452-471.

[WARD79] WARD, M., AND Y. T. CHIEN, "A Pictorial Database Management System which uses Histogram Classification as a Similarity Measure," *Proceedings of COMPSAC 79*, IEEE Computer Society, 1979, 153-156.

[YANG78] YANG, C. C., AND S. K. CHANG, "Encoding Techniques for Efficient Retrieval from Pictorial Databases," *Proceedings of IEEE Computer Society Conference on Pattern Recognition and Image Processing*, IEEE Computer Society, June 1978, 120-125.

E X E R C I S E S

1. It is of great importance to find an efficient algorithm for finding the optimal GH_m hypercube encoding. It is interesting to see that the optimal problem can be related with a bipartite graph problem. Let $S = \{i_1, i_2, \ldots, i_{(m-1)}\}$ be a *handle sequence* from $\{1, 2, \ldots, n\}$. We use $GH(S)$ as a short notation of $GH(x_{i_1}, \ldots, x_{i_{(m-1)}};$ $a_{i_m}, \ldots, a_{i_n}; b_{i_m}, \ldots, b_{i_n})$, and use $H(S)$ to denote the set of handle vectors derived from S. Let $S_1 = \{i_1, i_2, \ldots, i_{(k-1)}\}$ and $S_2 = \{j_1, j_2, \ldots, j_{(l-1)}\}$ be two disjoint *handle sequences* from $\{1, 2, \ldots, n\}$. We construct a bipartite graph $G = (V_1 \cup V_2, E)$ as follows:

   For each handle vector α in $H(S_1)$, we create a vertex v_α; the collection of such vertices is denoted by V_1. Similarly, we create a vertex v_β for each handle vector β in $H(S_2)$ and denote it by V_2. If (α, β) is a handle vector in $H(S_1 \cup S_2)$, we add an edge from v_α to v_β; the set of such edges is denoted by E. Prove the following:

   If the number of GH encoded hypercubes derived from handle sequence $S_1 \cup S_2$ is x, then there exists a vertex v_α in V_1 and a vertex v_β in V_2 such that the degree of v_α is greater than or equal to $x / |V_1|$ and the degree of v_β is greater than or equal to $x / |V_2|$.

2. Let N be the total number of nodes in a quadtree, B the number of black nodes which represent uniform black regions, W the number of white nodes which represent uniform white regions, and G the number of gray nodes which are internal nodes of a quadtree. Show that $N = 4G + 1 = (4(B + W) - 1)/3$.

3. Give the quadtree representation of the two binary pictures (Figure 6.9, p. 144) by drawing quadtrees. Briefly discuss the effect of transitions and rotations on quadtree representation.

4. Suppose we use the following data structure to represent a quadtree. Each node in a quadtree is represented as a record with four pointers to its four sons, a pointer to its father, and a field indicating the node type. Design an algorithm to perform the union operation of two quadtrees representing binary pictures, and show the time complexity of the algorithm.

5. Write an algorithm to convert a binary image into its quadtree representation. Each node of the quadtree is represented as a record with four pointers to its four sons, a pointer to its father, and a field indicating the node type.

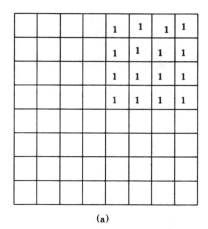 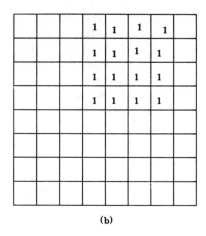

(a)   (b)

Figure 6.9   Binary pictures for Exercise 3.

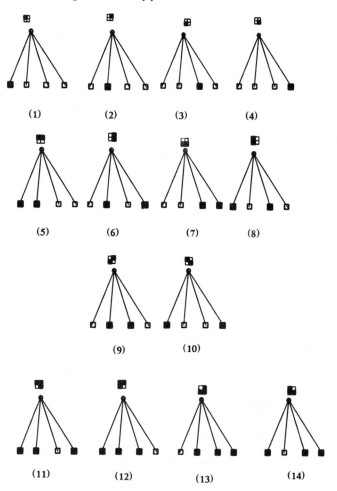

Figure 6.10   Subtrees for Exercise 6.

6. A *p-quadtree* is defined as follows:

Let Q be a quadtree with N nodes. If any of the 14 subtrees shown Figure 6.10 (p. 144) appear in Q, it is replaced by a corresponding leaf node which is denoted by the icon shown above each subtree in the figure.

The resultant quadtree is called *p-quadtree* because a total of 16 primitive picture patterns are used instead of only two primitive picture patterns in the original quadtree representation. Apparently, p-quadtree has fewer nodes than the original quadtree, and operations are speeded up accordingly. Compute the average saving of nodes in a p-quadtree compared to the original quadtree.

Part II

Chapter 7

Pictorial Knowledge Representation

In previous chapters we mainly dealt with physical pictures. Techniques for physical picture representation, picture processing, and picture coding were discussed. In this chapter, we will discuss various methods of knowledge representation for logical pictures. Our emphasis is on semantic network representation as a unifying approach for pictorial knowledge representation. One reason is that a semantic network offers an intuitive representation for pictorial knowledge (see Section 7.1). Moreover, since the basic representation is a graph, a semantic network can be generalized to represent complex logical pictures as attributed hypergraphs (Section 7.2.1). A semantic network can also be converted to a relational representation. Therefore, graph matching techniques (Sections 7.3, 7.4, and 7.5) and graph labeling techniques (Section 7.6) discussed in this chapter can be used as tools in pictorial query processing, which will be discussed in Chapter 8.

Once pictorial knowledge is formally represented, we can then apply formal inference procedures to deduce new knowledge, answer users' queries, and so on. The fundamental concepts of formal inference and reasoning are reviewed in Appendix III.

7.1 SEMANTIC NETWORKS

Consider the scene shown in Figure 7.1. It consists of three objects: an armchair, a highchair, and a stool.

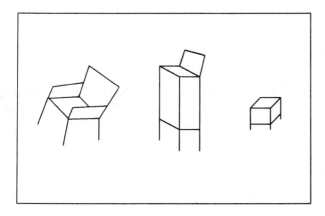

Figure 7.1 A scene consisting of an armchair, a highchair, and a stool.

The facts are expressed by the following statements:

armchair is chair

highchair is chair

stool is chair

armchair is wide

highchair is high

stool is low

armchair is to the left of highchair

highchair is to the left of stool

highchair is between armchair and stool

We can represent the preceding collection of knowledge by logical predicates.

```
IS-A(armchair,chair)

IS-A(highchair,chair)

IS-A(stool,chair)

SHAPE(armchair,wide)

SHAPE(highchair,high)

SHAPE(stool,low)

LEFT-OF(armchair,highchair)

LEFT-OF(highchair,stool)

BETWEEN(highchair,armchair,stool)
```

Let us collect all facts about the armchair. This is called a unit or a frame. In this representation, we take an object-oriented approach, so that all the facts about a certain object can be grouped together.

```
armchair
IS-A(armchair,chair)
SHAPE(armchair,wide)
LEFT-OF(armchair,highchair)
```

We will ignore the BETWEEN predicate for the time being. We can rewrite the preceding unit as follows. We introduce a binary predicate, EQ, to test the equality of its two arguments.

```
armchair
EQ(IS-A(armchair),chair)
EQ(SHAPE(armchair),wide)
EQ(LEFT-OF(armchair),highchair)
```

In the preceding representation, SHAPE is no longer a predicate. It is a function, mapping object sets into object sets. For example, SHAPE(armchair) is "wide." Following the treatment given by [NILSSON80], this representation can be more concisely rewritten as follows:

```
EQ(SHAPE(armchair),wide)
```

is written as

```
SHAPE: wide
```

Therefore, we have

```
armchair
IS-A: chair
SHAPE: wide
LEFT-OF: highchair
```

This frame concisely describes an object and it has three slots. Each slot has a slot-name, such as IS-A, SHAPE, LEFT-OF. Each slot also has a slot-value, such as chair, wide, highchair. We can also call slot-names the attribute names and slot-values the attribute values. Thus, each object has a number of attributes (or properties). Of all the attributes, one particular attribute, usually the IS-A attribute, denotes the object type. For example, armchair is a chair, so the object type of "armchair" is "chair." The frame can be graphically depicted as in Figure 7.2.

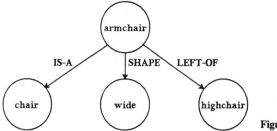

Figure 7.2   A semantic net

In the preceding semantic net, the objects armchair, wide, chair, and highchair are nodes. The labeled arcs represent their relations. In the simple semantic net, only binary relations which can be represented by labeled arcs, are allowed. Thus a semantic net is a labeled directed graph. The facts about the armchair, highchair, and stool can now be represented as in Figure 7.3. Again, in Figure 7.3, we temporarily ignore the BETWEEN ternary relation.

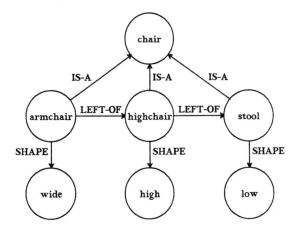

Figure 7.3 A semantic network representation of the scene in Figure 7.1, ignoring BETWEEN relation.

In this example, the IS-A relation is the set-membership relation—that is, $EQ(IS-A(x), y)$ if x is an element of y. Therefore, we sometimes use the notation EL(x,y).

We now try to handle the BETWEEN(highchair,armchair,stool) relation. Since this is a ternary relation, to represent it in the semantic net, we must make certain modifications. There are two possible approaches. The first approach uses a hypergraph, where each arc can be connected to a set of nodes. Therefore, the arc labeled BETWEEN should have three end-nodes: "armchair," "highchair," and "stool."

The second approach converts the BETWEEN relation into a set of binary relations as follows: We introduce a *relation instance*, which is one occurrence of the BETWEEN relation. Let us call it *B*1. The object *B*1 is represented by the following frame:

```
B1
        IS-A(B1,between)
        ONE-END(B1,armchair)
        MIDDLE(B1,highchair)
        ONE-END(B1,stool)
```

or more concisely,

```
B1
        IS-A: between
        ONE-END: armchair
        MIDDLE: highchair
        ONE-END: stool
```

The complete semantic net is as shown in Figure 7.4.

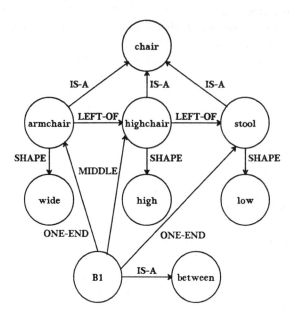

Figure 7.4 The complete semantic net representation of the scene in Figure 7.1.

The preceding technique of introducing object instances not only can be used to convert ternary (or n-ary) relations into binary relations, but also can be used to represent multiple occurrences of objects of the same type. Consider a scene consisting of sky, a little house, and the prairie. The frames are the following:

```
P1
        IS-A: sky
        COLOR: blue
        ABOVE: P2
        ABOVE: P3


P2
        IS-A: house
        COLOR: white
        BELOW: P1
        SIZE: little


P3
        IS-A: prairie
        COLOR: brown
        BELOW: P1
        BELOW: P2
```

The *IS−A* relation in *P*1 frame and *P*3 frame means "denote." The *IS−A* relation in *P*2 frame means "element-of." A third meaning of *IS−A* relation is "subset-of." Only the "element-of" interpretation of *IS−A* relation allows for property inheritance.

Another point worth noting is that some relations may be derivable from other relations. For example, *ABOVE*(*x*, *y*) is the same as *BELOW*(*y*, *x*). With such equivalence, the preceding frames can be simplified:

```
P1
      IS-A: sky
      COLOR: blue
      ABOVE: P2
      ABOVE: P3


P2
      IS-A: house
      COLOR: white
      SIZE: little
      ABOVE: P3


P3
      IS-A: prairie
      COLOR: brown
```

In the preceding, we have multiple occurrences of the ABOVE relations, which can be made more precise by modifying the frames and introducing relation instances as follows:

```
P1
      IS-A: sky
      COLOR: blue


P2
      IS-A: house
      COLOR: white
      SIZE: little


P3
      IS-A: prairie
      COLOR: brown


above1
      IS-A: above
      UP: P1
      DOWN: P2


above2
      IS-A: above
      UP: P1
      DOWN: P3
```

(Cont'd on p. 152)

```
                         above3
                           IS-A: above
                           UP: P2
                           DOWN: P3
```

The complete semantic net is illustrated in Figure 7.5.

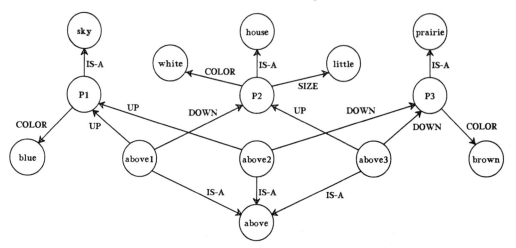

Figure 7.5. A complete semantic net representation of the scene of sky, house, and prairie.

Finally, we can also express the frames as objects in a database. Each object in the database has a type and other attributes. Objects with identical type can be grouped into an object class. The database is as follows:

```
Object class 1:  {(TYPE,sky), (NAME,P1), (COLOR,blue)}
Object class 2:  {(TYPE,house), (NAME,P2), (COLOR,white), (SIZE,little)}
Object class 3:  {(TYPE,prairie), (NAME,P3), (COLOR,brown)}
Object class 4:  {(TYPE,above), (NAME,above1), (UP,P1), (DOWN,P2)}
                 {(TYPE,above), (NAME,above2), (UP,P1), (DOWN,P3)}
                 {(TYPE,above), (NAME,above3), (UP,P2), (DOWN,P3)}
```

This database realization of a knowledge base enables us to use a database management system to manage a knowledge base.

7.2 APPLICATIONS OF SEMANTIC NETWORKS

As just discussed, a semantic network is a labeled directed graph, where both nodes and arcs are labeled by attributes. Depending on our interpretation, the semantic network can be applied in many different ways. We will review several applications in this section.

It should also be noted that a semantic network like the one shown in Figure 7.5 can be represented by a collection of logical propositions. For image understanding applications, the semantic net representation is sometimes more convenient. For planning and logical inferences, the logical representation is often preferred.

7.2.1 Attributed Hypergraphs

A. K. C. Wong and his co-workers at the University of Waterloo have proposed attributed hypergraphs for the representation of 3-D objects for computer vision [WONG82]. In their model, an attribute pair is an ordered pair (A_i, a_i), where A_i is the attribute name, and a_i is the attribute value. An attribute set is represented by $\{(A_1, a_1), ..., (A_n, a_n)\}$. An attributed graph $G = (V, A)$ is a graph whose vertex set is V and arc set is A, where both vertices in V and arcs in A can be associated with attribute sets.

The objects used in Wong's experiment consist of planar surfaces. To extract 3-D information from 2-D images, a structured lighting technique is used. As shown in Figure 7.6, the grating board has circular apertures. Therefore, ellipses will be created on the planar surfaces of the object. By estimating the lengths of the major and minor axes of the ellipse and the angle between them, one can estimate the orientation of the planar surface.

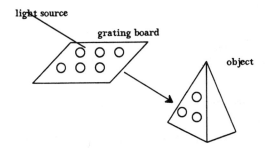

Figure 7.6 Illustration of extracting 3-D information from 2-D image.

After preprocessing, the constituent surfaces of an object are recognized. One then can proceed to describe each surface by an attributed graph. For example, the following graph describes the surface $S1$ shown in Figure 7.7.

$G_1 (V_1, A_1)$

$v_1\{(\text{type,line}),(\text{length,5})\}$
$v_2\{(\text{type,line}),(\text{length,5})\}$
$v_3\{(\text{type,line}),(\text{length,4})\}$
$v_4\{(\text{type,circle}),(\text{radius,1})\}$
$a_{12}\{(\text{type,connection}),(\text{line2},v_1),(\text{line2},v_2),(\text{angle},46^o)\}$
$a_{13}\{(\text{type,connection}),(\text{line1},v_1),(\text{line2},v_3),(\text{angle},67^o)\}$
$a_{23}\{(\text{type,connection}),(\text{line1},v_2),(\text{line2},v_3),(\text{angle},67^o)\}$

In G_1, the vertices v_1, v_2, and v_3 describe the three line segments of the surface area, and v_4 describes the circle in this area. The arcs a_{12}, a_{13}, and a_{23} describe the connections between the line segments and the angle between them.

Each surface of the object can thus be described by an attributed graph. These are called primitive attributed graphs. The primitive attributed graphs are combined to form a complete description of the object. To obtain the combined description, one

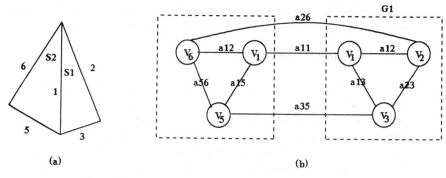

Figure 7.7. (a) A 3-D object; (b) its hypergraph representation.

can use an attributed hypergraph. Each hyper-vertex corresponds to a primitive attributed graph, and each hyper-arc is the set of arcs connecting two primitive attributed graphs that correspond to two hyper-vertices.

As an example, the other surface (surface S_2) of the object shown in Figure 7.7 can be described by the following attributed graph:

$G_2 (V_2, A_2)$

$v_1\{(\text{type,line}),(\text{length},5)\}$
$v_5\{(\text{type,line}),(\text{length},4)\}$
$v_6\{(\text{type,line}),(\text{length},5)\}$
$v_7\{(\text{type,circle}),(\text{radius},1)\}$
$a_{16}\{(\text{type,connection}),(\text{line}1,v_1),(\text{line}2,v_6),(\text{angle},46^o\ )\}$
$a_{15}\{(\text{type,connection}),(\text{line}1,v_1),(\text{line}2,v_5),(\text{angle},67^o\ )\}$
$a_{56}\{(\text{type,connection}),(\text{line}1,v_5),(\text{line}2,v_6),(\text{angle},67^o\ )\}$

The two graphs G_1 and G_2 are connected as follows:

$a_{11}\{(\text{type,common-line}),(\text{line},v_1)\}$
$a_{26}\{(\text{type,connection}),(\text{line}1,v_2),(\text{line}2,v_6),(\text{angle},70^o\ )\}$
$a_{35}\{(\text{type,connection}),(\text{line}1,v_3),(\text{line}2,v_5),(\text{angle},110^o\ )\}$

In the preceding, the arc a_{11} indicates the line segment v_1 is a common-line of the two surfaces. Arcs a_{26} and a_{35} specify the connection between v_2 and v_6, v_3, and v_5, respectively. The hypergraph $G = (V, A)$ is as shown in Figure 7.7(b). The hyper-vertex set is $V = \{G_1, G_2\}$, and the hyper-arc between G_1 and G_2 is the arc set $\{a_{11}, a_{35}, a_{26}\}$.

The procedure just described can be recursively applied to construct very complex objects: We describe planar surfaces by primitive attributed graphs, then construct hypergraphs with surface descriptions as hyper-vertices, and then construct hypergraphs with objects as hyper-vertices, and so on.

To recognize an object or object descriptions, we first construct the hypergraph describing the object as just outlined. Then we search the model database, which also consists of preconstructed hypergraphs describing typical objects. We try to match the object hypergraph with a model hypergraph, and report the best match as the recognition result.

An example is illustrated in Figure 7.8. Figure 7.8(a) is the same as Figure 7.7(b), which illustrates the constructed object hypergraph. Figure 7.8(b) illustrates the model graph for a pyramid. Because the object has hidden surfaces, the object hypergraph will only partially match the model hypergraph. The matching also proceeds recursively. If we try to match two hyper-vertices, then the corresponding subgraphs must also match.

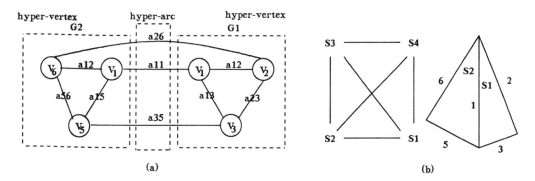

Figure 7.8 (a) Hypergraph representation of a pyramid; (b) a model graph for a pyramid.

The precise definitions of a match, a partial match, and the best match depend on applications. Techniques for efficient relational graph matching are topics being actively investigated by several research groups. The basic technique will be discussed in Section 7.4.

7.2.2 Location Networks

Another interesting (and different) interpretation of a semantic network is the location network [RUSSELL79], which can be used to compute potential search areas in an image. In the location network, each node is associated with an operation, an argument list, and a result node name. An example is illustrated in Figure 7.9.

Suppose we know that the object we are searching for is close to objects A or B but not too close to either one, then we can proceed to compute the potential search areas as follows:

Each area will be represented by a point set. We first form the union of areas A and B. The result is U. We then form the area C_1, any point of which is within the distance of X to U. We also form the area C_2, any point of which is within the distance of Y to U. (Naturally, X should be chosen greater than Y). We then take the difference of C_1 and C_2, which is the potential search area D. This sequence of operations can be represented by the location network as illustrated in Figure 7.9. Therefore, location networks allow for orderly geometric inference.

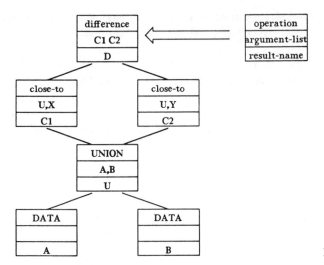

Figure 7.9   Location network example.

7.3 GRAPH MATCHING AND APPLICATIONS

Semantic networks can be implemented with ease using artificial intelligence languages such as LISP, KRL, and so on. In this section, we will use a direct implementation to illustrate the graph matching problem and its applications.

Referring again to the semantic network G shown in Figure 7.3 which is redrawn here in Figure 7.10, we can represent it by two arrays V and A. Array V stores the vertex names, and array A stores the starting vertex, ending vertex, and name of arcs.

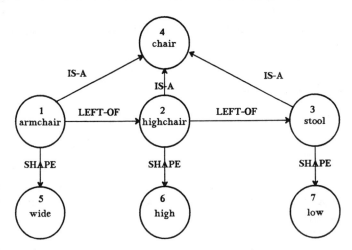

Figure 7.10   The semantic network G.

Mathematically, V and A are defined as follows:

$$V : N \to S$$
$$A : N \times N \to S \cup \{e\}$$

where $N = \{1, ..., n_{obj}\}$ is the index set for the vertices,

S is a finite nonempty set of names, and

e is a special symbol not in S, indicating "no arc."

We can then write programs to perform specific operations on the semantic network. For example, the following algorithm finds all the relations (or arc names) involving an object with the name obj-name.

```
all-relations(obj-name)
begin
        for i=1 to n_obj
        begin
                if V[i] = obj-name then key=i
        end;

        for i=1 to n_arc
        begin
                if A[i,start] = key then print(obj-name,V[A[i,end]],V[i]);
                if A[i,end] = key then print(V[A[i,start]],obj-name,V[i]);
        end
end
```

We now illustrate query answering using a semantic network to motivate the subgraph matching problem. Suppose we want to answer the query: "What is to the left of the highchair?"

This query can be formulated as a semantic network with variable names, as shown in Figure 7.11(a). Notice one node is marked X, indicating this is a variable node.

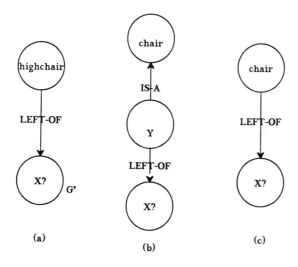

(a)

(b)

(c)

Figure 7.11 Query answering using semantic network.

We can attempt to match the semantic network G' of Figure 7.11(a) with the semantic network G of Figure 7.10. Since G' is a simpler graph, it can only be matched to a subgraph of G. The matching also assigns a value to the variable X —

that is, X is assigned the value "stool." Therefore, as we solve the subgraph matching problem, we also answer the query just posed.

Figure 7.11(b) illustrates the semantic network for the query: "What is to the left of the chair?" Now there are two variables X and Y, because "chair" is a generic concept. In actual usage, it is possible that the query is represented by the graph shown in Figure 7.11(c) because we do not know beforehand that "chair" is a generic concept. The inference system should have the capability to transform the graph of Figure 7.11(c) into that of Figure 7.11(b), and vice versa.

The graph of Figure 7.11(b) can be matched to two subgraphs of Figure 7.10. In one instance, X is highchair and Y is armchair. In another, X is stool and Y is highchair. Therefore, the answer to the query is ambiguous. It can be highchair or stool. The subgraph matching problem generally does not have a unique solution.

As a final example, the question: "What is near the highchair?" can be translated into a graph shown in Figure 7.12(a). Since "near" is not an arc name for the original graph G, the matching will fail unless the inference system can transform this query graph into two graphs, as shown in Figure 7.12(b). The answer is then the union of X and Y.

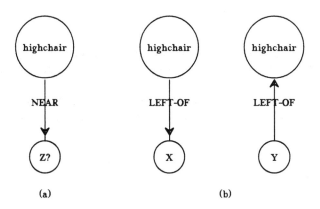

Figure 7.12 Query representation as subgraph matching.

(a) (b)

The subgraph matching problem for semantic networks can be formally stated as follows: Let $G'(V,A)$ and $G(V,A)$ be two labeled directed graphs defined as follows:

$$V' : N' \rightarrow S \cup X$$
$$A' : N' \times N' \rightarrow S \cup X \cup \{e\}$$

where   N' = $\{1,...,n'_{obj}\}$ is the vertex index set
   S is the arc name set
   X is the variable name set, and
   e is special symbol indicating "no arc."

$$V : N \rightarrow S$$
$$A : N \times N \rightarrow S \cup \{e\}$$

The subgraph matching problem is to find a one-to-one-into-mapping T, such that

1. for all i in N', $V'[i] = V[T(i)]$
(corresponding vertices have identical names)

2. for all i, j in N', if $A'[i,j]$ is not e, then $A'[i,j] = A[T(i),T(j)]$ (corresponding arcs have identical names)

In **2**, if one arc name is a variable, it will automatically match anything except e. For nonexact matching, the equality sign in **1** and **2** should be interpreted more liberally. For example, there may be a certain similarity measure on S, so that as long as the two names are sufficiently similar, they are considered a match.

Also, equality testing may be performed by an inference system, so that a rule is invoked to evaluate the equality of two names (two concepts). For example, "NEAR" and "LEFT-OF" can be inferred to mean the same.

Subgraph matching generally can be accomplished by a backtrack searching technique. To continue the previous example of matching the graph G' of Figure 7.11(a) to G of Figure 7.10, we may proceed as follows. We attempt to match all nonvariable names in V' to names in V. Since it is assumed that all vertex names are unique, the nonvariables in V' should match corresponding nonvariables in V. We are then left with only the variables in V', denoted by $V'-S$. We try to substitute the variables by names one by one, and check for consistency using **2**. In other words, arc names must also match. Whenever there is inconsistency, we backtrack to try another variable substitution. The backtrack search is illustrated in Figure 7.13. If vertex names are not unique, we must try all combinations.

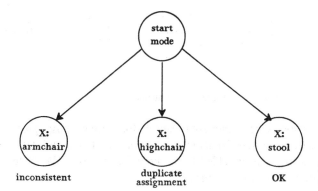

Figure 7.13 Matching by backtrack searching technique.

There are many variations of the graph matching problem. We have already seen that subgraph matching is applicable to query processing. The next example illustrates that partial graph matching is applicable to computer vision in robotics.

Suppose the robot is given the following command: "Pick up size-3-nut in the pan to-the-left-of conveyor-belt."

The initial image is illustrated in Figure 7.14(a), and the corresponding initial knowledge base (represented by a semantic network) is shown in Figure 7.14(b). Initially, only two pans and the conveyor belt have been recognized by the vision system. Therefore, the knowledge base only has information about these three entities.

The input command contains the following query: "What size-3-nut is in the pan to-the-left-of the conveyor-belt?" This query is represented by the graph of Figure 7.15(a). It is clear it cannot be matched to any subgraph of Figure 7.14(b). In fact, we only want a partial match, as shown in Figure 7.15(b).

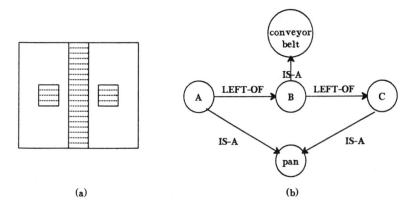

(a)   (b)

Figure 7.14   (a) Scene of conveyor belt and (b) its semantic net representation.

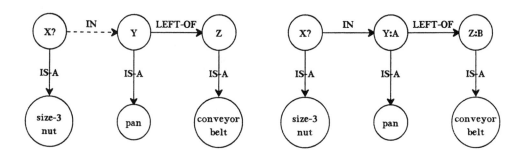

Figure 7.15   Partial graph matching.

The partial match helps us to locate subimage *A* for further image processing. We attempt to identify an object (size-3-nut) in this region. If it is found, this object (and its attributes, such as location) is added to the knowledge base. The system can then direct the robotic arm to pick up this object.

7.4 GRAPH MATCHING ALGORITHMS

In Section 7.3, we gave the formal definition of subgraph matching for semantic networks and demonstrated the applications of graph matching, including motion understanding (where we are dealing with unlabeled graphs), 3-D object description and recognition (using hypergraphs), locating subimages in image understanding, and so on.

The subgraph matching problem has many variations. If we allow for nonexact matching, we need not match identical node names and identical arc names. Also, some of the nodes may have no matching nodes. We therefore need a measure for the goodness of matching, defined as follows:

$$\text{Matching-Cost} = \sum_{i \text{ in } N', T(i) \text{ defined}} \text{COSTN} \, (V'[i], V[T(i)]) \quad \text{(template cost)}$$

$$+ \sum_{i,j \text{ in } N', T(i), T(j) \text{ defined}} \text{COSTA} \, (A'[i,j], A[T(i), T(j)]) \quad \text{(spring cost)}$$

$$+ \sum_{i \text{ in } N', T(i) \text{ undefined}} \text{COSTM}' \, (V'[i]) \quad \text{(missing cost: input graph)} \quad (7.1)$$

$$+ \sum_{j \text{ in } N \text{ no } i \text{ in } N' \text{ such that } T(i)=j} \text{COSTM} \, (V[j]) \quad \text{(missing cost: reference graph)}$$

In the preceding, *COSTN* is the cost of matching two similar nodes, sometimes called the "template cost." *COSTA* is the cost of matching two similar arcs, sometimes called the "spring cost." *COSTM'* and *COSTM* are the costs of "missing nodes." There may be some nodes in G' which cannot be matched to nodes in G (that is, $T(i)$ undefined). There may also be some nodes in G which cannot be matched to nodes in G' (that is, no $T(i)$ is equal to j). The situation is illustrated in Figure 7.16.

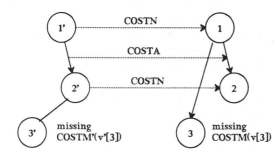

Figure 7.16   Cost definition for nonexact matching.

If we make *COSTN* and *COSTA* infinite, we are requiring exact node matching and exact arc matching, but we are allowing missing nodes in matching. Therefore, the "best match" in this case is the one which minimizes the cost of missing nodes or, equivalently, the one which maximizes the number of exact matches.

If we make *COSTM'* and *COSTM* infinite, we do not allow missing nodes in either G' or G. The subgraph matching problem becomes a graph matching problem. If we make *COSTM'* infinite, we are requiring no missing nodes in G' —that is, G' must be totally embedded in G. This is the original subgraph matching problem. In the most general case, the cost functions *COSTN*, *COSTA*, *COSTM'*, and *COSTM* are all finite. This is the general relational matching problem.

Graph matching can be done by constructing an auxiliary data structure, called an *association graph*. We illustrate the technique by an example.

In Figure 7.17(a), two graphs G and G' are shown. We construct the association graph $G'' = (V'', A'')$ as follows:

$V'' = \{(i,j): i \text{ in } N, j \text{ in } N', V[i] = V'[j]\}$
$A'' = \{((i1, j1), (i2, j2)): (i1, j1) \text{ and } (i2, j2) \text{ in } V'', A[i1, i2] = A'[j1, j2]\}$

In other words, V'' is the set of all possible matching among nodes. A'' is the set of all compatible node matchings. The "best match" problem in the case of infinite *COSTN* and *COSTA* is to find the largest set of compatible node matchings. This is equivalent to finding the maximal clique in the association graph, where a *clique* is a fully connected subgraph of G'', and a *maximal clique* is a clique whose node set is not

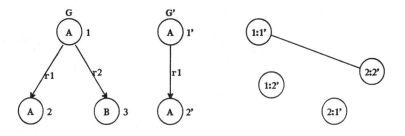

Figure 7.17 Illustration of nonexact match.

a proper subset of a node set of another clique. Therefore, the problem is reduced to finding the maximal clique.

In the example in Figure 7.17, the only possible matching is $T(1') = 1$, $T(2') = 2$. Another example is illustrated in Figure 7.18. Figure 7.18(a) shows the objects. Figure 7.18(b) represents the semantic networks corresponding to these two objects. E indicates an edge, C a corner, and S a short edge. The arcs in Figure 7.18(b) indicate adjacent relations. A maximal clique is shown in Figure 7.18(c), and the matching assignments are

$$T(2') = 1, T(3') = 2, T(1') = 5, T(4') = 3 .$$

The clique finding algorithm is as follows:

```
clique-finding(G")
begin
    LIST = { };
    while there are changes in LIST do
        begin
            for every X in LIST do
                begin
                    Y = V" - X;
                    for every y in Y, if y is connected to all x in X
                    then put X ∪ {y} back into the LIST;
                end
        end
end
```

As an example, the graph G'' is shown in Figure 7.19.

We initialize the *LIST* to { }. After the first iteration, we have *LIST* = { {1}, {2}, {3}, {4} }. After the second iteration, we have *LIST* = { {1,2}, {1,3}, {1,4}, {2,3} }. After the third iteration, we have *LIST* = { {1,2,3}, {1,4} }. Since there are no more changes, the cliques are {1,2,3} and {1,4}. The maximal clique is {1,2,3}.

It should be noted that in the clique finding algorithm, we should remove duplicates from the *LIST* in every iteration.

A generalization of the clique is an *r-connected component*, which is defined as a subgraph in which each node is connected to at least r other nodes. A clique with n nodes is an $(n-1)$-connected component.

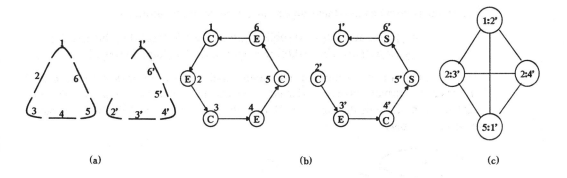

(a)   (b)   (c)

Figure 7.18   An example of nonexact matching.

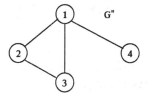

Figure 7.19   An example of clique-finding.

To find r-connected components, we start by finding all cliques with $r + 1$ nodes. Then, when we add new nodes to the cliques using the preceding algorithm, we only require the new node to be connected to r nodes.

For the general relational matching problem, in the association graph each node has a cost (*COSTN*) and each arc has a cost (*COSTA*). Each time we find a clique (r-connected component), we also compute its cost according to Equation (7.1). The clique with minimal cost is chosen as the "best match."

7.5 MATCHING ATTRIBUTED GRAPHS

The graph matching technique discussed in Section 7.4 can be extended to attributed graph matching. As we have seen in semantic networks representation, the objects and relations sometimes have multiple attributes instead of a single name.

The *attributed graph* $G = (V, A)$ is a graph, where

$$V : N \rightarrow \text{abstract object space}$$
$$A : N \times N \rightarrow \text{abstract object space}$$

Each abstract object is of the form $\{(A_1, a_1), (A_2, a_2), ..., (A_n, a_n)\}$. As an example, the cup illustrated in Figure 7.20 consists of three regions obtained by a segmentation algorithm:

$$v_1\{(\text{type,region}),(\text{shape,ellipse}),(\text{compactness},0.9)\}$$
$$v_2\{(\text{type,region}),(\text{shape,rectangle}),(\text{compactness},0.8)\}$$
$$v_3\{(\text{type,region}),(\text{shape,ellipse}),(\text{compactness},0.85)\}$$

The relations (arcs) among these objects also have multiple attributes:

$$a_{12}\{(\text{type,adj}),(\text{obj}1,v_1),(\text{obj}2,v_2),(\text{distance},1.5),(\text{big}1,0.8),(\text{big}2,1.25)\}$$
$$a_{23}\{(\text{type,adj}),(\text{obj}1,v_2),(\text{obj}2,v_3),(\text{distance},1.1),(\text{big}1,2),(\text{big}2,0.5)\}$$

The relations a_{12} and a_{23} are both adjacency relations between objects obj1 and obj2. The distance attribute gives the distance between their centers of gravity. The big1 attribute is the ratio of the size of obj1 over the size of obj2, and the big2 attribute is the inverse of big1.

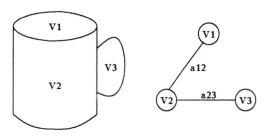

Figure 7.20 Example of an attributed graph.

To match attributed graphs, we must first define what we mean by a match of two objects. Object v_1 matches object v_2, if

$$|a_{1i} - a_{2i}| < T_i, \quad 1 \le i \le n$$

where a_{1i} is the i-th attribute of v_1, a_{2i} is the i-th attribute of v_2, and T_i is a given threshold.

Some objects may have missing attributes due to object occlusion and limitations of image processing algorithms. Therefore, it is sometimes necessary to consider a partial match, defined as follows: Object v_1 partially matches object v_2, if either a_{1i} is undefined, or

$$|a_{1i} - a_{2i}| < T_i, \quad 1 \le i \le n$$

The matching of two arcs (two relations) can be similarly defined. With the matching criteria thus defined, we can apply the matching algorithms of Section 7.4.

In Section 7.3, we discussed the application of hypergraphs for the description of 3-D objects. The reader is again referred to Figure 7.7 for an example of a hypergraph.

A hypergraph is induced by a partitioning of the vertex set V of a graph G = (V,A) as follows:

Example

Let $(V_1, V_2, ..., V_m)$ be a partition of V into disjoint nonempty subsets. This partitioning induces a hypergraph $GH = (VH, AH)$ where each hyper-vertex in VH is a subgraph of V, and each hyper-arc in AH is a set of arcs connecting subgraphs in VH. Therefore, hyper-vertex $G_i = (A_i, A_i)$ has vertex set V_i, and arc set

$$A_i = \{(v_j, v_k): v_j, v_k \ in \ V_i \ and \ (v_j, v_k) \ in \ A\}$$

The hyper-arc A_{ij} between hyper-vertices G_i and G_j is

$$A_{ij} = \{(v_m, v_k): v_m \ in \ V_i, v_k \ in \ V_j, (v_m, v_k) \ in \ A\}$$

To match two hypergraphs, we can consider them as ordinary graphs and directly apply the previous technique. However, this may be computationally inefficient. If we have model graphs for the hyper-vertices in a knowledge base, we can proceed as follows:

STEP 1. Construct subgraphs corresponding to regions obtained by some segmentation algorithm. These are the hyper-vertices of the input hypergraph.

STEP 2. Detect relations among the segmented regions. These are the hyper-arcs of the input hypergraph.

STEP 3. Perform structural matching, by matching reference hypergraph against input hypergraph, and matching reference models against input subgraphs.

An example is illustrated in Figure 7.21. The high-level hypergraph matching is illustrated in Figure 7.21(a), and the low-level hypervertex matching is illustrated in Figure 7.21(b).

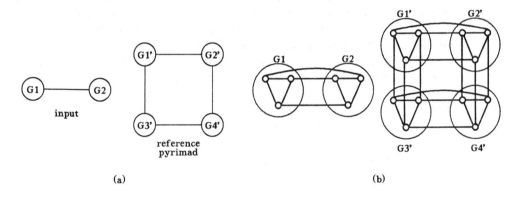

Figure 7.21 Matching of hypergraphs.

In 3-D object recognition, it is sometimes insufficient to match two hypergraphs, as illustrated in Figure 7.22. In this case, we must take another view of the object, and repeat the preceding processing.

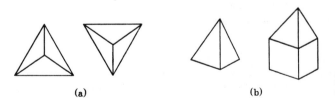

Figure 7.22 (a) Top view of two objects; (b) side view of two objects.

7.6 GRAPH LABELING ALGORITHMS

In graph labeling, we try to match an input graph to a model graph (reference graph) or to a number of model graphs. An example is illustrated in Figure 7.23, where we try to match vertices to vertices. The vertices in the input graph have adjacent relations, and the matching must not violate constraints imposed by the adjacent relations of the model graph.

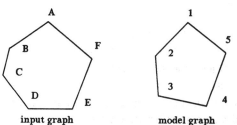

input graph   model graph   **Figure 7.23** Graph labeling problem.

For example, in Figure 7.23, if vertex A is assigned label 1, and vertex B is assigned label 2, no constraints are violated.

If, on the other hand, vertex A is assigned label 1, and vertex B is assigned label 3, then, although A and B are adjacent in the input graph, the corresponding vertices 1 and 3 will not be adjacent in the model graph, thus violating the constraint.

A general statement of the labeling problem is as follows: We are given a set of objects, a set of relations between objects, a set of labels, and a set of constraints. The goal is to assign a label to each object, so that the constraints are not violated. This labeling problem is called the *consistent labeling problem*.

Example 1.

The problem illustrated in Figure 7.23 can be stated as follows:

Objects: $\{A, B, C, D, E, F\}$

Relations: $M(A,B) = M(B,C) = M(C,D) = M(D,E) = M(E,F) = M(F,A)$
= 1 where $M(X,Y) = 1$ if X and Y are connected by a line.

Labels: $\{1, 2, 3, 4, 5\}$

Constraints:

1. $G(A) = \{1,2,3\}$, $G(B) = \{1,2,3\}$, $G(C) = \{1,2,3\}$, $G(D) = \{3,4\}$, $G(E)$ = $\{3,4\}$, $G(F) = \{1,4,5\}$, where $G(X)$ is the set of labels for X.

2. $M(1,2) = M(2,3) = M(3,4) = M(4,5) = M(5,1) = 1$.

3. if $M(X,Y) = 1$ then $M(L(X), L(Y)) = 1$.

Goal: Find consistent labeling function L.

Example 2

In graph coloring, no two adjacent nodes may have the same color. Suppose there are three nodes connected into a triangle. Nodes X and Y can be colored red or green. Node Z can be colored green or blue. The graph coloring problem can be stated as follows:

Objects: $\{X, Y, Z\}$

Relations: $M(X,Y) = M(Y,Z) = M(Z,X) = 1$.

Labels: $\{R, G, B\}$

Constraints:

1. $G(X) = \{R, G\}$, $G(Y) = \{R, G\}$, $G(Z) = \{G, B\}$.

2. if $M(X, Y) = 1$ then $L(X)$ not equal to $L(Y)$.

Goal: Find consistent labeling function L.

To find a consistent labeling L, we can apply an exhaustive tree search method. An example for finding the consistent labeling for the graph coloring problem in Example 2 is illustrated in Figure 7.24.

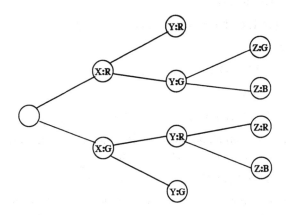

Figure 7.24 Tree search algorithm.

The backtrack search procedure is as follows:

```
consistent-labeling(i)
begin
     for j=1 to n_label
     begin
         if label-j can be assigned to object-i and
             label-j is consistent with previous assignments and
             consistent-labeling(i+1) is "true"
         then begin assign label-j to object-i;
                     return("true");
             end;
     end;
     return("false");
end
```

Another technique is relaxation labeling. Initially, each set Gi contains the set of labels compatible with object-i. We then check to see whether certain constraints will further reduce the size of Gi. The following procedure can be invoked as many times as needed, until no further changes are made:

```
relaxation-labeling(G)
begin
    for i=1 to n_object
        for j=1 to n_label
        begin
            if label-j is in Gi and inconsistent
            with all labels in another set Gk
            then label-j is removed from Gi
        end
    end
```

As an example, suppose initially

$$G(X) = \{R\}, G(Y) = \{R,G\}, G(Z) = \{G,B\} .$$

After the first iteration, we have

$$G(X) = \{R\}, G(Y) = \{G\}, G(Z) = \{G,B\} .$$

After the second iteration, we have

$$G(X) = \{R\}, G(Y) = \{G\}, \text{ and } G(Z) = \{B\} .$$

In this example, the relaxation algorithm converges to a consistent labeling solution. However, if we pick the wrong initial sets, for example,

$$G(X) = \{R,G\}, G(Y) = \{R,G\}, G(Z) = \{G\},$$

then the procedure will fail to find a solution. Also, even when the algorithm converges, the set $G(X)$ need not contain only one element. Therefore, we should then apply the exhaustive tree search algorithm.

In addition to the exhaustive tree search algorithm and the relaxation algorithm, there is a third class of *stochastic labeling algorithms*. The objective now is no longer to find consistent labeling but to find the "optimal" labeling defined in a certain sense. It is possible that the optimal labeling is inconsistent, but the optimal labeling should be "most probably consistent."

For each object i, let $P_{i(m)}$ be the weight (or probability) that label m is the correct label for object i. In stochastic labeling algorithms, we try to adjust the $P_{i(m)}$'s by iteration. If the $P_{i(m)}$'s converge to certain values, then we pick, for each object i, the label m which maximizes $P_{i(m)}$.

How do we update the $P_{i(m)}$'s? Different stochastic labeling algorithms utilize different update operations. The central idea is to estimate the *compatibility matrix* $M = [P_{ij}(m/n)]$. The term $P_{ij}(m/n)$ is the weight (or probability) that the object i has the correct label m, given the fact that object j has label n. Clearly, if the assignment of label m to object i is inconsistent, $P_{ij}(m/n)$ should be close to zero, and vice versa. To iteratively update the $P_i(m)$'s, we can apply the following formula:

$$P_i(m) = \sum_j C_{ij} [\sum_n P_{ij}(m/n) P_j(n)]$$

The inner sum is the expectation that object i has label m, given object has label j. $P_i(m)$ is thus the weighted sum of such expectations. In stochastic labeling, we must first provide estimates for C_{ij} and $P_{ij}(m/n)$ which should be somehow related to the consistency constraints and object relations. Once we have these parameters and an initial $P_i(m)$, we can apply the update operations iteratively until $P_i(m)$ converges. Examples of matching polygonal figures representing regions using stochastic labeling can be found in [BHANU84].

REFERENCES

[BALLARD82] BALLARD, D.H. AND C.M. BROWN, *Computer Vision*, Prentice-Hall, Inc., Englewood Cliffs, New Jersey, 1982.

[BHANU84] BHANU, B., AND O. D. FAUGERAS, "Shape Matching of Two-Dimensional Objects," *IEEE Trans. on PAMI*, Vol. PAMI-6, No. 2, March 1984, 137-156.

[NILSSON80] NILSSON, NILS J., *Principles of Artificial Intelligence*, Tioga Publishing Co., 1980.

[RUSSELL79] RUSSELL, D. M., "Where do I look now?", *Proc. PRIP*, August 1979, 175-183.

[WONG82] WONG, A. K. C., AND S. W. Lu, "Representation of 3-D Objects by Attributed Hypergraphs for Computer Vision," *Tech. Report*, University of Waterloo, 1982.

EXERCISES

1. Express the following statements as a collection of predicates: IS-A, SHAPE, LEFT-OF, and BETWEEN.

>   pool table is a table
>
>   coffee table is a table
>
>   dining table is a table
>
>   card table is a table
>
>   work table is a table
>
>   pool table is wide
>
>   coffee table is low
>
>   dining table is round
>
>   card table is square
>
>   work table is high
>
>   pool table is to the right of the coffee table
>
>   coffee table is to the left of the dining table
>
>   dining table is between the pool table and the coffee table
>
>   card table is to the right of the pool table
>
>   work table is between the card table and the pool table

2. Express each of the following objects as a frame: pool table; coffee table; dining table; card table; and work table.

3. Express each of the following objects as a semantic network, ignoring the BETWEEN relationship, as in Figure 7.3: pool table; coffee table; dining table; card table; and work table.

4. Add the BETWEEN relationship to the preceding semantic network, as in Figure 7.4.

5. Consider a scene consisting of a lovely boat, the ocean surface, and a small fish described by the following frames:

```
P1
          IS-A: boat
          COLOR: white
          ABOVE: P2
          ABOVE: P3
P2
          IS-A: ocean
          COLOR: green
          BELOW: P1
          ABOVE: P3
P3
          IS-A: fish
          COLOR: brown
          BELOW: P2
          SIZE: small
```

Draw the associated semantic network, as in Figure 7.5, by modifying the frames with the introduction of relation instances for ABOVE.

6. Given the following 3D cube, draw the hypergraph representation.

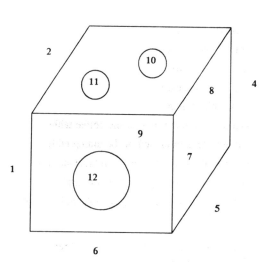

Pictorial Knowledge Representation   Chap. 7

7. Write a program to accept the description of two graphs, compute the association graph, apply the clique-finding algorithm to find the largest maximal clique, and output the "best match." Test your program on the following input data:

V1	A1	V2	A2
1 P	1 2 F	1 P	1 2 F
2 R	2 3 F	2 R	2 3 F
3 P	3 5 F	3 P	3 4 F
4 R	4 5 F	4 P	
5 P	4 5 F		
6 R	6 1 F		

Chapter 8

Pictorial Database System Design

Two problems can be distinguished in designing pictorial databases: the storage, retrieval, and manipulation of a large number of pictures; and the storage, retrieval, and manipulation of pictures of great complexity. Traditionally, researchers in image processing have concentrated on working with a few pictures. However, new applications for pictorial information systems generally require that the systems be capable of handling a large number of pictures, some of which are also very complex. Consequently, new techniques must be investigated for the efficient, flexible retrieval of pictorial information from large pictorial databases.

In [CHANG77], an approach to designing an integrated database system for tabular data, graphical data, and image data is described. It is based on generalizations of the relational approach to database design [CHANG76]. The main idea is to represent pictorial information by both logical pictures and physical pictures. A logical picture can be regarded as a model of the real image. It is defined as a hierarchically structured collection of picture objects. The logical picture can thus be stored as relational tables in a relational database and manipulated using a relational database manipulation language. Inquiries concerning the attributes of picture objects can also be handled by this relational database management system. Once a logical picture has been identified for retrieval, the corresponding physical picture can be generated on the output device by retrieving the physical picture from an image store which is specially designed for the storage of image data.

This chapter first describes the design of an integrated pictorial database system to support generalized zooming which can be used for flexible information retrieval and manipulation for a pictorial database system. This system is implemented for interactive map data retrieval and manipulation in a distributed database environment called the DIMAP (Distributed Image Management and Projection). In Section 8.19, capabilities of the DIMAP system are described. Generalized zooming concepts, including vertical zoom, horizontal zoom, and diagonal zoom, are discussed. Section 8.2 describes the relational database RAIN, which is a component of DIMAP. The concept of logical pictures and physical pictures, and the correspondence of maps and d-maps, are discussed in Section 8.3. Section 8.4 describes the image store. Techniques for frame staging are discussed in Section 8.5. Picture algebra is a comprehensive set of operations for logical/physical picture manipulation, which is described in Section 8.6. Section 8.7 describes the picture query translation system. The syntax of a picture query specified in GRAIN, the concept of a pictorial database skeleton for the specification of picture data semantics, a GRAIN translation algorithm, GRAIN query examples, and dynamic zooming examples are presented.

8.1 A PROTOTYPE PICTORIAL DATABASE SYSTEM

8.1.1 System Overview

The goal of the DIMAP project is to design an integrated pictorial database system which combines a relational database management system, RAIN, with an image store management system, ISMS, to enable the user to perform various zooming and panning operations and to browse through the pictorial database. The DIMAP system provides a pictorial information retrieval language called the GRAIN language. The integrated pictorial database management system, which includes the RAIN subsystem and the ISMS subsystem, is illustrated in Figure 8.1.

8.1.2 Display Terminal

The user interacts with the DIMAP system via a display terminal. The display terminal has the following features:

   a. A color raster monitor with good resolution (512 by 512 pixels)
   b. Two joysticks—one for panning, the other for zooming
   c. A cursor for pointing at picture objects in the window
   d. A functional keyboard

A user views a map through a window in a CRT screen. The window size in the present system is 512 by 512, corresponding to the CRT screen size as well as the x-y size of one frame buffer. It is possible to display more than one (variable-sized) window on the screen at a time. It's possible to view a large map by panning the window in any direction over the map using a joystick. Panning proceeds in starts and stops: smooth panning is possible over an area nine times the area covered by a single window; when panning is unidirectional there is sometimes jerkiness due to loading of frame buffers.

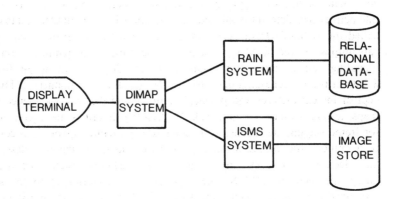

Figure 8.1 An integrated pictorial database management system.

8.1.3 Vertical Zoom

By pushing a joystick forward, the user zooms (vertically) in for a more detailed view of a map. The current map is replaced by a more detailed map. Pulling the joystick back causes an outward zoom and loss of detail apparent in the current map.

Since the map set is organized hierarchically (see Section 8.3 and Figure 8.5), some picture objects in the current map may correspond to more detailed lower-level maps. The user can also zoom in on a single picture object and request more detailed information on this picture object. If this picture object is indeed enlargeable, the current map will be replaced by another map corresponding to this picture object.

8.1.4 Generalized Zoom

Since the DIMAP system makes use of the relational database system RAIN, the user may ask questions about the nongraphical attributes of picture objects appearing in a map. A list of all attributes known to the DIMAP system about a particular picture object is obtained simply by pointing at the picture object and striking a button. A menu of attributes appears in the window near the picture object. The user may then ask questions about those attributes. The cursor can be controlled in several ways: through the keyboard, using a joystick, or via a data tablet pen. A light pen can also serve the same function.

With the relational database system RAIN, the DIMAP system can provide generalized zoom capabilities to retrieve picture objects based on their logical attributes. The concept of *horizontal zoom* (H-zoom) is illustrated in Figure 8.2. A *zoom window* is first displayed on the CRT screen, whose vertical axis corresponds to various picture objects in a picture file, and whose horizontal axis corresponds to a user-supplied *selection index* (which is obtained either by direct computation or by table look-up). For example, one selection index could be the degree of similarity of a picture object with a given reference picture object. The *zoom line* can then be moved to set a threshold for the selection of picture objects for display. If the zoom line is moved to the left, more picture objects will be selected. Thus, we have a wide-angle view of the picture file. If the zoom line is moved to the right, fewer picture objects will be selected, meaning a close-up (telephoto) view of the picture file. This type of zoom is called horizontal zoom because we are zooming in on subsets of picture objects belonging to a picture file. The traditional *vertical zoom* (V-zoom), on the other hand, provides close-up or wide-angle views of a single picture.

Once the zoom line is set, the *view line* can be moved to select a picture object for display. The corresponding picture then appears in the display window. With a larger screen, more than one viewing window may be provided.

Using functional keys, it may be possible to compute characteristics for a set of picture objects thus selected using the zoom line. We may sketch typical picture objects and atypical picture objects of the picture object set and display their attributes. In the case of raster images, an average picture object (in the sense of averaging the gray levels) can be painted, and its average attribute values displayed. We may also obtain a variable-valued logical description of the picture object set using VVL reduction techniques, extract additional features from the picture object set using pattern recognition techniques, and obtain structural information from the picture object set using syntactic parsing techniques [FU74]. Attribute values and texts associated with picture objects can also be displayed.

Figure 8.3 illustrates picture retrieval by successive horizontal zooms. By moving the view line from one position to another and striking a function key, all picture objects between these limits having a selection index above the zoom threshold will be selected. A reduced picture file can then be constructed. The zoom line can again be used to further reduce the picture object set, perhaps using a different (user-supplied) selection index. Finally, by striking another function key, the view line is set in the automatic mode, and pictures appear one by one in the viewing window in rapid succession. If these pictures are successive frames ordered chronologically, a movie is produced.

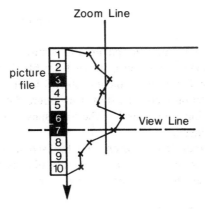

Figure 8.2 Horizontal zoom (H-zoom).

The concept of horizontal zoom can be further generalized to provide correlation capabilities among picture files. This is called *diagonal zoom* (D-zoom), as illustrated in Figure 8.4. Suppose picture files A and B are to be correlated, based on a (user-defined) relation among picture objects. For example, picture file A may consist of

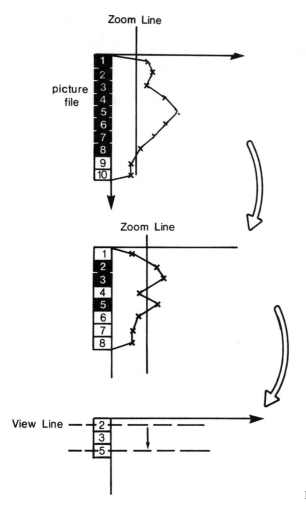

Figure 8.3 Successive horizontal zooms.

prototypes of various types of cars, and picture file B may consist of picture objects to be classified. The user may first select a subset from file A by setting zoom line A. All picture objects in file B related to picture objects in this subset of file A can be selected (using the correlation matrix as shown in Figure 8.4). The user may further prune the resulting set using zoom line B. The final subset of selected picture objects in file B can then be displayed.

To summarize, V-zoom and H-zoom can be used to select subsets of picture objects from a single picture file. D-zoom can be regarded as generalized H-zoom and can be used to select related subsets of picture objects from multiple picture files.

8.1.5 Map Overlay and Panning

A map is composed of a collection of *overlays* (see Figure 8.5) which the user may select individually. To concentrate on selected features, the user tunes out overlays simply by pushing buttons. A terrain map, for example, may show elevation contours,

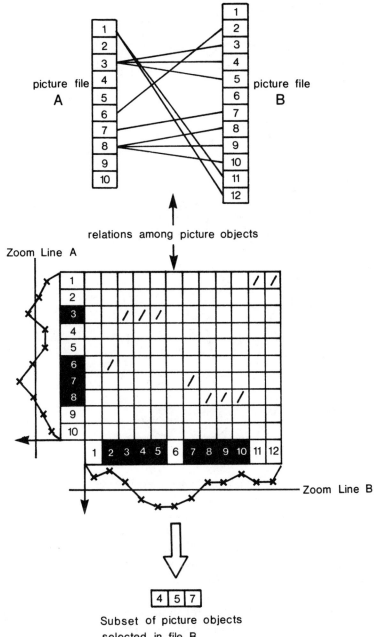

picture file **A**

picture file **B**

relations among picture objects

Zoom Line A

Zoom Line B

Subset of picture objects
selected in file B

Figure 8.4   Diagonal zoom (D-zoom).

roads, vegetation, and cities. These four features could be plotted separately, perhaps on clear plastic sheets. When the sheets are overlaid, a complete map is obtained.

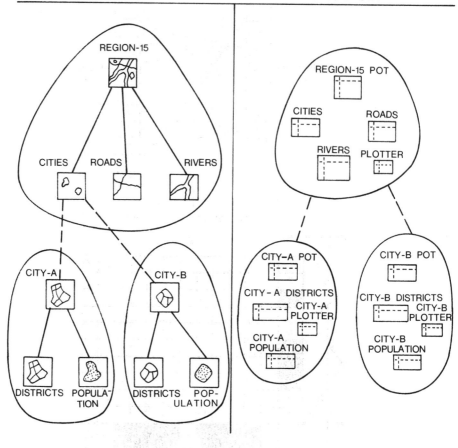

Figure 8.5 Correspondence of map set and d-map set.

In conventional maps, on paper, "what you see is what you get." The map reader can't tune out certain features to concentrate on others. There is no such constraint in the DIMAP system. At any time the user may show a single or many features in a particular region. The only restriction is that features which interfere visually with one another may not be displayed at the same time. Consider, for example, the two features "vegetation" and "political system." Assume both are area features, meaning their frames consist of colored (or shaded) regions in the viewing window. Displaying both simultaneously would produce a masking effect. The color actually seen by the user would not be the intended color of either, unless the intended color of the two areas happens to be the same; and in the latter case information would surely be distorted because there's little chance that the vegetation and the political system would correspond in an exact way.

The dynamic overlay capability of the DIMAP system is implemented through the use of the image planes (see Section 8.4). At load time, features (picture object set) can be arbitrarily associated with a particular image plane. The user can then move the display window horizontally over an image plane from one frame to another, which is called *panning*.

8.2 RELATIONAL DATABASE SYSTEM RAIN

8.2.1 Basic Concepts of Relational Model

The relational database is comprised of a collection of files. There are two types of files in the relational database: elementary files and composite files.

1. Elementary Files: An elementary file is a relational table in Third Normal Form. In the database, all composite files must be composed from elementary files. Since an elementary file is a relational table, all valid relational algebraic operations can be applied to an elementary file to extract the desired information.

An elementary file consists of a number of records (or rows, tuples), each record being of the form $(v_1, v_2, ..., v_n)$, where v_i belongs to the descriptor domain of descriptor K_i.

2. Composite Files: A composite file is a relational table which is defined in terms of other relational tables using certain composition rules. As an example, R_1 and R_2 are two constituent files. A composite file F can be defined as the vertical concatenation of R_1 and R_2, or

$$F = R_1 // R_2$$

where $//$ is the vertical concatenation operator, provided that R_1 and R_2 have identical descriptor sets. Similarly, a composite file F can be defined as the union of two constituent files R_1 and R_2, or

$$F = R_1 + R_2$$

where $+$ is the union operator, provided that R_1 and R_2 have identical concatenated keys.

A concatenated key is a subset of the descriptor set, which takes on unique values for every record in a file.

The last composition rule is the horizontal concatenation rule. A composite file F can be defined as the horizontal concatenation of constituent files R_1 and R_2, or

$$F = R_1 (*K_1) R_2$$

by equi-joining the two relational tables on descriptor K_1, where $*$ denotes the equi-join operator, and K_1 is the key for both R_1 and R_2.

In horizontal concatenation, the constituent files can also be joined on a common concatenated key, in which case the concatenation operation is written as $(*K_1, K_2, ..., K_n)$, where $\{K_1, ..., K_n\}$ is the common concatenated key.

8.2.2 Database Manipulation Language RAIN

The database manipulation language is based on relational algebra. An algebraic language is chosen for two reasons. First of all, an algebraic language is flexible and can easily be extended. The language can be easily embedded in a host language, so that the powerful instruction set of the host language can be used to write application programs or to design flexible user interfaces. Therefore, the database manipulation language is considered to be a low-level language. The end user will communicate with the database system via more flexible user interfaces described later. The application programmer will write application programs in a host language, with embedded procedure calls or subroutine calls to invoke RAIN.

The second reason for choosing an algebraic language is that it permits easy definition of structurally composed files. Although relational tables are useful as a unifying viewpoint for the end user, in implementing a realistic database system on a small computer, performance considerations cannot be overlooked. When a database grows larger and larger, the efficient storage and retrieval of possibly very large files becomes the primary concern of the database manager. In such cases, it is natural to consider breaking up or decomposing a large file into smaller pieces. The algebraic database manipulation language can be used to define structurally composed files and to dynamically restructure the files so that storage requirements and processing time can be reduced.

The database manipulation language can be used in two ways: (a) as a query language for direct query specification, and (b) as a low-level database manipulation language whose commands are embedded in a host language. In the former case, the user can invoke the RAIN interpreter directly to have an interactive session with RAIN. In the latter case, application programs are written in a host language, with embedded procedure calls to the RAIN interpreter to execute database manipulation commands.

8.2.3 Database Definitions

Several examples of database definitions will be given. The vertical concatenation of files can be defined as follows:

$$
\begin{aligned}
&\texttt{DEFINE CFILE F(K}_1\texttt{ , K}_2\texttt{ , K}_3\texttt{ , K}_4\texttt{ , K}_5\texttt{)}\\
&\qquad\texttt{STRUCTURE (//R}_1\texttt{ R}_2\texttt{)}\\
&\texttt{DEFINE EFILE R}_1\texttt{ (K}_1\texttt{ , K}_2\texttt{ , K}_3\texttt{ , K}_4\texttt{ , K}_5\texttt{)}\\
&\texttt{DEFINE EFILE R}_2\texttt{ (K}_1\texttt{ , K}_2\texttt{ , K}_3\texttt{ , K}_4\texttt{ , K}_5\texttt{)}
\end{aligned}
$$

Similarly, the horizontal concatenation of files can be defined as follows:

$$
\begin{aligned}
&\texttt{DEFINE CFILE F(K}_1\texttt{ , K}_2\texttt{ , K}_3\texttt{ , K}_4\texttt{ , K}_5\texttt{)}\\
&\qquad\texttt{STRUCTURE (*R}_1\texttt{ R}_2\texttt{)}\\
&\texttt{DEFINE EFILE R}_1\texttt{ (K}_1\texttt{ , K}_2\texttt{ , K}_3\texttt{)}\\
&\texttt{DEFINE EFILE R}_2\texttt{ (K}_1\texttt{ , K}_4\texttt{ , K}_5\texttt{)}
\end{aligned}
$$

In the definition of elementary or composite files, a characteristics clause can be included to describe concisely the contents of this file. Access and update can also be controlled by other clauses, as illustrated in the following example:

```
DEFINE EFILE R₁ (K₁ , K₂ , K₃)
        CHARACTERISTICS (K₁ ≤ '200')
        RETRIEVAL (K₃ = 'X')
        DELETION (USERID = 'SMITH')
        MODIFICATION (USERID = 'SMITH')
```

The preceding example provides the following information: the name of the elementary file is R_1, with descriptors K_1, K_2 and K_3; every record in R_1 has K_1 less than or equal to 200; all records with K_3 equal to 'X' can be retrieved by any user; the only user allowed to delete and/or modify records is 'SMITH'. (USERID is a reserved keyword. Other such keywords are PASSWORD, GROUPID, and so on.)

It can be seen that the subpartition of a composite file (or conceptually, the subregions of a two-dimensional relational table) can be assigned different protection conditions. Therefore, if part of the database is confidential and should never be made public, that portion could be separated out as a constituent file and given the most restrictive protection condition. This confidential file can also be stored in a separate storage volume with tight security control. Thus, the structured database protection scheme just described can be very useful to the database manager in a distributed system environment.

8.2.4 Database Operations on Composite Relational Files

In general, there are four types of database operations to be considered: insertion of a tuple, retrieval of tuples satisfying certain conditions, deletion of tuples satisfying certain conditions, and modification of tuples satisfying certain conditions. In the RAIN language, these commands are listed as D_1, D_2, D_3, and D_4. The execution of these database operations are explained next.

In what follows, Ec, Er, Ed, and Em denote logical expressions for the characteristics, retrieval protection condition, deletion protection condition, and modification protection condition of a relational file, respectively. Cr, Cd, and Cm denote logical expressions for the retrieval condition, deletion condition, and modification condition of the user query, respectively. Tuples in a relational file will be denoted by u,v,w, and so on.

1. Insertion: To insert a tuple u into a file, the tuple u should satisfy the characteristic condition Ec of that file—that is, Ec(u)=1. If this condition is satisfied for an elementary file, an insertion of u can be performed. The new tuple can be appended to the end of the file (entry sequenced) or inserted based on a certain indexing scheme (index sequenced). For a composite file, similar insertion commands are issued against all constituent files. Thus, parallel processes can be created to perform simultaneous insertions against the constituent files.

2. Retrieval: To retrieve tuples satisfying retrieval condition Cr, the logical expression Cr∧Ec∧Er should not be a logical zero. If this condition is satisfied for an elementary file, a tuple u can be retrieved, if Cr(u)=1, Er(u)=1, and Ec(u)=1. For a composite file, similar retrieval commands are issued against all constituent files.

3. Deletion: To delete tuples satisfying deletion condition Cd, the logical expression Cd∧Ed∧Er should not be a logical zero. If this condition is satisfied for an elementary relation, a tuple u can be deleted if Cd(u)=1 and Ed(u)=1. For a composite file, similar deletion commands are issued against all constituent files.

4: Modification: To modify tuples satisfying modification condition Cm, the logical expression Cm∧Em∧Er should not be a logical zero, and the modified tuples should also satisfy the characteristic condition Ec. For an elementary relation, a tuple u can be replaced by a new tuple v, if Cm(u)=1, Em(u)=1, and Ec(v)=1. For a composite file, similar modification commands are issued against all constituent files.

Insertion, deletion, modification, and retrieval are the four basic database operations performed by the relational database management system. Other relational algebraic operations can be built on top of these basic database operations.

8.2.5 Modular Design Approach

During the design of RAIN, there are several goals to accomplish. First, the complexity of development work should be reduced—for example, each program module can be tested independently; changes can be made without affecting other program modules; and so on. Second, the system should be portable. Third, the system should be expandable fairly easily. We can achieve these goals by taking a modular approach using self-descriptive database files and self-contained program modules.

A database file is *self-descriptive* if the file contains all the necessary information to process the file—for example, number of records, number of attribute descriptors, and so on. This means that each database file consists of two parts: an information block (header) and a data block. Data stored in the information block (header) is used to describe data in the data block. An obvious advantage is that the information block serves as the communication area between the program module and the database file. To process a database file, program modules do not have to consult with any directory or data dictionary to retrieve information about the database file.

A program module is *self-contained* if each program module represents a separate process. The interaction between program modules can be achieved in various ways—either via the process communication facilities supported by the operating system or via the self-descriptive files.

We can now use the approach of structured programming to describe the program modules. A few examples for the more important modules are presented next.

1. Define efile:

```
DEFINE EFILE s sno S2 key sno

input:   command-line
output: error-messages
files:   new-file s
processing:   parse command-line;
              construct header for new-file s.
```

2. Input Data:

```
READ s from sdata

input:   command-line
output:  error-messages
files:   s, sdata
processing:   parse command-line;
              interpret header of s;
              while there are more lines in sdata file
              begin
                      read next line from sdata;
                      convert line into row;
                      insert row into s
              end
```

3. Output Data:

```
WRITE s to sdata

input:   command-line
output:  error-messages
files:   s, sdata
processing:   parse command-line;
              interpret header of s;
              while there are more rows in s
              begin
                      retrieve next row of s;
                      expand row into line;
                      write line into sdata
              end
```

4. Print Relation:

```
PRINT s n1,n2

input:   command-line
output:  printed report
files:   s
processing:   parse command-line;
              interpret header of s;
              for i=n1 to n2
              begin
                      retrieve ith row of s;
                      expand row into line;
                      pretty-print row
              end
```

5. Projection:

```
PROJECT t = s[k1,k2]

input:      command-line
output:     error-messages
files:      s, t
processing:  parse command-line;
             interpret header of s;
             construct header of t;
             while there are more rows in s
             begin
                     retrieve next row of s;
                     extract projected attributes to construct new-row;
                     insert new-row into t
             end
```

6. Restriction:

```
RESTRICT t = s <sno=='S1'>

input:      command-line
output:     error-messages
files:      s, t
processing:  parse command-line;
             interpret header of s;
             construct header of t;
             while there are more rows in s
             begin
                     retrieve next row of s;
                     if test(row) = 1 then insert row into t
             end
```

7. Equi-Join:

```
JOIN t = s1 (*sno) s2

input:      command-line
output:     error-messages
files:      s1, s2, t
processing:  parse command-line;
             interpret header of s1;
             interpret header of s2;
             construct header of t;
             while there are more row-1 in s1
                  while there are more row-2 in s2
                  begin
                          if match(row-1,row-2)=1 then
                          insert row-1,row-2 into t
                  end
```

From the preceding program descriptions, we can identify the following common submodules:

- insert (tuple)
- retrieve (tuple)
- delete (tuple)

- modify (tuple)
- interpret (header)
- construct (header)
- convert (external input-line into internal row)
- expand (internal row to external output-line)
- test (whether row satisfies restriction condition)
- match (two rows for equi-join)
- extract (projected attributes)

Once these submodules have been implemented, it is relatively straightforward to implement the preceding modules.

8.3 CONCEPT OF LOGICAL VS. PHYSICAL PICTURES

A map isn't stored in the relational database in the way it appears in the window to the user. Rather, maps are generated by various processes that transform relational data into a visual form. The overall process of transforming relational data for display is called *materialization*. Clearly, there is a close correspondence between information in the relational database and information on the display screen. In fact, it's the same information represented in two different ways. In [CHANG77], it was proposed that only logical pictures are stored in the relational database, and physical pictures are stored in a separate image store.

To make the distinction between logical pictures and physical pictures conceptually clear, the following terminology is adopted:

Relational Database	Image Store
d-map set	map set
d-map	map
d-frame/logical picture	frame/physical picture/image
relation	picture object set/features/overlay
tuple	picture object/feature

A *map set* is a hierarchical collection of maps whose logical representation is called a d-map set. A *d-map set* is the entire collection of relations in the database. The correspondence of map set and d-map set is illustrated in Figure 8.5.

In Figure 8.5, the top map is REGION-15 consisting of three overlays: CITIES, ROADS, and RIVERS. In the CITIES overlay, there are two enlargeable picture objects—CITY-A and CITY-B—each corresponding to another map. The map CITY-A in turn consists of two overlays: DISTRICT and POPULATION.

A *map* is composed from one or many overlays whose logical representation is called a d-map. A *d-map* is a set of relations in the database which defines a complete map. The correspondence of map and d-map is illustrated in Figure 8.6. In addition to the relations CITIES, ROADS, and RIVERS, there are two special relations POT and PLOTTER, whose functions will be explained soon.

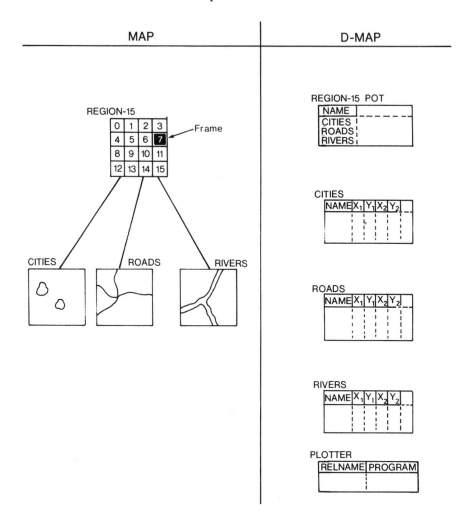

Figure 8.6 Correspondence of map and d-map.

The smallest unit for visual display is called a *frame,* whose logical representation is called a d-frame. A *d-frame* is a set of relations from which a single frame buffer may be loaded. Each relation in a d-frame corresponds to a group of *picture objects* (that is, *features*) of the same class. The correspondence of frame and d-frame is illustrated in Figure 8.7. It should be noted that these d-frame relations are restricted relations obtained from the d-map relations.

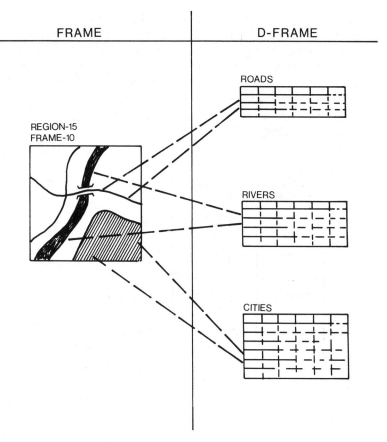

Figure 8.7 Correspondence of frame and d-frame. (d-frame relations are restricted relations obtained from d-map relations.)

The *physical picture* in a frame is also called an *image*. Thus, physical picture, frame, and image are regarded as synonymous; the logical representation is called a *logical picture*.

For each d-map, there is a special relation called POT (Picture Object Table), which contains detailed definitions of all the d-map relations.

Since all picture objects represented in a d-frame relation are of the same class, their visual interpretations are similar. The visual interpretations of tuples in the relation PEOPLE, for example, are alike insofar as they all depict a head, two arms, and two legs. We associate with each d-frame relation a graphics program that can draw a stereotypical picture object that is characteristic of the class of picture objects corresponding to the relation. The graphics program associated with PEOPLE knows, of course, how to draw people. It doesn't know, however, how to draw specific people, like "Mary Scott" or "Ray Roth." It takes the information needed to draw a specific person (assuming it's capable of drawing details about people) from the tuple corresponding to the person in question.

A typical d-frame is illustrated in Figure 8.7. As shown in Figure 8.8, there is a graphics program associated with every relation in the d-frame. The association is made via a special relation named PLOTTER. The information the program needs to create a particular frame is found in this associated relation. This implies that the graphics program must somehow communicate with the RAIN database system.

Support for materialization—that is, the process through which relations are given a visual interpretation—is one of DIMAP's central tasks. The problem is how to associate a d-frame with a frame buffer so that materialization may proceed as quickly as possible, leaving a pleasing visual impression with the user. This problem will be discussed in Section 8.5.

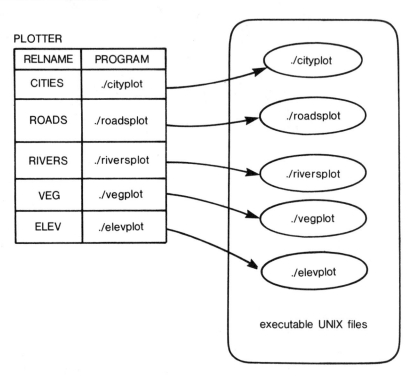

Figure 8.8 PLOTTER relation.

8.4 THE IMAGE STORE

A detailed system diagram is illustrated in Figure 8.9. From the user's viewpoint, the DIMAP system can be used to retrieve a logical picture, called a d-frame, which is stored in relational tabular form. A logical picture, or a d-frame, consists of a number of relational tables which are retrieved from the pictorial database using GRAIN commands. The GRAIN commands can be used to retrieve pictorial information the user needed via attribute information, structural relationships, similarity measures, and complex image processing operations such as color level and gray-level manipulation. At the bottom level, the ISMS system can be used to materialize logical pictures into physical pictures, called picture frames or simply frames. Using the display and print commands provided by the GRAIN language, the user can have flexible access to graphic,

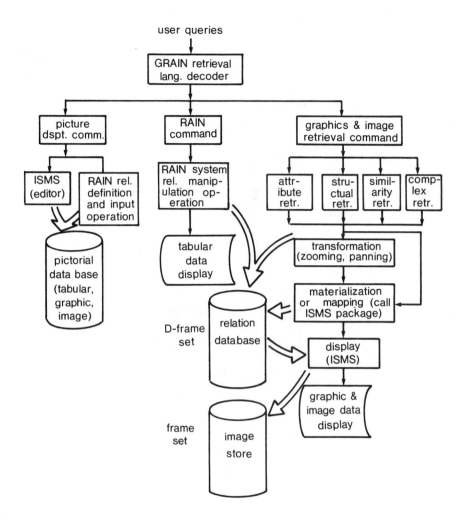

Figure 8.9 Detailed system diagram of DIMAP.

image, and tabular information. The design of the integrated pictorial database system, the relational database system RAIN, and the image store management system ISMS, can be found in [CHANG77], [WALSER78], and [REUSS77a], respectively.

The viewing window is refreshed out of the *image store* and consists of four *image planes,* as depicted in Figure 8.10. The basic unit in the image store is a four (or larger)-bit register called an *image cell.* The four bits can be used to code color or gray-level information. On display, the value in an image cell is interpreted visually as a point in a picture. Thus, an image store cell corresponds to a pixel. Each image plane has 2048 by 2048 memory cells and is partitioned into nine areas called *frame buffers.* Each frame buffer has 512 by 512 memory cells; thus, a frame buffer has the same number of memory cells as the viewing window has pixels.

Ideally, the image store would be implemented in hardware. This would be expensive in practice, however. To reduce cost, the frame buffers in the present

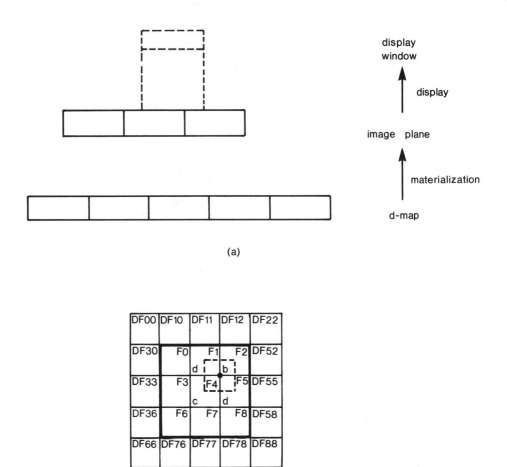

(a)

(b)

Figure 8.10 (a) Frame buffer staging concepts; (b) panning of window on image plane.

DIMAP system are disk-resident. The result is a less expensive, but slower, system. The storage requirement (in UNIX blocks) of the disk-resident frame buffers is computed as follows: Since one frame buffer has $512 \times 512 \times 4$ bits $= 131,072$ bytes $= 256$ UNIX blocks, and one image plane has 9 frame buffers, or $256 \times 9 = 2304$ UNIX blocks, the total storage requirement for four image planes is 9216 UNIX blocks, which can be accommodated by a reasonably large disk system.

It's assumed that a typical digitized map is so large that it won't fit within a single viewing window, nor even within a single image plane. This means that pixels in the map greatly outnumber points on the display screen. Thus it's necessary to partition the information associated with the map. Such a partition is called a frame.

In the simplest case, a map fits entirely within one frame buffer. Thus the x dimension of the map is the same or less than a frame buffer's maximum width; and likewise for the map's y dimension and the frame buffer's maximum height. The d-map for such a map consists of just one d-frame. A frame buffer may be loaded from this single d-frame, and the map may be viewed in its entirety within the buffer without panning.

In the worst case, the map is very large and the d-map consists of a large number of d-frames $DF_1,..., DF_n$. Since the user can view only one frame at a time, it will often be necessary to move the window from one frame to another. Moving the window horizontally over a map is called *panning*. Using the image store, it should be possible to achieve a smooth (if slow) panning.

The panning problem, from the database point of view, is to load the frame buffers from the proper d-frames as the user moves the window over the map. It should appear to the user that he is peering down through a window that can be moved laterally in any direction.

8.5 TECHNIQUES FOR FRAME STAGING

In dynamic zooming, zoom operations are performed by dynamically constructing a d-frame using pictorial retrieval commands. The advantage of the dynamic zoom is its flexibility. The disadvantage of the dynamic zoom is that it may be too time-consuming to construct d-frames dynamically. For efficiency reasons, we need also to consider the problem of the *staging* of d-frames.

The problem can be conceived as in Figure 8.10(a), where a window is shown over an image plane. The image plane, in turn, is (conceptually) over a d-map. Since the map is larger than the image plane, it isn't possible to have the entire map in the image plane at one time. Relations from the d-map must, therefore, be materialized on a selected basis into the image plane. It may appear to the user that the window may move anywhere over the map, even though, plainly, this isn't physically possible. We need an algorithm which will indicate which frame to load from which relation and when.

A potential solution is depicted in Figure 8.10(b). The image plane, consisting of nine frame buffers (shown from the "top"), is emphasized by heavy black lines. The viewing window is shown dashed, and the d-map (corresponding to a collection of d-frames in the relational database) is shown underneath the image plane. It's helpful to notice that Figure 8.10(b) is a top view of the arrangement shown in Figure 8.10(a).

To see the solution to the frame buffer staging problem (and, as a corollary, the panning problem), first imagine that the window (shown dashed) is positioned precisely over the central frame buffer. With the window in this position, the problem is simple: just let hardware project the image in the central frame buffer up to the CRT screen. But now notice that if the user moves the viewing window at all, it will partially cover not just one but four frame buffers. Precisely which four buffers are affected can be determined by noting which of the four central vertices is covered. It's easy to see that only one vertex may be covered at a time. Suppose vertex b is covered. This indicates that the viewing window is moving toward the upper right hand corner of the d-map. There's a strong likelihood that frames lying in that vicinity will have to be displayed. This is taken as a cue by the system to mean that the available frame buffers— F_0, F_3, F_6, F_7, and F_8—are to be loaded. Assuming there are procedures for properly loading map frame buffers into the viewing window, the question is: from which d-frames should the frame buffers be loaded? A staging rule that would work in the case illustrated in Figure 8.10(b) is as follows:

If the window covers vertex b, then DF_{11} is materialized into F_0, DF_{12} into F_3, DF_{22} into F_6, DF_{52} into F_7, and DF_{55} into F_8.

Other staging rules can be similarly formulated.

8.6 PICTURE ALGEBRA

To process queries in a relational pictorial database, relational algebra is not sufficient. Therefore, in what follows, a *picture algebra* is described for the pictorial information system. This picture algebra can be implemented as software modules operating on image files, which can be either *logical pictures* or *physical pictures*.

8.6.1 Materialization and Representation Conversion

Picture materialization is used to convert logical pictures into physical pictures or images ready for visualization. Representation conversion is used, for example, to transform the boundary representation of a pixel-filled area to a matrix representation of a linear feature.

Areal Feature

1. `MAT picture1 la picture2 pa "<condition>"`

This command materializes a logically represented area picture (la picture1) into a physically represented area picture (pa picture2) with a certain <condition>. The <condition> clause is optional. If no <condition> is specified, a binary picture is assumed. "la" and "pa" are optional, too. For example: The command "MAT p1 la p2 pa " value > 3 " ", transforms a logical picture p1 into a physical picture p2:

```
p1:         x   y   value
            --------------
            1   1   5
            1   3   3
            1   4   3
            2   1   5              p2:    5  0  0  0
            2   2   5       MAT           5  5  0  0
            2   4   3                     5  5  5  5
            3   1   5       ⟹            5  0  0  0
            3   2   5
            3   3   5
            3   4   5
            4   1   5
            4   4   3
```

As another example, if the command is: "MAT p1 la p2 pa," then the resultant physical picture p2 is:

```
p2:             1  0  1  1
                1  1  0  1
                1  1  1  1
                1  0  0  1
```

2. `DMAT picture1 pa picture2 la "K1"`

The optional domain name "K1" refers to the interpretation of pixel values in the materialized physical picture "picture2." For example: the command "DMAT p1 pa p2 la "landuse" " transforms the physical picture p1 into a logical picture p2:

```
                                          p2:x   y   landuse
p1:    5   0   3   3        DMAT          ---------------
       5   5   0   3                       1     1      5
       5   5   3   3         ⟹             1     3      3
       5   0   3   3                       1     4      3
                                           2     1      5
                                           2     2      5
                                           2     4      3
                                           3     1      5
                                           3     2      5
                                           3     3      3
                                           3     4      3
                                           4     1      5
                                           4     3      3
                                           4     4      3
```

If the command is "DMAT p1 pa p2 la," then the resultant "p2" is similar to the one just shown, without the column with domain descriptor "landuse."

3. `ATB picture1 la picture2 la "<condition>"`
   `ATB picture1 pa picture2 pa "<condition>"`
   `ATB picture1 la picture2 pa "<condition>"`
   `ATB picture1 pa picture2 la "<condition>"`

The various ATB operations convert a fill-in area representation to a boundary representation of the same area.

4. `BTA picture1 la picture2 la "<condition>"`
   `BTA picture1 pa picture2 pa "<condition>"`
   `BTA picture1 la picture2 pa "<condition>"`
   `BTA picture1 pa picture2 la "<condition>"`

The various BTA operations convert a boundary area representation to a fill-in area representation. The following diagram illustrates the relationships among the preceding four types of commands.

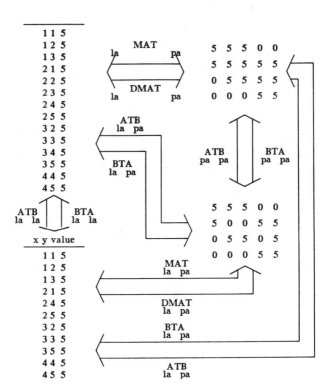

Linear Feature

1. `MAT picture1 ll picture2 pl "<condition>"`

This command materializes a vector format linear feature into a raster image. For example, the command "MAT p1 ll p2 pl" transforms logical picture p1 into physical picture p2:

```
p1:    st-x  st-y  en-x  en-y      MAT          1 1 1 1 1 1 1 1 1 1
       -----------------------     ====>        0 0 0 0 0 0 0 0 0 1
        1     1     1     10                     0 0 0 0 0 0 0 0 0 1
        1     10    5     10                     0 0 0 0 0 0 0 0 0 1
                                                 0 0 0 0 0 0 0 0 0 1
```

2. `DMAT picture1 pl picture2 ll "<condition>"`

This is the inverse operation of 1 just illustrated.

3. `LTA picture1 ll picture2 ll "<condition>"`

LTA is the command to convert a vector formatted linear feature into raster form and then convert it into a logical picture for storage in a relational file. For example, the command "LTA p1 l1 p2 l1" performs the following transformation:

```
p1: as before

p2: x    y
    ─────────
    1    1
    1    2
    1    3
    1    4
    1    5
    1    6
    1    7
    1    8
    1    9
    1    10
    2    10
    3    10
    4    10
    5    10
```

Point Feature

1. `MAT picture1 lp picture2 pp "<condition>"`

2. `DMAT picture1 pp picture2 lp "K1"`

These two commands are similar to the ones defined before.

8.6.2 Geometric Property

Unary Picture Operations.

Areal Feature

1. `AREA picture temp "<condition>"`

This command performs area calculation for pictures (in either logical or physical representation) and stores the result in an elementary relational file "temp." The file "temp" has two domains: picture-name and area.

2. `PERIM picture temp "<condition>"`

This command calculates the perimeter of an areal feature "picture," and the result is stored in an elementary relational file "temp" with two domains: picture-name and perimeter.

3. `CENT picture temp "<condition>"`

This command is used to calculate the centroid of an area picture, and the result is stored in an elementary relational file "temp" with three domains: picture-name and centroid x- and y-coordinates.

4. `LEFT picture1 picture2 "<condition>"`
   `RIGHT picture1 picture2 "<condition>"`
   `TOP picture1 picture2 "<condition>"`
   `BOTTOM picture1 picture2 "<condition>"`

The preceding commands are used to find the different portions of "picture1" with respect to the relative location specified in <condition>, and the result is stored in "picture2". If <condition> is omitted, the centroid location is assumed.

Linear and Point Features

1. `LENGTH picture temp "<condition>"`

This command is used to calculate the length of a line picture and stores the result in an elementary relational file "temp" with two domains: picture-name and length.

2. `LOCATION picture temp "<condition>"`

This command calculates the coordinates of a point picture and stores the result in an elementary relational file "temp" with three domains: picture name, x-coordinate, and y-coordinate.

Spatial Relationship Operations. Spatial relationship operations are employed to retrieve picture objects satisfying certain spatial relationships or to test spatial relationships among picture objects.

1. `WEST picture1 picture2 ... INTO picture0`
   `EAST picture1 picture2 ... INTO picture0`
   `NORTH picture1 picture2 ... INTO picture0`
   `SOUTH picture1 picture2 ... INTO picture0`
   `INSIDE picture1 picture2 ... INTO picture0`
   `TOUCH picture1 picture2 ... INTO picture0`
   `THROUGH picture1 picture2 ... INTO picture0`
   `BETWEEN picture1 picture2 INTO picture0`

These commands are used to find picture objects to the west (east, north, south, inside, touch, through) of "picture1," "picture2," ..., and store the result in picture file "picture0." The elementary relational file corresponding to "picture0" is as follows:

```
picture0:    pictobj
             --------
             highway1
             lake1

                .
                .
                .
```

where picture objects highway1, lake1, ..., are pictures defined in the pictorial database.

2. TESTW picture1 picture2 INTO temp
   TESTE picture1 picture2 INTO temp
   TESTN picture1 picture2 INTO temp
   TESTS picture1 picture2 INTO temp
   TESTI picture1 picture2 INTO temp
   TESTTH picture1 picture2 INTO temp
   TESTTO picture1 picture2 INTO temp
   TESTON picture1 picture2 INTO temp

The elementary relational file "temp" will get a single tuple "TRUE" if "picture2" is located to the west (east, north, south, inside, through, touch, on) of "picture1." Otherwise, it contains "FALSE."

3. DISTANCE picture1 picture2 INTO temp

In this command, "picture1" and "picture2" must be either areal features or point features. If the picture is an areal picture, its centroid will be used in distance calculations. The distance between "picture1" and "picture2" will be stored in an elementary relational file "temp" with distance as the only domain name.

Logical Operations

1. HORC picture1 picture2 ... INTO picture0

This command is the horizontal concatenation operation. This operation is useful when two or more different pictorial files of the same geographic region are to be integrated into a new pictorial file. For example, "vegetation" and "soil-type" features can be combined into a single pictorial file by horizontal concatenation. The new pictorial file has four domains: x-coordinate, y-coordinate, vegetation, and soil-type.

2. VERC picture1 picture2 ... INTO picture0

Vertical concatenation is used to integrate similar pictorial files in two or more different geographic regions. For example, two "soil-type" picture files covering different regions can be combined into one, using vertical concatenation.

3. OVERLAY picture1 picture2 ... INTO picture0 WITH "<condition>"

The <condition> is used to specify the result of common areas among those overlying pictures. Binary operators such as ADD, SUB, DIV, MAX, MIN, AVG, AND, OR, MULT, and XOR can be specified within the <condition>. It should be noted that OVERLAY differs from HORC, in that all feature domains are combined into a single domain (they are all retained as separate domains in the HORC command).

4. `INTERSECT picture1 picture2 ... INTO picture0 WITH "<condition>"`
   `UNION     picture1 picture2 ... INTO picture0 WITH "<condition>"`

After executing this command, the intersection or union of the areas is stored and the result is specified by "<condition>."

Similarity Operation and Vertical Zoom.

1. `SIMILAR picture1 WITH "M1" INTO picture0`

In this command, "M1" is the program to calculate the similarity measure. If "picture1" is an elementary picture file, then this command is equivalent to horizontal zooming. The picture objects similar to "picture1" will be stored in "picture0." If "picture1" consists of several elementary picture files, then this command is equivalent to diagonal zooming. The elementary relational file for "picture0" is

picture0:	pictobj	similarity index
	high1	0.6
	high5	0.2
	.	.
	.	.
	.	.

2. `ZOOMI picture1 temp "<condition>"`
   `ZOOMO picture1 temp "<condition>"`

ZOOMI zooms into detailed representation of "picture"; if it is successful, the relational file "temp" will get the single tuple "TRUE"; otherwise, "FALSE." ZOOMO is the command to go back to a higher level in the pictorial structure.

8.6.3 Transformation

Picture Transformations.

1. `MAG picture1 picture2 scale`

This command magnifies "picture1" into "picture2" by a factor of "scale."

2. TRANS picture1 picture2 transx transy

This command translates "picture1" into "picture2" by moving it (transx,transy).

3. ROT picture1 picture2 rotx roty angle

This command rotates "picture1" into "picture2" by "angle" degree.

Viewing Transformations.

1. WINDOW w1 x1 y1 x2 y2

This command defines a window "w1" of size (x1, y1, x2, y2).

2. MASKI picture1 picture2 WITH w1
   MASKO picture1 picture2 WITH w1

MASKI masks the interior of "picture1" with window "w1" to produce "picture2," and MASKO masks the exterior of "picture1".

3. PAN picture1 picture2 WITH w1 transx transy

This command performs the panning operation. The window "w1" is translated by (transx, transy) and then is used to mask out the exterior of "picture1" to produce "picture2." Thus, it is equivalent to

```
TRANS w1 w2 transx transy
MASKI picture1 picture2 WITH w2
```

Scale Change. Suppose the vegetation data is stored in relation "vgrl." The command,

```
PAINT -v vgrl x y lx ly scale scalex scaley to frame1
```

should have the following effect:

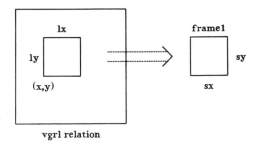

vgrl relation

In other words, the rectangle with its lower left corner at (x, y) and a size of (lx, ly) in the relation "vgrl" is materialized into a frame "frame1" whose real size is (sx, sy), and $sx = lx / scalex$, $sy = ly / scaley$.

In case the clause "scale scalex scaley" is omitted, the default frame size is (lx, ly).

Consequently, we need to store the following information in the header of a picture file:

1. $(x0, y0, Lx, Ly)$—original size of the picture or its minimal enclosing rectangle MER.
2. (x, y, lx, ly)—size of the picture shown in frame.
3. (xw, yw, lxw, lyw)—position and size of viewing window.
4. (sx, sy)—real size of the frame.
5. $(scalex, scaley)$—scale changes.

It should be noted that 1, 2, and 3 are all in terms of coordinates of "logical" pictures. Only 4 represents real frame coordinates.

8.7 THE PICTURE QUERY TRANSLATION SYSTEM

In the previous sections, we have described a generalized zooming technique which can be used for flexible information retrieval and manipulation for a pictorial database system. A typical zooming example could be that we start from a map of the United States and successively zoom into Illinois State and Cook County.

In this section, we describe a picture query language, GRAIN, and the translation algorithm to translate a user's query into picture algebraic statements. First, we discuss the general picture query translation system. An elementary picture query language is discussed in Section 8.7.1. Using this query language to input a pictorial information retrieval request, the concept of files is transparent to the user. In other words, the user need not know how data is stored in the pictorial database and how the picture files are linked. To do this, a pictorial database skeleton which is a condensed or approximate representation of a pictorial database is needed. The description of this pictorial database skeleton which is a model of the pictorial database as understood by the user is given in Section 8.7.2. The translation algorithm and some picture query translation examples are described at the end of this section.

Figure 8.11 shows the general organization of the picture query translation system. In this translation system, the user specifies a picture query in a language called GRAIN, which is similar to the elementary query language (EQL) proposed by Chang and Ke [CHANG78b]. The PQ translator will translate user queries into picture algebra operations according to the syntax rules of GRAIN and the pictorial database skeleton. The pictorial database skeleton includes a pictorial relational schema [CHANG78b] and a pictorial conceptual schema [CHANG79a]. The details of pictorial relational schema and conceptual schema will be described in Section 8.7.2. The detailed flowchart of the PQ translator is illustrated in Figure 8.12.

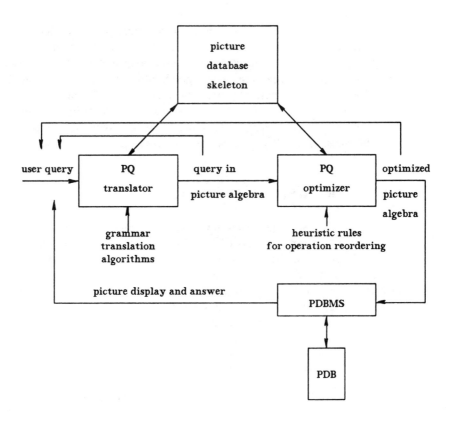

Figure 8.11   The general organization of picture query translator.

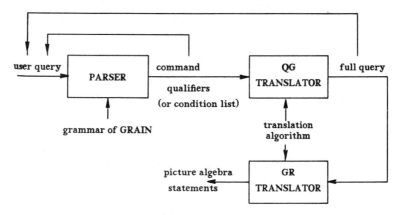

Figure 8.12   The PQ translator.

The user query is first processed by a PARSER routine which translates this query into standard internal form (that is, the internal representation of entities and their relationships). It consists of a command and a list of qualifiers. The PARSER will detect any syntax errors by consulting the grammar of GRAIN. The output of the PARSER is accepted by the QG translator which translates user's input query into a query graph which is a connected graph associating picture files and descriptors. The GR translator then translates this query graph into picture algebraic statements.

The translated picture algebraic statements from GR translator will be accepted by the PQ optimizer which will do tree evaluation according to cost estimation of operations in picture algebra, and reordering of the operation sequence by predefined heuristic rules. Then, it generates the optimized operation sequence ready for execution.

8.7.1 Parser and Syntax of Picture Query

To translate the user's query into the internal representation, we use the restricted pattern matching approach [WEIZENBAUM66, CHANG79a, CHANG78b]. This parser is very simple, since the input language of GRAIN is chosen to guarantee the simplicity of the parser and to provide the user with an easy-to-use interface. The parser is driven by the pictorial database skeleton of the pictorial database. It not only recognizes the query but also analyzes its syntactic structure.

A typical picture query language in GRAIN has the following structure:

a. $get \begin{bmatrix} all \\ <descriptor-list> \end{bmatrix}$; <condition-list>; into <relation-name>.

b. $\begin{bmatrix} paint \\ sketch \end{bmatrix} \begin{bmatrix} picture \\ <picture-relational-file> \end{bmatrix}$; <condition-list>; into <frame-name>.

c. show   <frame-name>

d. load   <database-name>

The keyword "get" is used to retrieve information associated with part or all attribute descriptors of picture objects which satisfy the condition specified in the query. The result is displayed in tabular form. No picture object's shape or geometrical description is shown in graphical or image form. The keywords "paint" and "sketch" are used to sketch picture objects in graphical form or to paint picture objects in image form. If the statement "into frame-name" is included, the picture objects satisfying the query condition will be stored in a frame instead of being displayed on the graphical terminal. Later, this frame can be referred to or displayed by using the keyword "show." Since the overall structure of the pictorial database is organized hierarchically to zoom into detailed picture objects at different levels of the pictorial database, the keyword "load" is used to load a database node and change it to active status.

A typical condition list is of the following form:

$$\begin{bmatrix} similar \\ spatial/structural \\ keyword \\ not \end{bmatrix} \begin{bmatrix} <descriptor> \\ <descriptor><opr>... \\ <literal> \end{bmatrix} \text{ using <program-name>}$$

In GRAIN, a user's query is a sequence of statements separated by semicolons and terminated by a period.

8.7.2 Pictorial Database Skeleton

The concept of a database skeleton has been applied to the translation of an elementary query language for the relational database [CHANG78b]. This database skeleton is a condensed description of a database which reflects the user's understanding of the data and the intended use of the database. It contains the functional relations among database entities, the semantic relations among database entities, and the contents description of database entities. These database entities include relational files and attribute descriptors. To take into account the special characteristics of picture data in the pictorial database, the concept of the database skeleton has been extended to form the pictorial database skeleton. This pictorial database skeleton will be considered a model of a pictorial database. In addition to the preceding interrelationships among database entities, the pictorial database skeleton keeps track of more information such as spatial relations, structural relations, and similarity relations among pictorial database entities.

In [CHANG78a,78b], an information graph is used to represent the essential semantic/functional relation of a database skeleton. A pictorial information graph for an example of a pictorial database is illustrated in Figure 8.13. A map corresponding to this pictorial database is shown in Figure 8.14. In Figure 8.13, attributed descriptions of picture objects are stored in relations RIVER, BRIDGE, HIGHWAY, CITY, and their geometrical descriptions are stored in LIN_RIVER, POIBRID, LIN_HIGH, and REG_CITY, respectively. The relation POT (picture object table) stores all picture objects and their types (linear, areal, or point).

In Figure 8.13, the relations ON and THROUGH are two spatial relations which could be generated by invoking spatial operators of the picture algebra before this pictorial database skeleton has been created. The other spatial relations may not exist. For example, the intersection relation between rivers and highways does not exist in the current pictorial database skeleton. If a picture query mentions the intersection relation among rivers and highways, then picture algebra command "INTERSECT" should be executed to perform the necessary spatial analysis. The functional relations in this diagram include: r<d>, the dependency relation; r<fd>, the full dependency relation; r<eq>, the equivalence relation; r<c>, the containment relation; and r<s>, the attribute similarity relation. The spatial relation in this information graph can be represented as a semantic network. For example, the relational file "ON" lists the bridges (bname) on the rivers (rname), so that the descriptors "bname" and "rname" have a semantic relation "ON." Conversely, descriptors "rname" and "bname" have a semantic relation "UNDER."

There is a special relation between attribute descriptor and relational file r<ar> in the information graph of Figure 8.13, indicated by a heavy line. Since the description of picture objects usually includes both attributed and geometrical description, two separate relational files are used to store this information. Where to find this information is important for the pictorial query translator, because the user's query may involve attributed description or geometrical description or both. For example, if a user asks about the area size of a city, and this information is not stored in its attributed description relational file, then the picture operation, AREA, should be executed, which finds the geometrical relational file of this city to apply Simpson's rule for area calculation (or to apply other methods of calculating area). Therefore, whenever spa-

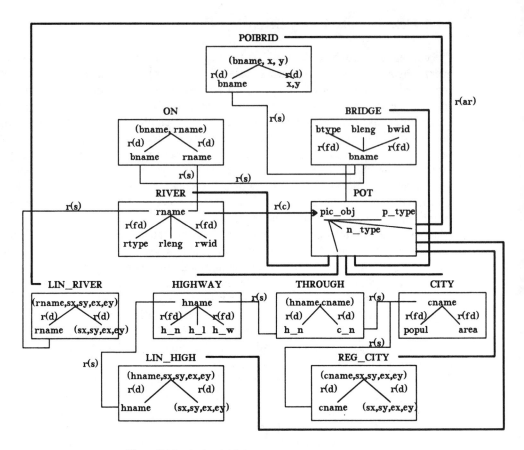

Figure 8.13 A pictorial information graph of example pictorial database.

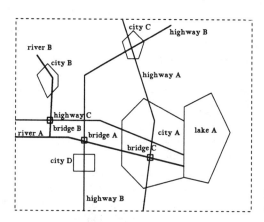

Figure 8.14 A map of example pictorial database.

tial analysis and similarity computation are needed, this special relation r<ar> should be maintained.

If the spatial relational files, similarity index relational files, and picture-oriented attribute descriptors do not exist in the pictorial database, then the information graph representing pictorial relational schema (PRS) does not contain enough information for pictorial elementary query translation. The D-type conceptual graph representing pictorial conceptual schema (PCS) needs to be introduced [CHANG79a]. This D-type conceptual graph can be used to represent a mathematical function, a predicate, or a derivation rule. Figure 8.15 illustrates several D-type (data-flow) conceptual graphs.

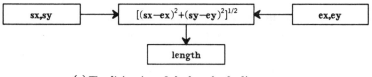

(a) The dirivation of the length of a line segment

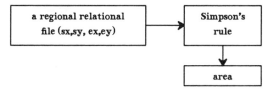

(b) The derivation of the area of a region

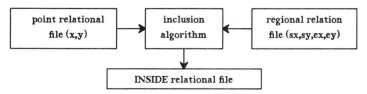

(c) The derivation of INSIDE relational file.

Figure 8.15   Three examples of D-type conceptual graphs.

8.7.3 GRAIN Translation Algorithm and Query Examples

In the picture query language translation system, we classify pictorial information retrieval into four categories: attribute, spatial/structural, similarity, and complex retrieval. The complex retrieval for pictorial information is the combination of attribute retrieval, spatial/structural retrieval, and similarity retrieval. Some examples will be illustrated in the following section.

Attribute Retrieval.   In attribute retrieval, picture objects are retrieved by their logical attributes. These attributes may physically exist in certain relational files, or they may be virtual attributes defined by D-type conceptual graphs. If an attribute is a virtual attribute, during attribute retrieval some calculation involving picture algebra is needed. For example, the following query retrieves attributes of a picture object with the name 'cityc':

```
get popul, area; pictobj equal 'cityc'.
```

The foregoing query can be translated using similar techniques as that for elementary query translation [CHANG78b]. In order to sketch the line drawing for picture object with city name (cname) equal to 'cityc', the picture query is:

```
sketch picture; cname equal 'cityc'.
```

Spatial/Structural Retrieval.   In spatial/structural retrieval, picture objects are retrieved by spatial relation and/or structural properties. The structure of a picture object is specified by its component/container. The spatial relations among picture objects are: intersection, through, adjacency, and so on. The following query is used to retrieve the highways passing through two cities:

```
sketch highway; through (cname equal 'cityd'
and cname equal 'cityc').
```

To sketch the city adjacent to a given lake, the query is

```
sketch city; adjacent (lname equal 'lakea').
```

Similarity Retrieval.   Similarity retrieval can be used to retrieve picture objects which are similar to a given picture object using certain similarity measures. For example, to retrieve all highways similar to a given highway 'highc', the query is:

```
sketch highway; similar (hname equal 'highc') using 'M1'.
```

If the similarity relation does not exist, the procedure "M1," will be executed to measure similarity.

Complex Retrieval.   As just mentioned, this retrieval is the combination of the preceding three types of retrieval commands. For example, to sketch the city whose area is greater than '500' and located to the west of a given city 'cityb', the query is

```
sketch city; west (cname equal 'cityb') and area greater than '500'.
```

By analyzing the characteristics of these retrieval commands, the overall strategy for translation of pictorial queries is presented in Figure 8.16.

Some examples of picture queries specified in the natural language, GRAIN, and picture algebra are listed next:

Q1. Display the soil type of the area occupied by a coniferous forest.

GRAIN:
```
paint picture; soil.x similar to forest.x; soil.y similar to forest.y;
forest.type equal to 'coniferous';
```

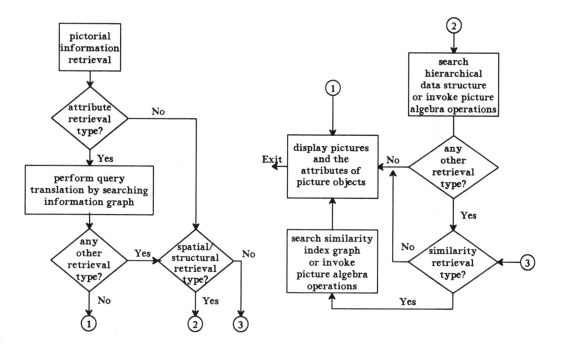

Figure 8.16　Translation strategy.

Picture Algebra:

```
RESTRICT t1 = forest<type=='coniferous'>
PROJECT t2 = t1[x, y]
JOIN t3 = t2 (*x, y) soil
PAINT t3
ERASE t1, t2, t3
```

Q2. Display the portion of a highway 'h1' within a city 'c1' boundary.

GRAIN:

```
paint highway; highway equal to 'h1'; within (city equal to 'c1');
```

Picture Algebra:

```
RESTRICT t1 = lin_high<hname=='h1'>
LTA t1 t2
RESTRICT t3 = reg_city<cname=='c1'>
BTA t3 t4
JOIN t5 = t2 (*x, y) t4
PAINT t5
ERASE t1, t2, t3, t4, t5
```

Q3. Get all highways passing through a city 'c1' boundary.

GRAIN:

```
get highway; through (city equal to 'c1')
```

Picture Algebra:

```
PROJECT t1 = highway[hname]
RESTRICT t2 = city<cname=='c1'>
THROUGH t1 t2 INTO t4
PRINT t4
ERASE t1, t2, t3, t4
```

Q4. Get all picture objects which are to the west of object 'w1' and the area of each object is greater than '100'.

GRAIN:

```
get picture; west (object equal to 'w1'); area greater than '100';
```

Picture Algebra:

```
RESTRICT t1 = pot<data_type=='areal'>
AREA t1 t2
RESTRICT t3 = t2<area ≥ '100'>
PROJECT t4 = t3[pic-obj]
WEST w1 t5
PROJECT t6 = t5[pic-obj]
JOIN t7 = t4 (*pic-obj) t6
PRINT t7
ERASE t1, t2, t3, t4, t5, t6, t7
```

Finally, we illustrate panning and zooming operations in GRAIN.

Panning. To pan around a certain portion of land occupied by forest, the command is

```
paint picture; name equal 'forest'; (forest.x less than or equal '40') and
(forest.x greater than or equal '70') and (forest.y less than or equal '20')
and (forest.y greater than or equal '30').
```

Zooming. Three kinds of zoom—horizontal zoom, vertical zoom and diagonal zoom—are supported:

1. Horizontal Zoom (H-zoom): To select the land occupied by coniferous forest and mixed forest, the commands are

```
paint picture; name equal 'forest'; forest.class greater than '1'.
```

2. Vertical Zoom (V-zoom): For V-zoom within a map, it is almost the same as panning transformation, except that the origin and coordinate spacing should be specified.

```
paint picture; name equal 'forest'; (forest.x greater than or equal '20') and
(forest.x less than or equal '40') and (forest.y greater than
or equal '10') and (forest.y less than or equal '30'); ((forest.x minus
'2') mod '2') equal '0'; ((forest.y minus '4') mod '2') equal 0.
```

For V-zoom on enlargeable picture objects, we first select a picture object and then load a new d-map corresponding to that picture object.

```
load CITY-A.
sketch picture.
```

3. Diagonal Zoom (D-zoom): This is the generalized H-zoom operation. This transformation finds all picture objects which are similar to a group of picture objects. For example, to find all highways which are similar to two highways 'h1' or 'h2', the command is

```
get picture; similar (highway.name equal 'h1') or similar
(highway.name equal 'h2') using 'M2'; into TEMP.
```

R E F E R E N C E S

[CHANG80] CHANG, DAVID, AND S. K. CHANG, "Frame Staging Techniques for Pictorial Database," *Technical Report,* Knowledge Systems Laboratory, University of Illinois at Chicago Circle, 1980.

[CHANG79a] CHANG, S. K., AND K. S. KE, "Translation of Fuzzy Queries for Relational Database System," *IEEE Trans. on Pattern Analysis and Machine Intelligence,* Vol. PAMI-1, No. 3, IEEE Computer Society, July 1979, 281-294.

[CHANG79b] CHANG, S. K., B. S. LIN, AND R. WALSER, "A Generalized Zooming Technique for Pictorial Database Systems," *Proceedings of National Computer Conference, AFIPS,* Vol. 48, 1979, 147-156.

[CHANG78a] CHANG, S. K., AND W. H. CHENG, "Database Skeleton and Its Application to Logical Database Synthesis," *IEEE Trans. on Software Engineering,* Vol. SE-4, No. 1, IEEE Computer Society, January 1978, 18-30.

[CHANG78b] CHANG, S. K., AND J. S. KE, "Database Skeleton and Its Application to Fuzzy Language Translation," *IEEE Trans. on Software Engineering,* Vol. SE-4, No. 1, IEEE Computer Society. January 1978, 31-44.

[CHANG78c] CHANG, S. K., J. REUSS, AND B. H. MCCORMICK, "Design Considerations of a Pictorial Database System," *International Journal on Policy Analysis and Information Systems,* Vol. 1, No. 2, Knowledge Systems Laboratory, UICC, January 1978, 49-70.

[CHANG77] CHANG, S. K., J. REUSS, AND B. H. MCCORMICK, "An Integrated Relational Database System for Pictures," *Proceedings of IEEE Workshop on Picture Data Description and Management,* IEEE Computer Society, 1977, 49-60.

[CHANG76] CHANG, S.K., M. O'BRIEN, J. READ, R. BOROVEC, W.H. CHENG, AND J.S. KE, "Design Considerations of a Database System in a Clinical Network Environment," *Proc. of National Computer Conference,* New York, June 1976, 277-286.

[CHANG76] CHANG, T.L., "Similarity Measures," *Proceedings of Third International Joint Conference on Pattern Recognition,* San Diego, California, November 1976.

[CODD70] CODD, E.F., "A Relational Model of Data for Large Shared Data Banks," *Communications of the ACM.,* Vol. 13, No. 6, June 1970.

[FU74] FU, K.S., *Syntactic Methods in Pattern Recognition.* Academic Press, 1974.

[KUNII74] KUNII, T., S. WEYL, AND J.M. TENENBAUM, "A Relational Database Schema for Describing Complex Pictures with Color and Texture," *Proceedings of the Second International Joint Conference on Pattern Recognition,* Lyngby-Copenhagen, Denmark, August 1974.

[McKEOWN77] McKEOWN, JR., D.M., AND D.R. REDDY, "A Hierarchical Symbolic Representation for an Image Database," *Proceedings of IEEE Workshop on Picture Data Description and Management,* Chicago, April 21-22, 1977, 40-44.

[REUSS77a] REUSS, J.L., "Introduction to the Image Store Management System," *Technical Report,* Knowledge Systems Laboratory, University of Illinois at Chicago Circle, March 1, 1977.

[REUSS77b] REUSS, J.L., S.K. CHANG, AND B.H. McCORMICK, "Paging Techniques for a Pictorial Database," *Technical Report,* Knowledge Systems Laboratory, University of Illinois at Chicago Circle, June 15, 1977.

[WALSER78] WALSER, R., ET AL., "RAIN Version 2 Specification," *Technical Report of Knowledge Systems Laboratory,* KSL-20, September 1978.

[WEIZENBAUM66] WEIZENBAUM, J., "ELIZA—A Computer Program for the Study of Natural Language Communication Between Man and Machine," *Comm. ACM,* Vol. 9, No. 1, ACM, January 1966, 36-45.

E X E R C I S E S

1. Explain differences among the following: vertical zoom, horizontal zoom, diagonal zoom.

2. Give the definition of an elementary file EF with descriptors, A, B, C, and D, such that every record in EF has A greater than 500; all records of B equal to 'Y' can be retrieved by any user; and the only user allowed to delete and/or modify records is 'JONES'.

3. Explain what condition(s) must be satisfied for a tuple to be inserted in composite relational files.

4. How is a database file self-descriptive?

5. Explain the difference between logical vs. physical picture.

6. What is a map set?

7. What is the panning problem?

8. What is a database skeleton?

9. Explain the difference between an attribute retrieval and a similarity retrieval.

10. Write the following query in the GRAIN language:

> Find all the farms which are to the east of a river *and*
> the area of farm land is less than 100 acres.

Chapter 9

Indexing and Abstraction

In chapter eight, we went through nearly all aspects of pictorial database design by describing an example—the DIMAP system. Emphasis was put on basic concepts and implementation. In this chapter, we present an approach for picture indexing and abstraction in a more formal and theoretical way. The concepts logical picture and physical picture were introduced in previous chapters; we will formally define them here. Picture query language for the DIMAP system was described in the last chapter; we will give the general view of the picture query here in this chapter. Picture indexing facilitates information retrieval from a pictorial database consisting of picture objects and picture relations. To construct picture indexes, abstraction operations to perform picture object clustering and classification are formulated. To substantiate the abstraction operations, we also formalize syntactic and semantic abstraction rules. We then illustrate, using examples, how to apply these abstraction operations to obtain various picture indexes and how to construct icons to facilitate accessing of pictorial data.

In traditional database systems, the use of indexing to facilitate database accessing has been well established. Although there were suggestions to use picture icons as picture indexes [TANIMOTO76], no theoretical framework has been established for picture indexing. In this chapter, we attempt to provide such a conceptual framework for picture abstraction, indexing, and retrieval.

In Section 9.1, picture objects, picture relations and logical pictures are introduced. In Section 9.2, we discuss picture query. Section 9.3 presents structured picture retrieval using picture trees. Examples are presented to illustrate the concept of picture indexing. In Section 9.4, two types of abstraction operations are introduced. Type-1 abstraction performs clustering and indexing, and type-2 abstraction performs classification and cross-indexing. Conceptually, type-1 abstraction performs generalization and integration, and type-2 abstraction performs differentiation. They can be recursively applied to obtain various picture indexes. In Sections 9.5 and 9.6, we present abstraction rules, which include both syntactic and semantic abstraction rules. In Section 9.7, we illustrate by example how to construct icons to facilitate accessing of pictorial data, and theorems showing abstraction rules are "sound" and "characteristic", and are proven in Section 9.8.

9.1 THE LOGICAL PICTURE

Researchers in image processing and pattern recognition have traditionally regarded pictures as two-dimensional arrays of pixels (or picture elements), which are called *physical pictures* in this chapter. Instead of such physical pictures, *logical pictures* are stored in the pictorial database. Physical pictures can either be stored in a separate image store or converted into logical picture representation. Logical pictures consist of picture objects and relational objects. We begin by defining picture objects.

A *picture object* consists of a set of attribute triples: (attribute-name, attribute-value, evaluation-rule). Attribute-name and attribute-value need no further explanation. The purpose of the eval-rule will be explained later. A picture object v always has a *type* attribute (or attribute set), which is the classification category of that object, and a *name* attribute (or attribute set), which is the unique identifier of that object. Other attributes are optional. A *picture object class* $V = \{v_1, v_2, ..., v_n\}$ is a set of picture objects having the same type. Therefore a picture object class always has a unique type.

As an example, $v = \{$(type, "river", eval-rule), (name, "Kwei", eval-rule), (pp,*,eval-rule)$\}$, refers to a picture object of type "river" whose name is "Kwei" and whose physical picture attribute is pp. The physical picture attribute pp is really a pointer. The physical picture can be accessed by invoking the eval-rule, which retrieves the corresponding physical picture from an image store and presents it to the user [CHANG79]. For the other two attributes, the eval-rule simply presents the attribute values as strings to the user.

As another example, the picture objects v_i are pixels, and $v_i = \{$(type,"pixel",eval-rule), $(x,x_i,$eval-rule), $(y,y_i,$eval-rule), $(c,f(x_i, y_i),$eval-rule)$\}$, where (x,y) is name of the pixel, and $f(x_i, y_i)$ is the pixel value at point (x,y). The pixel set

$$\{ v_i : v_i.type = pixel \land 1 \leq v_i.x \land v_i.x \leq 256 \land 1 \leq v_i.y \land v_i.y \leq 256 \}$$

is a picture object class. Depending on the keyword in the picture query (see Section 9.2), the evaluation rule can present the pixels in either numerical or gray-level form.

The foregoing examples illustrate the first use of the evaluation rule: when an attribute value is specified, the evaluation rule is invoked to interpret it and present it to the user. The second use of the evaluation rule is to interpret virtual attributes. When an attribute value is unspecified (as indicated by a question mark), the evaluation rule is invoked to evaluate it.

An attribute is *real* if its attribute value is specified. Otherwise it is *virtual*. A picture object is real if all its attributes are real. Otherwise it is virtual.

Virtual attributes and virtual objects are very useful in pictorial information systems, because it is often time consuming to extract all relevant information from the physical pictures beforehand. Virtual attributes allow the user to leave these attributes unspecified. When such virtual attributes are referenced, the evaluation rule is invoked to evaluate them, sometimes by invoking image processing algorithms to extract new information from the physical pictures, and sometimes by combining other real attribute values. The D-type conceptual graph discussed in Section 8.7.2 serves the same purpose.

As an example, the name attribute can be defined as a virtual attribute composed from other attributes. For example, to define a pixel object, we have $v = \{(\text{type},\text{"pixel"}, \text{eval-rule}), (\text{name}, ?, \text{equal}(x,y)), (x, 10, \text{eval-rule}), (y, 2, \text{eval-rule}), (c, 5, \text{eval-rule})\}$, and the name attribute is really the combination of the x and y coordinates of the pixel. The evaluation rule specifies name is equal to (x,y). It is therefore a virtual attribute.

A relational object also consists of a set of attribute triples: (attribute-name, attribute-value, eval-rule). Again, an attribute is interpreted if its value is specified and is evaluated if its value is unspecified.

A relational object always has a *type* attribute (or attribute set), which characterizes this relation, and a *name* attribute (or attribute set), which is unique for this relation. Other attributes are optional. The relational object's name can also be a virtual attribute defined in terms of other attributes. Usually the name is specified by a list of (type,name) pairs for picture objects entering that relationship.

As an example of a relational object, to define "bridge $b1$ is over river Kwei," we have $r = \{(\text{type},\text{"over"}, \text{eval-rule}), (\text{name}, ?, \text{equal}(\text{type1},\text{name1},\text{type2},\text{name2})), (\text{type1},\text{"bridge"}, \text{eval-rule}), (\text{name1},\text{"b1"}, \text{eval-rule}), (\text{type2},\text{"river"}, \text{eval-rule}), (\text{name2},\text{"Kwei"}, \text{eval-rule})\}$. In this example, name is a virtual attribute defined as (type1,name1, type2,name2). If there is no confusion about types, we may define a relational object's name as (name1, name2). On the other hand, if we are specifying a relation among picture object classes, we can define a relational object's name as (type1,type2).

A relational object class is a set of relational objects having the same type. For example, several relational objects having the same type "over" can be grouped into a relational object class.

A *logical picture* consists of a collection of picture objects V and a collection of relational objects R.

9.2 PICTURE QUERY

We now describe the retrieval of picture objects from logical pictures. First we present the concept of the picture query set and the picture query.

A *picture query set QS* is a subset of a collection of picture objects V. In other words, QS is the set of picture objects to be retrieved. In the picture query language, the query set QS is usually specified by a picture query Q.

A *picture predicate Q* is a logical function from V to $\{0, 1\}$. Q induces a partition of V into two subsets: $QS = \{v_i : Q(v_i) = 1\}$ and $QN = \{v_i : Q(v_i) = 0\}$. A *picture query Q* uses a picture predicate to specify QS, its corresponding picture query set.

The picture predicate of a picture query can be specified as a conjunction of logical clauses relating attributes and their values [CHANG79]. The retrieval target of a picture query is specified in the "get" clause, "sketch" clause, or "paint" clause. The keyword "get" means to retrieve the picture query set. The keyword "sketch" will produce a line drawing from the retrieved picture query set. The keyword "paint" will generate a raster image from the retrieved picture query set. Several examples will be presented soon. In these examples, we will write (attribute-name, attribute-value) instead of (attribute-name, attribute-value, eval-rule), whenever a standard evaluation rule is assumed.

Example 1

Get the bridge over the river Kwei.

Query 1: get w_1 ; w_1 is "bridge"; w_1 over w_2 ; w_2 is "river"; w_2.name is "Kwei".

In the foregoing query, (w_1 is "bridge") is a shorthand notation for (w_1.type is "bridge"). (w_1 over w_2) is a shorthand notation for (r.type is "over"; r.name1 is w_1.name; r.name2 is w_2.name). Therefore, the above query in set-theoretic notation is:

$$\{w_1 :(\exists r)(\exists w_2)(w_1.type=bridge) \wedge (r.type=over) \wedge (r.name1=v_1.name)$$

$$\wedge (r.name2=w_2.name) \wedge (w_2.type=river) \wedge (w_2.name=Kwei)\}$$

If we allow for the substitution of picture object variables by their types, then the preceding query can be expressed more concisely as:

Query 2: get bridge; bridge over river; river.name is "Kwei".

The pictorial database contains the following picture objects and relational objects:

```
v₁{(type,"bridge"),(name,"b1"),(x,10),(y,13)}
v₂{(type,"bridge"),(name,"b2"),(x,20),(y,14)}
v₃{(type,"river"),(name,"Kwei"),(pp,*)}
v₄{(type,"river"),(name,"MeiKong"),(pp,*)}
r₁{(type,"over"),(name1,"b1"),(name2,"Kwei")}
r₂{(type,"over"),(name1,"b2"),(name2,"MeiKong")}
```

In r_1 and r_2, we have omitted the definition of virtual attribute name as (name1,name2), which can be accomplished by adding the virtual attribute, (name,?,equal(name1, name2)).

Example 2

Display the little house on the prairie.

Query 1: sketch w_1 ; w_1 is "house"; w_1.size is "little"; w_1 *on* w_2 ; w_2 is "prairie".
or more concisely

Query 2: sketch house; house.size is "little"; house on prairie.

Example 3

Zoom into a raster picture at resolution factor 2 and display the portion inside window (0,5; 0,5).

Query 1: paint w_1; w_1 is "pixel"; $w_1.r$ is 2; $0 \leq w_1.x$; $w_1.x \leq 5$; $0 \leq w_1.y$; $w_1.y \leq 5$.

or more concisely

Query 2: paint pixel; pixel.r is 2; 0≤pixel.x; pixel.x≤5; 0≤pixel.y; pixel.y≤5.

Since a hierarchical data structure seems to be the most natural in many image processing applications [CHIEN80], we next describe a picture tree which is a structured collection of logical pictures. To illustrate the concept of a picture tree, we present another example.

Example 4

Display the countries in Europe having cities with population over 100,000.

Query 1: sketch w_1; w_1 is "country"; w_1 *in* w_2; $w_2.type$ is "continent"; $w_2.name$ is "Europe"; w_1 contain w_3; w_3 is "city"; $w_3.population \geq 100000$.

or more concisely

Query 2: sketch country; country in continent; continent.name is "Europe"; country contain city; city.population $\geq$ 100000.

The database contains the following picture objects and relational objects:

NODE H_1:

v_1 {(type,"node"),(name,"H$_1$"),(x$_1$,1),(y$_1$,1),(x$_1$,1000),(y$_2$,1000),(pp,*)}

v_2 {(type,"continent"),(name,"Europe"),(pp,*)}

r_1 {(type,"contain"),(name1,"H$_1$"),(name2,"H$_2$")}

r_2 {(type,"contain"),(name1,"H$_2$"),(name2,"Europe")}

NODE H_2:

v_3 {(type,"node"),(name,"H$_2$"),(x$_1$,1),(y$_1$,1),(x$_2$,500),(y$_2$,500),(pp,*)}

v_4 {(type,"country"),(name,"France"),(pp,*)}

v_5 {(type,"country"),(name,"Germany"),(pp,*)}

r_3 {(type,"contain"),(name1,"H$_2$"),(name2,"H$_3$")}

r_4 {(type,"contain"),(name1,"H$_2$"),(name2,"H$_4$")}

r_5 {(type,"contain"),(name1,"H$_3$"),(name2,"France")}

r_6 {(type,"contain"),(name1,"H$_4$"),(name2,"Germany")}

r_7 {(type,"contain"),(name1,"Europe"),(name2,"France")}

r_8 {(type,"contain"),(name1,"Europe"),(name2,"Germany")}

NODE H_3:

v_6 {(type,"node"),(name,"H$_3$"),(x$_1$,1),(y$_1$,1),(x$_2$,260),(y$_2$,500),(pp,*)}

v_7 {(type,"city"),(name,"Paris"),(population,1000000),(pp,*)}

r_9 {(type,"contain"),(name1,"H$_3$"),(name2,"Paris")}

r_{10} {(type,"contain"),(name1,"France"),(name2,"Paris")}

NODE H_4:

v_8 { (type,"node"),(name,"H_4"),(x_1,240),(y_1,1),(x_2,500),(y_2,500),(pp,*) }

v_9 { (type,"city"),(name,"Bonn"),(population,800000),(pp,*) }

r_{11} { (type,"contain"),(name1,"H_4"),(name2,"Bonn") }

r_{12} { (type,"contain"),(name1,"Germany"),(name2,"Bonn") }

In the foregoing, the database consists of four collections of picture objects and relational objects, each being associated with a node in a *picture tree* PT, as illustrated in Figure 9.1. Intuitively, we can visualize a picture tree as a hierarchical tree structure with pictorial information (picture objects and relational objects) associated with each node in the tree.

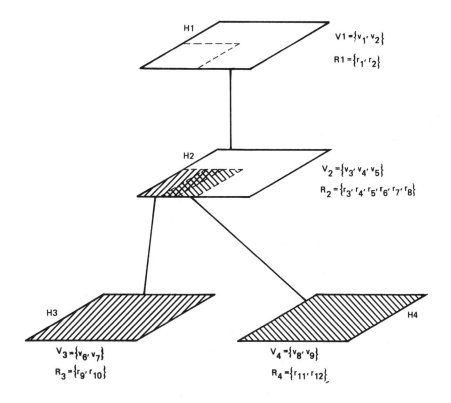

Figure 9.1 Picture tree for Europe database.

9.3 PICTURE INDEX

Given a picture query Q, the pictorial information retrieval problem then is to find QS, the picture query set, by searching the picture tree PT. To facilitate searching, we can conceptually transform a picture tree into a picture query tree as follows. Suppose H_i is a node in a picture tree. Let V_i be the collection of picture objects which can be retrieved from H_i, PS_i be the collection of picture objects which can be retrieved from the subtree with root node H_i, and P_i be the picture predicate corresponding to PS_i. A *picture query tree QT* is a tree having the same structure as the picture tree. Each node H_k of the query tree is of the following form:

$$H_k \ (P_{k1}, P_{k2}, ..., P_{k(mk)})$$

where mk is the number of successor nodes of H_k, and P_{ki} is the picture predicate corresponding to PS_{ki} for successor node H_{ki}. If $km = 0$, then H_k does not have any successor node. It can be seen that PS_1, the collection of picture objects retrievable from the tree with root node H_1, is the union of the V_i's. In other words, $PS_1 = V$.

Intuitively, the picture predicates P_{ki} in the picture query tree can be used to identify subtrees of interest. An example is illustrated in Figure 9.2. Figure 9.2(a) shows the picture tree. The collection of picture objects is

$$V = \{v_i : 1 \leq v_i.x_i \wedge v_i.x_i \leq 4 \wedge 1 \leq v_i.y_i \wedge v_i.y_i \leq 4\}$$

where each v_i is of the form $v_i\{(type,"pixel"), (x,x_i), (y,y_i), (c,f(x_i,y_i))\}$. The V_i's and PS_i's are

$$
\begin{aligned}
PS_1 &= V \\
V_1 &= \{\} \\
PS_2 &= V_2 = \{v_{13}, v_{14}, v_{23}, v_{24}\} \\
PS_3 &= \{v_{11}, v_{12}, v_{21}, v_{22}\} \\
V_3 &= \{\} \\
PS_4 &= V_4 = \{v_{31}, v_{32}, v_{41}, v_{42}\} \\
PS_5 &= V_5 = \{v_{33}, v_{34}, v_{43}, v_{44}\} \\
PS_6 &= V_6 = \{v_{12}\} \\
PS_7 &= V_7 = \{v_{11}\} \\
PS_8 &= V_8 = \{v_{22}\} \\
PS_9 &= V_8 = \{v_{21}\}
\end{aligned}
$$

The picture query tree is illustrated in Figure 9.2(b), and the picture predicates are

$$
\begin{aligned}
P_2 &= (v.type = pixel) \wedge (1 \leq v.x) \wedge (v.x \leq 2) \wedge (3 \leq v.y) \wedge (v.y \leq 4) \\
P_3 &= (v.type = pixel) \wedge (1 \leq v.x) \wedge (v.x \leq 2) \wedge (1 \leq v.y) \wedge (v.y \leq 2) \\
P_4 &= (v.type = pixel) \wedge (3 \leq v.x) \wedge (v.x \leq 4) \wedge (1 \leq v.y) \wedge (v.y \leq 2) \\
P_5 &= (v.type = pixel) \wedge (3 \leq v.x) \wedge (v.x \leq 4) \wedge (3 \leq v.y) \wedge (v.y \leq 4) \\
P_6 &= (v.type = pixel) \wedge (v.x = 1) \wedge (v.y = 2) \\
P_7 &= (v.type = pixel) \wedge (v.x = 1) \wedge (v.y = 1) \\
P_8 &= (v.type = pixel) \wedge (v.x = 2) \wedge (v.y = 2) \\
P_9 &= (v.type = pixel) \wedge (v.x = 2) \wedge (v.y = 1)
\end{aligned}
$$

A picture predicate P_i is not uniquely determined by the corresponding PS_i. The picture predicates just listed are only examples. It suffices that PS_i' corresponding to P_i includes PS_i.

To process a query Q, the picture query tree is searched recursively. The picture predicate P_{ki} associated with each node of the picture query tree is used to limit the search process. Initially, the *target set* TS is empty, and the root node is retrieved. For a node H_k, if $mk > 0$, then any successor node H_{ki} with nonempty intersection of P_{ki}

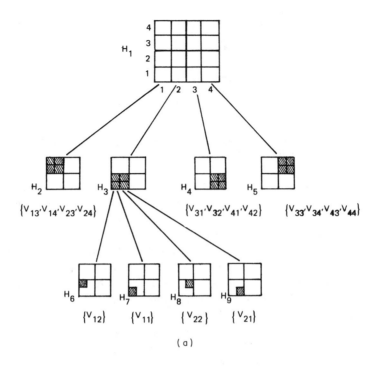

$$\{v_{13}, v_{14}, v_{23}, v_{24}\} \qquad \{v_{31}, v_{32}, v_{41}, v_{42}\} \qquad \{v_{33}, v_{34}, v_{43}, v_{44}\}$$

$$\{v_{12}\} \qquad \{v_{11}\} \qquad \{v_{22}\} \qquad \{v_{21}\}$$

(a)

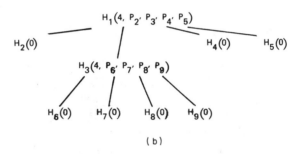

(b)

Figure 9.2 An example of (a) picture tree and (b) query tree.

and Q will be searched. Each time a node H_i is searched, TS is set to the union of previous TS and V_i. Finally, $QS = Q(TS) = \{v : v$ is in TS and $Q(v) = 1\}$.

In the preceding example, if the query Q is ((v.type="pixel") $\wedge$ (v.x ≤ 1)), then only nodes H_1, H_2, H_3, H_6, and H_7 need be searched. $TS = \{v_{11}, v_{12}, v_{13}, v_{14}, v_{23}, v_{24}\}$, and $QS = \{v_{11}, v_{12}, v_{13}, v_{14}\}$. Therefore, how to choose P_{ki} is important for limiting the search process.

The foregoing example suggests the concept of a *picture index*. In Webster's Third New International Dictionary (1971 Edition), "index" has the following definitions (among others):

1. A usually alphabetical list that includes all or nearly all items considered of special pertinence and fully or partially covered or merely mentioned in a printed or written work, that gives with each item the place where it may be found in the work;

2. Something that serves as a pointer or indicator;

3. Something in another (person or) thing that leads an observer to surmise a particular fact or draw a particular conclusion;

4. A sign whose specific character is causally dependent on the object to which it refers but independent of an interpretant.

The usual concept of an index in computer science is a combination of Webster's definitions 1 and 2. If we also consider Webster's definitions 3 and 4, we can see that the picture predicates associated with a node in the picture query tree can be considered picture indexes, because they can be used to surmise a fact or draw a conclusion about a picture and are at the same time dependent on the picture but independent of any interpretations. In other words, the picture index is used to help *focus* the search process to relevant subtrees. In a picture tree, at every node we can construct a picture index based on information contained in the subtree. The result is the picture query tree just described.

An index therefore has two meanings. In the pictorial database, it is an *index object* which is a relational object relating picture object classes. In pictorial information retrieval, this index object defines a *picture predicate*. Two general abstraction operations to construct a picture index will be described in the next section.

9.4 PICTURE INDEXING BY ABSTRACTION

Indexing is closely related to abstraction, which can be defined as the process of constructing new concepts from a given collection of concepts. Abstraction is a method of generating indexes. In the context of this chapter, we are interested in constructing new objects from a given collection of objects. The constructed objects can be subject to another level of abstraction operation, and so on.

Suppose we have picture objects $v_i \{(A_1, a_1), ..., (A_n, a_n), (X_1, x_{i1}), ..., (X_m, x_{im})\}$, where the a_j's are identical for all the objects, and the x_{ij}'s are different. We can perform an abstraction operation, called a *type-1 abstraction*, to create an *abstracted picture object class* $V_{1n} = \{v_1, ..., v_n\}$, where $(a_1, ..., a_n)$ is regarded as the common type of these objects. An *index object* $v_{1n} \{(A_1, a_1), ..., (A_n, a_n)(B_1, b_1), ..., (B_m, b_m)\}$ can also be created, where $a_1, ..., a_n$ is the type of this index object (which is also the type of the abstracted object class V_{1n}), and $b_1, ..., b_m$ are other attributes extracted from $v_1, ..., v_n$. This index object is a unary relational object, with its type corresponding to the abstracted object class V_{1n}.

Originally the objects v_i may be associated with a certain node H_i. After the type-1 abstraction operation, we can decide where to put the index object v_{1n} and the abstracted object class V_{1n}. For example, we can associate the object class V_{1n} with the original node H_i, and the index object v_{1n} with H_j, the predecessor node of H_i. The index object v_{1n} at H_j can thus be used to point to the object class V_{1n} at H_i. When we write the index object as $V_{1n} \{(A_1, a_1), ..., (A_n, a_n), (B_1, b_1), ..., (B_m, b_m)\}$, the extracted attributes $b_1, ..., b_m$ could be interpreted as the parameters of a logical predicate to characterize the set V_{1n}. How to determine this predicate will be discussed in the next two sections.

Therefore, it can be seen that indexing and abstraction are closely related. In the preceding, we have assumed that objects $v_1, ..., v_n$ share common attributes $a_1, ..., a_n$, which become their common type. If $v_1, ..., v_n$ do not share common attributes, they may be given a new common label by extending the objects' attributes by a common labeling attribute. In fact, this is the usual objective of clustering analysis. Therefore, we can describe the type-1 abstraction operation as follows.

TYPE-1 ABSTRACTION

STEP 1. *(Labeling)* A set of picture objects are given a common label. This can be accomplished by either (a) identifying common attributes with identical values or (b) extending the objects' attributes by a common labeling attribute.

STEP 2. *(Clustering)* The picture objects having the same label are clustered together to form a new picture object class, with the common label as its type.

STEP 3. *(Indexing)* A new relational object, called the *index object*, is created, which contains (a) a type which is the type of the picture object class created in STEP 2 and (b) other attributes extracted from the attributes of the picture objects in the same picture object class.

The abstraction operation can be applied recursively, so that the index objects can again be labeled, clustered, and indexed. An example of iterative abstraction is illustrated in Figure 9.3.

In Figure 9.3, we start with a collection of objects $v_1, ..., v_{12}$. They are clustered into four groups, and each group's objects are given a new common label g_1, g_2, g_3, and g_4, respectively. The index objects are $v_{13}\{(type,"g_1"), (lowkey,1), (highkey,3)\}$, $v_{14}\{(type,"g_2"), (lowkey,4), (highkey,6)\}$, $v_{15}\{(type,"g_3"), (lowkey,7), (highkey,9)\}$, and $v_{16}\{(type,"g_4"), (lowkey,10), (highkey,12)\}$. For example, in v_{13}, g_1 is a pointer to $\{v_1, v_2, v_3\}$, and the new attributes can be interpreted as a logical predicate $(1 \leq key) \wedge (key \leq 3)$ to denote that the range of the key is between 1 and 3. Now the index objects v_{13}, v_{14}, v_{15}, and v_{16} can be regarded as ordinary objects, and by performing another level of clustering operation, they can be grouped into object classes, and an additional level of index objects can be constructed. As illustrated in Figure 9.3, the final ISAM (Index Sequential Access Method) structure consists of the object classes $t_1, t_2, t_3, g_1, g_2, g_3$, and g_4.

Aggregation [SMITH77] is conceptually similar to type-1 abstraction. In aggregation, we retain only the common attributes, and the particular attributes are omitted in the abstraction (in our case, the index object). However, type-1 abstraction is more general than aggregation, because we allow for arbitrary extraction operation in step 3 of type-1 abstraction. Conceptually, type-1 abstraction is applied to perform generalization and integration, although the (integrated) index object may retain the combined characteristics of the indexed object class.

In addition to type-1 abstraction, we have another abstraction operation, *type-2 abstraction,* where a picture object is labeled and then decomposed into two or more picture objects.

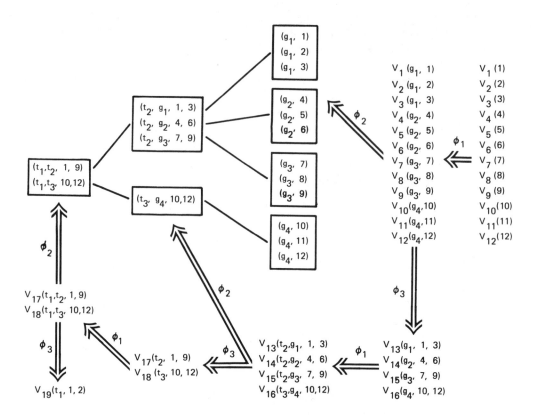

Figure 9.3 Type-1 abstraction example.

TYPE-2 ABSTRACTION

STEP 1. *(Classification)* A picture object is given a classification label. This label is added to the attribute list of that object.

STEP 2. *(Decomposition)* The picture object $v\{(A_1, a_1), ..., (A_n, a_n), (B_1, b_1), ..., (B_m, b_m), (C_1, c_1), ..., (C_k, c_k)\}$ is decomposed into two objects $v_1\{(A_1, a_1), ..., (A_n, a_n), (B_1, b_1), ..., (B_m, b_m)\}$ and $v_2\{(A_1, a_1), ..., (A_n, a_n), (C_1, c_1), ..., (C_k, c_k)\}$. The attributes $A_1, ..., A_n$ contain at least the name of the original object v. The attributes $B_1, ..., B_m$ contain the new label as the type of object v_1. The attributes $C_1, ..., C_k$ contain the old type as type of object v_2.

STEP 3. *(Cross-Indexing)* The new objects v_1 and v_2 are related by creating an index object, which is a relational object r_{12}. The name of this relational object is the (type,name) pairs of v_1 and v_2. The type of r_{12} is a newly created type code.

An example of type-2 abstraction is illustrated in Figure 9.4. In Figure 9.4, an object $v\{(type,"obj"), (name,"n1"), (pp,*)\}$ is classified as "table." This object is then decomposed into two objects, $v_1\{(type,"table"), (name,"n1")\}$, and $v_2\{(type,"obj"), (pp,*)\}$. The relational object for cross-indexing is $r_{12}\{(type,"cross"), (name, ?,$

equal(type1, name1, type2, name2)), (type1,"table"), (name1,"n1"), (type2,"obj"), (name2,"n1")}. It can be seen that *icons* [TANIMOTO76] can be constructed by type-2 abstraction. In the foregoing example, v_1 is the icon, v_2 is the physical object represented by the icon, and r_{12} relates them.

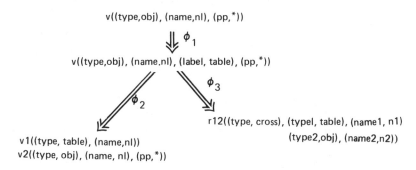

Figure 9.4 Type-2 abstraction example.

Type-2 abstraction can also be applied before or after the application of type-1 abstraction. For example, we can first classify objects as tables. The logical table object and the physical table object can be separated using the decomposition rule in type-2 abstraction. The table objects can then be clustered into a table object class, using type-1 abstraction. An index can then be established to point to the table object class.

Type-1 abstraction is conceptually similar to *qualified vertical decomposition,* and type-2 abstraction is similar to *horizontal decomposition,* as discussed in [CHANG80]. Both abstraction operations can be followed by another step to realize the abstract objects as relational tables.

STEP 4. *(Realization)* For each picture object class thus created, a relational table can be created whose name is the same as the type of the picture object class and whose attributes are the same as that of the picture object class, less the type attribute.

In other words, the picture object classes and the relational object classes can be realized as relational tables in a natural way, so that a relational database approach can be used to support a pictorial database. On the other hand, we can also use an artificial intelligence language such as LISP to define the objects directly. Therefore, there are several feasible approaches to implement the pictorial database as a collection of picture objects and relational objects.

9.5 SYNTACTIC ABSTRACTION RULES

The two types of abstraction operations just discussed do not specify how clustering or decomposition should be performed. To make abstraction operations more substantive, we now consider various types of abstraction rules. In this section, we describe syntactic abstraction rules using the concepts of mathematical logic [MENDELSON79, ROGERS71, STEEN72] and learning theory [BANERJI80, DIETTERICH81, HAYES78, VERE75]. For this purpose, each object $v\{(A_1, a_1), ..., (A_n, a_n)\}$ can be regarded as representing a logical conjunction of the form

$$A_1(v, a_1) \wedge A_2(v, a_2) \wedge \cdots \wedge A_n(v, a_n)$$

where $A_i(v, a_i)$ is a property predicate, meaning the value of attribute A_i of object v is a_i. If we use the notation of Section 9.1, we can also express the logical conjunction as

$$(v.A_1 = a_1) \wedge (v.A_2 = a_2) \wedge \cdots \wedge (v.A_n = a_n)$$

We will use C_v to denote the corresponding logical conjunction for an object v.

In what follows, the symbol -> denotes logical inference. The symbol => denotes logical implication. The symbol <=> denotes logical equivalence. The notation $(\forall x / D)i$, as opposed to [REITER78], denotes "for all x in domain D of type i," and the notation $(\exists x / D)i$ denotes "there exists x in domain D of type i." If all attributes of an object are of the same type, the subscript i will be dropped.

By *syntactic rules of abstraction* we mean the following three rules of inference:

Rule of Projection:

If U and V are conjunctive predicates, we have

$$U \wedge V \rightarrow U.$$

Rule of Bounded Generalization:

Let Q be an $(m + n)$-place conjunctive predicate, and Q(a) be the shorthand notation for

$$(\forall x_1 / D_1) \cdots (\forall x_m / D_m) Q(x_1, \cdots x_m, a_1, ..., a_n)$$

where $0 \le m$ and $1 \le n$.
We have

$$Q(a) \rightarrow (\forall x_1 / D_1) \cdots (\forall x_m / D_m)(\forall y_1 / \{a_1\}) \cdots (\forall y_n / \{a_n\})Q(x_1, ..., x_m, y_1, ..., y_n).$$

Rule of Extension:

If $Q(x)$ is true for all x in domain D_1, and Q(x) is also true for all x in domain D_2, then we have

$$(\forall x / D_1)_i Q(x) \wedge (\forall x / D_2)_i Q(x) \rightarrow (\forall x / D_1 \cup D_2)_i Q(x)$$

that is, $Q(x)$ is true for all x in domain $D_1 \cup D_2$.

We write $U]- V$, if V can be deduced from U by the application of one of the foregoing three syntactic abstraction rules. *A predicate U is a syntactic abstraction of C_v*, if there exist $C_1, ..., C_n$, $n \ge 1$, such that

$$C_v = C_1]- C_2]- \cdots]- C_n = U.$$

A rule of inference U -> V is *sound* if and only if U => V is true with respect to every interpretation—that is, V logically follows from U. We can formally prove that the preceding three rules of syntactic abstraction are sound [CHANG82b]. Moreover, both the converse of the rule of bounded generalization and the rule of extension are also sound.

Suppose we have an inference $U \rightarrow V$. We say $U \rightarrow V$ is a *characteristic inference* if $U \Rightarrow V$ is true under an interpretation I, which implies $V \Rightarrow U$ is also true under the same interpretation I. Otherwise, $U \rightarrow V$ is called a *condensed inference*.

Characteristic inferences are information "lossless" in the sense the U can be recovered from V. It will be proved in Section 9.8 that both the rule of bounded generalization and the rule of extension are characteristic inferences. The rule of projection [ZADEH79], on the other hand, is a condensed inference.

The converse of the rule of bounded generalization is called the *rule of particularization*, and the converse of the rule of extension is called the *rule of restriction*. Although they are not regarded as abstraction rules, both can be formally proved as sound and characteristic inferences.

The choice of abstraction rules is such that we prefer to have characteristic inference. For example, we could formulate a rule of *existential generalization* $Q(a) \rightarrow (\exists x)i\; Q(x)$ to replace the rule of bounded generalization $Q(a) \rightarrow (\forall x/\{a\})i\; Q(x)$. But the new rule, although still a sound rule, is no longer a characteristic inference and therefore is not information "lossless."

As an application of syntactic abstraction, we present the following example.

We have three objects represented by the following predicates:

$$P_1(v_1, a) \wedge P_2(v_1, b) \wedge P_3(v_1, c)$$

$$P_1(v_2, a) \wedge P_2(v_2, b) \wedge P_3(v_2, c)$$

$$P_1(v_3, a) \wedge P_2(v_3, b) \wedge P_3(v_3, c)$$

By applying the rules of bounded generalization and extension, we obtain the following:

$$[\forall x/\{v_1, v_2, v_3\}]\; [P_1(x, a) \wedge P_2(x, b) \wedge P_3(x, c)]$$

Therefore, in type-1 abstraction, we can cluster v_1, v_2, and v_3 to form an index object class.

On the other hand, the rule of projection is used in type-2 abstraction to obtain a decomposition of objects.

9.6 SEMANTIC ABSTRACTION RULES

In this section, we discuss semantic abstraction rules. A *semantic abstraction rule* $U \underset{I}{\vdash} V$ in S is a rule of inference in a finite set $S = \{U_i \rightarrow V_i\}$ associated with an interpretation I such that for each $(U_i \rightarrow V_i)$ in S,

1. The number of literals in V_i is less than that of U_i, and
2. $U_i \Rightarrow V_i$ is true under I.

It should be emphasized that semantic abstraction rules are valid *only with respect to a certain interpretation.*

A semantic abstraction M of a predicate C_v with respect to an interpretation I is obtained by repeated application of semantic abstraction rules:

$$C_v = C_1]_{\overline{I}} \; C_2]_{\overline{I}} \; \cdots \;]_{\overline{I}} C_n = M, \quad n \geq 1 \; .$$

As an example of semantic abstraction, what [SMITH77] has referred to as the generic hierarchy can be expressed by a set of semantic rules of abstraction as follows:

> For all v of type 'object',
> is(v, truck) $\vee$ is(v, helicopter) -> is(v, motorized-vehicle)
> is(v, helicopter) $\vee$ is(v, glider) -> is(v, air-vehicle)
> is(v, air-vehicle) $\vee$ is(v, land-vehicle) $\vee$ is(v, water-vehicle)
> -> is(v, vehicle)

As another example, in a domain where there is a linear ordering on the individual elements—for example, a finite subset of the natural numbers—we may add a semantic rule of abstraction under the interpretation of arithmetics as follows:

$$D = \{ n_1, ..., n_k \} \rightarrow D = [min(D) \; ... \; max(D)]$$

where $[a \; ... \; b]$ denotes a closed interval, and $min(D)$, $max(D)$ are values of the min, max functions of D, respectively.

The foregoing semantic rules also facilitate the concept of extensional database [MINKER78].

As a final example, in [YAMAGUCHI81], the concept of generic tuples was presented. The abstraction reported in [YAMAGUCHI81] can be expressed by a combination of syntactic and semantic abstraction rules, provided that the rule of existential generalization is incorporated as a semantic abstraction rule. We begin with the following collection of predicates,

> class(v_1, *warship*) $\wedge$ *tonnage* (v_1, 10000)
> class(v_2, *warship*) $\wedge$ *tonnage* (v_2, 15000)
> class(v_3, *warship*) $\wedge$ *tonnage* (v_3, 20000)

We first perform the rule of existential generalization to derive

> ($\exists v$)ship class(v, warship) $\wedge$ tonnage(v, 10000)
> ($\exists v$)ship class(v, warship) $\wedge$ tonnage(v, 15000)
> ($\exists v$)ship class(v, warship) $\wedge$ tonnage(v, 20000)

Then by repeated applications of rules of bounded generalization and extension, we can obtain

> ($\forall y$/ {10000, 15000, 20000})tonnage
> ($\exists v$)ship class(v, warship) $\wedge$ tonnage(v, y)

Now using the semantic rule of abstraction on the linear-ordered domain of natural numbers we finally derive

> ($\forall y$/ [10000 .. 20000]) tonnage
> ($\exists v$)ship class(v, warship) $\wedge$ tonnage(v, y)

Using the notation of Section 9.1, we have the following predicate to serve as the abstracted index:

$$(v.type = ship) \wedge (v.class = warship) \wedge (v.tonnage \geq 10000) \wedge (v.tonnage \leq 20000)$$

The corresponding index object is:

$$v \ \{(type,"ship"), (class,"warship"), (low\text{-}tonnage, 10000), (high\text{-}tonnage, 20000)\}$$

9.7 LATENT QUERIES AND ICONS

The last example in Section 9.6 illustrates the power of semantic abstraction [KING81, MICHALSKI80]. By incorporating syntactic and semantic abstraction rules into the abstraction operations described in Section 9.4, we can construct picture indexes for a picture tree, thereby facilitating pictorial information retrieval. Similar techniques may also be useful for a conventional database [ULLMAN81] to perform database abstraction, or applied to other artificial intelligence problems [FISHMAN75, POWELL78].

We can now present an example of a *latent query*. In Section 9.4, type-1 abstraction is employed to construct an ISAM index, where the object classes are $t_1, t_2, t_3, g_1, g_2, g_3$, and g_4. Typical objects are

$$v_{17}\{(type,"t_1"), (type1,"t_2"), (lowkey,1), (highkey,9)\}$$
$$v_{13}\{(type,"t_0"), (type1,"g_1"), (lowkey,1), (highkey,3)\}$$
$$v_2\{(type,"g_1"), (key,2)\}$$

To retrieve an object with key equal to "skey", we have the following query:

$$Q(skey) = \{w.key: (\exists u)(\exists v)\ u.type="t_1" \wedge u.lowkey \leq "skey" \wedge$$
$$"skey" < u.highkey \wedge u.type1 = v.type \wedge v.lowkey \leq "skey" \wedge$$
$$"skey" < v.highkey \wedge v.type1 = w.type \wedge w.key = "skey"\}$$

The foregoing query Q(skey) specifies how the ISAM index is to be searched by matching the type attribute with the type1 attribute. In other words, the type1 attribute serves as a pointer to another object class having the same type. If this query Q(skey) is also stored in the database and invoked whenever we need to retrieve objects from the ISAM structure, it becomes a latent query.

Another technique is to introduce a virtual object for the ISAM structure. The virtual object w is defined as

$$w \ \{(type,"isam",eval\text{-}rule), (key,?,Q(skey))\}$$

where the evaluation rule for the key attribute is the latent query Q(skey). To retrieve an object with key equal to 2, we can use the following query:

$$\{w: w.type="isam" \wedge w.key="2"\}$$

which will invoke the latent query Q(2) to access the ISAM index to find the object with key equal to 2. In other words, we use the icon w, which stands for an ISAM structure, to retrieve objects in that structure.

Therefore, an *icon* is a virtual object set whose evaluation rule is in the form of a latent query. It can be seen that generic tuples [YAMAGUCHI81] are conceptually similar to icons. The difference between an index and an icon is that an index points to another object class (or classes in the case of cross-indexing), whereas an icon is a virtual object set. In other words, *an index points to something, whereas an icon stands for something.*

As a final example, the query to get all ships of 14000 tons in the Pacific is:

$$Q(14000) = \{v: (\exists \ u) \ u.type="ship" \wedge u.low\text{-}tonnage \leq 14000 \wedge$$
$$14000 < u.high\text{-}tonnage \wedge$$
$$u.class = v.type \wedge v.tonnage=14000 \wedge v.area="Pacific"\}$$

This query utilizes an index object (see the last example of Section 9.6) to expedite the search process. Again, an icon can be constructed which stands for all ships of 14000 tons in the Pacific.

$$w \ \{(type,"ship14000",eval\text{-}rule), (tonnage,?,Q(14000))\}$$

9.8 PROOFS FOR ABSTRACTION RULES

In this section, we shall prove that both rule of bounded generalization and rule of extension are sound and characteristic. A first-order theory of many-sorted logic [STEEN72] will be employed that incorporates the arithmetic system and axiomized set theory. Moreover, the following notations are used in this section:

Notation	Connotation
$\wedge$	conjunction
v	disjunction
=>	implication
<=>	biconditional
]-	deduction
->	inference
$(\forall \ x)i$	typed universal quantification over x of type i
$(\exists \ x)i$	typed existential quantification
:	membership
{ }	set
$\cup$	union

Sometimes the meta-symbol pair [ ] is used in place of the regular ( ) to improve the legibility.

We won't prove that the rule of projection is sound since it's obviously a basic theorem; to prove the soundness of the other two syntactic rules, it suffices to show that they are derivable from axioms and other theorems. In the first place, we list some axiom schemata [MENDELSON79] necessary to the proofs:

For all typed well-formed formulae U, V, and W,

- Axiom schema 1. $U \ => \ (V => U)$
- Axiom schema 2. $[\ U => (V => W) \ ] \ => \ [\ (U => V) => (U => W) \ ]$

- Axiom schema 3. $(\forall x)i \ U(x) \ \Rightarrow \ U(t)$ where t is an individual constant/variables of type i and free for x.
- Axiom schema 4. $(\forall x)i \ (U \Rightarrow V) \ \Rightarrow \ [\ U \Rightarrow (\forall x)i \ V \ ]$ where U is free of x.
- Axiom schema 5. $(x = y) \ \Rightarrow \ [\ U(x, x) \Rightarrow U(x, y) \ ]$
- Axiom schema 6. $(\forall y)i \ (\exists D)j \ (\forall x)i \ [\ (x : D) <\Rightarrow x = y \ ]$

Two primary rules of inference are respectively:

- Modus Ponens $U, U \Rightarrow V \rightarrow V$
- Rule of Generalization $U \ \rightarrow \ (\forall x)U$

In addition, three theorems are needed:

- **Theorem 1.** $U \Rightarrow V, V \Rightarrow W \ ]\text{-} \ U \Rightarrow W$
- **Theorem 2.** $]\text{-} (x = y) \Rightarrow (y = x)$
- **Theorem 3.** $]\text{-} \ [(\forall x)i \ U(x) \wedge (\forall x)i \ V(x)] <\Rightarrow (\forall x)i \ [\ U(x) \wedge V(x) \ ]$

Finally, $(\forall x / D)i \ Q(x)$ is formally defined as $(\forall x)i \ [\ (x : D) \Rightarrow Q(x) \ ]$.

Lemma 1. The rule of bounded generalization is sound.

Proof: $(y = x) \ \Rightarrow \ [\ Q(y) \Rightarrow Q(x) \ ]$ By instance of Axm schm 5, where both x and y are free in Q.

$(x = y) \ \Rightarrow \ (y = x)$ By Theorem 2.
$(x = y) \ \Rightarrow \ [\ Q(y) \Rightarrow Q(x) \ ]$ By Theorem 1.
$[\ (x = y) \Rightarrow Q(y) \ ] \ \Rightarrow [\ (x = y) \Rightarrow Q(x) \ ]$ By Axm schm 2 and Modus Ponens.
$Q(y) \ \Rightarrow \ [\ (x = y) \Rightarrow Q(y) \ ]$ By Axm schm 1.
$Q(y) \ \Rightarrow \ [\ (x = y) \Rightarrow Q(x) \ ]$ By Theorem 1.
$(\forall x)i \ (\ Q(y) \ \Rightarrow \ [\ (x = y) \Rightarrow Q(x) \ ] \ )$ By rule of generalization.
$Q(y) \ \Rightarrow \ (\forall x)i \ [\ (x = y) \Rightarrow Q(x) \ ]$ By Axm schm 4.
$(\forall y)i \ (\ Q(y) \ \Rightarrow \ (\forall x)i \ [\ (x = y) \Rightarrow Q(x) \ ] \ )$ By rule of generalization.
$Q(\alpha) \ \Rightarrow \ (\forall x)i \ [\ (x = \alpha) \Rightarrow Q(x) \ ]$ By Axm schm 3.
$Q(\alpha) \ \Rightarrow \ (\forall x)i \ [\ (x : \{\alpha\}) \Rightarrow Q(x) \ ]$ Mainly by Axm schm 6 and notation of { }, i.e. $[\ (x : D) <\Rightarrow (x = \alpha) \ ]$ if and only if D is interchangable with $\{\alpha\}$, where x is an individual variable and α, an individual constant.
$Q(a) \ \Rightarrow \ (\forall x / \{a\})i \ Q(x)$ Mainly by definition. $\qquad\qquad \square$

An additional theorem is needed for proof of the next lemma:

Theorem 4. $U \Rightarrow W, V \Rightarrow W \ ]\text{-} \ (U \vee V) \Rightarrow W$

Lemma 2. The rule of extension is sound.
Proof: (Outlined as follows)

$(\forall x / D1)i \ Q(x) \ <\Rightarrow \ (\forall x)i \ [(x : D1) \Rightarrow Q(x)]$ By definition.
$(\forall x / D2)i \ Q(x) \ <\Rightarrow \ (\forall x)i \ [(x : D2) \Rightarrow Q(x)]$ By definition.
$(\forall x)i \ [\ ((x : D1) \ \Rightarrow \ Q(x)) \ \wedge \ ((x : D2) \ \Rightarrow \ Q(x)) \ ]$ By Modus Ponens and Theorem 3.

$(\forall\ x)i\ [\ ((x : D1) \vee (x : D2))\ =>\ Q(x)\ ]$ By rule of projection and Theorem 4.

$(\forall\ x)i\ [\ (x : (D1\ \bigcup D2))\ =>\ Q(x)\ ]$ By definition of union.   □

In the following part, we shall prove that both rule of bounded generalization and rule of extension are characteristic. (Note that rule of projection is only a condensed abstraction rule.) Some other necessary theorems are added for proofs:

Theorem 5. $U => V, U => W$]- $U => (V \wedge W)$

Theorem 6.]- $(\forall\ y)i\ (\exists\ x)i\ [x = y]$

Theorem 7. From U, V]- W, we have U]- $(V => W)$

Theorem 8. $U(x)$]- $(\exists x)U(x)$

Theorem 9.]- $(\exists x)[U(x) => V(x)] => [(\exists\ x)U(x) => (\exists\ x)V(x)]$

Theorem 10.]- $(\exists\ x)V => V$ for V free of x

Lemma 3.   The rule of bounded generalization is characteristic.

Proof: Since this rule is sound, we have to show that $(\forall\ x/\{a\})i\ Q(x)\ =>\ Q(a)$ is logically valid, i.e. true with respect to every interpretation. Following is an outline of a proof sequence.

$(x = y)\ =>\ [\ Q(x) => Q(y)\ ]$ By Axm schm 5.

$(\forall\ y)i\ (\ (x = y)\ =>\ [\ Q(x) => Q(y)\ ]\ )$ By rule of generalization.

$(x = a)\ =>\ [\ Q(x) => Q(a)\ ]$ By Axm schm 3.

$(\forall\ x/\{a\})i\ Q(x)$ Premise.

$(\forall\ x)i\ [(x = a) => Q(x)]$ Mainly by definition, and notation of $\{\ \}$.

$(x = a)\ =>\ Q(x)$ By Axm schm 3.

$(x = a)\ =>\ [\ Q(x) \wedge (\ Q(x) => Q(a)\ )\ ]$ By Theorem 5.

$Q(x) \wedge (\ Q(x) => Q(a)\ )$ Premise.

$Q(a)$ By rule of projection and Modus Ponens.

$Q(x) \wedge (\ Q(x) => Q(a)\ )$]- $Q(a)$ By definition of deduction.

]- $(\ Q(x) \wedge (Q(x) => Q(a))\ =>\ Q(a)\ )$ By Theorem 7.

$(x = a)\ =>\ Q(a)$ By Theorem 1.

$(\exists x)\ [(x = a) => Q(a)]$ By Theorem 8.

$(\exists\ x)[x = a] => (Ex)Q(a)$ By Theorem 9.

$(\exists\ x)Q(a) => Q(a)$ By Theorem 10.

$(\exists\ x)[x = a] => Q(a)$ By Theorem 1.

$(\forall\ y)i\ (\exists\ x)i\ [x = y]$ By Theorem 6.

$(\exists\ x)[x = a]$ By Axm schm 3.

$Q(a)$ By Modus Ponens.

$(\forall\ x/\{a\})i\ Q(x)$]- $Q(a)$ By definition of deduction.

]- $((\forall\ x/\{a\})i\ Q(x)) => Q(a)$ By Theorem 7.   □

Lemma 4.   The rule of extension is characteristic.

Proof: Like for lemma 3, we also have to prove that the converse of rule of extension is sound, but the proof outline in lemma 2 can be totally reversed while maintaining its logical validity; thus the converse of rule of extension has been proved to be sound.   □

9.9 DISCUSSION

In summary, this chapter presents an approach for picture indexing and abstraction. Starting with a collection of picture objects V and relational objects R, abstraction operations can be applied to construct abstracted objects and index objects, where the corresponding picture predicates are obtained using the syntactic and semantic abstraction rules. These picture objects can be incorporated into structured picture queries to facilitate pictorial information retrieval. Therefore, we can formulate image database search strategies, navigation strategies, and so on, as latent queries expressed in terms of various index objects, picture objects, and relational objects. Finally, such latent queries can be used to construct icons, which are symbolic representations of picture objects.

Structured picture queries as formulated in this chapter can be adapted for execution on a highly parallel computer. The hierarchical structure of the picture tree leads us to consider parallel processing algorithms. The investigation of suitable programming languages to specify image processing and parallel processing algorithms for structured picture retrieval in a picture tree is a research problem requiring further investigation. This language should also be user friendly so that the user can specify icons at will and navigate in the image database using icons. A preliminary design of such an image processing language can be found in [CHANG85].

R E F E R E N C E S

[BANERJI80] BANERJI, R. B., AND T. M. MITCHELL, "Description Languages and Learning Algorithms," *Internat. J. Policy Analysis and Information Systems,* June 1980, 202.

[BITNER79] BITNER, J. R., "Heuristics That Dynamically Organize Data Structures," *SIAM Journal on Computing,* Vol. 8, No. 1, February 1979, 104-107.

[BROWN79] BROWN, M. R., "A Partial Analysis of Random Height-Balanced Trees," *SIAM Journal on Computing,* Vol. 8, No. 1, February 1979, 37-39.

[CHANGNS79] CHANG, N. S., AND K. S. FU, "A Relational Database System for Images," *TR-EE 79-28,* Dept. of Electrical Engineering, Purdue University, May 1979.

[CHANG85] CHANG, S. K., E. JUNGERT, S. LEVALDI, G. TORTORA,, AND T ICHIKAWA, "An Image Processing Language with Icon-Assisted Navigation," *IEEE Transactions on Software Engineering*, Vol SE-11, No. 8, August, 1985, 811-819.

[CHANG78] CHANG, S. K., J. REUSS, AND B. H. MCCORMICK, "Design Considerations of a Pictorial Database System," *International Journal on Policy Analysis and Information Systems,* Vol. 1, No. 2, Knowledge Systems Laboratory, UICC, January 1978, 49-70.

[CHANG79] CHANG, S. K., B. S. LIN, AND R. WALSER, "A Generalized Zooming Technique for Pictorial Database Systems," *Proceedings of National Computer Conference, AFIPS,* Vol. 48, 1979, 147-156.

[CHANG80] CHANG, S. K., AND W. H. CHENG, "A Methodology for Structured Data Base Decomposition," *IEEE Transactions on Software Engineering,* Vol. SE-6, No. 2, March 1980, 205-218.

[CHANG82a] CHANG, S. K., "A Methodology for Picture Indexing and Encoding," in *Picture Engineering,* (K. S. Fu and K. L. Kunii, Eds.), Springer Verlag, Berlin 1982, 33-53.

[CHANG82b] CHANG, S. K., AND S. H. LIU, "Indexing and Abstraction Techniques for a Pictorial Database," *Proceedings of International Conference on Pattern Recognition and Image Processing,* June 14-17, 1982, Las Vegas, 422-431.

[CHIEN80] CHIEN, Y. T., "Hierarchical Data Structures for Picture Storage, Retrieval and Classification," in *Pictorial Information Systems,* (Chang and Fu, Eds.), Springer-Verlag, West Germany, 1980, 39-74.

[DAATE79] DATE, C. J., *Introduction To Database Systems.* Addison-Wesley, 1979.

[DIETTERICH81] DIETTERICH, T. G., AND R. S. MICHALSKI, "Inductive Learning of Structural Descriptions," *Artificial Intelligence,* Vol. 16, 1981, 262-289.

[FAGIN80] FAGIN, R., A. O. MENDELSON, AND J. D. ULLMAN, "A Simplified Universal Relation Assumption and Its Properties," *RJ2900, IBM Research Technical Report,* Nov. 1980, 7.

[FISHMAN75] FISHMAN, D. H., AND J. MINKER, "π-Representation: Clause Representation for Parallel Search," *Artificial Intelligence,* Vol. 6, No. 2, 1975, 102-127.

[GOTLIEB81] GOTLIEB, L., "Optimal Multi-Way Search Trees," *SIAM Journal on Computing,* Vol. 10, No. 3, August 1981, 422.

[HAYES78] HAYES-ROTH, F., AND J. MCDERMOTT, "An Interference Matching Technique for Inducing Abstractions," *Comm. ACM,* Vol. 21, 1978, 401-410.

[KING81] KING, J. J., "Query Optimization by Semantic Reasoning," *Report STAN-CS-81-857,* Dept. of Computer Science, Stanford University, May 1981.

[LIU81] LIU, S. H., AND S. K. CHANG, "Picture Covering by 2-D AH Encoding," *Proceedings of IEEE Workshop on Computer Architecture for Pattern Analysis and Image Database Management,* Hot Springs, Virginia, November 11-13, 1981.

[McKEOWN77] McKEOWN, JR., D. M., AND D. J. REDDY, "A Hierarchical Symbolic Representation for Image Database," *Proceedings of IEEE Workshop on Picture Data Description and Management,* IEEE Computer Society, April 1977, 40-44.

[MAIER79] MAIER, D., "An Efficient Method for Storing Ancestor Information in Trees," *SIAM Journal on Computing,* Vol. 8, No. 4, November 1979, 599-618.

[MENDELSON79] MENDELSON, E., *Introduction to Mathematical Logic.* D. Van Nostrand, 1979, 59-85 and 173-176.

[MICHALSKI80] MICHALSKI, R. S., AND R. L. CHILAUSKY, "Developing an Expert System for Soybean Disease Diagnosis," *Internat. J. Policy Analysis and Information Systems,* Dec. 1980, 128.

[MINKER78] MINKER, J., "An Experimental Relational Data Base System Based on Logic," in *Logic and Data Bases,* (H. Gallaire and J. Minker, Eds.), Plenum Press, 1978, 107.

[POWELL78] POWELL, P. B., AND P. THOMPSON, "Natural Languages and Voice Output for Relational Data Base Systems," *Proc. of Nat. Conf., ACM,* 1978, 585-595.

[REITER78] REITER, R., "Deductive Question-Answering on Relational Data Bases," in *Logic and Data Bases,* Plenum Press, 1978, 150.

[REUSS78] REUSS, J. L., AND S. K. CHANG, "Picture Paging for Efficient Image Processing," *Proceedings of IEEE Computer Society Conference on Pattern Recognition and Image Processing,* IEEE Computer Society, May 1978, 69-74.

[ROGERS71] ROGERS, R., *Mathematical Logic and Formalized Theories.* North-Holland, 1971, 99.

[SHAPIRO79] SHAPIRO, L. G., AND R. M. HARALICK, "A Spatial Data Structure," *Technical Report #CS 79005-R,* Dept. of Computer Science, Virginia Polytechnic Institute and State University, August 1979, 35.

[SMITH77] SMITH, J. M., AND D. C. P. SMITH, "Database Abstraction: Aggregation and Generalization," *ACM Trans. on Database Systems,* Vol. 2. No. 2,1977, 105-133.

[STEEN72] STEEN, S. W. P., *Mathematical Logic.* Cambridge University Press, 1972, 115-119.

[TANIMOTO76] TANIMOTO, S. L., "An Iconic/Symbolic Data Structuring Scheme," in *Pattern Recognition and Artificial Intelligence,* Academic Press, 452-471, 1976.

[VERE75] VERE, S. A., "Induction of Concepts in the Predicate Calculus," *Proc. of the 4th International Joint Conf. on Artificial Intelligence,* 1975, 281-287.

[YAMAGUCHI82] YAMAGUCHI, K., AND T. KUNII, "A Data Structure for Picture Database Computers," in *Picture Engineering,* Software Engineering Series No. 3, IBM Japan, 1982, 199-254.

[ZADEH79] ZADEH, L. A., "A Theory of Approximate Reasoning," *Machine Intelligence,* Vol. 9, Halsted Press, 1979, 172-177.

[ZAISHNAVI80] ZAISHNAVI, V. K., H. P. KRIEGEL, AND D. WOOD, "Optimum Multiway Search Trees," *Acta Informatica,* Vol. 14, 1980, 119-133.

E X E R C I S E S

1. The following is a physical picture. Please give the logical picture representation. Let's assume that the name of the road is "1st drive," the building at lower left corner is "hotel," the building at upper right corner is "church," and there is a car on the road.

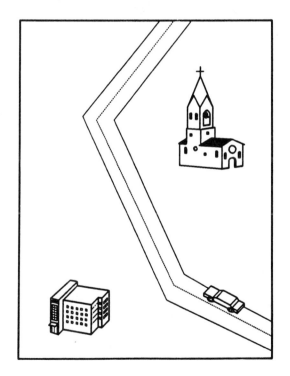

2. Refer to the logical picture representation of the picture in the previous problem. Give the set-theoretic specification of the following query:

```
get the black car on a driveway that surrounds a church.
```

3. Construct a binary tree index by type-1 abstraction for the picture in problem 1.

Chapter 10

Iconic Indexing by 2D Strings

In pictorial information retrieval, we often want to retrieve pictures satisfying a certain picture query—for example, "find all pictures having a tree to the left of a house." In previous chapters, we discussed various approaches for pictorial information retrieval, including relational database queries (Chapter 8), quadtrees (Chapter 6), picture trees (Chapter 9), and so on. We present in this chapter a new way of representing a picture by a *2D string*. A picture query can also be specified as a 2D string. The problem of pictorial information retrieval then becomes a problem of 2D subsequence matching. This approach thus allows an efficient and natural way to construct *iconic indexes* for pictures.

In Section 10.1, we describe the 2D string representation as the symbolic projection of a picture and define the absolute 2D string, normal 2D string, and reduced 2D string. Picture matching by 2D subsequence matching is discussed in Section 10.2. In Section 10.3, a method called *orthogonal relations*, used to specify spatial relations between objects, is used to obtain a symbolic representation of pictures. Spatial reasoning based on 2D string representation is discussed in Section 10.4. Section 10.5 is on the visualization of symbolic pictures represented as 2D strings. Section 10.6 discusses applications to iconic indexing using 2D strings.

10.1 2D STRING REPRESENTATION OF SYMBOLIC PICTURES

Let V be a set of symbols, or the vocabulary. Each symbol could represent a pictorial object, a pixel, and so on. Let A be the set $\{\ '='\ ,\ '<'\ ,\ ':'\ \}$, where $'='$, $'<'$, and $':'$ are three special symbols not in V. These symbols will be used to specify spatial relationships among pictorial objects.

A *1D string* over V is any string $x_1 x_2 \cdots x_n$, n $\geq$ 0, where the x_i's are in V.

A *2D string* over V, written as (u, v), is defined as

$$(x_1\, y_1\, x_2\, y_2\ \cdots\ y_{n-1}\, x_n, x_{p(1)}\, z_1\, x_{p(2)}\, z_2\ \cdots\ z_{n-1}\, x_{p(n)})$$

where

$\quad x_1\ \cdots\ x_n$ is a 1D string over V

$\quad p: \{1\,,\, ...\,,\, n\} \to \{1\,,\, ...\,,\, n\}$ is a permutation over $\{1\,,\, ...\,,\, n\}$

$\quad y_1\ \cdots\ y_{n-1}$ is a 1D string over A

$\quad z_1\ \cdots\ z_{n-1}$ is a 1D string over A

We can use 2D strings to represent pictures in a natural way. As an example, consider the picture shown in Figure 10.1.

Figure 10.1 A picture f.

The vocabulary is $V = \{a\,,\, b\,,\, c\,,\, d\}$. The 2D string representing the picture f is

$$(\ a = d < a = b < c, a = a < b = c < d\ )$$

$$= (x_1\, y_1\, x_2\, y_2\, x_3\, y_3\, x_4\, y_4\, x_5,\quad x_1\, z_1\, x_3\, z_2\, x_4\, z_3\, x_5\, z_4\, x_2)$$

where

$\quad x_1\, x_2\, x_3\, x_4\, x_5$ is $a\ d\ a\ b\ c$

$\quad x_1\, x_3\, x_4\, x_5\, x_2$ is $a\ a\ b\ c\ d$

$\quad p$ is $1\ 3\ 4\ 5\ 2$

$\quad y_1\, y_2\, y_3\, y_4$ is $\ = < = <$

$\quad z_1\, z_2\, z_3\, z_4$ is $\ = < = <$

The symbol $'<'$ denotes the left-right spatial relation in string u and the below-above spatial relation in string v. The symbol $'='$ denotes the spatial relation "at the same location as." The symbol $':'$ denotes the relation "in the same set as." Therefore, the 2D string representation can be seen as the *symbolic projection* of picture f along the x- and y- directions.

A *symbolic picture f* is a mapping $M \times M \rightarrow W$, where $M = \{1, 2, \cdots, m\}$, and W is the power set of V (the set of all subsets of V). The empty set $\{\}$ then denotes a null object. In Figure 10.1, the "blank slots" can be filled by empty set symbols, or null objects. The preceding picture is

$$
\begin{array}{lll}
f(1,1) = \{a\} & f(1,2) = \{\} & f(1,3) = \{d\} \\
f(2,1) = \{a\} & f(2,2) = \{b\} & f(2,3) = \{\} \\
f(3,1) = \{\} & f(3,2) = \{c\} & f(3,3) = \{\}
\end{array}
$$

We now show that, given f, we can construct the corresponding 2D string representation (u, v), and vice versa, such that all left-right and below-above spatial relations among the pictorial objects in V are preserved. In other words, let $\mathbf{R}_1$ be the set of left-right and below-above spatial relations induced by f. Let $\mathbf{R}_2$ be the set of left-right and below-above spatial relations induced by (u, v). Then $\mathbf{R}_1$ is identical to $\mathbf{R}_2$ for the corresponding f and (u, v).

It is easy to see that from f we can construct the 2D string (u, v). The foregoing example illustrates the algorithm. In the formal algorithm, we will first construct 2D string (u', v') where u' and v' contain symbols in W. Then, u' and v' can be rewritten as follows: If we see a set $\{a,b,c\}$, we write "a:b:c." If we see a null set $\{\}$, we simply remove it (that is, we write a null string). We can rewrite '= <', '< =', and '< <' to '<', and '= =' to '=', so that redundant spatial operators are removed. The operators '=' and ':' can also be omitted. The algorithm now follows.

```
2Dstring(f,m,u,v,n)
begin
  /*we assume f is m by m square picture*/
  n = m × m;
  for j from 1 until m
    for k from 1 until m
    /*we are looking at f(j,k)*/
    /*construct string  x₁ · · · xₙ */
      begin
      i = k + (j-1) m;
      xᵢ = f(j,k);
    /*construct string  x_p(1) · · · x_p(n) */
      p(i) = j + (k-1) m;
      end
  /*construct y string and z string */
  for i = 1 until n-1
    if i is multiples of m
      then  yᵢ = zᵢ = '<'
      else  yᵢ = zᵢ = '=';
  /*rewrite strings u and v*/
  while strings u and v contain rewritable substrings
    apply the rewriting rules (see following explanation):
```

```
r1. {a₁, a₂ , · · · , aₖ} is rewritten as a₁ : a₂ :  · · ·  : aₖ
    {}  is rewritten as null string
r2. '= ='  is rewritten as  '='
    '= <'  is rewritten as  '<'
    '< ='  is rewritten as  '<'
    '< <'  is rewritten as  '<'
r3. '=' is rewritten as null string
r4. ':' is rewritten as null string /*reduced string only*/;
```
end

As an example, for the picture f shown in Figure 10.1, if we apply the procedure "2Dstring" without the rewriting rules, we obtain

1. $(\{a\} = \{\} = \{d\} < \{a\} = \{b\} = \{\} < \{\} = \{c\} = \{\}, \{a\} = \{a\} = \{\}$
   $< \{\} = \{b\} = \{c\} < \{d\} = \{\} = \{\})$

Now we apply rewriting rule r1 to obtain

2. $(a == d < a = b =<= c =, a = a =<= b = c < d ==)$
   (absolute 2D string)

Since the 2D string of 2 contains all the spatial operators, it is a precise encoding of the picture f. The 2D string of 2 is called an *absolute 2D string*. This coding is obviously inefficient. In fact, one string suffices to represent f precisely. Therefore, we can apply rewriting rule r2 to obtain

3. $(a = d < a = b < c, a = a < b = c < d)$

In the foregoing 2D string representation, we keep only the *relative* positioning information, and the *absolute* positioning information is lost. If we also omit the '=' symbols by applying rewriting rule r3, we obtain

4. $(ad < ab < c, aa < bc < d)$ (normal 2D string)

The same procedure can be applied to pictures whose "slots" may contain multiple objects (that is, object sets). For example, if in figure 10.1, $f(1,3)$ is $\{d,e\}$ instead of $\{d\}$, then the 2D string representation is

5. $(ad:e < ab < c, aa < bc < d:e)$ (normal 2D string with sets)

The 2D strings of 4 and 5 are called *normal 2D strings*.

If the ':' symbols are also omitted by applying rewriting rule r4, we obtain the following *reduced 2D string*:

6. $(ade < ab < c, aa < bc < de)$ (reduced 2D string)

We note that in a reduced 2D string representation, there is no apparent difference between symbols in the same set and symbols not in the same set. In the preceding example, the local substring (that is, the substring between two '<'s, or one '<' and an end-marker) "ade" might also be encoded as "aed," "dae," "dea," "ead," or "eda." In other words, for reduced 2D strings, a local substring is considered to be equivalent to its permutation string.

10.2 PICTURE MATCHING BY 2D STRING MATCHING

Two-dimensional string representation provides a simple approach to perform subpicture matching on 2D strings. The *rank* of each symbol in a string u, which is defined as one plus the number of '$<$' preceding this symbol in u, plays an important role in 2D string matching. We denote the rank of symbol b by $r(b)$. The strings "$ad < b < c$" and "$a < c$" have ranks as shown in Table 10.1:

TABLE 10.1

Ranks of Strings	
string v	string u
a d < b < c	a < c
1 1 2 3	1 2

A substring where all symbols have the same rank is called a *local substring*.

A string u is *contained* in a string v, if u is a subsequence of a permutation string of v.

A string u is a *type-i 1D subsequence* of string v, if

a. u is contained in v and

b. if $a_1 w_1 b_1$ is a substring of u, a_1 matches a_2 in v, and b_1 matches b_2 in v, then

(type-0) $r(b_2) - r(a_2) \geq r(b_1) - r(a_1)$ or $r(b_1)-r(a_1) = 0$

(type-1) $r(b_2) - r(a_2) \geq r(b_1) - r(a_1) > 0$ or $r(b_2) - r(a_2) = r(b_1) - r(a_1) = 0$

(type-2) $r(b_2)-r(a_2) = r(b_1)-r(a_1)$

Now we can define the notion of type-i ($i = 0,1,2$) 2D subsequence as follows. Let (u,v) and (u',v') be the 2D string representation of f and f', respectively. (u',v') is a *type-i 2D subsequence* of (u,v) if (a) u' is a type-i 1D subsequence of u, and (b) v' is a type-i 1D subsequence of v. We say f' is a *type-i subpicture* of f.

In Figure 10.2, f_1, f_2, and f_3 are all type-0 subpictures of f; f_1 and f_2 are type-1 subpictures of f; only f_1 is a type-2 subpicture of f. The normal 2D string representations are

$$\begin{array}{ll} f & (ad < b < c, a < bc < d) \\ f_1 & (a < b, a < b) \\ f_2 & (a < c, a < c) \\ f_3 & (ab < c, a < bc) \end{array}$$

Therefore, to determine whether a picture f' is a type-i subpicture of f, we need only determine whether (u',v') is a type-i 2D subsequence of (u,v). The picture matching problem thus becomes a 2D string matching problem.

In type-1 subsequence matching, each local substring in u should be matched against a local substring in v. In Table 10.1, substring "a" in u is a subsequence of

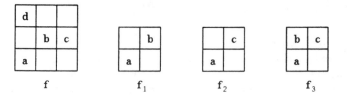

Figure 10.2 Picture matching example.

"ad" in v, and substring "c" in u is a subsequence of "c" in v. Notice the skipping of a rank is allowed in type-1 subsequence matching. Therefore, the type-1 subsequence matching problem can be considered a two-level subsequence matching problem, with level-1 subsequence matching for the local substrings, and level-2 subsequence matching for the "super-string" where each local substring is considered a super-symbol, and super-symbol u_1 matches super-symbol v_1 if u_1 is a subsequence of v_1.

Type-2 subsequence matching is actually simpler, because the rank cannot be skipped. That is to say, if local substring u_1 of u matches local substring v_1 of v, then substring u_i of u must match substring v_i of v for any i greater than 1. In the example shown in Table 10.1, v = "a < c" is not a type-2 subsequence of "ad < b < c."

Augmented 2D strings will be introduced in Section 10.5. For augmented 2D strings, we can define the notion of 2D subsequence as follows:

(u',v',p') is a type-i 2D subsequence of (u,v,p), if

a. (u',v') is type-i 2D subsequence of (u,v), and

b. if x'_i of u' matches x_j of u, then $x'_{p'(i)}$ of v' matches $x_{p(i)}$ of v.

Since augmented 2D strings will be seen to be the preferred representation, we present here only the procedure for augmented 2D string matching. By applying procedure "2DmatchA" once, we can check to see if (u',w') is a type-i 2D subsequence of (u,w) for i = 0, 1, or 2. A similar procedure "2Dmatch" can be written to handle absolute, normal, or reduced 2D string matching. The reader should skip this part in first reading, and study the procedure after having read Section 10.5.

```
2DmatchA(u', w'; u,w; i)

begin

1. convert (u', w') to (x',r',s',p')=(x'(1)...x'(N),r'(1)...r'(N),s'(1)...s'(N
     p'(1)...p'(N)) using procedure CA(u', w'; x',r',s',p');
   convert (u,w) to (x,r,s,p)=(x(1)...x(M),r(1)...r(M),s(1)...s(M),p(1)...p(1
     using procedure CA(u,w; x,r,s,p);
   while N ≤ M execute the following steps
```

```
      /* check if (u', w') is type-i 2D subsequence of (u,w) for i=0,1,2 */
2.for j from 1 until M
 begin
    if x(p(j))=a, let j belong to match(a)
 end
 for n from 1 until N
 begin
    MI(n)=match(x'(p'(n)))
 end
3.for n from 1 until N-1
 begin
    MC={}  /* {} denotes empty set */;
    while k belongs to MI(n) and j belongs to MI(n+1)
    begin
      call procedure d(n+1,j; n,k);
      if return "yes"
          let k belong to a(j,n+1,1);
      while n>1
      begin
          AP=a(k,n,1);
          for m from 2 until n
          begin
            a(j,n+1,m)={};
            while la belongs to AP
             begin
              call procedure d(n+1,j; n-m+1,la);
                if return "yes"
                    let la belong to a(j,n+1,m);
             end
            AP={lp | whenever la belongs to a(j,n+1,m) such that
              lp belongs to both a(la,n-m+1,1) and a(k,n,m)}
          end
      end
    if all a(j,n+1,m), m=1,...,n are not empty
        let j belong to MC
   end
   if MC is empty
      emit "no" and stop
   else MI(n+1)=MC
 end
 emit "yes"
end
```

```
d(m,j; n,k)
begin
  if j=k
    return "no";
  if  [r(p(j))-r(p(k))][r(p'(m))-r(p'(n))] ≥ 0 and
        (when i=0) [s(j)-s(k)][s'(m)-s'(n)] ≥ 0
                   |s(j)-s(k)| ≥ |s'(m)-s'(n)|
                   |r(p(j))-r(p(k))| ≥ |r'(p'(m))-r'(p'(n))|
        (when i=1) s(j)-s(k) ≥ s'(m)-s'(n)>0 or s(j)-s(k)=s'(m)-s'(n)=0
                   |r(p(j))-r(p(k))| ≥ |r'(p'(m))-r'(p'(n))|>0 or
                   r(p(j))-r(p(k))=r'(p'(m))-r'(p'(n))=0
        (when i=2) s(j)-s(k)=s'(m)-s'(n)
                   r(p(j))-r(p(k))=r'(p'(m))-r'(p'(n))
      return "yes"
  else
      return "no"
end

CA(u,w; x,r,s,p)
begin
 /* convert (u,w)=(u(1)...u(L), w(1)...w(K)) to (x,r,s,p)=(x(1)...x(N),
      r(1)...r(N), s(1)...s(N),p(1)...p(N)) */
 m=0;
 for l from 1 until L
 begin
   if u(l) ≠ '<'
      begin x(l-m)=u(l); r(l-m)=m+1 end
    else m=m+1
 end
 n=0;
 for k from 1 until K
 begin
   if w(k) ≠ '<'
      begin s(k-n)=n+1; p(k-n)=w(k) end
    else n=n+1
 end
end
```

This procedure can be divided into three major steps.

Step 1 converts (u,w) and (u',w') to (x,r,s,p) and (x',r',s',p'), respectively. String x over A consists of symbols appearing in u string, r is the corresponding rank string, s is another rank string corresponding to string y which consists of symbols appearing in v string, and p is the permutation function. The same is true for (u',w') and (x',r',s',p').

Step 2 constructs the initial matching tables $MI(n) = \{ j \mid$ whenever $y(j) = x(p(j)) = x'(p'(n)) = y'(n) \}$ for $n = 1, 2, ..., N$.

Step 3 checks to see if there exists a type-i subsequence in (u,w) which matches (u',w').

Given a 2D string (u, w), convert it to (x, r, s, p) using procedure CA. String $p(1)p(2) \ldots \ldots p(n)$, where n is equal to or less than the length of p, determines a 2D subsequence of (u, w). We denote the 2D subsequence by $(u, w)/n$. In the following, we consider (x, r, s, p) and (x', r', s', p') as they are in procedure 2DmatchA.

Lemma 1. In the procedure 2DmatchA, each path from an ancestor in $a(k, n, n-1)$ to k determines a length-n 2D subsequence in (u, w), and the subsequence matches $(u', w')/n$.

Since a path from an ancestor in $a(k, n, n-1)$ to k is actually a path consisting of indexes to elements of p, so the path determines a 2D subsequence of (u, w). It is easy to prove Lemma 1 by induction on n.

The procedure 2DmatchA works as follows: At first, MI(2) is examined to see if there are j in MI(2) and k in MI(1) such that the conditions listed in procedure $d(2, j; 1, k)$ are satisfied. If they are, let j belong to MC and k belong to $a(j, 2, 1)$. Then MI(2) is reduced to MC. Generally, if MI(n) has been reduced so that for each k in MI(n), all the ancestor sets $a(k, n, m)$, $m = 1, \ldots, n-1$, are not empty, and each path from an ancestor in $a(k, n, n-1)$ to k determines a length-n subsequence which matches $(u', w')/n$, then consider j in MI(n+1). An ancestor la in AP can be added to $a(j, n+1, m)$ only if the conditions listed in procedure $d(n+1, j; n-m+1, la)$ are true; thus the path from la to k is extended to j. If all $a(j, n+1, m)$, $m = 1, \ldots, n$, are not empty, j is put into MC, and then MI(n+1) is reduced to MC. It is apparent that each path from an ancestor in $a(j, n+1, n)$ to j determines a length-$(n+1)$ subsequence which matches $(u', w')/(n+1)$. Thus, by induction, if all MI(n), $n = 2, \ldots, N$ after reduction are not empty, then there exists at least one type-i 2D subsequence in (u, w) which matches (u', w'). The converse is also true. In conclusion, we have the following theorem.

Theorem 1. Procedure 2DmatchA$(u', w'; u, w; i)$ gives the correct results for type-i 2D subsequence matching—that is, it emits "yes" if and only if (u', w') is a type-i 2D subsequence of (u, w), where $i = 0, 1$, or 2.

Procedure 2DmatchA(.) has a running time of $O(M) + O(n^2 \times lp^3)$, where lp denotes the maximal length of matching tables MI(n), $n = 1, \ldots, N$. In fact, step 1 and step 2 can be completed in the time $O(M) + O(N)$. For each j in MI(n+1), the construction of $a(j, n+1, m)$, $m = 1, \ldots, n$, in step 3 needs time $O(n \times lp^2)$. Since the number of elements contained in MI(n+1) is not greater than lp, and the length of n loop is $N-1$, so the time spent on step 3 is $O(n^2 \times lp^3)$. And the total time spent on this procedure is $O(M) + O(N^2 \times lp^3)$. If, on the average, lp can be considered M/N, then the running time of procedure 2DmatchA(.) is $O(M^3/N)$.

Through a little modification, procedure 2DmatchA can be used to list all type-i 2D subsequences in (u, w) that match (u', w'). See [CHANG87] for details.

10.3 ORTHOGONAL RELATIONS

With the progress in the field of pictorial information systems, spatial data structure becomes one of the important factors in the design of pictorial information systems. Thus, to find a method that easily describes the spatial relations between objects is a basic issue in the design of pictorial information systems. In the following, a method called *orthogonal relations* is presented.

In terms of enclosing rectangles of objects, three types of spatial relations between objects can be identified. These are for objects with

1. nonoverlapping rectangles
2. partly overlapping rectangles
3. completely overlapping rectangles

The case with nonoverlapping rectangles is trivial and will never cause any problems in describing their mutual spatial relations because the object relations are simple. The other two might sometimes cause problems, especially when one of the objects partly surrounds the other or two objects surround one another.

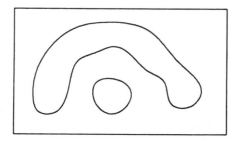

Figure 10.3 Objects with overlapping rectangles.

Figure 10.3 demonstrates a problem of this latter type. The fundamental issue here is to find a method that easily describes the relations between the objects. The method is called *orthogonal relations*, because it deals with spatial relations that are orthogonal to each other.

The basic idea is to regard one of the objects as a "point of view object" (PVO) and then view the other object in four directions (north, east, south, and west). Hence, at least one or at most four subparts of the other object can be "seen" from the PVO. The part of the object that actually is "seen" is in the interval where the two rectangles overlap, partly or completely. This is illustrated in Figure 10.4 and Figure 10.5.

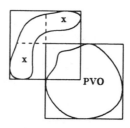

Figure 10.4 The PVO and its corresponding orthogonal relations for partly overlapping MERs.

The subobjects segmented by PVO are called *relational objects* of the original object. In Figures 10.4 and 10.5 relational objects are marked with an "x." The relational objects can be regarded as point objects—that is, a point located at the centroid of the rectangle that encloses each relational object. It is a fairly simple operation to identify and generate these points from a given segmented image. The next step is then

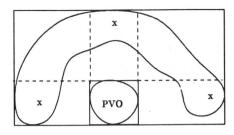

Figure 10.5 The PVO and its corresponding orthogonal relations for completely overlapping MERs.

to identify the relation between the objects by using the 2-D projection method described in Section 10.1.

Since relational objects of an object are regarded as points, a sparse vector description of the original object is generated. From this viewpoint it does not matter whether the original object is of a closed or linear type. This makes the methods powerful. However, it is of importance that the subobjects are interpreted correctly. Figure 10.6(a) shows a correct interpretation of a north and a west segment, while the interpretation of the same element in Figure 10.6(b) is erroneous.

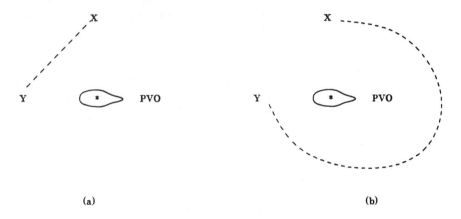

(a)   (b)

Figure 10.6 (a) A correct and (b) an erroneous interpretation of orthogonal relations.

Section 10.5 gives more details on the ruled-based interpretation of symbolic pictures obtained using orthogonal projections.

The technique of finding orthogonal relations is described in the following algorithm:

```
Ortho(x,y)
begin
  /*this procedure finds the orthogonal relations
    of object x with respect to object y*/

  /*find the minimum enclosing rectangle of x and y*/
  find Mer(x); find Mer(y);
```

```
/*find the four relational objects of object y intersecting
   with the extensions of object x*/
y-W = W-extension(Mer(x)) ∩ Mer(y);
y-E = E-extension(Mer(x)) ∩ Mer(y);
y-N = N-extension(Mer(x)) ∩ Mer(y);
y-S = S-extension(Mer(x)) ∩ Mer(y);

return( {y-W,y-E,y-N,y-S} );
end
```

The technique of finding orthogonal relations can be applied to obtaining the symbolic representation of a picture which preserves the spatial relations between objects in the picture. The symbolic picture then can be encoded into a 2D string representation which can be used for iconic indexing, to derive complicated spatial relations, and so on. First we process the image and recognize the objects. Then, for each object x, we find its orthogonal relational objects with respect to object y. If the number of orthogonal relational objects is less than 2, the MERs of objects x and y are disjointed. Therefore, we need not do further processing. If the number of orthogonal relational objects is greater than or equal to 2, then we will add them to the list Rel(y). After all object pairs have been processed, we have for each object y a list of orthogonal relational objects Rel(y). The object y can then be segmented into |Rel(y)| segments. The reference point of each segment is the center point of each orthogonal relational object. All the reference points constitute a symbolic picture which can then be converted to 2D string representation.

The algorithm now follows:

```
OrthoSegment(f,u,v)
begin
  /*object recognition*/
  recognize objects in the picture f;

  /*initialization*/
  for each object x
   Rel(x) is set to empty;

  /*find orthogonal relations*/
  for each pair of objects x and y
   begin
   find Ortho(x,y) /*orthogonal relations of object x
                 with respect to object y*/;
   if |Ortho(x,y)|>1 then Rel(y)=Rel(y) ∪ Ortho(x,y);
   find Ortho(y,x) /*orthogonal relations of object y
                 with respect to object x*/;
   if |Ortho(y,x)|>1 then Rel(x)=Rel(x) ∪ Ortho(y,x);
   end
```

```
/*segmentation*/
for each object x
 segment x into objects listed in Rel(x);

/*2D string encoding*/
apply procedure 2Dstring(f,m,u,v,n);
end
```

An example is given next. The original image contains objects 'a', 'b', and 'c', where 'c' is a linear object, and 'a', 'b' are point objects and 'c' is a line object, as shown in Figure 10.7(a).

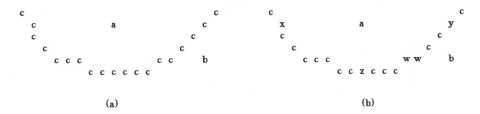

(a)   (b)

Figure 10.7   (a) Original image; (b) its segmentation.

After applying the Procedure Ortho, we find that Ortho(a,c) = $\{x, y, z\}$, and Ortho(b,c) = $\{w, y\}$. Therefore, object 'c' contains four relational objects. 'x', 'y', 'z', and 'w', as shown in Figure 10.7(b). The center of each relational object is used as the reference point of each segment. In this way, all orthogonal spatial relations are preserved. The 2D string encoding of the picture is $(u, v) = (x < za < w < by, z < wb < xay)$.

10.4 SPATIAL REASONING

Spatial reasoning may be thought of as the inferring of a consistent set of spatial relationships among the objects in a picture. Spatial reasoning is important in computer vision and robotics as well as pictorial information systems. This section describes spatial reasoning based on 2D string representation.

When retrieving pictures from a pictorial information system, one of the most powerful methods we have for discriminating among the pictures is the perception of spatial relationships that exist between objects in the desired picture. This makes the ability to make queries on these relationships an important attribute of a pictorial information system. A simple tabular account of these relationships soon overwhelms the system due to their combinatorial nature. Also, the addition of a new fact may require a major reconfiguration of the pictorial database. For these reasons, a more practical implementation will store the information as facts from which these relations can be derived as they are needed, along with a set of rules for deriving them. In this form, new facts are easily assimilated by the system.

The 2D string representation is an efficient, yet powerful, data structure for preserving the needed information while at the same time providing an index for the picture. If we consider only point objects, we can see that the 2D string gives us an unambiguous account of the simple relations such as *north*, *south*, *east*, *west*, and their aliases— *over, under,* and *next to.* A query asking for all pictures with a lake east of a mountain is translated into a pattern matching problem where "lake" is to the left of "mountain" in the strings representing the east-west relation. The correct answer for a query on lakes northeast of mountains is simply the intersection of the set of lakes north of mountains with that set east of mountains. The 2D string may be constructed at different resolutions, thus allowing us to make our queries as fuzzy or as precise as necessary.

The user of a pictorial information system may ask the system such questions as "What objects are situated between a lake and a forest in this picture?" or "Is there a gas station east of the highway in the picture?" This type of query might be of interest in cases where a large number of pictures are archived at a central site. By examining these relations, along with the picture's icons, users at remote sites can retrieve those pictures of interest while operating on a small fraction of the information stored at the central site.

Besides the simple spatial relations such as *north*, *south*, *east*, *west*, and their aliases— *over, under* and *next to*—we need to derive more complicated and useful spatial relations such as *surrounded by*, *partly surrounded by*, *same position as*, and so on. In considering how to derive these types of relationships, we need to know how the 2D string representation is constructed. The input to this string construction process is a labeled, segmented image. Each connected object has a unique label. In the case where each object labeled is a point object, there is no ambiguity in the construction process. The 2D string can be constructed by sorting the objects into two lists by their position in the east-west and north-south directions and separating the object labels with '<' markers. However, consider the following more difficult example in Figure 10.8.

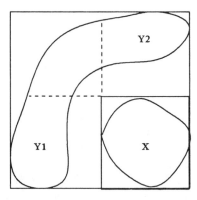

Figure 10.8 A partly surrounded object.

For an object X partly surrounded by another object Y in Figure 10.8, we will have a 2D string of the following type: $(Y1 < X \ Y2, Y1 \ X < Y2)$. In other words, part 1 of Y is west of X, and part 2 of object Y is at the same north-south level as object X; part 1 of Y is at the same west-east level as object X, and part 2 of Y is north of object X.

We know that the object with the primary label Y is connected; therefore we can deduce that X is partly surrounded by Y on its west and north sides. In this case, we had X lying inside the minimum enclosing rectangle of Y. For this reason we split the large object (Y) into two parts based on the orthogonal projections of the small object (X). A recursive application of this principle leads to the desired string representation. In general, an object with the symbolic label X may be divided into parts $X1, X2, \cdots, Xn$ during the string construction process. We use this knowledge of the construction process to interpret the string.

In a similar manner, we can find the *surrounded by* relations by looking for combinations of string patterns which give rise to this situation. We must have an object with one part south, east, north, and west of an object with (at least) four parts. In deriving the *surrounded by* and *partly surrounded by* relations, a picture with a large number of objects will generate a large number of partial solutions as the algorithm attempts to find the *north*, *south*, *east*, and *west* relations as subgoals and then unify those subgoals at a higher level. Many of the spurious partial solutions can be suppressed by recalling that an enclosing object must have multiple parts. Therefore we don't generate "the dog is east of the car" as a partial solution to the query "Which objects surround the car?"

The way the relation *near* is treated is to consider objects which have no other objects between them as being *near* one another. This solution is the best we can give in our representation, since the 2D string contains no metric information, and it is reasonably intuitive. If we have X near Y and the set Z between X Y, then Z is the empty set.

At the lowest level, we have four basic relations: east-of (X, Y), same-east-position (X, Y), north-of (X, Y), and same-north-position (X, Y). From these we have two more relations since east-of (X, Y) implies west-of (Y, X), and north-of (X, Y) implies south-of (Y, X). We then combine these six relations to form northeast, northwest, southeast, and southwest. Building on these basic relations and our knowledge of the way the 2D string is represented, we find still more relations such as *surrounded by* and *near*. All of these relations can be traced back to the process of searching through the basic 2D string representation.

The next step is to add domain-specific knowledge to the rule base. These rules could have several functions. One type of rule can be used to prune our search tree by the application of semantic knowledge. For instance, knowledge of the relative size of objects can be used to halt the generation of subgoals in the *surrounded by* relation if the object "inside" the relation is always bigger than the object surrounding it. We can suppress the generation of relations which are always true such as "the median strip is near the highway."

We could also add rules which allow us to make higher-level queries. For example, a simple rule might state that we can travel between two cities if there is a highway between the two cities and at the same position as the cities. The addition of a layer of rules such as this is easy due to the structure of the reasoning system as a collection of rules. The design facilitates the tailoring of the system to the user and to domain-specific applications. Different users can specify different databases of rules which they can maintain or change as they see fit.

Another class of rules that are easy to add are categorical rules such as "is-a" and "instance-of." The addition of this type of rule, along with an advanced recognition module, makes the spatial reasoning system very powerful. We could construct a list of "interesting" objects and make queries such as "Show me all interesting objects north of the river." The list of objects would then be compared with those objects north of the river, and the intersection of the two sets would be the response.

An extension of the approach to spatial reasoning will take into account the following types of information: metric information, shape, orientation, and topology. Metric information could take the form of an indication of the scale of the image along with the closest distance between adjacent components of the 2D string. This would allow the spatial reasoning system to answer queries concerning distances between objects in the image and the shortest distance between objects. Shape information could be given by a chain code or some other approach. The orientation of objects allows us to distinguish those cases where objects have the same projections along both east-west and north-south axes. Topological information allows us to assign multiple symbolic names to the logical components of connected objects. All of this information could be extracted during the segmentation phase.

Another approach would be to add attributes to the objects. This would allow queries such as "Find all cities with a population greater than 100,000 which are located on a lakeshore."

10.5 VISUALIZATION OF SYMBOLIC PICTURES

We now ask the following question: Given the 2D string representation, can we visualize the objects in the original picture?

From the 2D string (u, v), we can easily reconstruct the symbolic picture which the 2D string (u, v) represents. As an example, suppose the 2D string is $(x_1 \, x_2 < x_3 \, x_4 < x_5, x_2 \, x_3 \, x_4 < x_1 \, x_5)$. We first construct the picture shown in Figure 10.9(a), based on the 1D string u, by placing objects having the same spatial location (that is, objects related by the '=' operator) in the same "slot".

Next, we use the 1D string v to construct the final picture Figure 10.9(b).

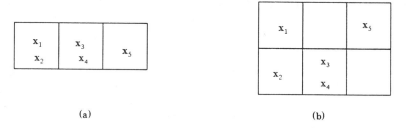

(a)   (b)

Figure 10.9   Picture reconstruction from 2D string.

The algorithm follows:

```
2Dpicture(f,m_1,m_2,u,v,n)
begin
  /*find out the size of the picture*/
  m_1 = 1 + number of '<' in string u;
  m_2 = 1 + number of '<' in string v;
  /*find out the x-rank and y-rank of each object*/
  for i from 1 until n
    begin
    x-rank of x_i = 1 + number of '<' preceding x_i in u;
    y-rank of x_p(i) = 1 + number of '<' preceding x_p(i) in v;
    end
  /*we construct an m_1 by m_2 picture f*/
  for j from 1 until m_1
    for k from 1 until m_2
      f(j,k) = the set of all objects
               with x-rank j and y-rank k;
end
```

In the procedure "2Dpicture," we assume the permutation function p is given. If all the objects in a 2D string are distinct, the permutation function p is unique. If, however, there are identical symbols in the 2D string, then in general there are many permutation functions. For example, the picture f of Figure 10.1 has 2D string representation $(u,v) = (ad < ab < c, aa < bc < d)$. Let the u string be "$x_1 x_2 < x_3 x_4 < x_5$". Then the v string is either

$$"x_1 x_3 < x_4 x_5 < x_2" \quad \text{or} \quad "x_3 x_1 < x_4 x_5 < x_2"$$

We can use either permutation function in the foregoing procedure "2Dpicture," which will always reconstruct a picture. However, the reconstructed picture could be different from the original picture. In the preceding example, the reconstructed picture is actually unique and unambiguous. However, this may not always be the case. The problem of ambiguity was investigated in detail in [CHANG87].

Another consideration is the uniqueness of the 2D string representation. As just stated, given any 2D string (u,v) and its permutation function p, the procedure "2Dpicture" will always reconstruct a picture. However, only for the reduced 2D string representation is the 2D string generated from the reconstructed symbolic picture always identical to the original 2D string, because the local substrings and their permutation strings are considered equivalent.

The foregoing considerations suggest that we can include the permutation function p in the 2D string representation. Then, we will have no ambiguity in picture reconstruction, and the 2D string representation is also unique.

Therefore, we define an *augmented 2D string* (u,v,p), where (u,v) is the reduced 2D string as previously defined, and p is the permutation function. With the augmented 2D string, picture f of Figure 10.1 is represented by

7. $(ad < ab < c, aa < bc < d, 13452)$ (augmented 2D string)

In actual coding, the second string v can be replaced by

$$w = p(1)z(1)p(2)z(2) \dots z(n-1)p(n)$$

In other words, the symbols in v are replaced by the permutation indexes:

8. $(ad < ab < c,\ 13 < 45 < 2)$ (augmented 2D string)

We will use the notation (u, v, p) to denote an augmented 2D string, although in actual coding we will use (u, w). For augmented 2D strings, the procedure "2Dpicture" can be applied directly by including p as an additional input parameter. Procedure "2Dstring" of Section 10.1 should be replaced by the following procedure.

```
2DstringA(f,m; u,w)
begin
   /* we assume f is m by m square picture */
   n=0;
   for i from 1 until m do
      begin
         for j from 1 until m do
            begin
               if f(i,j) is not empty
                  for s in f(i,j)
                     begin
                        n=n+1;
                        q(i,j) = q(i,j) ∪ {n}
                     end
            end
      end
   l=0; u='null'  /* 'null' denotes null string */
   for i from 1 until m do
      begin
         for j from 1 until m do
            begin
               if f(i,j) is not empty
                  l=l+ size-of(f(i,j));
                  u=u.f(i,j)   /* '.' denotes concatenation operator */
            end
         if i<m and l<n
            u=u.<
      end
   k=0; w='null';
   for j from 1 until m do
      begin
         for i from 1 until m do
            begin
               if f(i,j) is not empty
                  k=k+ size-of(f(i,j));
               w=w.q(i,j)
            end
         if j<m and k<n
            w=w.<
      end
end
```

The foregoing procedure "2DstringA" generates an augmented 2D string representation, where the function size-of(S) returns the number of elements in a set S.

If there is no overlapping between objects' enclosing rectangles—that is, in some sense we can treat the objects as "point objects" by substituting every symbol with its icon—we can get an approximate visualization of the original picture. However, if the objects are pieces of a segmented object, we must somehow reconstruct (and reconnect) the segmented pieces.

We can, of course, retrieve the original images or the compressed images from the image database. This is time consuming. An alternative is to use spatial reasoning to find out the spatial relations between objects or object segments from 2D string representation and then apply *connection rules* to reconnect the segments from a reconstructed symbolic picture.

For symbolic pictures derived by using the orthogonal relation method, by successively using the rules discussed in Section 10.3, we can obtain for every object its orthogonal relational objects. How do we reconnect these segments to form an integrated object? In fact, there are many ways to reconnect these segments. Figure 10.6 shows two ways to reconnect segments into an integrated object. Figure 10.6(a) shows a correct interpretation of a north and a west segment, while the interpretation of the same element in Figure 10.6(b) is erroneous. The natural interpretation is to look clockwise. Hence, nine different combinations can be identified.

2 points: N - E, E - S, S - W, W - N
3 points: N - E - S, E - S - W, S - W - N, W - N - E
4 points: N - E - S - W

No other interpretations are allowed. However, a single object may be "viewed" by more than one PVO. After the relational objects with respect to each PVO are reconnected, we need some work to connect the intermediate objects together. Figure 10.10 shows an example of how the connection is done. In the connection procedure, spline functions can be used to get smooth and reasonable lines, in the absence of shape information. So far what we have is a picture of lines and points. By expanding lines representing areal objects to an appropriate extent, an approximate visualization of the original image is achieved. If we associate attributes with the symbols in a symbolic picture, more reaslistic visualization can be achieved. The more interesting issue is "Can we implement the visualization independent of how the symbolic pictures are abstracted from original images?" In this case, we have no a priori knowledge about the structure of the symbolic picture. We can use some general knowledge—for example, "if there is no bridge on a river, a road cannot cross the river"—and some connection rules to reconnect the pieces of objects.

In fact, if more connection rules are added into the knowledge base of the connection procedure, more realistic visualizations can be achieved. Also, by checking the visualized pictures during the experimental stage, the connection rule set can be expanded and improved gradually, leading to a practical visualization program. Figure 10.11 shows the experimental results using Interlisp-D on a Xerox 1108 Lisp machine. Figure 10.11(a) and 10.11(b) are two symbolic pictures, where symbols F, L, B, and

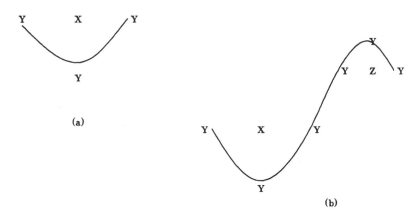

Figure 10.10 (a) Reconnection of orthogonal relational objects; (b) connection of intermediate objects.

R represent *forest*, *lake*, *barn—house*, and *road*, respectively. Figure 10.11(c) and 10.11(d) are the visualizations of Figure 10.11(a) and 10.11(b), respectively.

10.6 ICONIC INDEXING

To construct the iconic index using 2D strings, we can proceed as follows: First, we apply image processing and pattern recognition techniques to segment the image and recognize the objects in the image. For the object-oriented picture, we use the techniques discussed in Section 10.3 to obtain a symbolic representation of the picture. Then the symbolic representation is converted to a 2D string representation which is stored in the pictorial database as an iconic index for the picture. Since we extract every object in the original image and each object is indexed by including a symbolic name in the 2D string representation, we call the preceding indexing method *complete 2D string indexing*. Generally, we can have *partial 2D string indexing* by extracting and indexing only on interesting objects.

The 2D string representation is ideally suited to formulating picture queries. In fact, we can easily imagine that the query can be specified graphically by drawing an iconic picture on the screen of a personal computer. The graphical representation can then be translated into the 2D string representation using the procedure "2Dstring" described in Section 10.1. This approach combines the advantage of the query-by-example approach—where a query is formed by constructing an example—and the concept of icon-oriented visual programming systems. Pictorial information retrieval is then transformed into the problem of 2D subsequence matching. The query, represented by a 2D string, is matched against the *iconic indexes,* which are the 2D

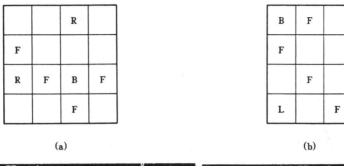

		R	
F			
R	F	B	F
		F	

(a)

B	F	
F		
		F
L		F

(b)

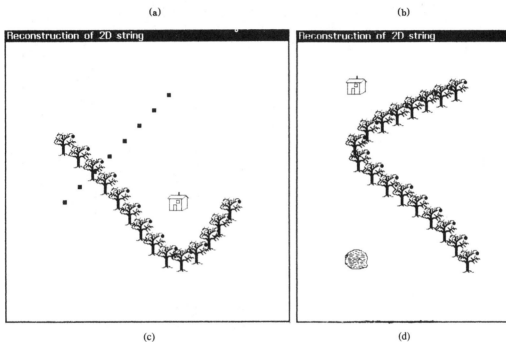

(c) (d)

Figure 10.11 Examples of visualization on Xerox 1108 Lisp machine. Symbolic pictures of (a) road, forest, and barn-house; (b) barn-house, forest, and lake; (c) visualization on Xerox 1108 Lisp machine of (a); (d) visualization of (b).

string representations of the pictures in the database. Those pictures whose iconic indexes match the query 2D string are retrieved.

The early experimental results on 2D string matching were conducted on a PDP11/70 minicomputer system. Figure 10.12(a) shows a picture which is a map overlay of lakes. This picture was digitized, and the lake objects were classified into small lakes, medium-sized lakes, and large lakes. The resultant symbolic picture is shown in Figure 10.12(b). The user can specify a query by giving a query pattern, as shown in Figure 10.13. Figures 10.13(a) and (b) are queries to retrieve type-1 and type-2 subpictures respectively. By applying the 2D string matching algorithms, the matched subpictures are found. When there are several matched subpictures, the results (the coordinates of retrieved objects) are all displayed.

Figures 10.13(c) and (d) illustrate queries containing variables. For example, Figure 10.13(c) shows such a query pattern: "find the pictures in which there is

Sec. 10.6   Iconic Indexing   **255**

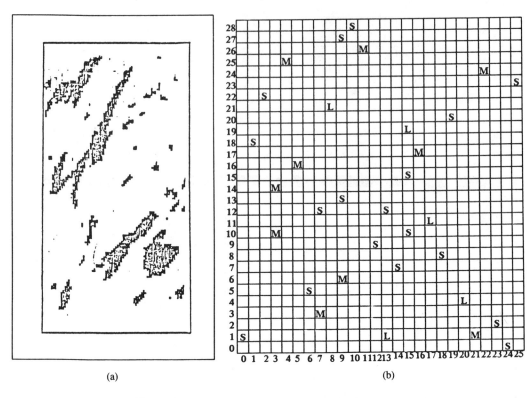

(a)   (b)

Figure 10.12   (a) A picture of lakes; (b) a symbolic picture of lake objects.

something (unknown) whose relative spatial relations with large lakes are implied by the pattern." The corresponding 2D string for this query contains a symbol Z, which is a variable or "wild-card" character that can match any symbol other than the operator symbols. It is easy to see that various queries can be expressed implicitly by 2D strings, and we can also answer these queries by using 2D string matchings. These examples illustrate the potential applications of our approach to pictorial information retrieval.

```
QUERY PATTERN ( TYPE-1 )
L,   ,
 ,L,
 , ,L


RESULT:
*(20,4)   (17,11)  (15,19)
*(20,4)   (17,11)  (8,21)
*(20,4)   (15,19)  (8,21)
*(17,11)  (15,19)  (8,21)
```

Figure 10.13   Query patterns and retrieval results.

(b) QUERY PATTERN (TYPE-2)
       S,

        ,

         ,M

       RESULT:
       *(7,3) (6,5)
       *(11,26) (10,28)

(c) QUERY PATTERN (TYPE-1)
        ,L, ,

         , ,Z,

         , , ,L

       L, , ,

       RESULT
       *(13,1) (20,4) (18,8) (17,11)
       *(13,1) (20,4) (18,8) (17,11) (16,17) (15,19)
       *(13,1) (17,11) (16,17) (15,19)

(d) QUERY PATTERN (TYPE-2)
       , , , ,L, , ,

       , , , , , , ,

       , , , , , , ,

       , , , , ,Z, ,

       , , , , , , ,

       , , , , , , ,

       , , , , , , ,

       , , , , , , ,L

       , , , , , , ,

       , , , , , , ,

       L, , , , , , ,

       RESULT:
       *(13,1) (20,4) (18,8) (17,11)

Figure 10.13 *cont'd.*

Recently, a prototype pictorial information system was developed at the University of Pittsburgh. The distinction of this pictorial information system is that it uses the 2D string as an iconic indexing to the pictorial database. One of the many features of the system is that it supports a lot of drawing functions to allow users to draw a picture (query example) of object icons on a working window. Figure 10.14 is such an instance of query-by-example on the system. The semantic meaning of the query is "find the picture(s) with two houses and a car, and the spatial relations between the two houses and the car are the same as it implies in the query picture." When the user completes the query picture, the system will interpret it and convert it into 2D string representation and then do the matching. The matched 2D string index (or indexes) in the pictorial database can be visualized. Figure 10.15 is the response of the system to this query—that is, the response is a visualized picture of matched 2D string(s).

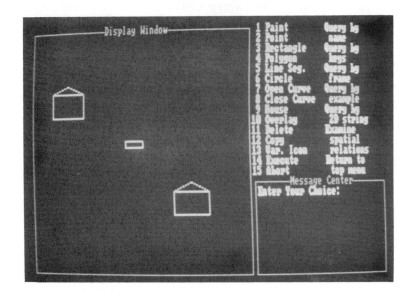

Figure 10.14 Query by example.

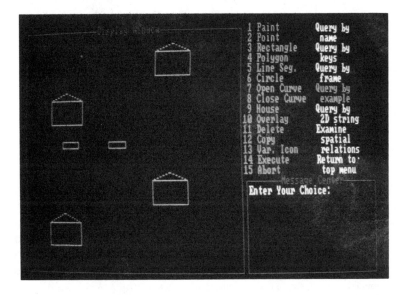

Figure 10.15 Response to query by example.

Figure 10.16 is the original image from which the matched 2D string is extracted. Note that the orientation of the cars in the original image and that in the visualized picture is not the same; but we can get rid of this by binding some attributes to 2D strings.

Figure 10.16 Town picture.

The iconic index not only can be used in pictorial information retrieval, but it also provides an efficient means for *picture browsing*. Since we can visualize a picture from its 2D string representation, we can apply a visualization procedure to reconstruct an *icon picture* from the iconic index. In this picture browsing mode, we need only access the iconic indexes instead of retrieving the actual pictures from the image database. For some applications, the picture browsing technique might be very useful.

R E F E R E N C E S

[BASL85] BASL, P. J., AND R. C. JAIN, "Three-Dimensional Object Recognition," *ACM Computing Surveys,* Vol. 17, No. 1, March 1985, 75-145.

[CHANGNS79] CHANG, N. S., AND K. S. FU, "Query-by-Pictorial-Example," *Proceedings of COMPSAC 79,* IEEE Computer Society, 1979, 325-330.

[CHANG71] CHANG, S. K., "The Reconstruction of Binary Patterns from Their Projections," *Communications of the ACM,* Vol. 14, No. 1, January 1971, 21-25.

[CHANG81] CHANG, S. K., AND T. KUNII, "Pictorial Database Systems," *IEEE Computer Magazine Special Issue on Pictorial Information Systems,* Edited by S. K. Chang, November 1981, 13-21.

[CHANG84A] CHANG, S. K., AND S. H. LIU, "Indexing and Abstraction Techniques for Pictorial Databases," *IEEE Transactions on Pattern Analysis and Machine Intelligence,* July 1984, 475-484.

[CHANG84B] CHANG, S. K., AND O. CLARISSE, "Interpretation AND Construction of Icons for Man-Machine Interface in an Image Information System," *IEEE Proceedings of Languages for Automation,* Nov. 1-3, 1984, 38-45.

[CHANG85] CHANG, S. K., "Icon Semantics - A Formal Approach to Icon System Design," *Technical Report,* Information Systems Laboratory, Illinois Institute of Technology, August 1985.

[CHANG87] CHANG, S. K., Q. Y. SHI, AND C. W. YAN, "Iconic Indexing by 2D Strings," *IEEE Tran. on PAMI-9,* No. 3, May 1987, 413-428.

[HIRSCHBERG77] HIRSCHBERG, D. S., "Algorithms for the Longest Common Subsequence Problem," *Journal of the ACM,* Volume 24, 1977, 664-675.

[HUNT77] HUNT, J. W., AND T. G. SZYMANSKI, "A Fast Algorithm for Computing Longest Common Subsequences," *Communications of the ACM,* Volume 20, 1977, 350-353.

[SAMET84] SAMET, H., "The Quadtree and Related Data Structures," *ACM Computing Survey,* Vol 16, No. 2, June 1984, 187-260.

E X E R C I S E S

1. The following are two symbolic pictures. Find the augmented 2D string representations of these two symbolic pictures.

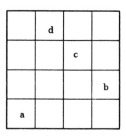

(a)   (b)

2. Apply procedure 2DmatchA to the augmented 2D strings obtained in problem 1. Trace the procedure and answer the question:

   Is picture B a type-1 subpicture of picture A?

3. Let (u, v) be a reduced 2D string and (x, y) another reduced 2D string. Is the following statement true?

> if (a) x is a substring of u and
> (b) y is a substring of v
> then the symbolic picture represented by (x, y) is a
> subpicture of the symbolic picture represented by (u, v).

Explain why.

4. Design a small pictorial database containing ten images using the 2D string iconic indexing technique. Each image contains simple objects such as house, car, trees, and so on. The pictorial database should be able to handle queries given as 2D strings.

5. Design an algorithm to check to see if any given string pair (u, v) forms a reduced 2D string—that is, for any string pair (u, v), is there a symbolic picture such that (u, v) is a reduced 2D string representation of the symbolic picture?

6. Design an algorithm to find all the orthogonal spatial relations in a symbolic picture which is represented as an augmented 2D string.

Chapter 11

Visual Languages

In Part I of this book, we dealt with principles of picture coding, physical picture representation and picture processing. In Figure 1.1 (reproduced here), the schematic diagram of a pictorial information system, we can see Part I covers the principles and techniques for the subsystem corresponding to the blocks "picture input device," "picture processor," and "picture communication interface." Part II concentrates on pictorial database design, and covers the principles and techniques for the subsystem corresponding to the blocks "picture storage system" and "pictorial database." In Part III of this book, we will concentrate on the rightmost block, "picture output device." In other words, we will concern ourselves with the design of the visual user interface and describe principles and techniques for visual languages and icon-oriented system design.

Visual languages can be classified into four types: languages supporting visual interaction, visual programming languages, visual information processing languages, and iconic visual information processing languages. In this chapter we survey recent research in these four types of visual languages and introduce the concept of generalized icons to provide a unified framework for the design of visual languages. Applications of various types of visual languages are also surveyed.

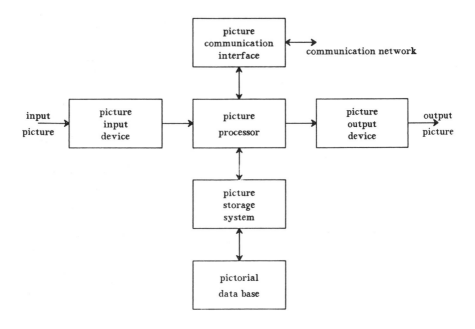

Figure 1.1 The pictorial information system.

11.1 CLASSIFICATION OF VISUAL LANGUAGES

The combination of graphics, image, video, and microelectronics technology has made it feasible to design low-cost image information systems to create, transmit, display, manipulate, and retrieve visual information. Research in visual languages has also gained momentum due to recent interest in multimedia communications [ACEVES85, LODDING82]. However, the term "visual language" means different things to different people. To some, it means the objects handled by the language are visual. To others, it means the language itself is visual. To the first group of people, "visual language" means "language for processing visual information" or "visual information processing language." To the second group of people, "visual language" means "language for programming with visual expression" or "visual programming language."

In visual information processing languages, the objects to be dealt with usually have an inherent visual representation. They are images or pictorial objects which are then associated with a certain logical interpretation. On the other hand, the languages themselves may not have a visual representation. These languages are usually based on traditional "linear" languages, enhanced by library subroutines or software packages to deal with visual objects. Application domains of visual information processing languages include image processing, computer vision, robotics, image database management, office automation, and image communications.

In visual programming languages, the objects to be dealt with usually do not have an inherent visual representation. They include traditional data types such as arrays, stacks, queues, and application-oriented data types such as forms, documents, databases, and so on. To achieve a user-friendly person-machine interface, we would like to present these objects visually. For the same reason, the languages themselves also should be presented visually. In other words, both programming constructs and rules to combine these programming constructs should be visually presented. Application domains of visual programming languages include computer graphics, user interface design, database interface, form management, and computer aided design.

The foregoing two types of visual languages do not exhaust all the possibilities. The objects to be dealt with by a visual language can be inherently visual, or inherently nonvisual but with imposed visual representation. The programming language constructs can be visual or linear. Therefore, there are *four types* of visual languages, which are summarized in Table 11.1 (column 3 will be explained later).

TABLE 11.1

Visual Languages' Classification	Objects to Be Dealt With	Transformation of Objects	Languages' Visibility
Languages Supporting Visual Interaction	logical objects with visual representation	$(X_m, e) \rightarrow$ (X_m, X'_i)	linearly represented constructs
Visual Programming Languages	logical objects with visual representation	$(X_m, e) \rightarrow$ (X_m, X'_i)	visually represented constructs
Visual Information Processing Languages	visual objects with imposed logical representation	$(e, X_i) \rightarrow$ (X'_m, X_i)	linearly represented constructs
Iconic Visual Information Processing Languages	visual objects with imposed logical representation	$(e, X_i) \rightarrow$ (X'_m, X_i)	visually represented constructs

The four types of visual languages are indeed different. A unifying concept for these visual languages is that they all deal with different aspects of generalized icons. Generalized icons consist of object icons and process icons. An *object icon* is a dual representation of an object, written as (X_m, X_i), with a logical part X_m (the meaning) and a physical part X_i (the image). In visual programming languages, we are dealing with (X_m, e)—that is, objects with logical meaning but no visual image. (The symbol 'e' denotes a null object.) The visual representation is then imposed—that is, we must transform (X_m, e) into (X_m, X'_i) so it can be visualized. In visual information processing languages, we are dealing with (e, X_i)—that is, objects with a visual image but whose logical meaning must be assigned. In other words, we must transform (e, X_i) into (X'_m, X_i). The transformations of object icons are summarized in column 3 of Table 11.1.

The objects handled by a visual language can thus be considered object icons or icons with a logical part and a physical part representing an object. Similarly, the programming language constructs in a visual language can be considered *process icons* or icons with a logical part and a physical part representing a computation process. The distinction between an object icon and a process icon depends on both context and interpretation. For example, the road sign of a diagonal line inside a circle can be interpreted as a "stop-sign" by a computer vision system. It is an object icon under this latter interpretation. On the other hand, it could also be interpreted as a "halt" command by a mobile robot. It is a process icon (or action icon) under this interpretation. The concept of *generalized icon* encompasses both object icons and process icons (or action icons). We can then study the syntax and semantics of icon interpretation for both isolated icons and a spatial arrangement of icons.

The concept of generalized icons as object icons and process icons leads to a general approach for designing visual languages. First we ask the question, How can we represent visual objects logically? And conversely, How can we represent logical objects visually? This consideration leads to the concept of object icons. Then we ask the question, How can we represent programming constructs visually and specify algorithms in a visual language? This consideration leads to the concept of process icons (or action icons).

This chapter is organized into four main sections: the Section 11.2 surveys both visual programming languages and languages supporting visual interaction. Section 11.3 surveys iconic and visual information processing languages; Section 11.4 describes two types of visual languages for database systems; and Section 11.5 discusses cognitive aspects in visual information processing. Some concluding remarks are then given.

11.2 VISUAL PROGRAMMING LANGUAGES AND LANGUAGES SUPPORTING VISUAL INTERACTION

11.2.1 Performance Measures for Visual Languages

Shu [SHU86] gave a survey of visual programming languages and proposed a dimensional framework for analysis so that visual programming languages can be characterized and compared.

To evaluate whether the visual language approach is adequate or not for an intended application of a certain type of user, three questions can be asked:

- Is the visual language adequate in visualization?
- Is the visual language adequate in representing processes?
- Is the visual language adequate in representing objects?

The three questions correspond to the three dimensions in Shu's performance measure of visual programming languages. These are:

1. Visibility (adequacy in visualization).
2. Level of a language (adequacy in representing processes by procedural or nonprocedural means).
3. Scope of a language (adequacy in representing objects for different applications).

The level of a language is an inverse measure of the amount of details that a user has to give to the computer to achieve the desired results. The scope of the language, ranging from the general and widely applicable to the specific and narrowly applicable, depicts the application scope of a language. Shu used these three yardsticks to characterize visual languages (see Figure 11.1). For example, the Xerox Star System is high in visual content, but low in level and scope. On the other hand, Query-by-Example [ZLOOF81] is low in visual content and scope, but high in language level. The adequacy of visual languages is related to the cognitive aspects in visual information processing, which will be discussed later.

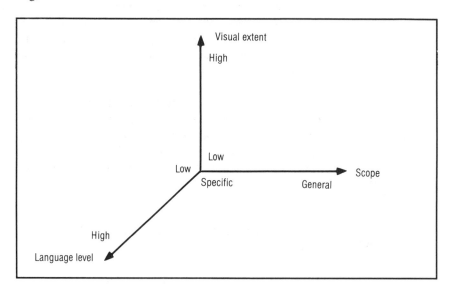

Figure 11.1 Three dimensions of visual programming languages (from S.K. Chang, "Visual Languages: A Tutorial Survey," *IEEE Software*, ©1987 IEEE).

11.2.2 Spatial Parsing

When a text-graphic object is used in communication, that object has meaning under a system of interpretation of a visual language. Lakin [LAKIN86] explores the parsing and interpretation of visual sentences—or visual communication objects—in visual languages. The objects to be dealt with are logical objects with visual representation. By analyzing their spatial arrangement, the underlying syntactic structure is recovered—which could denote a computation process or a complex structure subject to further interpretation. Lakin thus calls his approach "executable graphics." In our classification, spatial parsing is applicable to both visual programming languages and iconic visual information processing languages, although Lakin's work is more closely related to the former. As an example of spatial parsing, in the visual Lisp called 'Vennlisp' developed by Lakin, visual objects are used to direct computation, and the results of computation are also visual objects (see Figure 11.2). In a Vennlisp diagram, spatial enclosures are used to denote the nesting of function calls. Therefore, the spatial parser will first find the spatial enclosing relations among visual objects (using the up-left-first ordering rule) and then construct the corresponding parsing tree. A second example of parsing a visual sentence written in VIC (a visual language for aphasics) is illustrated in Figure 11.3. Since the VIC sentence is almost linear, the parser will recognize the individual icons and then construct the parsing tree. A third example of parsing a finite-state diagram is illustrated in Figure 11.4. Parsing in this example amounts to the tracing of arcs in a directed graph to construct the arc-node list.

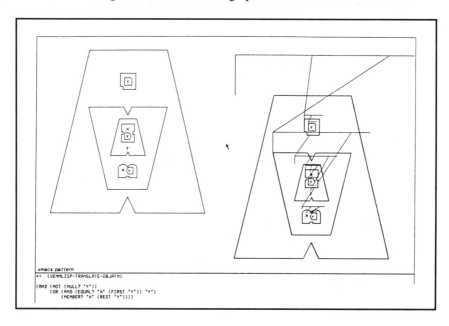

Figure 11.2 A Vennlisp Diagram and its parsed version (from S.K. Chang, "Visual Languages: A Tutorial Survey," *IEEE Software*, ©1987 IEEE).

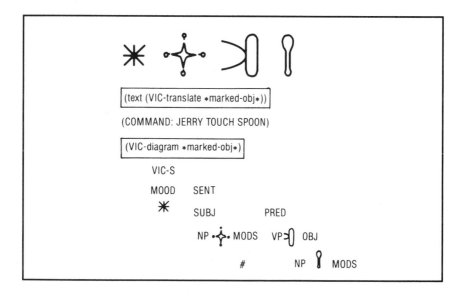

Figure 11.3 A visual sentence written in VIC (from S.K. Chang, "Visual Languages: A Tutorial Survey," *IEEE Software*, ©1987 IEEE).

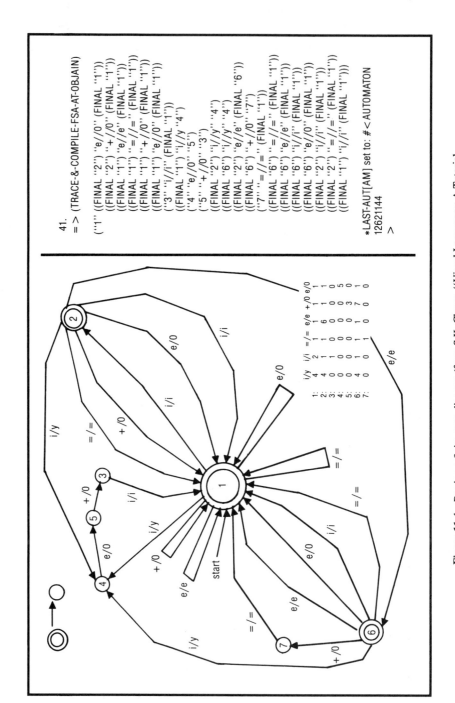

Figure 11.4 Parsing a finite-state diagram (from S.K. Chang, "Visual Languages: A Tutorial Survey," *IEEE Software,* ©1987 IEEE).

Spatial parsing of visual languages is rather application-dependent. In what follows, we take Vennlisp as an example to demonstrate the principles of spatial parsing of visual objects.

Visual objects in Vennlisp are text-graphics based on the so-called SAM-model of writing and drawing. Text-graphic objects of the SAM-model are either graphic atoms or patterns and can be defined as follows:

A text-graphic object is either a line or a pattern.
   A line is a draw-line or a character or a text-line.
      A draw-line is a vector chain drawn through one or more locations.
      A character is one or more draw-lines.
      A text-line is one or more characters.
   A pattern is a group of none or more lines and/or patterns.

Now writing and drawing on the screen become text-graphic object manipulation. In Vennlisp, the parser provides the functions for processing text-graphic forms and the facilities for the spatial searching in up-left-first ordering and enclosure testing. Figure 11.2 shows an example of Vennlisp form before and after parsing. The input of the parser is a text-graphic object consisting of atomic objects, each of which stands for an object or an operational object. For instance, x and y in Figure 11.2 can stand for a mouth and a face pattern of a face image. The outer-most atomic object is a sign of an "and" operation. The output of the parser, as shown on the right side of Figure 11.2, is a tree structure, which in fact follows Lisp exactly. The first member of each group is the name (actually, the name shape) of the function, and the rest of the members are arguments to the function. As matter of fact, the tree structure of the parsing result in Figure 11.2 can be translated into Lisp as

```
(AND (NOT (NULL? Y)) (OR (AND (EQUAL? Y) Y) (MEMBER? X(REST Y))))
```

The Vennlisp parser consists of two major steps. It first copies objects within the indicated region and sorts them according to their spatial position in the order of up-left to down-right. This is accomplished by the sort predicate higher-then-lefter-P. The up-left corner of two objects A and B are compared by the predicate; TRUE is returned if A is both higher and more left than B. When A is higher but more right, TRUE is returned only if the degree of higher is greater than that of righter. The sorting operation produces the up-left sorted list, which Lakin calls a flat-list.

The second step of the Vennlisp spatial parser is to form a result tree from the flat-list. We notice from Figure 11.2 that this type of visual language is characterized by the spatial enclosure relationships of visual atomic objects. The second step takes advantage of the fact that every encloser will appear earlier in the flat-list than all of the enclosees. But the reverse may be not true. That is to say, given two atomic objects A and B on the flat-list, if A is before B, B is either enclosed by A or parallel to A. Therefore the procedure for constructing the result tree can be as follows:

Each level of the result-tree is initialized with the first member of the flat-list. The parser then finds the atomic visual objects which are directly enclosed by the first member of the level from the rest of the flat-list. They should be the arguments of the function defined by the first member and be put on the end of the same level. The foregoing operation is recursively called by the parser until all members on the flat-list have been processed.

An evaluation operation is further performed on the parsing result tree by a Lisp function viz-eval. It translates user-defined functions and variables by looking them up on a visual association list.

Chang proposed more sophisticated parsing techniques for the spatial arrangement of objects using picture grammars and precedence grammars [CHANG70, CHANG71]. Picture grammar is designed to parse digitized pictures on a square grid. It is based on the fact that digitized pictures consist of elementary points (pixels). This can be demonstrated by the following example. Suppose we have an object set: a point (2,3) and a line with the coordinates of two end points (4,3) and (8,3). Then a set of grammar rules can be used to describe them:

```
1. h-dash(4,3,2)  := point(4,3,1) & point(5,3,1)
2. h-dash(6,3,2)  := point(6,3,1) & point(7,3,1)
3. h-line(4,3,4)  := h-dash(4,3,2) & h-line(6,3,2)
4. h-line(4,3,5)  := h-line(4,3,4) & point(8,3,1)
5. h-line(2,3,1+5+δ)  := point(2,3,1) & h-line(3+δ,3,5)
       δ = 1
```

where δ is a gap tolerance in a line. Similarly we can construct other grammar rules for lines other than horizontal and for any other shape.

Now we present the general definition of picture processing grammar:

Definition. A picture-processing grammar G is a quintuple (S,V,C,g,P), where S is the set of basic symbols, V is the set of vocabulary symbols, $C \subset V$ is the set of categorical symbols, g is a function from $V \cup S$ into the set of natural numbers, and P is the set of grammar rules. Each rule is of the form

$$\alpha\,(f\,(x_1,x_2,...,x_k)) := \beta_1\,(x_1)\ \&\ \beta_2\,(x_2)\ \&...\&\ \beta_k\,(x_k)$$

where $\beta_1, \beta_2,..., \beta_k \in V \cup S, \alpha \in V$, the number of parameters of the associate vector $\vec{x}_i$ is equal to $g(\beta_i)$, $1 \le i \le k$, and f is a partially computable function from $I^{\sum_{i=1}^{k} g(\beta_i)}$ *into* $I^{g(\alpha)}$, whose completion is also computable. It is required that $k \ge 1$.

According to the definition, rule 1 can be rewritten in the general form as

```
h-dash[f((4,3,1),(5,3,1))]  := point(4,3,1) & point(5,3,1)
```

A picture processing grammar may have a hierarchical structure and is defined as

Definition. A picture processing grammar $G = (S,V,C,g,P)$ is called *hierarchical* if and only if there is a nontrivial partition of the rules P into blocks $R_1, R_2,..., R_n$, $n > 1$, such that if α appears as the left-hand symbol of a rule in R_i, then it will never appear as a right-hand symbol of any rule in R_j, provided that $j < i$.

The parsing algorithm of the languages generated by hierarchical picture processing grammar is then as follows:

STEP 1. Partition the set of rules P into hierarchical blocks $R_1, R_2,..., R_n$.
STEP 2. i ← 1.

STEP 3. Apply rules in R_i in any sequence to reduce the picture. When no more reduction is possible, go to the next step.

STEP 4. If $i = n$ or the picture has been reduced to a categorical symbol, stop. Otherwise let $i \leftarrow i + 1$ and go to step 3.

The picture processing grammar just introduced was applied to analyze handwritten numericals. The grammar rules are divided into four groups. The first level rules are used to reduce a picture consisting of points to one consisting of horizontal strips. Imperfect strips can be recognized by adjusting δ to fill gaps. The second level rules are used to reduce the picture to one consisting of vertical lines (V-L) and horizontal lines (H-L). In the third level, L-shaped, U-shaped, and O-shaped figures are described. Finally, in the fourth or last level, the ten numerals are described in terms of their component parts.

Precedence grammar [CHANG70] is another spatial parsing grammar and can be used for 2-D mathematical expression analysis and printed page format analysis. Let us start explaining it, using a simple example. Suppose we have a mathematical expression a + (b). The structure specification scheme is then defined to describe these mathematical expressions. Assume that some or all primitive components are operators, each of which is uniquely associated with a region, a rectangular area on a 2-D plane, mathematically written as $L(X_c, Y_c, X_{min}, Y_{min}, X_{max}, Y_{max})$, where X_c, Y_c are coordinates of region centroid. A pattern U is a finite collection of primitive components. A frame F of a pattern U is the smallest region containing all primitive components of U.

The structure tree is then constructed by comparing precedence of operators in a pattern and dividing the pattern into one or several subpatterns. Further division is carried out on those subpatterns. Figure 11.5(b) is the structure tree of expression $a + (b)$, and Figure 11.5(a) is the frame partition corresponding to Figure 11.5(b). The operators "(" and ")" are grouped together because they are regarded as an operator pair. The structure specification scheme is then defined as a finite collection of these division rules. Thus we have the following formal definition:

A well-formed structure of a pattern U is a tree T whose nodes (or node-names) are operator sequences and regions such that

1. The root of the tree is the frame F of U.

2. Every primitive component of U appears as a member of some operator sequence that is a terminal node of T, and the set of all operator sequences of T is U.

3. If a region is a terminal node, then it is a nonessential region with respect to some division rule.

4. If a region is a nonterminal node, then its successor nodes constitute a division of it with respect to some division rule.

5. If operator w_1 and region R are successor nodes of some node, and operator w_2 is a successor node of R, then w_1 dominates w_2, or w_1 precedes w_2, or they are of equal precedence.

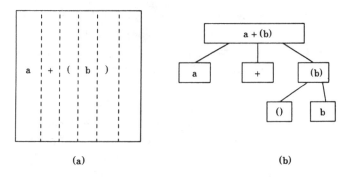

(a)   (b)

Figure 11.5 (a) A partition of the expression "$a + (b)$"; (b) structure tree of the expression "$a + (b)$".

Operator w_i dominates operator w_j, if w_j is contained in a region of w_i, but not conversely. The spatial parsing is carried out by first grouping the primitive components of U into operator sequences and then building up a structure tree T of U. To build up a structure tree T of U, we let F_0 be the frame of U. Let $w_1, w_2, ..., w_n$ be all the operator sequences of U. Construct two $n \times n$ precedence matrices M1 and M2 as follows: M1(i,j) is ">" if w_i dominates w_j, "<" if w_j dominates w_i, and blank otherwise. M2(i,j) is ">" if w_i precedes w_j, "<" if w_j precedes w_i, "=" if they are of equal precedence, and blank otherwise. All comparisons are done with respect to F_0. By using these two matrices M1 and M2, we choose w_i to divide F_0 with respect to w_i, such that w_i is in F_0, w_i is not dominated by any other w_j in F_0, and F_0 can be divided with respect to w_i into essential and nonessential regions that contain all other w's in F_0.

11.2.3 Visual Programming Environment

Visual programming deals with abstract objects which are not visual and do not have ready-made graphic images. The principle "what you see is what you get" sometimes does not apply. To provide a friendly interface by using a visual programming language for these abstract objects, it is necessary to devise suitable graphical representation or visual metaphors. That is the essence of visualization. Visualization is a necessary environment for visual programming. To demonstrate the importance of proper visualization, Jacob conducted an experiment letting human subjects visually cluster 50 points in a 9-D space. These points originally are from five normally distributed classes. To visualize the points, three graphical representations were used: (1) each point was represented by a 3×3 matrix, (2) each point was represented by a polygon of 9 vertices—the distance from the origin to each vertex was proportional to the point coordinates, and (3) each point was represented by a Chernoff face. The coordinates of the point controlled the variation of the features of the face. The experimental result showed that the face representation was superior to both the polygon and digit matrix. This is because the face representation abstracts the point features and represents them in the best way for human interpretation.

Visualization in a visual programming language should be designed in such a way that it can demonstrate the behavior of the user interface completely, precisely, and unambiguously. Visual programs are often directly executable in a visual programming environment.

Jacob describes the use of a visual programming language to represent an abstract computation process which does not have a direct graphical image. In his approach, the state transition diagram is used as a visual programming language for designing and specifying user interfaces [JACOB83, JACOB85]. The state diagram description of a simple desk calculator is illustrated in Figure 11.6(a), where "i command" indicates input, "o response" indicates output, and "Ai" indicates action which must be executed by the desk calculator [actions are defined in a separate program specification, as shown in Figure 11.6(b)].

Recently, significant activities have been taking place to use graphical (iconic) representations in software design and implementation [MARTIN85], such as data flow diagrams, HIPO charts, action diagrams, NS diagrams, and so on. Most of these representations can be considered languages supporting visual interaction. For example, the Nassi-Shneiderman (NS) diagram uses a two-dimensional representation for the three programming constructs: sequence, iteration, and selection [SHNEIDERMAN83]. However, the program statements are still written in a conventional programming language. Therefore, NS diagrams can be regarded as a language supporting visual interaction. The same can be said about the BOXER system, where the list data structures are manipulated graphically by creating and destroying boxes containing list elements.

The Programming-by-Rehearsal system [FINZER84] shown in Figure 11.7 is a visual programming environment implemented in SMALLTALK-80 on the Xerox Lisp Machine. It provides a powerful metaphor for visual programming—programming by rehearsal. The creation of a rehearsal world production involves the following steps: (a) auditioning the available performers by selecting their cues and observing their responses; (b) copying the chosen performers and placing them on the stage; (c) blocking the production; (d) rehearsing the production by showing each performer what actions should be taken in response to a cue or user input; (e) storing the production for later retrieval and execution. Each "performer" corresponds to an action icon, and the performers are grouped into "troupes" in different windows on the display screen (see Figure 11.7). This system is high in visual content, but low in its level and scope—only icons that can be seen can be manipulated. However, the program design process is quick, easy, and enjoyable, and a simple program can be made in less than thirty minutes.

Pict/D is an interactive graphical programming environment developed by Glinert and Tanimoto [GLINERT84] relying upon icons for visual programming. Pict/D users never touch a keyboard once the system is initialized. Instead, they draw programs using an input device like a joystick. The Pict/D prototype system allows the user to compose programs that do simple numeric calculations. Figure 11.8 shows a partial scenario of Pict/D programming. The flowchart is used as the metaphor in Pict/D programming. The major Pict/D subsystems include programming (represented by a flowchart icon); erasing (represented by a hand holding an eraser); an icon editor (represented by a hand writing with a pen); and a user library (represented by a shelf of books). The user can program an icon, edit it, or run its associated program. The resultant program can be denoted by a new icon created by the user using the icon editor and stored in the user library for future use. As it stands, Pict/D is quite suitable for

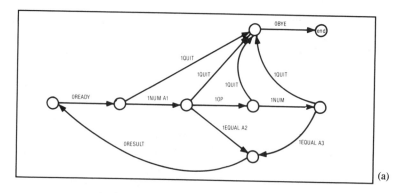

(a)

```
char prevop[100] = "+", prevnum[100] = "0";
```

A1: assign(*savenum1,viNUM);
```
     /*
      * assign is a built-in function that performs variable assignment
      */
```

A2: const(*voRESULT,savenum1);
```
     /*
      * The function const performs a constant mode calculation
      * Repeats previous operation with new operand num,
      * and returns answer in result
      */
     const(result,num) char **result, *num; {
         int ians; char strans[100];

             if (STREQ(prevop,"+")) ians=atoi(prevnum)+atoi(num);
             else if (STREQ(prevop,"−")) ians=atoi(num)−atoi(prevnum);
             else if (STREQ(prevop,"*")) ians=atoi(prevnum)*atoi(num);
             else if (STREQ(prevop,"/")) ians=atoi(num)/atoi(prevnum);

             sprintf(strans,"%d",ians);  assign(result,strans);
     }
```

A3: calc(*voRESULT,savenum1,viOP,viNUM);
```
     /*
      * The function calc performs calculator operation op
      * on operands num1 and num2, and returns answer in result
      */
     calc(result,num1,op,num2) char **result, *num1, *op, *num2; {
         int ians; char strans[100];

             if (STREQ(op,"+")) {
                     ians=atoi(num1)+atoi(num2);
                     strcpy(prevnum,num1);
             }
             else if (STREQ(op,"−")) {
                     ians=atoi(num1)−atoi(num2);
                     strcpy(prevnum,num2);
             }
             else if (STREQ(op,"*")) {
                     ians=atoi(num1)*atoi(num2);
                     strcpy(prevnum,num1);
             }
             else if (STREQ(op,"/")) {
                     ians=atoi(num1)/atoi(num2);
                     strcpy(prevnum,num2);
             }

             strcpy(prevop,op);
             sprintf(strans,"%d",ians);  assign(result,strans);      (b)
     }
```

Figure 11.6 (a) A finite-state diagram of a simple desk calculator; (b) actions called by the finite-state diagram. Part (a) is from S.K. Chang, ''Visual Languages: A Tutorial Survey,'' *IEEE Software*, © 1987 IEEE.

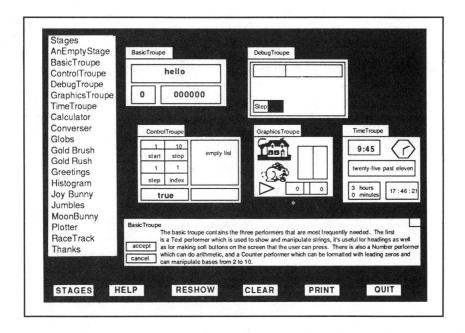

Figure 11.7 The programming-by-rehearsal world theater (from S.K. Chang, "Visual Languages: A Tutorial Survey," *IEEE Software*, © 1987 IEEE).

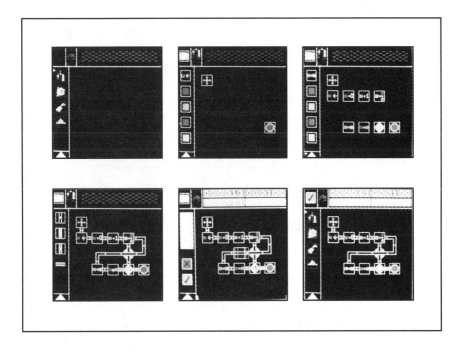

Figure 11.8 A partial scenario of programming in Pict/D (from S.K. Chang, "Visual Languages: A Tutorial Survey," *IEEE Software*, © 1987 IEEE).

novices, but to satisfy the expert user, its capabilities must be significantly expanded to increase its language level and scope. An interesting result in user response to Pict/D is that user acceptance seems to be a function of sex and age: Responses from female students were consistently more favorable than from male students, and the oldest third of the students gave consistently fewer favorable responses than the youngest third.

The form definition and manipulation language described by Yoshida and his co-workers [SUGIHARA86] deals with forms as objects which are essentially logical objects (form type F) with imposed visual representation (form instance I). The form model can be explained as

$$\text{FORM} ==> \{[\text{form type F}], (\text{from instance I})\}$$
$$==> \{[(\text{scheme S}), (\text{template } T_S)], (\text{form instance I})\}$$

The concepts appearing in the foregoing expression are formally defined as follows. Let Δ be a set of characters to be displayed, Γ be a set of attributes $\{A_1, A_2, ..., A_n\}$, and $\Sigma = \Delta \cup \Gamma$. A *regular expression* over Σ is a set of strings of any length, including empty set ϕ and null string λ. A scheme S is then recursively defined as

$$(S) := [r] \cup [(A)]$$

$$(A) := (S) \cup (S),(A)$$

where r is a *regular expression*. A *scheme* S_i is said to be a *(proper) subscheme* of a scheme S_j if S_i is a substring of S_j. In the preceding expression "," separates two subschemes in the same level. All subschemes concatenated by "$\cup$" are called *children* of their parents. A subscheme without child is called an *atom*.

Example :

A scheme S:

$$S = [[A_1], [A_2, A_3]], [A_4 \cup A_5^*], [[A_6], [[A_7 (',' A_8)^* 'and' A_8], [A_9]], [A_{10}]]$$

there are 11 subschemes:

$$\begin{aligned}
S_0 &= S \\
S_1 &= [[A_1, [A_2, A_3]] \\
S_2 &= [A_4 \cup A_5^*] \\
S_3 &= [[A_6], [[A_7 (',' A_8)^* 'and' A_8], [A_9]], [A_{10}]] \\
S_4 &= [A_1] \\
S_5 &= [A_2, A_3] \\
S_6 &= [A_6] \\
S_7 &= [[A_7 (',' A_8)^* 'and' A_8], [A_9]] \\
S_8 &= [A_{10}] \\
S_9 &= [A_7 (',' A_8)^* 'and' A_8] \\
S_{10} &= [A_9]
\end{aligned}$$

there are seven atoms $S_2, S_4, S_5, S_6, S_8, S_9, S_{10}$. The hierarchy of scheme S is shown in Figure 11.9.

A template represents a visual structure of a form. It is constructed by creating a corresponding diagraph for each atom r in S. This results in a layout graph in a template of scheme S, which is an acyclic diagraph $G_S = (V_S, E_S)$ such that

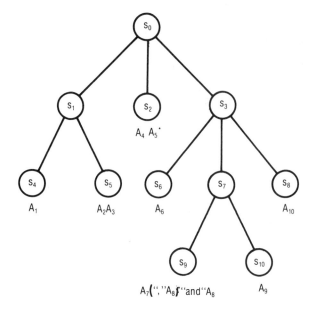

Figure 11.9 The hierarchy in the scheme S (from S.K. Chang, "Visual Languages: A Tutorial Survey," *IEEE Software*, ©1987 IEEE).

1. $V_S = \{v_{S_i} \mid S_i$ is a child of S$\}$.

2. $E_S \in V_S \times V_S$.

3. Each edge (v_{S_i}, v_{S_j}) is labeled by H and V. H represents that S_i must be placed on the left of S_j, V represents that S_i must be placed above S_j.

Figure 11.10 is a display format of the layout graph of scheme S in Figure 11.9. The layout graph is a visual template. The size of atoms are default; the positions of atoms are relative.

Each atom also has attributes $\{(A_1, x_1), ..., (A_k, x_k)\}$. Assigning attributes to atoms in a scheme will result in a *form instance*. The atoms of a form instance can have absolute size and position, which are determined by a layout algorithm.

The form definition language is a visual language to describe the form model just introduced. The form manipulation language is a nonprocedural language to create, retrieve, modify, and browse form instances.

The form definition and manipulation language is an example showing that special-purpose visual programming languages can have a limited scope—that is, in dealing with a special type of logical object. Since the language has "linear" representations, it can also be considered a language supporting visual interaction.

11.3 ICONIC AND VISUAL INFORMATION PROCESSING LANGUAGES

Iconic languages are visual languages with extensive or exclusive use of icons. An iconic language could be any of the four types of visual languages: visual

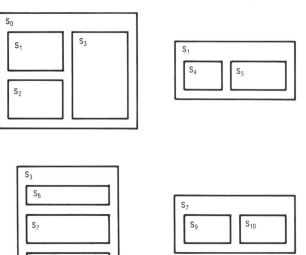

Figure 11.10 Visual templates of a structured form in Figure 11.9 (from S.K. Chang, "Visual Languages: A Tutorial Survey," *IEEE Software*, © 1987 IEEE).

programming languages, iconic visual information processing languages, languages for visual interaction, or visual information processing languages. In this section we first discuss some basic problems of iconic languages and then describe three iconic language examples.

11.3.1 Icon Concepts, Icon Communication, and Icon Design

Webster's dictionary defines an icon to be "an image; figure; representation; picture" [WEBSTER83]. Historically, the term "icon" has been associated primarily with religious images. It was introduced into computing to denote a symbolic representation that can be used to direct data manipulation operations. Korfhage and Korfhage [KORFHAGE86] examined this and related concepts, exploring the role of an iconic system as a user interface to computers. They define an iconography as a finite set of icons. A pictograph is defined as a structured set of related icons (such as icons for hotel, restaurant, and fuel, and action signs such as arrow), and an iconic sentence is defined as an iconic structure formed according to specific linguistic rules. An iconic sentence has a definite syntax for constructing the sentence, as well as semantic rules for its interpretation. The iconic sentences then form an iconic language. Korfhage and Korfhage found business-oriented iconographies are richer in object icons with strong textual elements, while graphics-oriented iconographies have a better stock of action icons. Hierarchical relationships can be handled with ease in an iconography (see Figure 11.11). The user should be able to combine icons to define more complex icons (see Figure 11.12) and construct new iconic sentences (see Figure 11.13). The user of an iconic language also needs the ability to define several levels of descriptive detail, including what information appears or disappears as the levels are changed. In addition, the user should have the ability to define several interlocking hierarchies of iconographies.

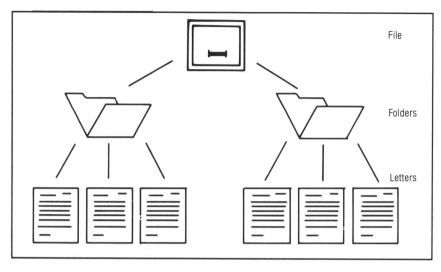

Figure 11.11 Hierarchical relationships among icons (from S.K. Chang, "Visual Languages: A Tutorial Survey," *IEEE Software*, ©1987 IEEE).

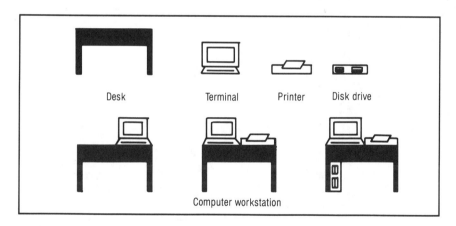

Figure 11.12 Construction of complex object icons (from S.K. Chang, "Visual Languages: A Tutorial Survey," *IEEE Software*, ©1987 IEEE).

Icon communication concerns the use of images to convey ideas or actions (commands) in a nonverbal manner. Lodding gives a taxonomy of icons, providing a classification by their design or their function [LODDING82]. By this taxonomy, there are three types of icons distinguished by their design and function (see Figure 11.14):

An icon image is chosen to relate to the idea or action either by resemblance (picture), by analogy (symbol), or by being selected from a previously defined and learned group of arbitrarily designed images (sign). To assure the correct interpretation of an icon image, we must carefully consider the following:

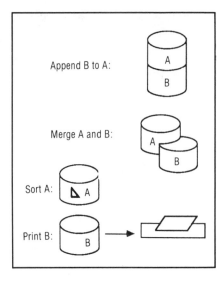

Figure 11.13 Construction of iconic sentences (from S.K. Chang, "Visual Languages: A Tutorial Survey," *IEEE Software*, © 1987 IEEE).

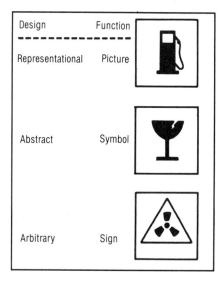

Figure 11.14 A taxonomy of icons (from S.K. Chang, "Visual Languages: A Tutorial Survey," *IEEE Software*, © 1987 IEEE).

- Design of the icon image.
- Selection of the caption associated with the image.
- The context in which the icon appears.

Iconic languages have their problems and drawbacks. As pointed out by Lodding, some icons are inherently ambiguous, while some can only be interpreted within a certain context [see Figure 11.15(a)]. As pointed out by Korfhage, since there is no commonly accepted universal set of icons, icons may evolve in time [see Figure 11.15(b) for various "file" icons]. Therefore, the design process of icons must be well thought out. Lodding suggests the design process of icons be divided into three distinct steps or phases: (a) choosing the representation, (b) rendering the design, and (c) testing the resulting icon.

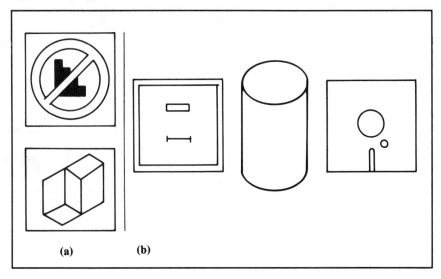

(a)   (b)

Figure 11.15   (a) Ambiguous icons; (b) evolution of the "file" icons (from S.K. Chang, "Visual Languages: A Tutorial Survey," *IEEE Software*, © 1987 IEEE).

The issue of icon design is investigated from a different angle by Montalvo [MONTALVO86], who identifies the central problem as the symbolic description of visual objects and their correspondence to concepts natural to people. To discover and validate the symbolic description of visual properties, Montalvo suggests the following approach: (a) the *denotation* between symbolic descriptions and visual properties can be validated by focusing on the conversation between user and system; (b) the Bongard diagrams can then be used to discover a natural and rich set of visual primitives. Figure 11.16 illustrates Bongard Problem #3. The problem is to find the minimal description that distinguishes the figures on the left from the figures on the right [BON-GARD70]. Once the visual properties have been isolated and made explicit, compositional operators can be used to construct understandable complex diagrams. In our conceptual framework, Montalvo's "denotation" is the correspondence between X_m and X_i in a generalized icon (X_m, X_i). What she proposes is a methodology to verify the natural correspondence between X_m and X_i, and to isolate the properties of X_i. Although the compositional operators are not yet fully understood, further research along this direction will lead to a better understanding of icon semantics.

11.3.2 Iconic Languages

PLAY.   Tanimoto and Runyan [TANIMOTO86] describe an interesting iconic programming system for children called PLAY. PLAY is an experimental computing environment for children that makes it possible to design dramatic characters, their movements and backgrounds, and to make up stories and view animated performances of them.

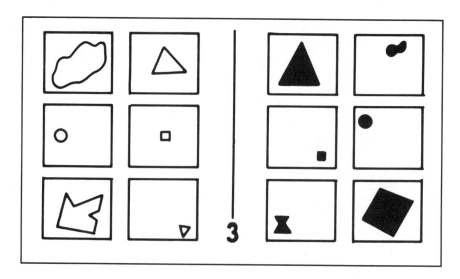

Figure 11.16 Bongard Problem #3 (from S.K. Chang, "Visual Languages: A Tutorial Survey," *IEEE Software*, ©1987 IEEE).

Instead of natural language, PLAY describes stories by iconic language. To form an overall description of a story, there should be two principal kinds of objects:

1. Characters play a central role and are active in a story, so that a set of character profiles should be created which describes not only the appearance of characters in various positions, but also how they look in the course of performing various movements. Based on characters, the script is constructed to give the overall description of a story.

2. Backgrounds which consists of large "mural" images should be created.

Each story is described by a script, which consists of a sequence of iconic sentences; the script appears somewhat like a comic strip (see Figure 11.17). An iconic sentence has one of two forms: (1) an action sentence, or (2) a background-loading command. An action sentence consists of three parts: (1) an icon designating a PLAY-thing, (2) an icon designating an action, and (3) a modifier which normally specifies a direction. Figure 11.17 shows a script on the top row of the picture, which consists of six icon sentences, each enclosed by a rectangle. The "action sentence," with its fixed syntax and semantics for icon interpretation, corresponds to Lakin's "visual sentence," Korfhage's "iconic sentence," or what Rohr calls "visual concept" (see Section 11.5).

Figure 11.17 also shows a PLAY screen layout. The "script window" is at the top of the screen. Below is a menu in iconic form, which may be used for entering various modes and for script editing. The large window occupying most of the screen is the "stage" in which the animation is normally performed. At the bottom of the screen are some icons for controlling the PLAY system. The performance proceeds in the stage window. Simultaneously, the script itself is animated in the script window. The system highlights the currently active event and scrolls the script to the left to bring a new portion onto the screen.

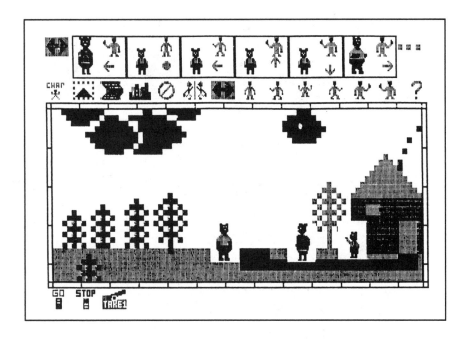

Figure 11.17 Icon sentence in PLAY (from S.K. Chang, "Visual Languages: A Tutorial Survey," *IEEE Software*, © 1987 IEEE).

The system structure of PLAY is shown in Figure 11.18. There are four kinds of program modules. *Animators* compute and manage the moving things to be displayed. *Editors* are used to design characters, scripts, and backgrounds. *Interpreters* for the scripts interpret the scripts and control the execution of performances. *Display-screen manager* manages display areas and keeps them in proper order.

PLAY has been successful with children as young as six years.

VICON. A general approach for designing icon-oriented software systems on a Lisp machine is described by Clarisse and Chang [CLARISSE86]. VICON's design is based on the concept of generalized icons discussed earlier. A generalized icon is implemented as an object with two types of attributes: the *aspects* of a generalized icon include such attributes as icon name, bitmap name, window name, menu and built-in functions associated with this menu, and so on; and the *relations* of a generalized icon include pointers to the parent icon, sibling icons, and child icons. The relational properties can be used to specify relation types, such as IS-A, IN-FRONT-OF, BEHIND, ON-TOP, ATTACHED-TO, and so on. A special property, CHILDLIST, can be used to organize icons in a hierarchical structure. An icon is presented by displaying its *icon image* inside its window datatype. The icon image is stored as a bitmap representation of the icon.

The graph representation of an icon system is a semantic network. An icon is interpreted as a node of a general semantic network, with each node being an icon name or sketch representation (node symbol) and each arc (or relational symbol) given the name (or visual representation) of one icon relation.

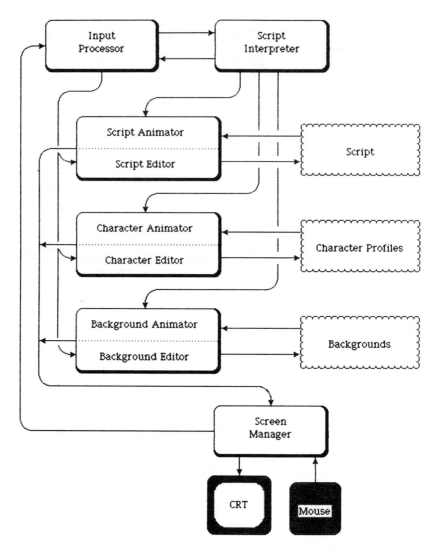

Figure 11.18 System structure of PLAY (from [CHANG86]).

VICON provides several basic operations on icon structures. They are classified in three categories: icon management, icon editing, and icon interpretation.

Icon management provides functions such as creating, opening, closing, saving, presentation, selection, and so on. When an icon is created by the function MAKE-ICON, it accepts as an argument an icon name, a window, or a bitmap. The function SAVEICON saves all the changes performed on an icon since the last time it was saved. It also checks to see if the icon sketch has been changed. The icon property list contains all the information to create the icon from scratch. A list of commands is produced to save an icon in a file. The Interlisp-D function MAKEFILE is then used to create the icon file, and LOAD is used to load it.

Icon images can be edited and combined using an *image editor*. The logical structure of an icon system is edited using a *structure editor*. In VICON, a general icon editor is the combination of an image editor, a structure editor, the structure-oriented lisp editor, and the text editor of Interlisp-D.

The icon interpreter performs icon interpretations according to icon types; in particular, it interprets system commands which are generated by the selection of icon sketches using the mouse. When the user has created a sufficient set of command icons for his applications, almost no typing is necessary to interact with VICON. Three buttons of the mouse are used to invoke the icon interpreter. The left button is used to attempt "evaluation" of an icon, the middle one is used to select icons as arguments in the context of a process icon, and the right one is used to execute an icon command, which originated from a left selection done earlier.

The following icon types are used in VICON by the icon interpreter:

1. Object icon. It can be used to represent a real object or an abstract object (for example, an icon relation). An object icon has a name or a sketch definition.

2. Transparent icon. An object icon having a mask property.

3. Command icon. An object icon whose function property is a special function or expression constructed to apply the command function to a set of icons selected from their icon sketch.

4. Process icon. A process icon is used to apply commands from a menu list on icons selected from the screen.

5. Menu icon. A set of icons collected in a menu definition.

6. User interface icons. A class of icons used for specific user interaction.

7. Icon instance. It is an instance of its original icon. It shares all its property values with the original icon except for the window and region.

8. Icon copy. A copy looks like the original but does not share any property. It can be modified without affecting the original icon.

9. Variable icon. It matches any other icon. A variable icon can have "relations" to other icons. This allows the definition of an abstract icon structure which matches any icon having the same structure.

This icon-oriented approach is ideally suited for the design of high-level structured graphic interfaces. Applications include pictorial database design (see Figure 11.19), computer-aided design of VLSI circuits (see Figure 11.20), expert system design, office information system prototyping, robotics, and so on. Icon-oriented software systems need not be restricted to the design of efficient user interfaces. It is demonstrated that an iconic language may be transformed into a high-level visual programming language or iconic visual information processing language by constructing the proper object icons and process icons in a generalized icon data structure. In other

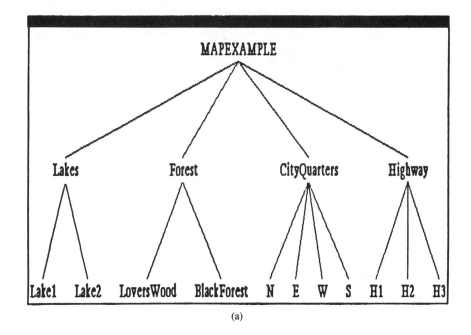

(a)

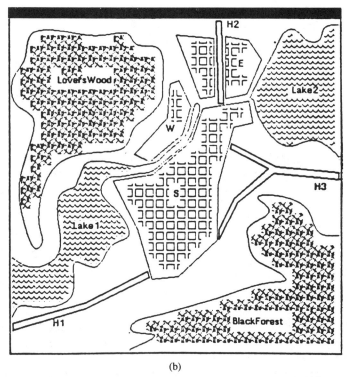

(b)

Figure 11.19 (a) Icon system of a map; (b) the corresponding map created from the icon system (from S.K. Chang, "Visual Languages: A Tutorial Survey," *IEEE Software*, ©1987 IEEE).

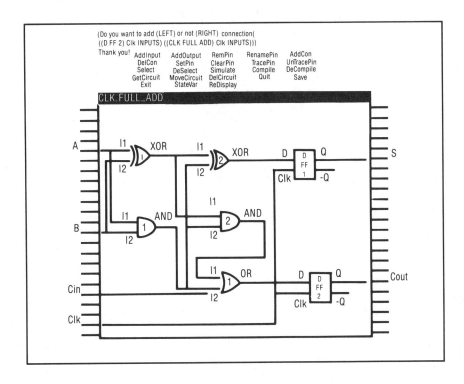

Figure 11.20 VLSI design using VICON (from S.K. Chang, "Visual Languages: A Tutorial Survey," *IEEE Software*, ©1987 IEEE).

words, VICON can be used as a tool for iconic visual language design for various applications.

11.3.3 HI-VISUAL

The HI-VISUAL language developed at Hiroshima University by Ichikawa and his co-workers [ICHIKAWA86] employs icons to represent objects of an application domain, as well as the computation processes they perform (see Figure 11.21). In other words, HI-VISUAL uses both object icons and process icons for visual interaction. Therefore, HI-VISUAL can be classified as an iconic visual information processing language in our classification scheme,

HI-VISUAL can also be considered a visual programming language. Let us use an example to give an overview of it. First the user selects an action icon TV CAMERA and puts it in a suitable place on the display. The system activates the icon immediately and returns the results to the user. The user then decides the next operation. Programming proceeds when another icon is connected to the output. If the result does not meet the user's requirements, the user can replace the preceding icons with suitable ones. Figure 11.21 shows a complete iconic program.

Conventional multiple window systems provide no data communication between executions of programs. To achieve the preceding programming features, the system should be able to accept the definition of the relationship between windows, assuming

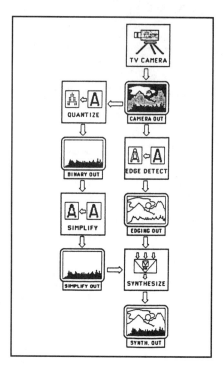

Figure 11.21 An image processing program in HI-VISUAL (from S.K. Chang, "Visual Languages: A Tutorial Survey," *IEEE Software*, ©1987 IEEE).

that a window corresponds to a program module at a certain level in a program hierarchy. A "hierarchical multiple window system" is used as a conceptual schema of HI-VISUAL, which is shown in Figure 11.22. In this hierarchical system, virtual displays at various levels are referred to as *desks*. The part enclosed by a dotted line square is referred to as a *region_frame,* and the part enclosed by a bold line square, a *viewport*. A region_frame is mapped into a viewport by a mapping operation, which may include operations such as clipping, scale, translation, and so on.

To manage this hierarchical multiple window system, the following basic facilities are required.

1. Viewport management. Each viewport has three basic attributes (dimensions, location, and rotation angle) and a priority indicating the order of its appearance in an overlapped use of multiple viewports on a desk. Each viewport also has three additional attributes: (a) Opaque/transparent. When a viewport is in opaque status, it hides the scene of other underlying viewports. (b) Visible/invisible. (c) Frame-visible/invisible.

2. Appearance control. This is achieved by selection of four basic operations, "expand," "contract," "move," and "rotate," for the viewport and region_frame independently. The following is a list of all combinations of these four operations performed on viewports and region_frames:

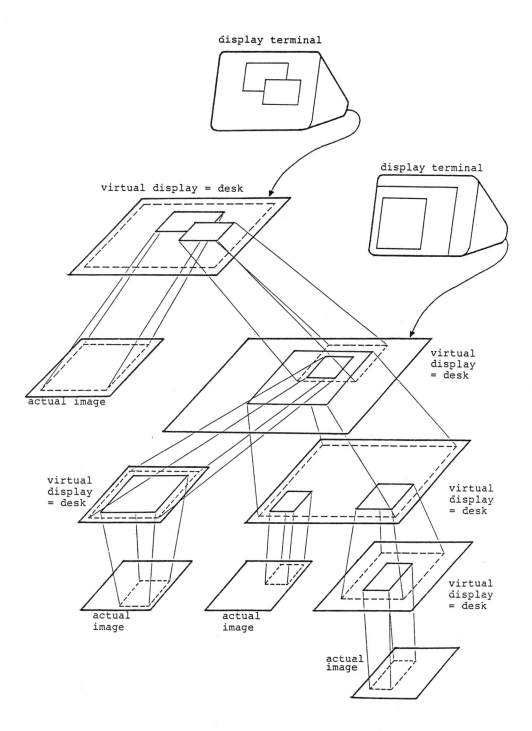

Figure 11.22 Hierarchical multiple window model (from [CHANG86]).

VIEWPORT

Region_Frame	Viewport				
	Hold	Expand	Contract	Move	Rotate
hold	-	enlarge	reduce	shift	w-rotate
expand	zoom-out	expose	-	-	-
contract	zoom-in	-	-	conceal	-
move	scroll	-	-	scan	-
rotate	r-rotate	-	-	-	co-rotate

3. Display priority reassignment.

The system structure based on the foregoing hierarchical multiple window system consists of three components and is illustrated in Figure 11.23(a). (a) The system_desk contains a region_frame, a desk, and operations to be applied to the system. The region_frame is connected to the desk. (b) The joint contains a desk and a set of region_frames connected to the desk. (c) The unit contains a physical image, a set of region_frames, and a set of operations to be applied to the physical image. The region_frame is connected to the physical image. According to the hierarchical multiple window system, a viewport is connected to a region_frame. Therefore, the structure of a system is a network such that (a) a root node is a system_desk, (b) leaf nodes are units, and (c) nonterminal nodes other than root nodes are joints. A structure of a system is shown in Figure 11.23(b).

I/O devices can be considered pre-defined units. The programmer then treats them in the same manner as user-defined units.

Now an icon can be located and moved to wherever the user wants, and the user can create a new icon-image by combining several predefined icon-images. This is shown in Figure 11.24. To manage an icon as a reference to an object or a procedure, a pointer is provided for a desk or an image for the association such as

```
icon_define(D:desk, O:object)
icon_define(A:image, S:procedure)
```

The HI-VISUAL language just described makes system development feasible by means of visual communications between programmer and computer.

11.4 VISUAL LANGUAGES FOR DATABASE SYSTEMS

In this section we describe two examples of visual languages for database systems.

Larson uses entity-relationship diagrams to represent a database description (see Figure 11.25) and allow the user to manipulate this graph to create different templates for displaying various types of data from the database [LARSON86]. This graphical description of the database can be used as the basis for various types of interfaces:

1. Interface for users working as form administrators to create form templates used to display data from the database.

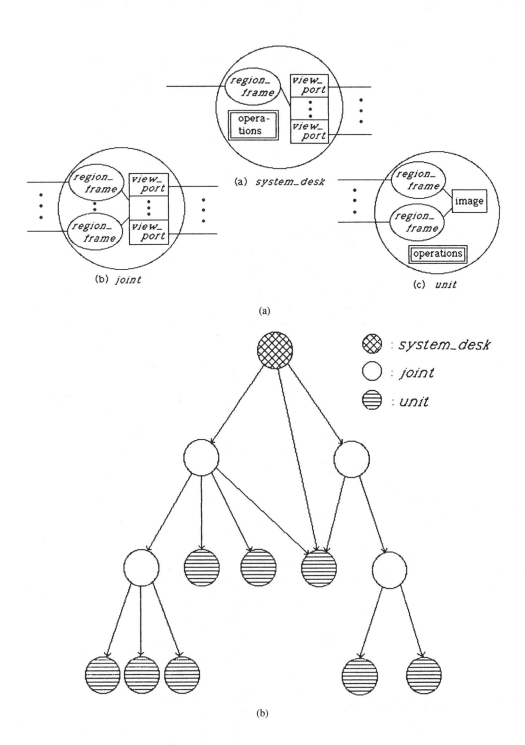

Figure 11.23 (a) Three components; (b) structure of the system (from [CHANG86]).

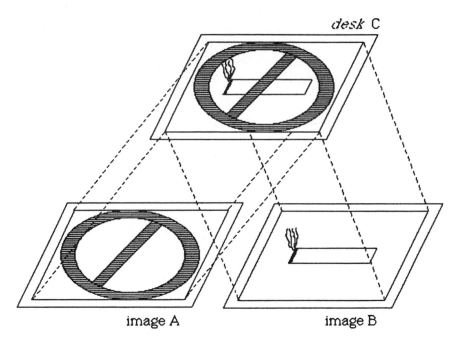

Figure 11.24 Creation of an icon image (from [CHANG86]).

2. Interface of DBMS users to formulate queries by directly manipulating the E-R graph,

3. Interface for novice users learning a traditional DBMS command language,

4. Interface for database administrators to design databases.

In what follows we explain the idea of implementing interfaces to create form templates. As already mentioned, all these interfaces are based on an E-R graph, and an E-R schema for a university database in Figure 11.25 are used as an example—where entity sets are represented by rectangles, attributes are represented by ovals, and relationships between entity sets are represented by diamonds.

Form templates correspond to portions of the database which are defined interactively using an E-R data model. These form templates are then used to formulate database queries and to guide the formatting and display of the results. The form building process is supported by the Form Pattern Language and takes the following four steps:

1. An E-R graph is first generated and displayed on the user's video screen by using the information of the database schema. This E-R graph relieves the user of the burden of remembering the exact contents of the database. The Form Pattern Language also provides various levels of visibility, such as turning off attribute visibility to enhance entity sets and relationship sets.

2. The user selects the portion of the database which is necessary to generate the desired form template. This is done on the E-R graph by trimming off the irrelevant information. The user can either point out the irrelevant entity sets, attribute sets, and

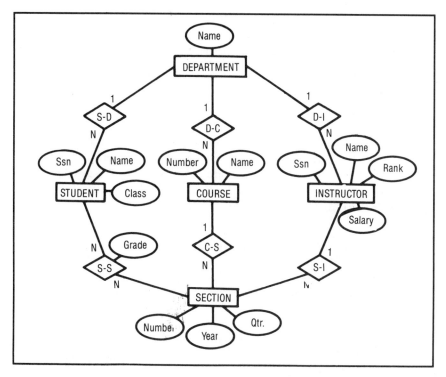

Figure 11.25 Entity-relation diagram of a university database (from S.K. Chang, "Visual Languages: A Tutorial Survey," *IEEE Software*, ©1987 IEEE).

relationship sets when the number of these irrelevant sets are small, or otherwise point out the relevant set.

3. The defined portion of the E-R graph is now to be converted into a tree structure. To aid in the conversion, the user identifies an entity set of primary interest. The designated entity set will become the root entity of the tree structure and the top-level or outermost template in the nested form template.

4. The system first converts the E-R graph defined in the preceding steps into a tree structure of entity sets and then into a nested form template. To convert an E-R graph into an entity tree, the attributes of a relationship are migrated from the relationship downward (from the root) to the entity set below the relationship in the tree, and all relationship diamonds are eliminated. In the hierarchical view, M:N and 1:N relationships are viewed as 1:N, while N:1 and 1:1 relationships are viewed as 1:1. Any two entity sets are merged to form a single entity set with attributes of both. The entity tree is then converted into a nested form template using the following rules:

a. The root of the entity tree becomes the top-left or outermost form template.

b. The tree is traversed, and all children nodes are converted into form templates nested inside the form template corresponding to their parent.

c. A default value for each attribute is placed on the same line and to the left of its attribute on the form template.

d. The appropriate information is stored in the form data directory for query processing afterwards. This includes (1) information about entities that were merged during the hierarchical conversion and (2) information about relationships connecting entities on the form.

e. A form template name corresponding to the entity name is placed at the top of each form template.

To illustrate the foregoing form template building procedure, Figure 11.26(a) is a schema subgraph selected from Figure 11.25. Figures 11.26(b) and (c) are the corresponding entity tree and form template. Users may now formulate database queries by filling in values to a form template. The results of the database queries are displayed using the format of the form template.

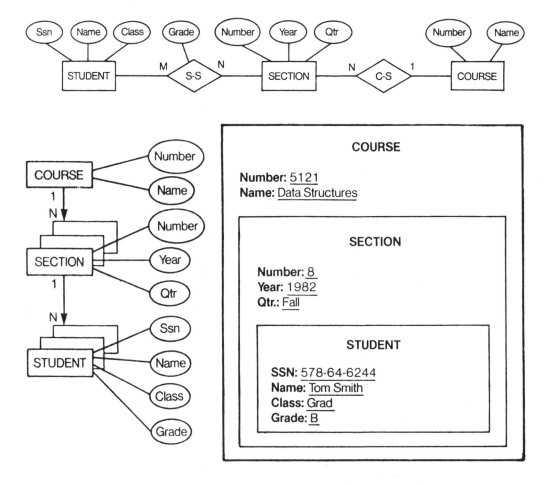

Figure 11.26 (a) Schema subgraph selected from Figure 11.25; (b) schema hierarchy; and (c) form template (from [CHANG86]).

Design of the logical structure of the database mainly involves E-R graph manipulation on the screen. When a final E-R graph is determined, an algorithm is used to translate the E-R graph into a database schema.

Herot reported a Spatial Data Management System (SDMS) which organizes and retrieves information by positioning it in a graphical data space examined through a color display [HEROT80]. SDMS simultaneously presents a world view and a detailed view of the database. This ensures that users are always aware of their current location in the database and can browse through the database to find what they want. The user can zoom in to the detailed view to get more detailed information. In what follows we will first describe the general idea of SDMS by giving an example, and then present the implementation of SDMS.

This example is a database of ships. The user can examine the database through two or more color displays. One display shows the world-view of the ships of several countries. A window is highlighted indicating the user's selection. The movement of the window is controlled by the user through a joy-stick. A detailed view within the window is displayed on the other screen. As the user zooms in, the shape, color, and associated attribute text become visible.

The ship icon conveys information stored in the corresponding tuple of a symbolic database. An *Icon-Class Description* defines some graphical operations to generate icons according to the attributes from corresponding tuples. An Icon-Class Description of a ship is as follows:

```
icon class cluster(r)
begin
maximum size is (110,60);
position is
    (case r.type begin
                "CV":       800
                "SSN":     1600
                "SSBN":    1600
                "SSGN":    1600
                "CGN":     2500

                 ...        ....
                "AO":      4000
                default    1600
                end
        case r,nat begin
                "US":      1200
                "UR":      2000
                default    2500
                end);
    template icon case r.type begin
                        "CV":       carrier
                        "SSN":      sub
                        "SSBN":     sub
                        "SSGN":     sub
                        "CGN":      cruiser

                         ...        ...
                        "AO":       oiler
                        default     cruiser
                        end;
```

```
        scale is r.beam*2 percent;
        color of region 1 is case r.ready  begin
                                           "1":   green
                                           "2":   yellow
                                           "3":   orange
                                           "4":   red
                                           default:gray
                                           end;
        attribute region r.nam from (5,16) to (70,28);
        attribute region r.ircs from (5,28) to (70,40);
        attribute region r.conam from (5,40) to (70,52);
        end;
```

In the preceding Icon-Class Description, the x and y coordinates of a ship icon on the screen are determined by the type and nationality of the ship, respectively. The template statement specifies the shape of the icon by selecting among a set of pictures previously drawn. The scale statement specifies the size of the icon as a function of the beam of the ship. The color statement gives the color to the ship icon according to its readiness. Three attribute region statements define the region for attribute text, such as name, international radio call sign, commanding officer, and so on. We have noted that besides the associated attributes of an icon, the appearance of an icon (position, color, shape, and size) also conveys information.

The graphics mechanism of SDMS is actually superimposed on the DBMS and therefore requires no modification of the user's original symbolic database, allowing SDMS to be used for accessing an existing (possibly shared) database. It is also possible to define multiple graphical views of the data, since the display mechanism is external to the database. The query language of SDMS is a combination of QUEL, the query language of INGRES, and additions made for the graphical environment of SDMS.

Now we are ready to discuss implementation of SDMS. An *icon* is the graphical representation of a tuple of a relation in a symbolic database management system. *Entities* are those tuples having graphical representations and are distinguished from other tuples. Now we have the concepts pair icon and entity. Icon and entity have no unique correspondence. *Links* should be created between icons and entities such that mapping between them is possible, and a selection of one implies a selection of the other. Links are created by associating a tuple with an icon. There are two types of associations in SDMS. The first type, the *specific association,* links a specific tuple to an existing icon. Such icons are often photographs or diagrams. For example, the icons for the employees in a personnel database can be the employees' photographs.

The second type, the *class association* generates new icons for one or more tuples in a relation. This was demonstrated in the ship database example. When a class association is made, an explicit data dependence is established between each entity and its corresponding icon. If an entity is updated, its corresponding icon is updated, If an entity is deleted, so is its corresponding icon. If a new tuple is added to the relation, it becomes an entity if it passes the qualification, and a new icon is created to represent it. The result is that the graphic data space always contains a representation for the given relation and can provide the graphical view of the relation.

An icon created by class association may appear at several levels of detail, and therefore several levels of zoomings are possible. For example, the icon for the ship might be drawn this way: at the topmost level (least detail), the ship appears as a small rectangle. The second level has a rough silhouette with the ship's name beneath it. The third level shows the ship's structure and all of its attributes.

The concept of *subicon* is another feature of an icon class in SDMS. For example, a subicon for each employee within a department can be created within the area of the department icon. The subicons move as their parent icon moves. If the parent icon is deleted, so are all its subicons and their links.

SDMS provides a graphical interaction to the database. It is easy to learn and operate. Even when a key cannot be precisely specified, retrieval is still possible. The user can browse through the database to locate a desired object. If a key can be precisely specified, on the other hand, it may be more efficient to type the key directly into the system.

Hoehne and his co-workers [HOEHNE86] describe an extension of the database language SQL to ISQL which provides tools for handling images in an interactive environment. It is implemented in a pictorial information system for radiology.

11.5 COGNITIVE ASPECTS IN VISUAL INFORMATION PROCESSING

As pointed out earlier, considerations of the cognitive aspects in visual information processing are important to decide the adequacy of visual languages for person-machine interaction. Weber and Kosslyn [WEBER86] compare and contrast human imagery and computer graphics systems with a twofold purpose: to explore ways in which graphics systems could be improved to better externalize mental imagery and to discover ways in which human imagery might be enhanced by using ideas from computer graphics. This research indicates that mental imagery has features not presently available in computer graphics, such as flexible conversion between object and large map representations, flexible image editing capabilities, zooming, and complex functions. There is firm evidence that both the "deep," long-term memory representations and the "surface," short-term memory representations are object-oriented. However, the human imagery system seems to be capable of handling both object and bit-mapped representations within the same display. There is also firm evidence that the human imagery system has the capability for continuous size scale changes (that is, zooming), and extensive editing capability seems to exist for any size of image, except where the image becomes so small that resolution is lost. Imagery really shows its advantages over graphics systems at the level of complex functions such as learning, programming, self-diagnosis, and repair. Also, the integration of imagery with semantic information is remarkable in the human imagery system. Conversely, computer graphics systems have features that would enhance the capability of human imagery. The large item capacity of computer graphic systems combined with long retention intervals probably is unattainable by the human imagery system. Therefore, properly designed systems supporting visual languages combining features of computer graphics, image, and video technology could enhance the human imagery system for better visual communication.

Studies by Rohr [ROHR84,86] demonstrate that there is a strong relationship between the degree of abstraction of an icon and its type of use. In general, object icons tend to be strongly pictorial, with the picture of the object reduced to its simplest elements. Process icons (or action icons) tend to be more abstract. Rohr discusses the adequacy of visual languages from the viewpoint of cognitive psychology. To decide whether visual languages can help, an analysis was made of how people represent different aspects of reality, what basic concepts they generally deal with, and what enables them to learn new concepts. The conclusion is that there is a real difference in the encoding of visual and linguistic information. Visual information encoded as spatial relations between objects leads to visual concepts, which are helpful in dealing with spatial functions and property transformations. However, highly abstract concepts such as existential functions are too complex to be expressed as visual concepts. It is, therefore, important to provide a specification language for iconic system structure description, so that we can decide how icons can be used effectively for expressing such system components.

11.6 DISCUSSION

Visual languages introduce a new dimension to person-machine communications and augment our ability to design a multimedia person-machine communication system. New programming paradigms invented by designers of visual languages could enrich or even one day replace classical programming languages. However, many issues remain to be explored. For example, few research projects have considered *dynamic icons,* which can be defined as complex icons whose constituent icons have a time-of-appearance attribute. A blinking traffic light signal is an example of a dynamic icon. Another topic to be considered is *icon dynamics,* or the time-sequenced interpretation of an iconic system. Icon dynamics can enhance a system's ability to provide a dynamic system trace, debugging aids, and simulation of a prototype (for example, a robot icon, a car icon, simulation of a VLSI icon, simulation of a flowchart icon, and so on.)

We also need to investigate the effectiveness and the limits of visualization. Rohr has demonstrated that different types of people, called "visualizers," "formalizers," and "verbalizers," have different acceptance levels for visual languages. How will visualization benefit an experienced programmer? How can we visualize more abstract programming concepts such as recursion? These and many other questions remain to be answered. As the various visual languages mature, there will be an increasing need for the empirical study and evaluation of these languages in terms of usability (ease of use), degree of meeting the requirements from the intended users, and productivity improvement.

In conclusion, visual languages and the concept of generalized icons can be studied fruitfully from many different perspectives, including computer graphics, formal language theory, educational methodology, cognitive psychology, and visual design. Cooperative, interdisciplinary research efforts can lead to better understanding of the visual communication process and the development of an effective methodology to design the next generation of visual languages.

R E F E R E N C E S

[ACEVES85] ACEVES, J. J. GARCIA LUNA, AND A. A. POGGIO, "Computer-Based Multimedia Communications," *Special Issue on Multimedia Communications, IEEE Computer,* Vol. 18, No. 10, October 1985, 10-11.

[BONGARD70] BONGARD, M., *Pattern Recognition.* New York: Hyden Book Co. (Spartan Books), 1970.

[BROWN85] BROWN, G. P., et al., "Program Visualization: Graphical Support for Software Development," *IEEE Computer,* Vol. 18, No. 8, Aug. 1985, 27-35.

[CHANG70] CHANG, S. K., "A Method for the Structural Analysis of Two-Dimensional Mathematical Expressions," *Information Sciences,* Vol. 2, 1970, 253-272.

[CHANG71] CHANG, S. K., "Picture Processing Grammar and its Applications," *Information Sciences,* Vol. 3, 1971, 121-148.

[CHANG85] CHANG, S. K., E. JUNGERT, S. LEVIALDI, G. TORTORA, AND T. ICHIKAWA, "An Image Processing Language with Icon-Assisted Navigation," *IEEE Transactions on Software Engineering,* August 1985, 811-819.

[CHANG86] CHANG, S. K., T. ICHIKAWA, AND P. LIGOMENIDES, eds., *Visual Languages,* Plenum Pub. Corporation, 1986.

[CHANG87] CHANG, S. K., "Visual Languages: A Tutorial and Survey," *IEEE Software,* Vol. 4, No. 1, Jan. 1987, 29-39.

[CHU86] CHU, KAI, "Cognitive Aspects in Chinese Character Processing," in *Visual Languages,* edited by S. K. Chang et al., Plenum Pub. Co., 1986.

[CLARISSE86] CLARISSE, O., AND S. K. CHANG, "An Icon Manager in Lisp," in *Visual Languages,* edited by S. K. Chang et al., Plenum Pub. Co., 1986.

[FINZER84] FINZER, W., AND L. GOULD, "Programming by Rehearsal," *Byte,* Vol. 9, No. 6, June 1984, 187-210.

[GLINERT84] GLINERT, E. P., AND S. L. TANIMOTO, "Pict: An Interactive Graphical Programming Environment," *IEEE Computer Magazine,* November 1984, 7-25.

[GRAFTON85] GRAFTON, R. B., AND T. ICHIKAWA (Eds.), *Special Issue on Visual Programming, IEEE Computer,* Vol. 18, No. 8, August 1985.

[HEROT80] HEROT, C. F., "Spatial Management of Data," *ACM Trans. on Database Systems,* Vol. 5, No. 4, 1980, 493-514.

[HOEHNE86] HOEHNE, K., "The ISQL Language - A Unified Tool for Managing Images and Non-Images Data Management System," in *Visual Languages,* edited by S. K. Chang et al., Plenum Pub. Co., 1986.

[ICHIKAWA86] ICHIKAWA, T., "HI-VISUAL: A Language Supporting Visual Interaction in Programming," in *Visual Languages,* edited by S. K. Chang et al., Plenum Pub. Co., 1986.

[JACOB83] JACOB, R. J. K., "Using Formal Specifications in the Design of a Human-Computer Interface," *Comm. of ACM,* Vol. 26, 1983, 259-264.

[JACOB85] JACOB, R. J. K., "A State Transition Diagram Language for Visual Programming," *IEEE Computer,* Vol. 18, No. 8, Aug. 1985, 51-59.

[KORFHAGE86] KORFHAGE, R. R., AND M. A. KORFHAGE, "Criteria for Iconic Languages," in *Visual Languages,* edited by S. K. Chang et al., Plenum Pub. Co., 1986.

[LAKIN86] LAKIN, F., "Spatial Parsing For Visual Languages," in *Visual Languages,* edited by S. K. Chang et al., Plenum Pub. Co., 1986.

[LARSON86] LARSON, J. A., "Visual Languages for Database Users," in *Visual Languages,* edited by S. K. Chang et al., Plenum Pub. Co., 1986.

[LODDING82] LODDING, K. N., "Iconics - A Visual Man-Machine Interface," *Proceedings of National Computer Graphics Association Conference,* Anaheim, California, 1982, Vol. 1, 221-233.

[MARTIN85] MARTIN, J., AND C. MCCURE, *Diagramming Techniques for Analysts and Programmers.* Prentice-Hall, 1985.

[MONTALVO86] MONTALVO, F. S., "Diagram Understanding: Associating Symbolic Descriptions with Images," *Proc. of Second IEEE Workshop on Visual Languages,* Dallas, Texas, June 1986.

[RAEDER85] RAEDER, G., "A Survey of Current Graphical Programming Techniques," *IEEE Computer,* Vol. 18, No. 8, Aug. 1985, 11-25.

[REISS85] REISS, S. P., "PECAN: Program Development Systems that Support Multiple Views," *IEEE Trans. on Software Engineering,* Vol. 11, No. 3, March 1985, 276-285.

[ROHR84] ROHR, G., "Understanding Visual Symbols," *Proc. of 1984 IEEE Workshop on Visual Languages,* Hiroshima, December 1984, 184-191.

[ROHR86] ROHR, G., "Using Visual Symbols," in *Visual Languages,* edited by S. K. Chang et al., Plenum Pub. Co., 1986.

[SHNEIDERMAN82] SHNEIDERMAN, B., "Multi-Party Grammars and Related Features for Defining Interactive Systems," *IEEE Trans. on Systems, Man, and Cybernetics, SMC-12,* 1982, 148-154.

[SHNEIDERMAN83] SHNEIDERMAN, B., "Direct Manipulation: A Step Beyond Programming Languages," *IEEE Computer,* Vol. 16, No. 8, 1983, 57-69.

[SHU86] SHU, N. C., "Visual Programming Languages: A Perspective and A Dimensional Analysis," in *Visual Languages,* edited by S. K. Chang et al., Plenum Pub. Co., 1986.

[SUGIHARA86] SUGIHARA, K., J. MIYAO, M. TAKAYAMA, T. KIKUNO, AND N. YOSHIDA, "A Visual Language for Form Definition and Manipulation," in *Visual Languages,* edited by S. K. Chang et al., Plenum Pub. Co., 1986.

[TANIMOTO86] TANIMOTO, S., AND MARCIA S. RUNYAN, "PLAY: An Iconic Programming System for Children," in *Visual Languages,* edited by S. K. Chang et al., Plenum Pub. Co., 1986.

[WEBER86] WEBER, ROBERT J., AND STEPHEN M. KOSSLYN, "Computer Graphics and Mental Imagery," in *Visual Languages,* edited by S. K. Chang et al., Plenum Pub. Co., 1986.

[WEBSTER83] *Webster's New Twentieth Century Dictionary,* Unabridged. 1983.

[ZLOOF81] ZLOOF, M. M., "QBE/OBE: A Language for Office and Business Automation," *IEEE Computer Magazine,* May 1981, 13-22.

E X E R C I S E S

1. Rank the following languages according to Shu's dimensions: Vennlisp, Pict/D, Cobol.

2. Construct a precedence matrix for the following operators: $\sqrt{}$, ÷, ( ), +, *

3. An icon is a dual representation of an object $\mathbf{X} = (X_m, X_i)$. Where X_m is the meaning of the icon, and X_i is the image of the icon.

An icon operator is used to transform elementary icons into more complex ones. Thus, if we have an icon representing swimming and the diagonal line which is generally understood to mean forbidden, the binary icon operator superpose can be used to construct a "no swimming" icon by combining the two elementary icons.

Give a list of icon operators (unary or binary) which transform the images of elementary icons to build up more complex icons.

4. One may consider a visual language in terms of the elementary icons of the language and the icon operators used to construct visual sentences in the language. These sentences are then subject to syntax analysis.

   Consider Pascal as a visual language. The elementary icons are the keywords, identifiers, and symbols (":=", ";", etc.) of the language. The icons are purely logical—they have no image. What icon operator is used to construct visual sentences (that is, programs)?

5. In spite of the fact that conventional programming languages are nonvisual, programming techniques suggesting a visual semantics have been proposed. Name two of these techniques.

6. Consider a blackboard activity of the type that occurs during a classroom lecture as a loosely structured visual language.

   Suggest some heuristics that might be useful in the parsing of this language.

7. List some of the distinguishing characteristics of icons as opposed to general symbols.

8. In the design of visual programming environments, capacity factors are often of crucial importance. Speed and the presence of a nonvisible buffer for when an image is larger than a viewing window are examples of these.

   List and discuss several others.

9. One area where attempts to visualize software have taken place is in program documentation.

   Give some examples of visualization in documentation.

10. Suppose we want to describe the set of horizontal straight lines on a two-dimensional grid. Any square on the grid is called a point. A dash is formed by concatenating two horizontally consecutive points, and a horizontal line is formed by concatenating more than two horizontally consecutive points.

    Use a picture grammar to completely describe horizontal lines so that we can use the grammar to determine whether a given set of points constitutes a line.

11. Of what use is the δ in the picture grammar?

    What will be the effect of increasing or decreasing δ ?

12. What are ambiguous icons? Why do they concern us? Suggest a way of dealing with this problem.

Chapter 12

Theory of Generalized Icons

In the previous chapter, we surveyed current research on visual languages and argued that visual languages can be designed based on the concept of *generalized icons*, which are dual representations of objects consisting of a logical part and a physical part. Generalized icons can be further classified into *object icons* and *process icons*. The main concepts concerning generalized icons can now be summarized.

An *icon system* is a structured set of related icons. A complex icon can be composed from other icons in the iconic system and therefore express a more complex visual concept. An *iconic sentence* (called visual sentence by Lakin, iconic sentence or action sentence by Tanimoto, and iconic statement by Korfhage) is a spatial arrangement of icons from an iconic system. A *visual language* is a set of visual sentences constructed with given syntax and semantics. *Syntactic analysis of visual language* (spatial parsing) is the analysis of the spatial arrangement of icons (that is, visual sentences) to determine the underlying syntactic structure. Finally, *semantic analysis of visual language* (spatial interpretation) is the interpretation of a visual sentence to determine its underlying meaning.

In this chapter, we will present the fundamentals of the theory of generalized icons. In Section 12.1, we give an example of pictorial database design using generalized icons. A formal specification of icon systems is presented in Section 12.2. Section 12.3 describes iconic operators to operate on generalized icons, and section 12.4 describes the evaluation procedure for complex icons. The issues of icon purity are discussed in Section 12.5. Finally, Section 12.6 discusses the relevance and applicability of the theory of generalized icons.

12.1 PICTORIAL DATABASE DESIGN USING ICONS

A simple example of icon construction will first be presented. An icon image corresponding to a picture can be constructed by obtaining the half-tone (binary) picture from the original picture. The binary picture, after size reduction, becomes the icon image. An example is illustrated in Figure 12.1. In Figure 12.1(a), the original picture is shown. Two types of half-tone pictures are shown in Figures 12.1(b) and (c). After size reduction, the icon images are shown in Figures 12.1(d) and (e). Icon images can also be constructed interactively. Line drawings can be created, and simple images can be combined to create more complex icon images.

We can now give a scenario for pictorial database design using icons. Figure 12.2(a) first shows an actual SEASAT picture. By applying picture processing and pattern recognition algorithms, certain ship-like objects in this picture can be reduced to object icons. Some more complex objects, such as the shore area, can be reduced to complex icons. The icon image construction techniques just described can be used to generate the icon images. The picture now becomes a picture consisting in part of the real picture and in part of object icons. Figure 12.2(b) illustrates the result. Second-level complex icons are then created, as shown in Figure 12.2(c). These icons are related hierarchically to consititute the picture tree. The final result is illustrated in Figure 12.2(d).

This example shows that by constructing icons we can design the pictorial database interactively. The resulting hierarchical structure then enables the user to navigate in the pictorial database using logical zooming techniques described in Chapters 8 and 9.

Generalized icons thus serve several purposes:

1. An icon, or a (physical representation, logical representation) pair, becomes the unit of information exchange among various software modules. This representation can be made self-descriptive, so that the interfaces among software modules become straight-forward.

2. The picture processing language can be based on the manipulation of icons. Moreover, as illustrated by the foregoing example, the pictorial database can be designed by constructing icons.

3. The user interface can be designed around icons. Icons also serve as the units for person-machine communications.

With the concept of generalized icons, it becomes possible for various software modules to be interfaced in a uniform way. As discussed in Chapter 11, the concept of generalized icons also serves to unify the various types of visual languages.

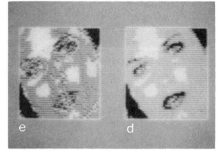

Figure 12.1 (a) Original picture; (b) half-tone picture of (a); (c) another half-tone picture of (a); (d) and (e) two icon images.

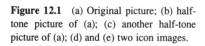

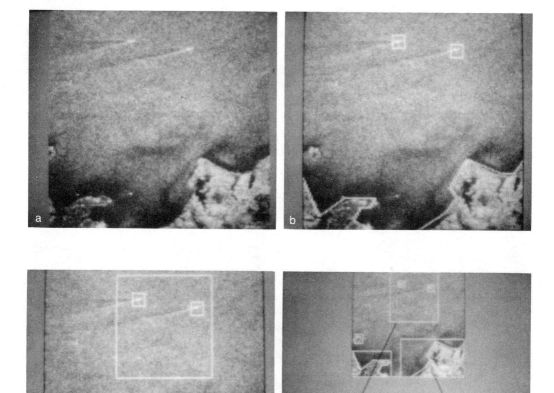

Figure 12.2 (a) Original picture; (b) icons are identified; (c) complex icons are added; (d) the picture tree.

12.2 FORMAL SPECIFICATION OF ICON SYSTEMS

We now present a formal specification of icon systems using generalized icons. A *generalized icon* is a dual representation of an object, written as (Am,Ai), with a logical part Am (the meaning) and a physical part Ai (the image). A formal *icon system* is a five-tuple G (VL, VP, S, xo, R), where

- VL is a set of logical objects
- VP is a set of physical objects
- S   is a finite, nonempty set of icon names

- *xo* is an element in S, denoting the head icon name
- R is a mapping from S into $2^{VL \cup S} \times VP$, denoting icon rules

The icon rules R specify icons as the dual representation by a set of logical objects and a physical object. Several examples will be presented next.

Example 1

For the pictorial database shown in Figure 12.2(d), the formal icon system is G1 ($\{c1, c2\}$, $\{po, p1, p2, p3, p4\}$, $\{xo, x1, x2, x3, x4\}$, *xo*, R1), where the icon rules R1 are

$$
\begin{array}{ll}
r1: & xo ::= (\{x1, x2\}, \text{ po}) \\
r2: & x1 ::= (\{x3, x4\}, \text{ p1}) \\
r3: & x2 ::= (\quad \{ \} \quad , \text{ p2}) \\
r4: & x3 ::= (\quad \{c1\} \quad , \text{ p3}) \\
r5: & x4 ::= (\quad \{c2\} \quad , \text{ p4})
\end{array}
$$

In the preceding, rule r1 specifies an icon *xo* with the logical part $\{x1, x2\}$ and the physical part po. Both $x1$ and $x2$ are icon names in S. Therefore, rule r1 says $x1$ and $x2$ are sub-icons of the icon *xo*. Rule r2 is similar to rule r1. Rule r3 specifies an icon $x2$, whose logical part is the null object and whose physical part is p2. In other words, $x2$ is really a "pure image." Rule r4 specifies an icon $x4$, whose logical part is $\{c1\}$ and physical part is p3. The object c1 is an element of VL and is used as a "label" for the physical image p3.

The icon system can be seen as a special type of picture grammar [FU74]. The icon grammar rules can also be expressed as commands in an iconic language (see [CHANG85] for a proposed language IPL). We give the following examples to illustrate elements of an interactive iconic language. In what follows, a command line is indicated by a colon. The system response, if any, follows the command line.

```
: X = ICON(Xm, Xi)       create an icon X with logical
                         part Xm and physical part Xi
: X                      display contents of icon X
  (Xm, Xi)
: VL(X)                  display logical part of X
  Xm
: VP(X)                  display physical part of X
  Xi
: MAT(Xm)                materialization of logical part Xm
  Xi                     as physical part Xi
: DMA(Xi)                dematerialization of physical part Xi
  Xm                     as logical part Xm
```

The foregoing iconic language can be implemented using icons in a direct manipulation interface [CLARISSE85]. The materialization operator MAT and dematerialization operation DMA will be discussed in the following section. The commands to create the five icons of Example 1 are:

```
x4 = ICON(    {c2}  , p4)
x3 = ICON(    {c1}  , p3)
x2 = ICON(    { }   , p2)
x1 = ICON( {x3,x4}, p1)
xo = ICON( {x1,x2}, po)
```

Example 2

Suppose we have a book organized as chapters containing sections, as illustrated in Figure 12.3.

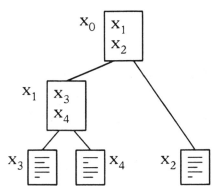

Figure 12.3 Icon system of a book (from [CHANG87a]).

The formal icon system is G2 ({COM}, {e,p2,p3,p4}, {$xo,x1,x2,x3,x4$}, xo, R2), where the icon rules R2 are

```
r1:    xo ::= ({COM,x1,x2}, e)
r2:    x1 ::= ({COM,x3,x4}, e)
r3:    x2 ::= (  { }  ,p2)
r4:    x3 ::= (  { }  ,p3)
r5:    x4 ::= (  { }  ,p4)
```

The symbol "e" denotes an "empty picture." Therefore, rule r1 specifies an icon xo with subicons $x1$, $x2$ and no physical image. The logical part of icon xo is actually {COM, $x1$, $x2$}, where COM is in *VL*, and $x1$, $x2$ are in *S*. The symbol "COM" is an *iconic operator* which operates on the subicons to create a new icon. The positional attributes of these subicons determine the order in applying the iconic operator.

The command VL(xo) will display the logical part of icon xo, and the system will respond by displaying {COM, $x1$, $x2$} which is evaluated to be COMm({$x1,x2$}), where the COMm operator is applied to the icon set {$x1,x2$} to display them. Therefore, VL(xo) is equivalent to listing the contents of "directory" xo. On the other hand, the command VP(xo) will generate a "blank picture," because the physical part of xo is "e."

The command VP($x2$) will display the physical part of icon $x2$, and the system will respond by displaying p2, the "contents" of "file" $x2$. On the other hand, the command VL($x2$) will generate no output, because $x2$ does not have a logical part.

Example 3

In clustering analysis, we often want to group physical objects p1, p2, ..., pn into different clusters, each with a different cluster name c1, c2,..., cm. To perform clustering, we have the following procedure:

```
CLU(c1,...,cm,p1,...,pn)
begin
  for i = 1 to m
  begin
    for j = 1 to n
    begin
      if class(pj) = ci then xij = ICON({ci},pj);
    end
    xi = ICON({xi1,...,xin}, e);
  end
end
```

As shown in Figure 12.4, each cluster is denoted by a single icon. For example, cluster ci is denoted by icon xi. This icon has its logical part $\{xi1,...,xin\}$, which is the set of icons in that cluster. It has no physical part. The icons xij have the same logical part ci (cluster name), with different physical parts pj. The command MAT(ci) will generate all the objects pi indexed by ci. The command VL(xi) will generate all icons xij indexed by ci.

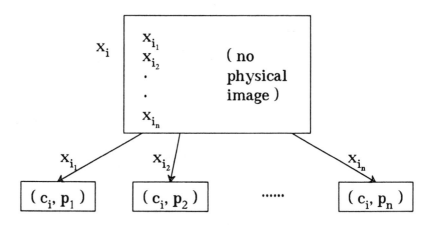

Figure 12.4   Icon system for clusters of objects (from [CHANG87a]).

Example 4

For the document illustrated in Figure 12.5 ("Form10"), the formal icon system is G4(VL, VP, S, xo, R4), where

$$VL = \{Getdate,Ltx1,Ltx2,Sgpwd\},$$

$$VP = \{WFrm10,Cnt10,Dat10,Hd10,$$
$$Txt1,Txt2,Lg1,Sg1,Sk1,Dsp1,$$
$$M1,Thk1\},$$

```
S = {Form10,Content10,Date,
     Header10,BigText,SmallText,
     Logo,Signature,Display,Mouse,
     Thinkjet},

xo = Form10
```

and the icon rules R4 are

```
r1:    Form10    ::= ( {Content10, Date,
                        Header10}, WFrm10  )


r2:    Content10 ::= ( {BigText  , SmallText,
                        Logo     , Signature,
                        Sketches}, Cnt10   )


r3:    Sketches  ::= ( {Display  , Mouse,
                        Thinkjet}, Sk1     )


r4:    Date      ::= ( {Getdate} , Dat10   )
r5:    Header10  ::= ( { }        , Hd10    )
r6:    BigText   ::= ( {Ltx1}     , Txt1    )
r7:    SmallText ::= ( {Ltx2}     , Txt2    )
r8:    Logo      ::= ( { }        , Lg1     )
r9:    Signature ::= ( {Sgpwd}    , Sg1     )
r10:   Display   ::= ( { }        , Dsp1    )
r11:   Mouse     ::= ( { }        , M1      )
r12:   Thinkjet  ::= ( { }        , Thk1    )
```

Rule r1 specifies the icon "Form10," which is the association of the logical part {Content10, Date, Header10} and the physical part "WFrm10." "WFrm10" in this example is a window datatype, as shown in Figure 12.5(b). Rule r5 specifies the icon "Header10," whose logical part is the null object and physical part is "Hd10," a bitmap datatype in this example. In other words, the icon "Header10" is a pure bitmap. Rule r9 specifies the icon "signature," whose logical part is "Sgpwd." "Sgpwd" is the label of a process which creates the signature after having verified the password entered by the user.

From the foregoing examples, it can be seen that an icon can be a pure physical picture ({ }, PICTURE), a pure logical label ({LABEL},e), a complex icon constructed from subicons ({OP, $x1,...,xn$}, PICTURE), or a complex icon related to subicons with an unspecified method of construction ({$x1,...,xn$}, PICTURE).

In the preceding, we have outlined a methodology for the formal specification of an icon system. For complex icons, we need to investigate how to construct an icon with a physical part (the image) and a logical part (the meaning) from subicons by applying iconic operators. In other words, we need to study icon semantics. We will approach this problem by developing an algebra on icons.

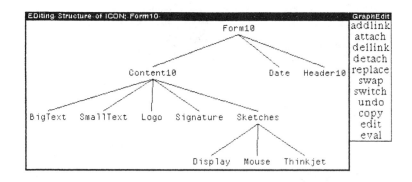

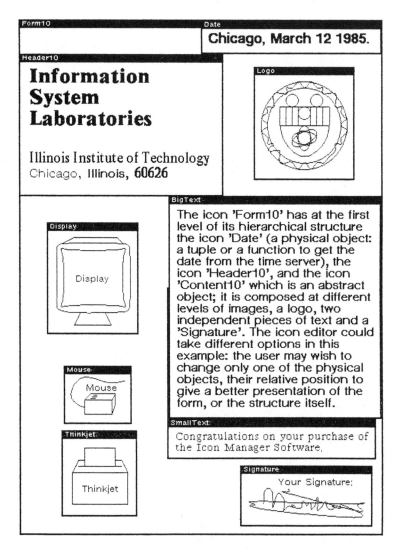

Figure 12.5 Icon system of a form.

12.3 AN ICON ALGEBRA

Iconic operators operate on generalized icons and change either the logical part (the meaning) or the physical part (the image) of an icon, or both. The concept of duality is essential: *iconic operators operate on the dual representations of icons.* In other words, the iconic operator operates simultaneously on logical and physical parts of an icon. An essential characteristic of the icon is that *the logical part and the physical part are mutually dependent.* Therefore, as the image of an icon is changed, so will its meaning, and vice versa.

An iconic operator OP has two parts: OPm for the logical operator, and OPi for the physical operator. We write

$$OP = (OPm, OPi)$$

A binary iconic operator OP has two arguments, X and Y:

$$OP(X, Y) = (OPm(X, Y), OPi(X, Y))$$

When there is no mutual dependency—that is, OPm does not depend on Xi or Yi, and OPi does not depend on Xm or Ym—we can write

$$OP(X, Y) = (OPm(Xm, Ym), OPi(Xi, Yi))$$

A unary iconic operator OP has only one argument X:

$$OP(X) = (OPm(X), OPi(X))$$

Again, when there is no mutual dependency, we can write

$$OP(X) = (OPm(Xm), OPi(Xi))$$

Let WL denote $2^{VL \cup S}$. The *materialization operator* MAT is a mapping from WL to 2^{VP}, and the *dematerialization operator* DMA is a mapping from VP to 2^{WL}.

A *pure icon* is an icon $X = (Xm, Xi)$, where $\{Xm\} = $ DMA(Xi) and $\{Xi\} = $ MAT(Xm).

For pure icons only, the logical part can be completely recovered from the physical part, and vice versa. This is possible only when MAT(Xm) and DMA(Xi) are both singletons. In general, MAT(Xm) may yield a set of icon images. For example, MAT("Mona Lisa") may be the original drawing for Mona Lisa, or a sketch of Mona Lisa. DMA(Xi) may also yield a set of icon meanings. Such impure icons will cause problems if used for a person-machine interface. In Section 12.5, we will give purity-preserving conditions for iconic operators.

A *physical iconic operator* operates only on the physical part of an icon—that is,

$$OP(X, Y) = (\text{DMA}(OPi(Xi, Yi)), OPi(Xi, Yi))$$

where X and Y are pure icons.

A *logical iconic operator* operates only on the logical part of an icon—that is,

$$OP(X, Y) = (OPm(Xm, Ym), \text{MAT}(OPm(Xm, Ym)))$$

where X and Y are pure icons.

The usual image processing operations can be regarded as physical iconic operators. Similarly, the usual logical operations on objects in a knowledge base can be regarded as logical iconic operators. We now investigate those generic operators which may affect both the meaning and the image of an icon. We will use Chinese character formation rules to explicate icon semantics [S. K. Chang, "Icon Semantics," *International Journal of Pattern Recognition and Artificial Intelligence*, 1(1), ©1987 World Scientific Publishing Co.] In what follows, we will use ($\{Xm\},Xi$) and (Xm,Xi) interchangeably.

1. Combination COM:

```
COM((Am,Ai), (Bm,Bi))
= (COMm(Am,Bm), COMi(Ai,Bi))
= (CONCEPT-MERGE(Am,Bm), SUPERPOSE(Ai,Bi))
```

Explanation: The images Ai and Bi are combined by superposition. At the same time, the conceptual merge of the meanings Am and Bm becomes the meaning of the resultant new icon. As an example, COM($\oslash$, $⫲$) = COM((do-not, $\oslash$), (road, $⫲$)) = (CONCEPT-MERGE(do-not,road), COMBINE($\oslash$, $⫲$)) = (no-entry, $⨁$). Two special cases of the COM operator are vertical combination VER and horizontal combination HOR.

2. Vertical Combination VER:

```
VER((Am,Ai), (Bm,Bi))
= (VERm(Am,Bm), VERi(Ai,Bi))
= (CONCEPT-MERGE(Am,Bm), VER-COMBINE(Ai,Bi))
```

Explanation: The images Ai and Bi are combined vertically. At the same time, the conceptual merge of the meanings Am and Bm becomes the meaning of the resultant new icon. As an example, VER(日 , 月) = (CONCEPT-MERGE(sun,moon), VER-COMBINE(日 , 月) = (change, 易). Notice the conceptual merge of "sun" and "moon" results in the new meaning "change."

3. Horizontal Combination HOR:

```
HOR((Am,Ai), (Bm,Bi))
= (HORm(Am,Bm), VERi(Ai,Bi))
= (CONCEPT-MERGE(Am,Bm), HOR-COMBINE(Ai,Bi))
```

Explanation: The images Ai and Bi are combined horizontally. At the same time, the conceptual merge of the meanings Am and Bm becomes the meaning of the resultant new icon. As an example, HOR(人 , 言) = (CONCEPT-MERGE(person,speech), HOR-COMBINE(人 , 言)) = (trust, 信). Notice the conceptual merge of "person" and "speech" results in the new meaning, "trust" or "faith."

4. Subtraction SUB:

```
SUB((Am, Ai), (Bm,Bi))
= (SUBm(Am,Bm), SUBi(Ai,Bi))
= (CONCEPT-DIFF(Am,Bm), REMOVE(Ai,Bi))
```

Explanation: The image *Bi* is removed (or subtracted) from the image *Ai*. As the same time, the conceptual difference of *Am* and *Bm* becomes the meaning of the resultant new icon. As an example: SUB((have, 有), (*Om,Oi*)) = (CONCEPT-DIFF(have,*Om*), REMOVE(有 ,*Oi*)) = (have-not, 冇), where (*Om,Oi*) is "some-object."

5. Inversion INV:

```
INV(Am,Ai)
= (INVm(Am), INVi(Ai))
= (CONCEPT-INV(Am), INVERT(Ai))
```

Explanation: The image of *Ai* is inverted. Image inversion could be further differented into "top-bottom," "left-right," or "black-white" inversion. At the same time, the conceptual inversion of *Am* becomes the meaning of the resultant new icon. As an example, INV(人) = INV((man, 人)) = INV(CONCEPT-INV(man), INVERT(人)) = (reversal, 𠈮). In this example, INVERT gives a top-bottom inversion of an image.

6. Marking MAR:

```
MAR((Am,Ai), (Om,Oi))
= (MAR(Am,Om), MAR(Ai,Oi))
= (CONCEPT-MARKING(Am,Om), MARK(Ai,Oi))
```

Explanation: The marking operator marks an image *Ai* with a "marker image" *Oi*. The marking usually denotes a place of emphasis. Therefore, the meaning of *Am* should be modified by incorporating this conceptual marking. As an example, MAR(木 ,low-marker) = ((CONCEPT-MARKING(tree,low-marker), MARK(木 ,low-marker)) = (stem, 本). The "low-marker" is a marking in the lower portion of an image. Similarly, a "high-marker" is a marking in the upper portion of an image. Therefore, MAR(木 ,high-marker) = ((CONCEPT-MARKING(tree,high-marker), MARK (木 ,high-marker)) = (branch, 末).

7. Enhancement ENH:

```
ENH((Am,Ai), (Bm,Bi))
= (ENHm(Am,Bm), ENHi(Ai,Bi))
= (CONCEPT-ENH(Am,Bm), Ai)
```

Explanation: The icon enhancement operator enhances the conceptual richness of an object *A* by adding some attributes of another object *B*. In the resulting new icon, the image of *A* remains unchanged. However, the images of *A* and *B* are usually similar so that conceptual inheritance can take place. The two icons *A* and *B* need not occur together in some context. As an example, ENH(馬 , 🐎) = (CONCEPT-ENH({}, 🐎 m), 馬 i) = (horse, 馬 i). The sketch 馬 is considered similar to the image of a horse. Therefore, the icon 馬 also acquires the attributes of "horse." Notice the icon 馬 originally has no meaning (hence the notation {}) and inherits all the attributes of "horse." As another example, ENH(易 , 蜴) = (CONCEPT-ENH(易 m, 蜴 m), 易 i) = (蜴 'm, 易 i). The two images 易 and 蜴 are considered similar. Since 蜴 , the chameleon, has the attribute "constantly changing," that attribute can be transferred to 易 by conceptual inheritance. This time, the icon 易 may already have some meaning, and the new attribute is added to the existing attributes.

8. Contextual Interpretation CON:

$$CON((Am,Ai), (Bm,Bi))$$
$$= (CONm(Am,Ai,Bm,Bi), CONi(Ai,Bi))$$
$$= (CONTEXT(Am,Ai,Bm,Bi), Ai)$$

Explanation: Contextual interpretation is achieved by considering icon A in the context of icon B. The two icons A and B occur together. The new meaning depends on both A and B. In the new icon, the image remains to be the image of Ai. Contextual interpretation can obviously incorporate a lot of additional attributes to enhance an icon. As an example, CON(鹿 , 土) = (CONTEXT(鹿 , 土), CONi(鹿 i, 土 i)) = (CONTEXT(鹿 , 土), 鹿) = (vanishing-deer, 鹿), where 鹿 (deer) and 土 (earth) are combined to form 塵 (sand), which has the attribute "vanishingly small."

9. Indexing IDX:

$$IDX(Am,Ai)$$
$$= (IDXm(Am), IDXi(Ai))$$
$$= (CONCEPT-REDUC(Am), IMAGE-REDUC(Ai))$$

Explanation: In iconic indexing, the conceptual meaning as well as the image of an icon is simplified so that a less complicated icon is constructed to serve as an index to the original icon. For the logical part (meaning) of an icon, the simplification is achieved by reducing the conceptual graph, or by tree pruning. For the physical part (image) of an icon, the simplification is achieved by obtaining the sketch, the silhouette, the contour, or the sub-region, of an image. A more detailed explanation of iconic indexing will be given in the following section. As an example, IDX(埋) = IDX(埋 m, 埋 i) = (IDXm(埋 m), IDXi(埋 i)) = (土 m, 土 i) = 土 .

10. Clustering CLU:

$$CLU((c1,e),...,(cm,e),(\{\},p1),...,(\{\},pn))$$
$$= \{ (ci,pj): 1 \leq j \leq n\}$$

Explanation: The objects to be clustered, $(\{\},pj)$, are images. The result of clustering will enhance the meaning of the images. The logical part added, ci, is usually a label. We say image pj is assigned to cluster ci. This is essentially the same as Example 3 of the previous section. Clustering is a special case of type-1 abstraction (see Chapter 9).

11. Cross-Indexing CRO:

$$CRO((Am,Ai), (Bm,Bi))$$
$$= (IDX(A), IDX(B))$$

Explanation: Cross-indexing, or type-2 abstraction, is used to relate two icons which are similar according to some criteria. They can be physically similar (having similar images) or logically similar (having similar meanings), or a combination of both.

12. Similarity Operator SIM:

$$SIM(X, Y) = (SIMm(Xm, Ym), SIMi(Xi, Yi))$$

Explanation: Similarity operator returns a "true" icon (true-m, true-i), or a "false" icon (false-m, false-i). True/false icons are pure icons. If SIM(X,Y) depends only on SIMi(Xi,Yi), the similarity operator tests the physical similarity of images. On the other hand, if SIM(X,Y) depends only on SIMm(Xm,Ym) the similarity operator tests the logical similarity of two images. The logical similarity of icons allows for variations of icon images. For example, (stop, ⊘) and (stop, ⓘ) are considered similar by logical similarity. (diner,⊗), (diner,⊕), (diner,⊡) are also considered similar by logical similarity.

13. Existence Operator EXI:

$$EXI(X, Y) = (EXIm(Xm, Ym), EXIi(Xi, Yi))$$

Explanation: The existence operator tests for the existence of X in Y and returns a true/false icon. We can test for the existence of the logical object Xm within Ym or the existence of the physical object Xi within Yi, or both.

The generic iconic operators just discussed can be used to construct arbitrarily complex icons. These operators are generic, in the sense that their semantics are not completely specified. For specific formal icon systems, we can use "custom-made" iconic operators to interpret icon objects.

12.4 EVALUATION OF COMPLEX ICONS

To evaluate a complex icon, we can apply a generic iconic operator INT recursively to construct an interpretation for a formal icon system G. Such icon semantics can be implicitly defined. Or we can explicitly define icon semantics by associating an iconic operator INT_j with each rule rj in R. The evaluation procedure is described next.

```
EVAL(xo)
begin
  exp = xo;
  while there is an icon x in exp
        and rule rj is x ::= (Xm, Xi)
    replace x in exp by INTj(Xm, Xi);
end
```

For example, head icon xo of Example 1 can be evaluated as follows:

1. xo

2. $INT1(\{x1, x2\}, po)$

3. INT1({INT2({$x3, x4$}, p1), $x2$}, po)

4. INT1({INT2({INT4({c1}, p3), $x4$}, p1),
       $x2$}, po)

5. INT1({INT2({INT4({c1}, p3),INT5({c2},
       p4)}, p1), $x2$}, po)

6. INT1({INT2({INT4({c1}, p3),INT5({c2},
       p4)}, p1),INT3({ },p2)}, po)

If all the INTi's are identical, we have

7. INT({INT({INT({c1}, p3),INT({c2}, p4)},
       p1),INT({ },p2)}, po)

Evaluation of the foregoing expression depends on the INT operator. For the image database of Example 1, INT may be defined as follows:

```
INT(A, B)
begin
   draw physical image B to scale;
   while there is another element u in set A
   begin
     if u is of the form INT(C,D)
        then INT(C,D)
        else draw logical object u to scale
        within image B;
   end
end
```

This INT operator creates an *image icon* ({ }, image) using the preceding recursive procedure. It will first draw image po. Within po, the sub-regions for p1 and p2 will be redrawn with greater detail. Within p1, the sub-regions for p3 and p4 will be redrawn with even greater detail. Moreover, p3 will be marked with label "c1," and p4 will be marked with label "c2."

In iconic indexing, we can use the generic iconic indexing operator IDX_j to replace the INT_j operator, so that we can reduce a complex icon specified by a formal icon system into a simpler icon. This new icon can then serve as an index to the original complex icon. Continuing with the foregoing example, the expression in 6 can be replaced by

8. IDX1({IDX2({IDX4({c1}, p3),IDX5({c2}, p4)}, p1),IDX3({ },p2)}, po)

The general form of the indexing operator IDX has been defined in Section 12.3. We now give a specific indexing operator IDX_j, which will behave differently for a different rule-index-set.

```
IDXj(A,B)
begin
  if j is in rule-index-set
    then return(union of logical part of
                 icons in A, B)
    else return({}, e)
end
```

With this indexing operator, suppose the rule-index-set is $\{1\}$, then we will reduce the preceding expression 8 into an icon: ($\{\}$, po). In other words, a low-resolution image po is used as an index. If the rule-index-set is $\{1,2,3,4,5,6\}$, then the indexing icon becomes ($\{c1,c2\}$, p0). In other words, the index has a logical part which is a set of subicons (in this case, a set of two ship-like objects) and a physical part which is a low-resolution image po.

The low-resolution images pi could be replaced by the 2D string representation of these images (see Chapter 10), in which case we can retrieve the icons by 2D strings.

Now we can generalize the concept of similarity among icons. Suppose X is a complex icon, and Y is a simpler icon. The two icons are similar, if SIM(IDX(X),Y) is true. The icon Y can also be considered to be an index of X. In icon-oriented information retrieval, we can use Y to retrieve similar icons in the set $\{W: \text{SIM(IDX}(W),Y) \text{ is true}\}$.

If we use 2D strings, SIM(IDX(X),Y) could be defined as $\text{SIM}i(Xi,Yi)$, which tests the similarity of the 2D strings.

It can be seen that iconic indexing is a powerful tool to construct indexes from a formal icon system. For a different application domain, we can define the appropriate indexing operators IDX$_j$ to create a specific indexing technique.

12.5 PURITY OF ICONS

In Section 12.3, we introduced a formal approach to specify icon systems. Iconic operators were presented which constitute an icon algebra to construct complex icons and define icon semantics. We also introduced the notion of pure icons. Only for pure icons can the logical part be completely recovered from the physical part, and vice versa. Impure icons will cause problems when used for a person-machine interface. In this section, we give purity-preserving conditions for iconic operators.

An icon is denoted by x, its formal identifier, or (X_m, X_i), where X_m is a subset of $VL \cup S$, and X_i is an element of VP. We will use the notations $x, (X_m, X_i), x(X_m, X_i)$, and (x, X_m, X_i), interchangeably, to denote an icon. Given an icon system G, we can determine the iconset RR, which is the set of all icons defined by G, or formally,

$$RR = \{ (x, X_m, X_i): \quad x ::= (X_m, X_i) \in R \} \tag{12.1}$$

An icon (x, X_m, X_i) can be one of the following types:

Elementary Icon: if $X_m \cap S$ is empty. In other words, X_m is subset of VL, so that x is of the form ({labels}, image). The labels could denote objects, procedures, or operators, so that the elementary icon could be an object icon, a process icon, or an operator icon.

There are special elementary icons. An *image icon* is one where X_m is empty, so x is of the form ({ }, image). A *label icon* is one where the physical part is null, so x is of the form ({labels}, e). Finally, a null icon is of the form ({ }, e).

Complex Icon: if $X_m \cap S$ is not empty. A complex icon points to other icons and defines icon relations. We can further distinguish the following types:

composite icon: if $X_m \cap VL$ is not empty. The icon x is of the form $(\{OP, y_1, \cdots, y_n\}, \text{image})$. In other words, x is composed from subicons $y_1, \cdots, y_n$ using the operator OP. The positional attributes of these subicons determine the order in applying the iconic operator.

structural icon: if $X_m \cap VL$ is empty. The icon x is of the form $(\{y_1, \cdots, y_n\}, \text{image})$. In other words, x is related to subicons $y_1, \cdots, y_n$, but the mechanism for composing x from $y_1, \cdots, y_n$ is unspecified.

Given an icon system G, we can classify all icons $x \in RR$ to *elementary* icons, *composite* icons, or *structural* icons.

Let WL denote the power set of $VL \cup S$, or the set of meanings. The *materialization* and *dematerialization* functions can now be defined.

The materialization function MAT is a partial function from WL to the power set of VP, defined as follows. For every X_m which appears in (x, X_m, X_i) of RR,

$$\text{MAT}(X_m) = \begin{cases} \{X_i : (x, X_m, X_i) \in RR\} \\ \textit{undefined for other } X_m \end{cases} \tag{12.2}$$

The dematerialization function DMA is a partial function from VP to the power set of WL, defined as follows. For every X_i which appears in (x, X_m, X_i) of RR,

$$\text{DMA}(X_i) = \begin{cases} \{X_m : (x, X_m, X_i) \in RR\} \\ \textit{undefined for other } X_i \end{cases} \tag{12.3}$$

We can now define pure icons as follows. An icon (X_m, X_i) is pure, iff

$$\begin{cases} \text{MAT}(X_m) = \{X_i\} \\ \text{DMA}(X_i) = \{X_m\} \end{cases} \tag{12.4}$$

For elementary icons, it is easy to determine directly their purity from MAT and DMA. An example follows.

Example 5

The icon set $RR1$ is
$$\begin{cases} (x_0, \{x_1, x_2\}, p_0), \\ (x_1, \{x_3, x_4\}, p_1), \\ (x_2, \{\ \}, p_2), \\ (x_3, \{c_1\}, p_3), \\ (x_4, \{c_2\}, p_4), \\ (x_5, \{c_2\}, p_5) \end{cases} \tag{12.5}$$

The MAT and DMA functions are

$$\left\{ \begin{array}{ll} \text{MAT}(\ \{\ x_1, x_2\ \}\ ) & = \{\ p_0\ \} \\ \text{MAT}(\ \{\ x_3, x_4\ \}\ ) & = \{\ p_1\ \} \\ \text{MAT}(\ \{\ c_1\ \}\ ) & = \{\ p_3\ \} \\ \text{MAT}(\ \{\ c_2\ \}\ ) & = \{\ p_4, p_5\ \} \end{array} \right. \qquad \left\{ \begin{array}{l} \text{DMA}(\ p_0\ ) = \{\ \{\ x_1, x_2\ \}\ \} \\ \text{DMA}(\ p_1\ ) = \{\ \{\ x_3, x_4\ \}\ \} \\ \text{DMA}(\ p_2\ ) = \{\ \} \\ \text{DMA}(\ p_3\ ) = \{\ \{\ c_1\ \}\ \} \\ \text{DMA}(\ p_4\ ) = \{\ \{\ c_2\ \}\ \} \\ \text{DMA}(\ p_5\ ) = \{\ \{\ c_2\ \}\ \} \end{array} \right. \qquad (12.6)$$

Icon x_3 is pure, while icons x_4 and x_5 are not. The icon x_2 is an image icon. It is pure in this example, but if the icon system has another image icon, x_2 will no longer be pure. Since image icons are physical images without any label, we usually do not think of them as pure icons.

If we use the foregoing partial functions MAT and DMA, then the structural icons x_0 and x_1 are also pure. Again, we usually do not think of structural icons as pure icons, because they normally represent iconic *relations*.

We now deal with composite icons and their purity. A composite icon $(x, X_m = \{\ OP, y_1, ..., y_n\ \}, X_i)$ is composed from subicons $y_1, ..., y_n$ as follows:

$$\left\{ \begin{array}{ll} X_m & = OP_m\ (y_1, ..., y_n) \\ X_i & = OP_i\ (y_1, ..., y_n) \end{array} \right. \qquad (12.7)$$

where $OP(y_1, ..., y_n)$ is an n-ary iconic operator.

Two conditions for *purity-preserving* the composition of composite icons can now be stated:

$$\text{MAT}(OP_m(y_1, ..., y_n)) = \{\ OP_i(\text{MAT}(Y_{m_1}), ..., \text{MAT}(Y_{m_n}))\ \} \qquad (C\text{-}1)$$

$$\text{DMA}(OP_i(y_1, ..., y_n)) = \{\ OP_m(\text{DMA}(Y_{i_1}), ..., \text{DMA}(Y_{i_n}))\ \} \qquad (C\text{-}2)$$

Condition (C-1) says that $\text{MAT}(X_m)$, or the materialization of X_m, is equal to the application of the operator OP_i on the individual materialization of the subicons $Y_{m_1}, ..., Y_{m_n}$. The condition (C-2) can be interpreted similarly.

The consequence of these purity-preserving conditions is stated in the next theorem.

Theorem: If $y_1, ..., y_n$ are pure icons, and the preceding purity-preserving conditions hold, then the composite icon x is also pure.

Proof: We need to show $\text{MAT}(X_m) = \{X_i\}$ and $\text{DMA}(X_i) = \{X_m\}$.

$$\begin{array}{ll} \text{MAT}(\ X_m\ ) & = \text{MAT}(OP_m(y_1, \cdots, y_n)) \\ & = \{\ OP_i(\text{MAT}(Y_{m_1}, \cdots, MAT(Y_{m_n}))\ \} \quad (because\ of\ C\text{-}1) \\ & = \{\ OP_i(\{\ Y_{i_1}\ \}, \cdots, \{\ Y_{i_n}\ \}\} \qquad (because\ Y_i\ are\ pure) \\ & = \{\ X_i\ \} \end{array} \qquad (12.8)$$

Similarly, we can show $\text{DMA}(X_i) = \{X_m\}$. □

Structural icons can be regarded as composite icons with an implicit operator STC. Therefore, if $(x, X_m = \{ y_1, \cdots, y_n \}, X_i)$ is a structural icon, we have

$$X_m = \text{STC}_m(y_1, \cdots, y_n) = \{ y_1, \cdots, y_n \}$$
$$X_i = \text{STC}_i(y_1, \cdots, y_n) = \text{STC}_i(Y_{i_1}, \cdots, Y_{i_n}) \tag{12.9}$$

For composite icon (x, X_m, X_i), the X_m part is formally denoted by $\{$OP, $y_1, \cdots, y_n \}$. By that we mean $\text{OP}_m(y_1, \cdots, y_n)$, but we will formally write $\{$OP, $y_1, \cdots, y_n \}$. If $\text{OP}_m(y_1, \cdots, y_n)$ really generates a new meaning, then the composite icon x becomes once more an elementary icon—that is

$$(x, X_m, X_i) = (x, \text{OP}_m(y_1, \cdots, y_n), \text{OP}_i(y_1, \cdots, y_n)) \tag{12.10}$$

If the purity conditions hold, this newly composed icon is also a pure icon. The implications of the purity-preserving conditions are the following:

C-1. If we find the meanings of all subimages, then we can combine them to find the meaning of the whole image.

C-2. If we find the images of all the partial meanings, then we can combine them to find the image of the whole meaning.

It should be noted that the purity-preserving conditions also imply:

$$\begin{cases} \text{OP}_m(y_1, \cdots, y_n) = \text{OP}_m(y_{m_1}, \cdots, y_{m_n}), & \text{and} \\ \text{OP}_i(y_1, \cdots, y_n) = \text{OP}_i(y_{i_1}, \cdots, y_{i_n}). \end{cases} \tag{12.11}$$

In other words, the operator $\text{OP}(y_1, ..., y_n) = (\text{OP}_m(y_{m_1}, \cdots, y_{m_n}), \text{OP}_i(y_{i_1}, \cdots, y_{i_n}))$.

The purity of a formal icon system can be defined by extending the icon system into a fuzzy icon system, based on the theory of fuzzy sets. The details are given in [CHANG87b].

12.6 DISCUSSION

Formal icon specification and the icon algebra form the basis of a design methodology for visual languages. The formal icon specification handles the static aspect of an icon system. The icon algebra handles the dynamic aspect of an icon system. The iconic indexing technique, together with the concept of icon similarity, allow the indexing and comparison of icons.

With a powerful icon algebra, we can write programs using these very-high-level operators to perform image processing, pictorial database design, document editing, robotic manipulation, VLSI design, and so on.

In application to document editing, the icon (Xm, Xi) represents documents. In (Xm, Xi), Xm is document structure and meaning, and Xi is external document presentation. A generic operator DOCUMENT(op, X, Y) then defines how documents can be combined and what its semantic effects are. The dematerialization operator DMA(Xi) gives the *symbolic reference* to document Xi. In document editing, the indexing operator can be used to reduce generalized icons "with histories" into some canonical form. In this way, each user may be dealing with a specialized document (including its history of changes), but a common canonical copy can be kept for public reference.

In application to robotic manipulation, the icon (Xm, Xi) may represent a robotic arm. In (Xm, Xi), Xm denotes the virtual arm, and Xi denotes the physical arm. Therefore, a generic robotic operator ROBOT(op, X) can be defined to manipulate the logical arm Xm and the physical arm Xi. In general, any agent can be thought of as an icon (Xm, Xi), with Xm representing the abstract model, and Xi the physical realization.

We can apply an icon system to VLSI design, where a VLSI icon represents a (design-specification, physical-layout) combination. In other words, in (Xm, Xi), Xm is a VLSI design specification, and Xi is a physical layout. We can have a generic iconic operator VLSI(op, X, Y) = (VLSIm(op, Xm,Ym), VLSIi(op, Xi,Yi)), where VLSIi(op, Xi,Yi) specifies how the two layouts are combined, and VLSIm(op, Xm,Ym) specifies how the two design specifications are merged.

The concept of generalized icons and icon algebra also provides a unified framework for the theory of pattern recognition. Conceptually, we can compare statistical pattern recognition, syntactical pattern recognition, and clustering analysis as follows:

In statistical pattern recognition, we are given an image $(\{ \ \}, pj)$ and we want to classify the image into class ci and obtain $(\{ci\}, pj)$. The transformation is

$$ENH((\{ \ \}, pj)) = (\{ ci \}, pj)$$

where ENH is an enhancement iconic operator.

In syntactical pattern recognition, we are given an image $(\{ \ \}, pj)$ and we want to construct a formal icon system G, whose head icon is xo. The transformation is

$$SYN((\{ \ \}, pj)) = xo$$

where SYN is a synthesizing process to construct an icon system G.

In clustering analysis, we are given images $\{p1, ..., pn\}$, and we want to cluster them into classes $\{c1, ..., cm\}$. The transformation is

$$CLU((\{ c1 \}, e), ..., (\{ cm \}, e), (\{ \ \}, p1), ..., (\{ \ \}, pn))$$
$$= \{ (\{ ci \}, pj): 1 \leq j \leq n \}$$

The theory of icons can also be applied to the design of icon-oriented user interfaces. A visual language compiler can be constructed, accepting the formal icon system, the iconic operators, and definition of basic icons as input. It can then parse a visual sentence to determine its syntactic structure and semantic meaning. More about the visual language compiler can be found in [CHANG87c].

The theory of icons or the theory of dual representation and its semantics therefore can be seen as of great importance in providing a methodology for visual language design, as well as for pictorial information system design.

R E F E R E N C E S

[CHANG85] CHANG, S. K., E. JUNGERT, S. LEVIALDI, G. TORTORA, AND T. ICHIKAWA, "An Image Processing Language with Icon-Assisted Navigation," IEEE Transactions on Software Engineering, August 1985, 811-819.

[CHANG87a] CHANG, S. K., "Iconic Semantics—Toward a Formal Theory of Icons," *International Journal of Pattern Recognition and Artificial Intelligence,* Vol.1, No.1, 1987, 103-120.

[CHANG87b] CHANG, S. K., G. TORTORA AND B. YU, "Icon Purity—Toward a Formal Theory of Icons," *International Journal of Pattern Recognition and Artificial Intelligence,* Vol.1, No.3-4, 1987.

[CHANG87c] CHANG, S. K., ET AL., "The SIL-ICON Compiler—An Icon-Oriented System Generator," Proceedings of 1987 IEEE Workshop on Languages for Automation, Vienna, Austria, 1987, 17-22.

[CLARISSE85] CLARISSE, O., AND S. K. CHANG, "An Icon Manager in Lisp," Proceedings of 1985 IEEE Workshop on Languages for Automation, Mallorca, Spain, June 28-29, 1985, 116-131.

[FU74] FU, K. S., "Syntactic Methods in Pattern Recognition," Academic Press, 1974.

E X E R C I S E S

1. Identify the pure icons, impure icons, image icons, label icons, elementary icons, and complex icons of the following icon system:

$x_0 ::= (\{x_1, x_2, x_3\}, \; p_0)$
$x_1 ::= (\{c_1\}, \; p_1)$
$x_2 ::= (\{c_2\}, \; p_1)$
$x_3 ::= (\{x_4, x_5\}, \; p_2)$
$x_4 ::= (\{\}, \; p_3)$
$x_5 ::= (\{c_3\}, e)$

2. In a simple menu-driven user interface, there is only one menu page, as illustrated in Figure 12.6.

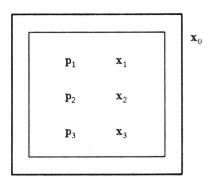

Figure 12.6 A single-page menu system.

The formal icon system *G1* for this menu page is given by

$$x_0 ::= (\{x_1, x_2, x_3\}, "p_1" \wedge "p_2" \wedge "p_3")$$
$$x_1 ::= (p_1, "p_1")$$
$$x_2 ::= (p_2, "p_2")$$
$$x_3 ::= (p_3, "p_3")$$

where the notation "p_i" denotes the actual image of p_i, and the operator $\wedge$ is the vertical concatenation operator to vertically concatenate two images.

The following iconic operators are defined:

$SEL_i (x_0) = x_i$ for i=1,2,3, selects a sub-icon x_i in menu icon x_0,

$EXEC (x_i)$ for i=1,2,3, invokes and executes process pi.

Therefore, x_1, x_2, and x_3 are *process icons*, and x_0 is a complex icon. The user can first select an icon from the menu x_0 (using the SEL_i operator). The EXEC operator can then be applied to invoke and execute the selected process.

A more complex, two-page menu system is illustrated in Figure 12.7.

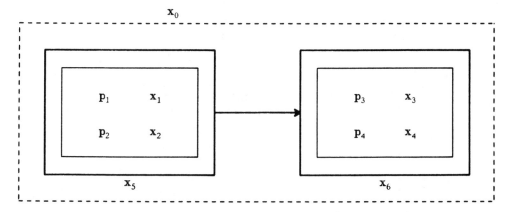

Figure 12.7 A two-page menu system.

The formal icon system *G2* for the two-page menu system is given by

$$x_0 ::= (CONNECT_m(\{x_5, x_6\}), CONNECT_i(\{x_5, x_6\}))$$
$$x_5 ::= (\{x_1, x_2\}, "p_1" \wedge " p_2")$$
$$x_6 ::= (\{x_3, x_4\}), "p_3" \wedge " p_4")$$
$$x_1 ::= (p_1, " p_1")$$
$$x_2 ::= (p_2, " p_2")$$
$$x_3 ::= (p_3, " p_3")$$
$$x_4 ::= (p_4, " p_4")$$

The following iconic operators are defined:

CONNECT($\{X,Y\}$) connects two object icons X and Y. CONNECT$_m(\{X,Y\})$ gives the logical relationship that icon Y is after icon X, and CONNECT$_i(\{X,Y\})$ is the sketch with two icon sketchs for X and Y connected by a directed arc from X to Y.

FIRST(X) gives the first subicon in the complex icon X.

NEXT(X) gives the next icon which is logically connected to X.

$SEL_i(X)$ selects the ith subicon in complex icon X.

a. Describe how the iconic operators operate on the icons of this formal icon system $G2$ to realize the menu-driven user interface.

b. Describe the tree menu system of Figure 12.8 as a formal icon system $G3$.

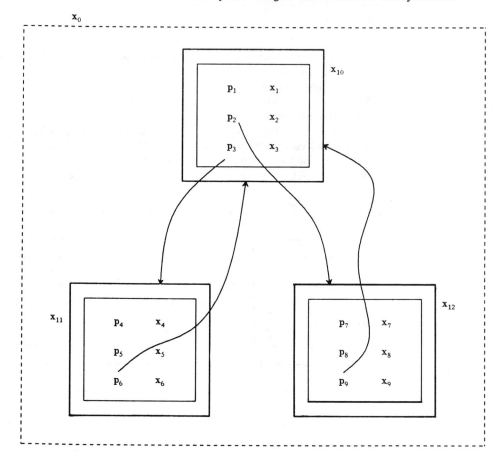

Figure 12.8 A tree menu system.

Appendix I

Fourier Transform and Filter Design

I.1 THE FOURIER TRANSFORM

The Fourier transform pair is given by

$$F(u,v) = \int_{-\infty}^{\infty} \int_{-\infty}^{\infty} f(x,y)\, e^{-j2\pi(ux+vy)}\, dx\, dy \tag{I.1}$$

$$f(x,y) = \int_{-\infty}^{\infty} \int_{-\infty}^{\infty} F(u,v)\, e^{-j2\pi(ux+vy)}\, du\, dv \tag{I.2}$$

The convolution of f and h is written as

$$g(x,y) = \int\int f(a,b)\, h(x-a,y-b)\, da\, db \tag{I.3}$$

$$\text{or} \quad g = f * h \tag{I.4}$$

where the symbol "*" denotes convolution.

The autocorrelation function R_f is defined as

$$R_f = f(x,y) * f(-x,-y) \tag{I.5}$$

The cross-correlation function R_{fg} is defined as

$$R_{fg} = f(x,y) * g(-x,-y) \tag{I.6}$$

The important properties of Fourier transform pairs are given next:

a. Addition theorem: $f(x,y) + g(x,y) \leftrightarrow F(u,v) + G(u,v)$

b. Similarity theorem: $f(ax,by) \leftrightarrow \dfrac{1}{|ab|} F(\dfrac{u}{a}, \dfrac{v}{b})$

c. Shift theorem: $f(x-a, y-b) \leftrightarrow e^{-j2\pi(au+bv)} F(u,v)$

d. Convolution theorem: $f(x,y)*g(x,y) \leftrightarrow F(u,v)G(u,v)$

e. Separable product: $f(x)g(y) \leftrightarrow F(u)G(v)$

f. Rotation: $f(x\cos\theta + y\sin\theta, \; -x\sin\theta + y\cos\theta) \leftrightarrow F(u\cos\theta + v\cos\theta, \; -u\sin\theta + v\cos\theta)$

g. Raleigh's theorem: $\iint f^2(x,y)\, dx\, dy = \iint |F(u,v)|^2\, du\, dv$

The discrete Fourier transform is written as

$$F(u,v) = \frac{1}{MN} \sum_{x=0}^{M-1} \sum_{y=0}^{N-1} f(x,y)\, e^{-j2\pi(\frac{ux}{M} + \frac{vy}{N})} \tag{I.7}$$

$$f(x,y) = \frac{1}{MN} \sum_{u=0}^{M-1} \sum_{v=0}^{N-1} F(u,v)\, e^{-j2\pi(\frac{ux}{M} + \frac{vy}{N})} \tag{I.8}$$

To express Equations (I.7) and (I.8) in matrix notation, we define two square matrices $[P]$ and $[Q]$ as follows: $[P]$ is M by M matrix whose element in the (x,u) position is

$$\frac{1}{M} e^{-j2\pi xu/M}$$

$[Q]$ is N by N matrix whose element in the (y,v) position is

$$\frac{1}{N} e^{-j2\pi yv/N}$$

The picture function is expressed as an M by N matrix $[f]$

$$[f] = \begin{bmatrix} f(0,0) & f(1,0) & \cdots & f(0,N-1) \\ \vdots & \vdots & & \vdots \\ f(M-1,0) & f(M-1,1) & \cdots & f(M-1,N-1) \end{bmatrix}$$

The discrete Fourier transform in matrix notation is

$$[F] = [P]\,[f]\,[Q] \tag{I.9}$$

The inverse transform is

$$[f] = [P]^{-1}\,[F]\,[Q]^{-1} \tag{I.10}$$

where $[P]^{-1}$ is an M by M matrix whose element in the (x,u) position is

$$e^{j2\pi xu/M}$$

$[Q]^{-1}$ is an N by N matrix whose element in the (y,v) position is

$$e^{j2\pi yv/N}$$

Suppose $M = N$—that is, $[f]$ is a square matrix. $[P][f]$ requires N^3 operations, and $[P][f][Q]$ requires $2N^3$ operations, where each operation is one multiplication and one addition. Those operations require complex arithmetic and floating-point operations. However, if a matrix can be expressed as a product of $\log N$ sparse matrices, the product of the matrix with a vector requires approximately $(N \log N)$ operations. In the fast Fourier transformation (FFT) algorithm, using clever matrix decompositions, only $(N^2 \log N)$ operations are required to perform the transformation.

Therefore, if we want to find $g = f * h$, with the fast Fourier transform algorithm, it is computationally efficient to transform into the frequency domain, take the multiplication of F and H, and then take the inverse transform.

To simplify computation, other transform matrices, such as the Hadamard transform, Haar transform, and so on, can be used. These transforms do not require complex arithmetic or floating-point computations and therefore are easier to compute.

The Hadamard matrix H consists of only $+1$ and -1. The rows (columns) are mutually orthogonal. The Hadamard $H_{2,2}$ matrix is defined as,

$$H_{2,2} = \begin{bmatrix} 1 & 1 \\ 1 & -1 \end{bmatrix}$$

The $H_{2n,2n}$ Hadamard matrix can be defined in terms of Hn,n Hadamard matrix as follows:

$$H_{2n,2n} = \begin{bmatrix} H_{n,n} & H_{n,n} \\ H_{n,n} & -H_{n,n} \end{bmatrix}$$

For example, the $H_{4,4}$ Hadamard matrix is

$$H_{4,4} = \begin{bmatrix} 1 & 1 & 1 & 1 \\ 1 & -1 & 1 & -1 \\ 1 & 1 & -1 & -1 \\ 1 & -1 & -1 & 1 \end{bmatrix}$$

The discrete Hadamard transform is expressed by

$$[F] = H_{M,M} \ [f] \ H_{N,N} \tag{I.11}$$

$$[f] = \frac{1}{MN} H_{M,M} \ [F] \ H_{N,N} \tag{I.12}$$

where M, N are powers of 2.

As an example, if the picture f is

$$[f] = \begin{bmatrix} 2 & 2 \\ 0 & 0 \end{bmatrix}$$

The Hadamard transform $[F]$ is

$$[F] = \begin{bmatrix} 1 & 1 \\ 1 & -1 \end{bmatrix} \begin{bmatrix} 2 & 2 \\ 0 & 0 \end{bmatrix} \begin{bmatrix} 1 & 1 \\ 1 & -1 \end{bmatrix} = \begin{bmatrix} 2 & 2 \\ 2 & 2 \end{bmatrix} \begin{bmatrix} 1 & 1 \\ 1 & -1 \end{bmatrix} = \begin{bmatrix} 4 & 4 \\ 0 & 0 \end{bmatrix}$$

The inverse Hadamard transform $[f]$ is

$$[f] = \frac{1}{4} \begin{bmatrix} 1 & 1 \\ 1 & -1 \end{bmatrix} \begin{bmatrix} 4 & 0 \\ 4 & 0 \end{bmatrix} \begin{bmatrix} 1 & 1 \\ 1 & -1 \end{bmatrix}$$

$$= \frac{1}{4} \begin{bmatrix} 8 & 0 \\ 0 & 0 \end{bmatrix} \begin{bmatrix} 1 & 1 \\ 1 & -1 \end{bmatrix} = \frac{1}{4} \begin{bmatrix} 8 & 8 \\ 0 & 0 \end{bmatrix} = \begin{bmatrix} 2 & 2 \\ 0 & 0 \end{bmatrix}$$

I.2 LINEAR SYSTEMS

The discrete convolution of f and h is written as

$$g(x,y) = \sum_a \sum_b f(a,b) h(x-a,y-b) \tag{I.13}$$

If f, h, and g are continuous functions, we can write,

$$g(x,y) = \int\int f(a,b) h(x-a,y-b) \; da \; db \tag{I.14}$$

$$\text{or} \quad g = f * h \tag{I.15}$$

Let the Fourier transform of f, g, and h be F, G, and H, respectively. Since $g = f * h$, we have

$$G = F H$$

In other words, the convolution of f and h in the spatial domain becomes the multiplication of F and H in the spatial frequency domain. In system identification, if we know F and G, then H can be found to be

$$H = G / F$$

In digital picture processing, the function h is called the *point spread function*. In linear system theory, the function h is called the *transfer function* or the *impulse response function*. Figure I.1 indicates the function h serving as a filter to obtain g from f.

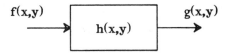

f(x,y) → [h(x,y)] → g(x,y)

Figure I.1 A linear system with transfer function $h(x,y)$.

The foregoing linear system has the following properties:

a. Linearity: $f_1 \rightarrow g_1$ and $f_2 \rightarrow g_2$ imply $f_1 + f_2 \rightarrow g_1 + g_2$. $f \rightarrow g$ implies $cf \rightarrow cg$.

b. Shift Invariance: $f \rightarrow g$ implies $f(x-a,y-b) \rightarrow g(x-a,y-b)$.

Conversely, if a system is linear and shift-invariant, we have $g = f * h$.

As an example of linear filtering, consider the transfer function $h(x,y)$ specified by

$$h(x,y) = \begin{cases} 1/9 & \text{if } -1 \le x, \; y \le 1 \\ 0 & \text{otherwise} \end{cases} \tag{I.16}$$

The discrete convolution is computed as follows:

$$g(x,y) = f(x-1,y+1)h(1,-1) + f(x,y+1)h(0,-1) + f(x+1,y+1)h(-1,-1) +$$
$$f(x-1,y)h(1,0) + f(x,y)h(0,0) + f(x+1,y)h(-1,0) +$$
$$f(x-1,y-1)h(1,1) + f(x,y-1)h(0,1) + f(x+1,y-1)h(-1,1)$$

I.3 FILTER DESIGN

The local operation in picture processing is the cross-correlation of f and h —that is, the convolution of $f(x,y)$ with $h(-x,-y)$, where f is the original picture function, h the local operator, and g the resultant picture function.

Linear filters can be implemented by convolution (that is, local operations) in the time or spatial domain, or by multiplication in the frequency or spatial frequency domain. Intuitively, filters are useful, because (a) we want to select (or emphasize) a part of the signal, and (b) we want to recover true signal from noise. In what follows, we will present a few examples of linear filters.

Example I.1

The low-pass filter is illustrated in Figure I.2. The $H(w)$ is a rectangular function $Rect(w)$.

$$Rect(w) = \begin{cases} 1 & |w| \le 1/2 \\ 0 & otherwise \end{cases}$$

The filter function $h(t)$ is therefore

$$h(t) = sinc(t) = \frac{\sin(\pi t)}{\pi t}$$

Using the fact

$$f(at) \leftrightarrow \frac{1}{|a|} F(\frac{\omega}{a})$$

we have

$$\frac{\sin(2a\pi t)}{2a\pi t} \leftrightarrow \frac{1}{2a} Rect(\frac{\omega}{2a})$$

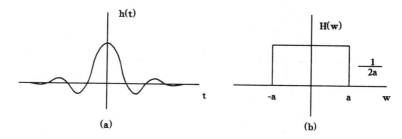

Figure I.2 (a) Low-pass filter $h(t)$; (b) $H(\omega)$.

When 'a' approaches infinity, $h(t)$ becomes a delta function, and $H(\omega)$ becomes a constant. Conversely, when 'a' approaches zero, $h(t)$ becomes a constant, and $H(\omega)$ becomes a delta function.

Example I.2

A band-limited filter, or band-pass filter, is illustrated in Figure I.3.

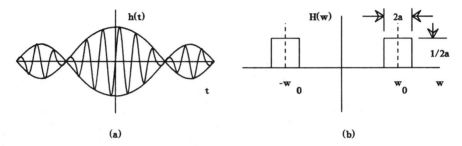

(a)   (b)

Figure I.3   (a) Band-limited filter $h(t)$; (b) $H(\omega)$.

The transfer function $H(\omega)$ can be regarded as the convolution of $rect(\omega/2a)$ with $Delta(\omega + \omega_0) + Delta(\omega - \omega_0)$. Since

$$2a \; \frac{\sin(2a\,\pi\,t)}{2a\,\pi\,t} \; \leftrightarrow \; Rect(\frac{\omega}{2a})$$

and

$$2\cos\omega t \; \leftrightarrow \; \delta(\omega - \omega_0) + \delta(\omega + \omega_0)$$

we have

$$h(t) \; = \; 2a \; \frac{\sin(2a\,\pi\,t)}{2a\,\pi\,t} \; 2\cos\omega t$$

This is a cosine wave in the envelope of a sinc envelope. When 'a' becomes small, $h(t)$ approaches a cosine wave.

Example I.3

The high-pass filter is illustrated in Figure I.4.

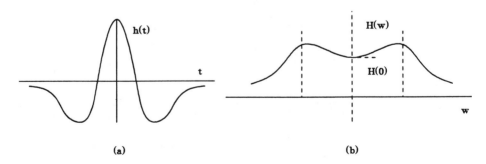

(a)   (b)

Figure I.4   (a) High-pass filter $h(t)$; (b) $H(\omega)$.

The characteristics of the high-pass filter are

a. It has a zero-frequency gain $H(0)$.

b. The high-frequency components are reinforced.

c. The filter falls back toward zero at very high frequencies. The curve $H(\omega)$ has the general shape of a butterfly (hence the name "butterfly filter").

To realize two-dimensional high-pass filters, we can use local operations such as

$$
\begin{array}{ccc}
-1 & -1 & -1 \\
-1 & 5 & -1 \\
-1 & -1 & -1
\end{array}
$$

To realize one-dimensional or two-dimensional filters using frequency or spatial frequency domain techniques, we can use

$$H(\omega) = H_1(\omega) - H_2(\omega) \; (one-dimensional \; filter)$$

or

$$H(u,v) = H_1(u,v) - H_2(u,v) \; (two-dimensional \; filter)$$

where H_1 is a broadband low-pass filter, and H_2 is a narrowband low-pass filter. As illustrated in Figure I.5, their difference would then have the general shape of a "butterfly."

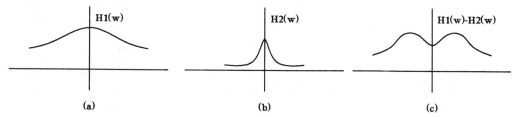

(a) (b) (c)

Figure I.5 The difference of (a) broadband and (b) narrowband filters becomes (c) a high-pass filter.

In digital picture processing, the zero-frequency gain $H(0)$ determines contrast in large flat areas. If we make $H(0)$ equal to zero, then a large flat area can become "hollow." In other words, when we enhance the boundary and sharpen the edges, the flat areas may become "washed out."

Suppose $H(\omega) = H_1(\omega) - H_2(\omega)$, then

$$H(0) = H_1(0) - H_2(0) = \int h_1(t) \, e^{-j \, 0} \, dt - \int h_2(t) \, e^{-j \, 0} \, dt = \int h_1(t) \, dt - \int h_2(t) \, dt$$

Therefore, the zero-frequency gain $H(0)$ is equal to the differences of the area under $h_1(t)$ and the area under $h_2(t)$.

The maximum frequency gain, H_{max}, occurs at high frequency, therefore

$$H_{max} = H_1(w_{max}) - H_2(w_{max}) \approx H_1(w_{max}) \leq H_1(0)$$

because $H_2(w_{max})$ is negligible at w_{max}.

I.4 OPTIMAL FILTER DESIGN

Suppose the noise is additive noise, so that

$$g(t) = f(t) + n(t)$$

We would like to recover $f(t)$ from $g(t)$. The optimal *Wiener filter* allows us to reconstruct an estimated input signal at minimum mean-square-error—that is,

$$\text{Mean-Square-Error} = E[e^2(t)]$$

is minimized, where

$$e^2(t) = [f(t) - \hat{f}(t)]^2$$

The Wiener filter is illustrated in Figure I.6.

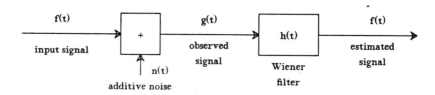

Figure I.6 Wiener filter.

We assume the noise function is unknown, but its power spectrum is known. The power spectrum $P_n(\omega)$ and autocorrelation $R_n(a)$ is a Fourier transform pair:

$$P_n(\omega) = F[R_n(a)] = F[\int n(t)\, n(t+a)\, da]$$

where F[ ] denotes the Fourier transform. So the problem can be restated as follows: Given the power spectrum of $f(t)$ and $n(t)$, determine $h(t)$ to minimize mean-square-error.

Let $P_{fg} = F\{R_{fg}\}$, where R_{fg} is the cross-correlation of f and g, which expresses our knowledge about the power of the observed signal due to the true signal. Let $P_g = F\{R_g\}$, where R_g is the autocorrelation of g, which expresses our knowledge about the power of the observed signal. We have

$$H_{op}(\omega) = \frac{P_{fg}(\omega)}{P_g(\omega)}$$

If signal and noise are uncorrelated, we have

$$H_{op}(\omega) = \frac{P_f(\omega)}{P_g(\omega) + P_n(\omega)}$$

From the preceding equation, we can see the effects of the optimal filter. When the signal-to-noise ratio is large at a particular frequency, we pass the signal. When the signal-to-noise ratio is small at a particular frequency, we suppress it. Since we only have general knowledge about the signal and noise, the Wiener filter allows us to estimate the true signal, to the best of our knowledge. The steps for designing a Wiener filter are as follows:

STEP 1. Estimate $f(t)$ from $g(t)$.

STEP 2. Estimate $n(t)$.

STEP 3. Calculate P_{fg} from R_{fg}, and P_g from R_g.

STEP 4. Compute $H_{op}(\omega)$ and use the Fourier transform to obtain $h(t)$.

STEP 5. Compute $\hat{f}(t)$.

As an example, suppose we have multiple copies of a noisy picture, f_i. We want to detect the boundary of objects in f. In step 1, we can get the average picture from f_i, as the estimated f. In step 2, we compute

$$n(x,y) = \frac{1}{N} + |f_i(x,y) - f(x,y)|$$

as the estimated noise function. In steps 3 and 4, the Wiener filter $h(x,y)$ is obtained. This filter is used to reconstruct $f(x,y)$. We can then use gradient operators to detect the boundary. Therefore, the Wiener filter is used basically to obtain a "smooth," "noise-free" picture. Unlike the averaging operation which is at best an ad hoc operation for picture smoothing, the Wiener filter is guaranteed to be optimal in the sense just defined.

R E F E R E N C E S

[CASTLEMAN79] CASTLEMAN, K.R., *Digital Image Processing*, Englewood Cliffs, New Jersey: Prentice-Hall, Inc., 1982.

Appendix II

Sampling, Quantization, and Histogramming

II.1 PICTURE SAMPLING

Given a spatially band-limited picture, we can determine the sampling strategy and the interpolation function, so that the picture can be reconstructed from the samples without errors. We will prove the sampling theorem in the one-dimensional case. The two-dimensional case is analogous.

Let $f(t)$ be a continuous function. Let $f(k\,T)$ be the value of f at kT, where k takes on integer values, and T is the sampling period. The sampling theorem says that we can express f in terms of the interpolation function g under certain conditions.

$$f(t) = \sum_{k=-\infty}^{\infty} f(kt)\ g(t - kT) \tag{II.1}$$

To prove (II.1), we assume f and g are continuous functions and Fourier transformable. Let $\delta(t)$ represent the Dirac Delta function, that is,

$$\delta(t) = 0 \quad \text{for} \quad t \neq 0, \quad \text{and}$$

$$\int_{-\infty}^{\infty} \delta(t)\, dt = 1$$

Clearly,

$$\int_{-\infty}^{\infty} f(s) \, g(t-s) \, \delta(s-kT) \, ds = f(kT) \, g(t-kT)$$

Therefore, the right-hand side of equation (II.1), denoted by $h(t)$, becomes

$$f'(t) = \sum_{k=-\infty}^{\infty} f(kT) \, g(t-kT) = \sum_{-\infty}^{\infty} \int f(s) g(t-s) \, \delta(s-kT) \, ds$$

or

$$f'(t) = \int_{-\infty}^{\infty} f(s) \, g(t-s) \, [\sum_{k=-\infty}^{\infty} \delta(s-kT)] \, dt \qquad \text{(II.2)}$$

The function $\sum_{k=-\infty}^{\infty} \delta(s-kT)$ is periodic with period T. Therefore, we can represent it by a Fourier series

$$\sum_{k=-\infty}^{\infty} \delta(s-kT) = \sum_{n=-\infty}^{\infty} a_n \, \exp \left[+j \, \frac{2\pi n}{T} \, s \right] \qquad \text{(II.3)}$$

where

$$a_n = \frac{1}{T} \int_{-T/2}^{T/2} \delta(s-kT)] \, \exp(-j \, \frac{2\pi n}{T} \, s) \, ds$$

$$= \frac{1}{T} \int_{-T/2}^{T/2} \delta(s) \, \exp(-j \, \frac{2\pi n}{T} \, s) \, ds = \frac{1}{T}$$

Thus

$$f'(t) = \int_{-\infty}^{\infty} f(s) \, g(t-s) \left[\sum_{n=-\infty}^{\infty} \frac{1}{T} \, \exp(+j \, \frac{2\pi n}{T} \, s) \right] ds \qquad \text{(II.4)}$$

Interchanging integration and summation, we obtain

$$f'(t) = \sum_{n=-\infty}^{\infty} \int_{-\infty}^{\infty} [f(s) exp(+j2(\pi n/T)s)] g(t-s)/T \, ds \qquad \text{(II.5)}$$

The term in the summation is the convolution of $f(t) \exp(+j \, (2\pi n/T) \, t)$ and $g(t)/T$. The Fourier transform of the convolution of two functions is the product of the Fourier transforms of these two functions. We have the following transform pairs:

$f(t)$	$\leftrightarrow$	$F(\omega)$
$f(t) \exp(+j \, 2\pi nt / T)$	$\leftrightarrow$	$F(\omega - (2\pi n / T))$
$g(t)$	$\leftrightarrow$	$G(\omega)$
$g(t) / T$	$\leftrightarrow$	$G(\omega) / T$

Therefore, $f'(t)$ will be identical to $f(t)$, if the following condition holds:

$$F(\omega) = \sum_{n=-\infty}^{\infty} [F(\omega - 2\pi n/T) \, G(\omega)/T] = \frac{G(w)}{T} \sum_{n=-\infty}^{\infty} F(\omega - 2\pi n/T) \qquad \text{(II.6)}$$

Equation (II.6) is in fact the *necessary and sufficient condition* for the exact reconstruction of $f(t)$ from its samples $f(k\,T)$.

We notice $F(\omega - 2\,\pi n/T)$ is $F(\omega)$ shifted by $(2\pi n/T)$. Therefore, if $f(t)$ is bandlimited—that is, $F(\omega) = 0$ for $|\omega| \geq 2\,\pi\,f_c$, then we can select T to be less than or equal to $1/2f_c$, to make sure that spectrum functions do not overlap, as shown in Figure II.1.

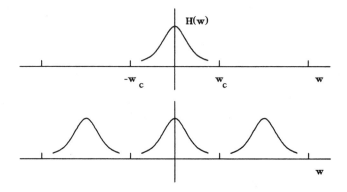

Figure II.1 $F(\omega)$ and the shifted $F(\omega - 2\,\pi n/T)$.

We can choose

$$G(\omega) = \begin{cases} T & |\omega| < 2\,\pi\,f_c \\ 0 & otherwise \end{cases}$$

With this $G(\omega)$, (II.6) is automatically satisfied. This band-limited filter $G(\omega)$ is illustrated in Figure II.2, and the time function $g(t)$ is

$$g(t) = \frac{1}{2\,\pi} \int_{-2\pi f_c}^{2\pi f_c} T\,e^{jwt}\,dw = \frac{\sin 2\,\pi\,f_c\,t}{\pi\,t/T} = sinc\,(2\,\pi\,f_c\,t)$$

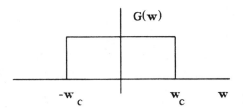

Figure II.2 The band-limited filter $G(\omega)$.

We have therefore demonstrated the following:

If the Fourier transform of $f(t)$ vanishes for $|\omega| \geq 2\,\pi\,f_c$, then $f(t)$ can be exactly reconstructed from samples taken $f_c/2$ apart (or closer).

We now turn our attention to the two-dimensional case. The spatial function $f(x,y)$ has its Fourier transform $F(u,v)$ given by

$$F(u,v) = \int\limits_{-\infty}^{\infty} \int\limits_{-\infty}^{\infty} f(x,y) \, e^{-j2\pi(xu+yv)} \, dx \, dy \tag{II.7}$$

The spatial frequency function $F(u,v)$ is again assumed to be spatial-frequency limited,

$$|u| \leq 2\pi f_c$$

$$|v| \leq 2\pi f_c$$

Corresponding to (II.1), we have the following two-dimensional sampling theorem:

$$f(x,y) = \sum_{m=-\infty}^{\infty} \sum_{n=-\infty}^{\infty} f(mT,nT) \, g(x-mT,y-nT) \tag{II.8}$$

Following similar arguments as presented above for the one-dimensional case, we obtain the following necessary and sufficient condition for equation (II.8) to hold.

$$F(u,v) = \frac{G(u,v)}{T^2} \sum_{m=-\infty}^{\infty} \sum_{n=-\infty}^{\infty} F(u-2\pi m/T, v-2\pi n/T) \tag{II.9}$$

The spatially band-limited filter is illustrated in Figure II.3.

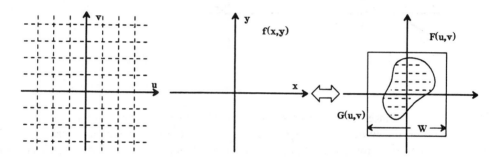

Figure II.3   (a) Sampling lattice, (b) the Fourier transform pair.

We have therefore demonstrated the following:

If the Fourier transform of f(x,y) vanishes over all but a bounded region of the spatial frequency space, then f(x,y) can be exactly reconstructed from samples taken on a regular sampling lattice of points spaced $f_c/2$ apart (or closer).

II.2 PICTURE RECONSTRUCTION FROM PROJECTIONS

In the preceding sampling strategy, we have taken samples using a sampling lattice in the spatial domain. Sometimes we can take samples from the projections of a picture function. As before, the spatial function $f(x,y)$ has its Fourier transform $F(u,v)$ given by

$$F(u,v) = \int\limits_{-\infty}^{\infty} \int\limits_{-\infty}^{\infty} f(x,y) \, e^{-j2\pi(xu+yv)} \, dx \, dy$$

If we set v to be 0, we obtain

$$F(u,0) = \int\limits_{-\infty}^{\infty} \int\limits_{-\infty}^{\infty} f(x,y) \, e^{-j2\pi xu} \, dx \, dy$$

$$= \int\limits_{-\infty}^{\infty} (\int\limits_{-\infty}^{\infty} f(x,y) \, dy) \, e^{-j2\pi xu} \, dx$$

$$= \int\limits_{-\infty}^{\infty} p(x) \, e^{-j2\pi xu} \, dx$$

where $p(x)$ is the projection of $f(x,y)$ on its x-axis. In other words, $F(u,0)$ is the Fourier transform of $p(x)$. Similarly, we can see that $F(0,v)$ is the Fourier transform of $p(y)$, the projection of $f(x,y)$ on its y-axis.

If we have many projections θ-degrees apart, their Fourier transforms will be on lines θ-degrees apart in the spatial frequency domain, as illustrated in Figure II.4.

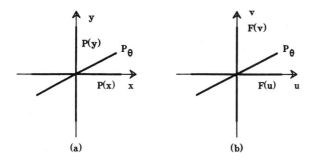

(a)   (b)

Figure II.4 Reconstruction from projections by interpolating the Fourier transform of the projections.

Since $F(u,v)$ is usually band-limited, we can use standard interpolation techniques to estimate $F(u,v)$ and then take the inverse Fourier transform to obtain $f(x,y)$. This is the basis for most of the computerized tomography reconstruction techniques. A schematic diagram is illustrated in Figure II.5.

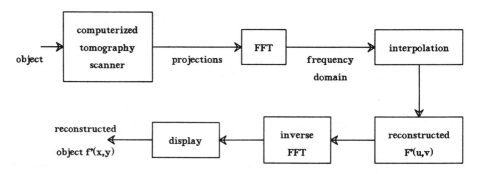

Figure II.5   Picture reconstruction from projections.

II.3 ALIASING PROBLEMS IN PICTURE SAMPLING

The aliasing effect is the phenomenon of picture distortion due to undersampling. An example is illustrated in Figure II.6.

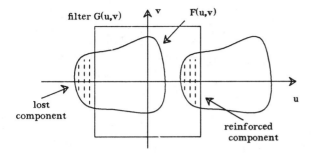

filter G(u,v)

F(u,v)

lost
component

reinforced
component

u

Figure II.6 Picture aliasing due to undersampling.

As seen in Figure II.6, $F(u,v)$ has nonzero components outside of the band-limited filter $G(u,v)$. This causes two problems:

1. Some spatial frequency components are reinforced, causing the appearance of false lines and edges, leading to a distorted image.
2. High spatial frequency components of $F(u,v)$ outside of $G(u,v)$ are lost, causing loss of resolution.

Because of the aliasing problem, periodic waveforms may change frequency and orientation. This is demonstrated by a simple example. Suppose the picture function is

$$f(x,y) = \cos 2\pi \omega_0 x$$

This picture consists of vertical bars representing the sinusoidal waveforms, as illustrated in Figure II.7(a). Its Fourier transform $F(u,v)$ is illustrated in Figure II.7(b), which consists of two Delta functions $2\omega_0$ apart,

$$\delta(u + \omega_0) + \delta(u - \omega_0)$$

Suppose the filter $G(u,v)$ is as shown in Figure II.7(c), where $\omega_0 = 0.75\ T$. In other words, the sampling rate is below ω_0. When $f(x,y)$ is reconstructed using equation (II.9), the original high frequency components fall outside the filter and are suppressed. On the other hand, high-frequency components from adjacent spectrum waveforms fall inside the filter region, leading to the following $F'(u,v)$, which is illustrated in Figure II.7(d).

$$\delta(\omega + \frac{1}{2}\omega_0) + \delta(\omega - \frac{1}{2}\omega_0)$$

The resultant waveform becomes a lower-frequency cosine waveform. If $f(x,t)$ is a time function, representing, for example, a turning wheel, then the wheel will be turning at a lower frequency.

A final example is illustrated in Figure II.8, where the original picture consists of slanted stripes. Again, due to undersampling, both the spatial frequency and the orientation of the Delta functions are changed, resulting in a picture consisting of stripes with different orientation and modified aliasing frequency.

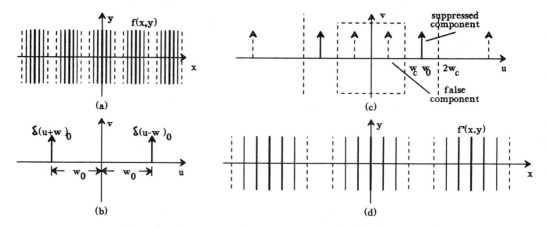

Figure II.7 An example of spatial aliasing. (a) Original cosine waveform; (b) $F(u,v)$; (c) filter $G(u,v)$ and effects of undersampling; (d) reconstructed cosine waveform.

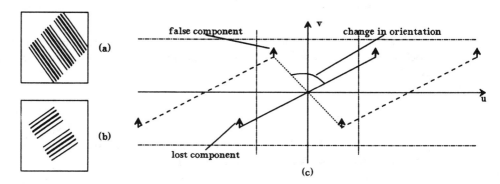

Figure II.8 Original picture (a) is changed to (b) due to spatial aliasing (c).

II.4 PICTURE QUANTIZATION

In digital picture processing, the picture samples must be quantized. The range of values of the samples must be divided into intervals, and all values within an interval will be represented by a single level.

Usually, we select quantization levels that are evenly spaced. An example is illustrated in Figure II.9(a). If a sample takes on a value in $[z_k, z_{k+1})$, it is assigned gray level q_k.

The point operation, thresholding, can be regarded as a quantization operation, where samples in $[z_1, z_2)$ are quantized to q_1 (binary 0), and samples in $[z_2, z_3)$ are quantized to q_2 (binary 1).

Although usually the quantization levels are evenly spaced, *tapered quantization,* or unequally spaced quantization levels are sometimes useful, if sample values in a certain range occur more frequently, as illustrated in Figure II.9(b). Representing the picture in this range with finer quantization may improve image quality. In what follows, we present a technique to find the optimal quantization levels [MAX60].

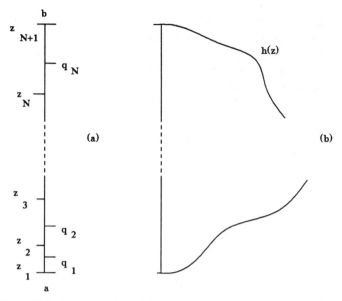

Figure II.9 (a) Quantization levels and (b) sample amplitude density function .

Let the quantization levels be $q_1, q_2, ..., q_L$. Let $h(z)$ be the histogram function (or sample amplitude density function). We define the *mean square quantization error* as follows:

$$E = \sum_{k=1}^{L} \int_{z_k}^{z_{k+1}} (z - q_k)^2 h(z) \, dz \tag{II.10}$$

To improve image quality, we can choose $(q_1, ..., q_L)$ and $(z_1, ..., z_L, z_{L+1})$ to minimize E. We take the partial derivatives of E with respect to z_k and q_k and set the results to zero.

$$\frac{\partial E}{\partial z_k} = (z_k - q_{k-1})^2 h(z_k) - (z_k - q_k)^2 h(z_k) = 0, \quad k = 2, ..., L \tag{II.11}$$

$$\frac{\partial E}{\partial q_k} = -2 \sum_{z_k}^{z_{k+1}} (z - q_k) h(z) = 0, \quad k = 1, ..., L \tag{II.12}$$

From (II.11), we have

$$(z_k - q_{k-1} + z_k - q_k)(z_k - q_{k-1} - z_k + q_k) h(z_k) = 0$$

and therefore,

$$z_k = \frac{q_{k-1} + q_k}{2} \quad k = 2, ..., L \tag{II.13}$$

In other words, the z_k's are halfway between the q_k's. From (II.12), we have

$$q_k = \frac{\displaystyle\int_{z_k}^{z_{k+1}} z \, h(z) \, dz}{\displaystyle\int_{z_k}^{z_{k+1}} h(z) \, dz} \tag{II.14}$$

In other words, q_k is the centroid of the portion of $h(z)$ between z_k and z_{k+1}.

The general problem of optimal quantization is as follows: Given $h(z)$, how do we select z_k and q_k according to equations (II.13) and (II.14)?

An iterative algorithm is as follows. We first select a tentative q_1. We then determine z_2 from (II.14), and q_2 from (II.13),..., until q_L. If z_{L+1} is not equal to the maximum value allowed, we must change q_1 and iterate until a satisfactory value of z_{L+1} is obtained.

If $h(z)$ is uniform—that is, $h(z) = p$,—then the z_k and q_k can be calculated directly. From (II.14),

$$q_k = \frac{0.5(z_{k+1} - z_k)}{z_{k+1} - z_k} = \frac{z_{k+1} + z_k}{2} \tag{II.15}$$

Equations (II.13) and (II.14) will be satisfied, if we choose

$$z_k = (k-1)/L \quad , k=1,2,...,L+1$$

$$q_k = \frac{2k-1}{2L} , \qquad k = 1, 2 ,..., L$$

II.5 THE HISTOGRAM FUNCTION

A global picture transformation, which is very useful in practical applications, is *histogramming*. A *histogram function* h(z) is defined as the number of pixels at gray level z, or

$$h(z) = \iint [f(x,y) = z] \, dx \, dy \tag{II.16}$$

From the histogram function $h(z)$, the *area function* $A(z)$ can be computed, which is the area of picture with gray level above threshold z.

$$A(z) = \int_z^\infty h(z) \, dz \tag{II.17}$$

from (II.17)

$$\frac{d A(z)}{dz} = -h(z)$$

and therefore,

$$h(z) = -\frac{d A(z)}{dz}$$

The integrated optical density (IOD) is defined as

$$IOD = \iint f(x,y) \, dx \, dy = \int z \, h(z) \, dz \tag{II.18}$$

Histograms are useful in many applications. They can be used in tapered quantization to improve image contrast (see section II.4). They can be used in finding the appropriate threshold for object detection. They can also be used in picture normalization by *histogram matching*. In this section, we explain the technique of histogram matching.

To improve image contrast, the *gray-level transformation* can be used. Gray-level transformation is also a point operation. It is illustrated in Figure II.10.

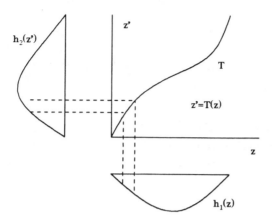

Figure II.10 Gray-level transformation.

The gray-level transformation T is defined by

$$z' = T(z) \tag{II.19}$$

where z is the old gray-level value, and z' the new gray-level value. $T(z)$ is usually a monotonic function in z. The transformation T can be used to transform one histogram, say $h1$, into another, say $h2$, by changing the gray levels of pixels. Since the areas under the two histogram curves must be equal and Δz and $\Delta z'$ are related by $z' = T(z)$, we have

$$h_1(z) \, \Delta z = h_2(z') \, \Delta z \tag{II.20}$$

Taking the limit, we obtain

$$h_1(z) = h_2(z') \frac{dT(z)}{dz} \tag{II.21}$$

Therefore,

$$h_2(z') = \frac{h_1(T^{-1}(z'))}{dT(z)/dz} \tag{II.22}$$

As an example, if $z' = a z + b$ (linear gray level transformation), then

$$z = (z' - b)/a$$

whence

$$h_2(z') = \frac{h_1[(z' - b)/a]}{a}$$

Intuitively, the constant b shifts the histogram left (b<0) or right (b>0), and the constant 'a' broadens (a>1) or narrows (a<1) the histogram.

In the foregoing, we are given one histogram h_1 and the gray-level transformation T, and we want to find the other histogram h_2. The problem of *histogram matching* can be posed as the following question: Given two histograms, how can we find a gray-level transformation T, so that one histogram can be converted into another?

If we assume h_1 and h_2 are continuous functions, a simple technique is illustrated in Figure II.11. The approach is to find two transformations T_1 and T_2 which will transform h_1 and h_2 into a uniform histogram, respectively. The composite transform

$$z' = T_2^{-1} [T_1(z)]$$

will then transform $h_1(z)$ into $h_2(z')$.

To find the transformations T_1 and T_2, we can use (II.22) to derive

$$c \frac{d T_1(z)}{dz} = h_1(z)$$

and

$$c \frac{d T_2(z)}{dz} = h_2(z)$$

Performing integration, we obtain

$$T_1(z) = \frac{1}{c} \int_0^z h_1(t) \, dt$$

$$T_2(z) = \frac{1}{c} \int_0^z h_2(t) \, dt$$

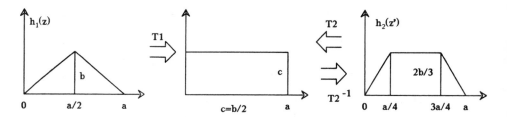

Figure II.11 Histogram matching technique.

As an example, the transformations T_1 and T_2 for the two histograms h_1 and h_2 shown in Figure II.11, are illustrated in Figures II.12(a) and (b), respectively. The transformation $T_1(z)$ is given next:

$$T_1(z) = \frac{1}{b/2} \int_0^z h_1(t) \, dt = \begin{cases} \dfrac{2z^2}{a} & 0 \le z \le \dfrac{a}{2} \\[2mm] a - \dfrac{2}{a}(a-z)^2 & \dfrac{a}{2} \le z \le a \end{cases}$$

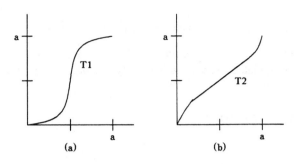

Figure II.12 The transformations (a) T_1 and (b) T_2.

If the picture function f is a digital picture function, then its histogram h is also a discrete function. The problem of finding an optimal gray-level transformation to match two histograms becomes a combinatorial problem. An algorithm was given in [CHANG78].

II.6 PICTURE ALGEBRAIC OPERATIONS AND ITS EFFECTS ON HISTOGRAMS

We now look at the effects of *algebraic operations* on histograms. The general form of a binary algebraic operation is

$$f_1 \; \theta \; f_2 = f_3$$

where θ denotes some operator.

II.6.1 Histogram of Added Pictures

Suppose the operation is

$$f_1 \qquad + \qquad f_2 \qquad = \qquad f_3$$

$$h_1(z_1) \qquad\qquad h_2(z_2) \qquad h_3(z)$$

Let $h_{12}(z_1, z_2)$ denote the two-dimensional histogram of f_3. In other words, $h_{12}(z_1, z_2)$ is the number of pixels in f_3, with

$$f_1(x,y) = z_1, \quad \text{and} \quad f_2(x,y) = z_2$$

Suppose

$$z_1 + z_2 = z$$

Then

$$z_2 = z - z_1$$

Therefore,

$$h_3(z) = \int h_{12}(z_1, z-z_1) \, dz_1$$

If the two pictures are uncorrelated, so that

$$h_3(z) = \int h_1(z_1) \, h_2(z-z_1) \, dz_1 = h_1(z_1) * h_2(z_2)$$

where the symbol * indicates h_3 is the *convolution* of h_1 and h_2. Therefore, we can see that the sum of the uncorrelated pictures will occupy a broader gray-level range than that of the component pictures.

II.6.2 Histogram of Subtracted Pictures

Suppose the operation is

$$f_1 \qquad - \qquad f_2 \qquad = \qquad f_3$$

$$h_1(z_1) \qquad\qquad h_2(z_2) \qquad\qquad h_3(z)$$

If $f_1(x,y) = f(x + \Delta x, y)$, $f_2(x,y) = f(x,y)$; in other words, one picture is the displacement of another, then

$$f_3 = f(x+\Delta x,y) - f(x,y) = \frac{f(x+\Delta x,y) - f(x,y)}{\Delta x} \Delta x = \frac{df}{dx} \Delta x$$

We can regard (df/dx) as a picture whose histogram is h'. This picture is then multiplied by a constant Δx. Therefore, the new histogram is

$$h_3(z) = \frac{h'\left(\dfrac{z}{\Delta x}\right)}{\Delta x}$$

This technique can be used to detect motion in time-sequenced pictures (elapsed photography). As an example, the pictures and their histograms are

```
      f1              f2              f3
   3  2  1         2  1  0         1  1  1
   3  2  1    -    2  1  0    =    1  1  1
   3  2  1         2  1  0         1  1  1


   h1(1)=3         h2(0)=3
   h1(2)=3         h2(1)=3       h3(1)=9
   h1(3)=3         h2(2)=3
```

II.7 PICTURE QUALITY

The common measures of digitized picture quality include: resolution, bits per pixel, and acutance.

Resolution is the distinguishability of small, close objects such as bars on a resolution chart. If the bar width is b units, the resolution can be expressed as 2b units, measured from one bar center position to the next bar center position. Another way of expressing resolution is the reciprocal of 2b, or 1/2b line-pairs per unit distance.

As an example, the bar width on a resolution chart is five mils, or five thousandths of an inch.

$$b = 5/1000 \ inch = 1/200 \ inch$$

The resolution is 10 mils, or

$$1/2b \; = \; 1000/10 \; = \; 100 \; line-pairs \; per \; inch.$$

A picture's quality is better if the resolution as expressed in lines per inch is large or as expressed in mils is small.

The next measure of a digital picture's quality is the number of bits per pixel (Bpp). A picture's quality is better if the number of bits per pixel is large.

The *acutance* is the average steepness of an edge in the output picture that results from a perfect step edge in the input. It is measured also in line pairs per inch and is normally the same as resolution.

R E F E R E N C E S

[CASTLEMAN79] CASTLEMAN, K. R., *Digital Image Processing*, Englewood Cliffs, New Jersey: Prentice-Hall, Inc., 1979.

[CHANG78] CHANG, S. K., AND Y. WONG,. "Optimal Histogram Matching by Monotone Gray Level Transformation," *Communications of the A.C.M.*, October 1978, 835-840.

[MAX60] MAX, J., *Quantizing for Minimum Distortion*, IRE Transactions on Information Theory, IT-6, 1960, pp. 7-12.

Appendix III

Inference
and Reasoning

III.1 INTRODUCTION TO PREDICATE CALCULUS

In Chapter 7, we discussed how to represent knowledge by semantic networks. The facts in the knowledge base are represented by statements, which are expressed as logical predicates. Some examples are shown next:

Statement	Predicate
Kim is female	FEMALE(Kim)
Kim is male	MALE(Kim)
Three is less than five	LESSTHAN(three,five)
Kim is mother	MOTHER(Kim)

In the preceding examples, each predicate has a name and a number of arguments. Such predicates are called *atoms*. The arguments of an atom may be functions of other arguments. For example, FEMALE(wifeof(John)) represents the statement, "The wife of John is female."

Atoms can be combined by logical connectives to form logical expressions called *clauses*. Some examples are given next:

348

Statement	Clause
Kim is female and a mother	FEMALE(Kim) ∧ MOTHER(Kim)
Kim is not male	~ MALE(Kim)
Kim is male or Kim is female	MALE(Kim) | FEMALE(Kim)
If Kim is mother then Kim is female	MOTHER(Kim) → FEMALE(Kim) or ~ MOTHER(Kim) | FEMALE(Kim)

The last example illustrates the clause "A → B," sometimes written as "IF A THEN B," is equivalent to "~A | B."

The expressive power of predicate calculus is further enriched by the introduction of *variables*. Some examples are given next:

Statement	Clause
Everyone is male or female	MALE(x) | FEMALE(x)
For all x, if x is mother then x is female	MOTHER(x) → FEMALE(y) or ~ MOTHER(x) | FEMALE(x)

Technically, each variable in a clause is considered *universally quantified*. In other words, a variable such as x is treated as signifying "every x" or "for all x." Thus, the following clause,

1. PERSON(x) ∧ PARENT(x) → MOTHER(x) | FATHER(x)

means "for every x, if x is a person and a parent, then x is either a mother or a father." The clause 1 can be rewritten as

2. ~(PERSON(x) ∧ PARENT(x)) | MOTHER(x) | FATHER(x)

Applying DeMorgan's law, we have

3. ~PERSON(x) | ~PARENT(x) | MOTHER(x) | FATHER(x)

If we insist on adding the universal quantifier, 3 should be written as

4. ($\forall x$) (~PERSON(x) | ~PARENT(x) | MOTHER(x) | FATHER(x))

The expressions 1, 2, 3, and 4 are all equivalent. Expressions of the form 1 are said to be in *clausal form syntax,* and expressions of the form 4 are said to be in *nonclausal syntax.*

A general expression for a clause in the clausal form syntax is

5. $A_1 \wedge A_2 \wedge \cdots A_n \rightarrow B_1 \mid B_2 \ldots \mid B_m$

where $A_1, \ldots, A_n$, and $B_1, \ldots, B_m$ are atoms. The foregoing expression is understood to mean

6. ($\forall x_1, \ldots, x_n$) $A_1 \wedge A_2 \wedge \cdots A_n \rightarrow B_1 \mid B_2 \ldots \mid B_m$

A *sentence* in clausal form is the logical conjunction of a set of clauses.

A well-formed formula (wff) in nonclausal form is any well-formed logical expression involving atoms, logical connectives, and existential quantifiers (written as ∃, signifying "there exists") and universal quantifiers (written as ∀, signifying "for all"). It is possible to convert from nonclausal form to clausal form and vice versa. Therefore, the two representations are equal in expressive power. We will now illustrate with an example.

Suppose we have a collection of facts, such as the predicates represented by a semantic network illustrated in Figure III.1, how do we represent the same collection of facts using predicate calculus?

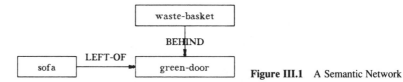

Figure III.1   A Semantic Network

The preceding semantic network represents the following predicates:

```
BEHIND(waste-basket, green-door)
LEFT-OF(sofa, green-door)
```

The intuitive meaning of the foregoing two predicates is "The waste-basket is behind the green-door, *and* the sofa is to the left of the green-door." Therefore, the set of predicates is interpreted to mean the logical conjunction of these predicates. In nonclausal form syntax, we have the expression

```
BEHIND(waste-basket, green-door) ∧ LEFT-OF(sofa, green-door)
```

In clausal form syntax, we write

```
→ BEHIND(waste-basket, green-door)
→ LEFT-OF(sofa, green-door)
```

In the foregoing, the left-hand side of each clause is null. If the left-hand side of a clause is null, the clause "→P" is interpreted to mean "P." On the other hand, if the right-hand side of a clause is null, the clause "P→" is interpreted to mean "~P." A null clause (both left-hand side and right-hand side are null) is understood to be a contradiction.

The preceding example shows that we can represent a semantic network as a well-formed formula in nonclausal form, or as a sentence (that is, a set of clauses) in clausal form. The advantage of this logical representation is that now we can apply *inference rules* to infer new facts, or prove theorems, from a given collection of facts.

III.2 INFERENCE BY THEOREM PROVING

The semantics of a logical expression depends on how we interpret it, by specifying the domain of discourse, the meaning of symbols and functions, the true/false values of atoms, and the meaning of the logical connectives. With respect to an interpretation, we can then evaluate the true/false value of a logical expression. A logical expression is *inconsistent* if it is false in every interpretation. It is *valid* if it is true in every interpretation.

A logical expression B logically follows from another logical expression A if every interpretation that makes A true also makes B true. In other words, the expression $(A \rightarrow B)$ is valid. A formal proof then is a sequence of inferences which establishes that $(A \rightarrow B)$ is valid. Standard inference rules include the following:

- Modus Ponens: $(A) \wedge (A \rightarrow B) \vdash (B)$
- Modus Tollens: $(\sim B) \wedge (A \rightarrow B) \vdash (A)$
- Projection: $A \wedge B \vdash A$
- Substitution: $(\forall x)_{D_x} P(x) \vdash P(a)$ where a is in D_x

Suppose we have (from figure III.1) the following facts, expressed in nonclausal form:

$$\text{BEHIND(waste-basket, green-door)} \wedge \text{LEFT-OF(sofa, green-door)} \qquad \text{(III.1)}$$

and we also know the following fact:

$$(\forall x,y) \ \text{BEHIND}(x,y) \rightarrow \text{INVISIBLE}(x) \qquad \text{(III.2)}$$

or "for any x and y, if x is behind y, then x is invisible." The conjunction of (III.1) and (III.2) yields, in Prenex normal form,

$$(\forall x,y) \ \text{BEHIND(waste-basket, green-door)} \wedge$$

$$\text{LEFT-OF(sofa,green-door)} \wedge (\sim \text{BEHIND}(x,y) \mid \text{INVISIBLE}(x)) \qquad \text{(III.3)}$$

If we substitute x by waste-basket, and y by green-door, we obtain

$$\text{BEHIND(waste-basket, green-door)} \wedge \text{LEFT-OF(sofa, green-door)} \wedge$$

$$(\sim \text{BEHIND(waste-basket, green-door)} \mid \text{INVISIBLE(waste-basket)}) \qquad \text{(III.4)}$$

By the projection rule, we obtain

$$\text{BEHIND(waste-basket, green-door)} \wedge$$

$$(\sim \text{BEHIND(waste-basket, green-door)} \mid \text{INVISIBLE(waste-basket)}) \qquad \text{(III.5)}$$

Since $(A \wedge (\sim A \mid B)) = (A \wedge \sim A) \mid (A \wedge B) = (A \wedge B)$, we obtain

$$\text{BEHIND(waste-basket, green-door)} \wedge \text{INVISIBLE(waste-basket)} \qquad \text{(III.6)}$$

Applying the projection rule once more, we finally have

$$\text{INVISIBLE(waste-basket)} \qquad \text{(III.7)}$$

In other words, we have proven (or derived the new fact) that the waste-basket is invisible.

The foregoing proof is by the direct manipulation of nonclausal forms, which is similar to our usual mathematical proof procedure. For mechanical reasoning, the non-clausal form is less commonly used than the clausal form. In clausal form, (III.3) becomes

$$\to \text{BEHIND(waste-basket, green-door)}$$
$$\to \text{LEFT-OF(sofa, green-door)}$$
$$\text{BEHIND}(x,y) \to \text{INVISIBLE}(x) \qquad\qquad\qquad\text{(III.8)}$$

To prove that "waste-basket is invisible," we can add the negation of this statement to (III.8) and attempt to derive a contradiction. Therefore we start from

$\to$BEHIND(waste-basket, green-door)	(III.9-a)
$\to$LEFT-OF(sofa, green-door)	(III.9-b)
BEHIND$(x,y) \to$ INVISIBLE(x)	(III.9-c)
INVISIBLE(waste-basket) $\to$	(III.9-d)

The nice thing about the clausal form in mechanical reasoning is that *a single inference rule suffices*. This inference rule, called the *resolution principle*, was first discovered by Robinson. The resolution principle involves matching the left-hand part of one clause *A* with the right-hand part of another clause *B*. When we perform the matching, substitution of variables is done to make atoms identical.

After the matching, the derived clause *C*, called the *resolvent*, consists of the unmatched left-hand and right-hand parts of *A* and *B*, instantiated by the matching substitution. Several variations of the resolution principle are given below:

1. $A1{\to}A2 \land A2{\to}A3 \vdash A1{\to}A3$ (if $A1 \to A2$ and $A2 \to A3$, then $A1 \to A3$)

2. $\to A1 \land A1{\to}A2 \vdash \to A2$ (Modus Ponens)

3. $A1,A2{\to}A3,A4 \land A4,A5{\to}A6,A7 \vdash A1,A2,A5{\to}A3,A6,A7$

For example, the left-hand part of (III.9-c) matches the right-hand part of (III.9-a), after *x* is substituted by waste-basket, and *y* is substituted by green-door. The resolvent of (III.9-a) and (III.9-c) is

$$\to \text{INVISIBLE(waste-basket)} \qquad\qquad\qquad\text{(III.9-e)}$$

But the resolution of (III.9-d) and (III.9-e) will result in a null clause, which means a contradiction. Thus, the theorem ("waste-basket is invisible") is proved.

A fundamental result in first-order logic (predicate calculus) is that any true theorem expressible in first-order logic is provable in finite time, and there is an algorithm to find the proof. However, it is undecidable whether this algorithm will terminate. The resolution principle preserves the *completeness* (all true theorems are provable) and *correctness* (no false theorems are provable) properties of first-order logic.

Many automated theorem provers use the resolution principle, or variations of the resolution principle, to find proofs or make inferences. We notice, although the resolution principle is very simple, its practical application depends very much on *how to reduce the search space when we attempt to perform matching.* We also note that the resolution principle is closely related to graph matching. In fact, we can represent the sentence (or clauses) by a (modified) semantic network and make inferences by applying the resolution principle to the semantic network.

III.3 INFERENCE USING SEMANTIC NETWORKS

As we have discussed in the clausal form of representation, the clauses in predicate calculus can be represented as

$$A_{11}, A_{12}, ..., A_{1n} \rightarrow B_{11}, B_{12}, ..., B_{1m}$$
$$A_{21}, A_{22}, ..., A_{2n} \rightarrow B_{21}, B_{22}, ..., B_{2m}$$
$$.....$$
$$A_{k1}, A_{k2}, ..., A_{kn} \rightarrow B_{k1}, B_{k2}, ..., B_{km}$$

The resolution rule is then repeatedly applied to the foregoing set of clauses to derive a contradiction (a null clause). The clauses can also be represented by a semantic network as follows. Each clause corresponds to a partition in a graph. By a notational trick, every unary relation is converted to an equivalent binary relation by repeating the argument, so that INVISIBLE(x) becomes INVISIBLE(x,x). Also, an arc is drawn as a thick line if it is a relation in the condition part of the clause and as a thin line if it is in the conclusion part of the clause. An example is given in Figure III.2(a). In Figure III.2(a), the semantic network represents

<table>
<tr><td>$\rightarrow$ BEHIND(waste-basket, green-door)</td><td>(III.9-a)</td></tr>
<tr><td>BEHIND(x,y) $\rightarrow$ INVISIBLE(x)</td><td>(III.9-c)</td></tr>
<tr><td>INVISIBLE(waste-basket) $\rightarrow$</td><td>(III.9-d)</td></tr>
</table>

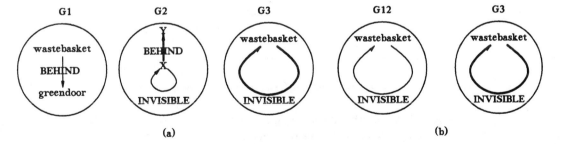

(a)   (b)

Figure III.2 (a) Original net; (b) new net.

To make inferences using this semantic network, we will merge partitions. When two partitions are merged, we first make variable substitutions, and then the corresponding arcs ($A{\rightarrow}B$) and ($A{\Rightarrow}B$) will cancel. Therefore, when we merge $G1$ and $G2$ of the graph shown in Figure III.2(a), after substituting x by "waste-basket" and y by "green-door," the resulting partition is $G12$, as shown in Figure III.2(b). The substitution of variables by values is called *binding,* which is a side effect of the inference process.

If we now try to merge $G12$ and $G3$, we have an empty partition which corresponds to the null clause in theorem proving. Therefore, we have proven the conclusion.

If we do not specify the theorem, we can still use the semantic network to infer new facts by merging partitions. Notice the newly derived facts are automatically added to the knowledge base. An example of inferring "Silo-30 is between river-1 and river-2" is given in Figures III.3(a) to (c). Again, in this inference process, binding of variables occurs as a side effect. The resultant graph Figure III.3(c), as well as the values of bounded variables, can be output to the user.

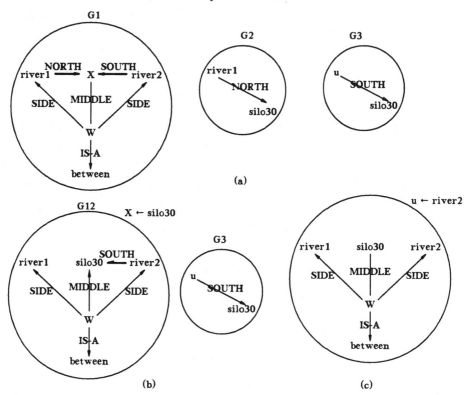

Figure III.3 Inferring "Silo-30" between river-1 and river-2.

If we allow for arbitrary mergings, we may derive many useless facts, and the knowledge base may become too large. Since we may impose additional structures on the semantic network, we can simulate, for example, attention focusing (or zooming), by stipulating that the merging take place only within a group of partitions. Of course, we then must forsake any claim about logical completeness (that is, all provable theorems can be derived).

Another restriction on the clauses is to allow a single atom on the right-hand side of the clause. Thus every clause (called the Horn clause) has the form

$$A_1, A_2, ..., A_n \rightarrow B$$

This may be considered as a procedure $B(A1,A2,...,An)$, where the name of the procedure corresponds to the conclusion, and the conditions become procedures to be invoked by this procedure. This line of thinking leads to the programming language PROLOG. In the semantic network representation of Horn clauses, every partition has a single thick line (or no thick line at all) which could be used as an index for the partition, thereby facilitating searching and merging.

If we consider a collection of Horn clauses, proving a conclusion leads to proving the premises, which again leads to proving of the premises of the premises. In PROLOG, this becomes the recursive evocation of procedures. This is commonly referred to as *backward chaining*. Another way is to think of the proof process as searching an AND/OR tree, as illustrated in Figure III.4.

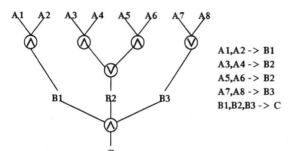

A1,A2 -> B1
A3,A4 -> B2
A5,A6 -> B2
A7,A8 -> B3
B1,B2,B3 -> C

Figure III.4 Searching the "AND/OR" tree.

In PROLOG, the premises (or subgoals) in a clause are processed strictly left-to-right, and clauses used to prove (or solve) a subgoal are processed in the order in which they occur in the input. This simple control mechanism is well suited to the specification of many algorithms. Although PROLOG is incomplete in that provable conclusions may not be derivable in PROLOG, its efficiency and algorithmic nature make it attractive for solving problems where the reasoning process is well focused, and the algorithm for reasoning is known.

III.4 INFERENCE USING PRODUCTION SYSTEMS

In the preceding, we saw that the clauses can be stored in a knowledge base. In this knowledge base, we can store both *data* (or facts) and *rules*. Therefore, it is conceptually useful to distinguish the two parts of the knowledge base: a *database* and a *rule base*.

In mechanical theorem proving, the dynamic addition/deletion/modification of facts and/or rules in this knowledge base is not allowed, except by the theorem prover itself in its application of the inference rule (such as the resolution rule).

If we allow arbitrary updates of this knowledge base and impose various restrictions on the inference mechanism, we then have the so-called *production system* or *rule-based system*.

The production system has three basic components:

1. A database (a collection of facts).
2. A rule base (a collection of rules).
3. An interpreter (to control the inference mechanism). In general, the interpreter of the production system operates by matching the condition (or situation, left-hand part) of the rule against facts in the database. If there is a match, the action part of the rule is invoked, which could result in the addition (deletion, modification) of facts in the database, or the addition (deletion, modification) of rules in the rule base, or the invocation of other arbitrary processes. A rule-based system, therefore, is very general, because the actions can be unconstrained.

As an example, the following rule can be regarded as a situation-action pair, which says that "a region whose color is green is also a region covered by grass":

$$(Green\,(REGIONx\,)) \rightarrow (Grass\,(REGIONx\,))$$

Translated into clauses, the foregoing rule might look like

$$REGION\,(x\,),COLOR\,(x\,,Green\,) \rightarrow COVERED-BY\,(x\,,Grass\,)$$

The interpreter will try to match the situation, or the left-hand part of the rule, with some pattern (or fact) in the database. If such a match can be found, the new fact (that the region is covered by grass) will be added to the database. In this case, except for some notational changes, we can see the production system is actually equivalent to a mechanical theorem-proving system. However, the following rule may also be incorporated into the production system:

$$(Green\,(Regionx\,)) \rightarrow (Notify\,(UserAdams\,))$$

Thus the system will send a message to Adams, when it discovers that region x is green. Such actions, although useful for a production system or an expert system, may lead to unforeseen consequences not achievable by any theorem prover.

The interpreter of the production system must identify the rules that are applicable and decide which is to be applied next. Various ad hoc restrictions can be imposed to make the production system more efficient. For example, rules might be linearly ordered and scanned sequentially by the interpreter. The first applicable rule will be used, and the scanning then resumes from the beginning or from the current rule. Both backward chaining and forward chaining may be employed. Domain-dependent knowledge may also be employed by the interpreter in determining the application of rules. Such special restrictions on the inference mechanism of the interpreter will increase its efficiency.

The production system is the heart of an expert system. An *expert system* can be thought of as a computer program that performs an intellectually demanding task about as well as most human experts. Some of the best known expert systems include the following:

a. MYCIN, developed to offer consultation in a limited area of medicine.
b. DENDRAL, created to aid in analyzing organic chemical compounds.
c. PROSPECTOR, programmed to aid in selecting sites for mineral exploration.

In addition to the database, the rule base, and the interpreter which controls the inference mechanism for the production system, the expert system also has the following components:

4. A knowledge acquisition component, which is a sophisticated program designed to communicate with a human expert to transfer the facts and rules that are used by the human expert into the knowledge base.
5. A user interface, which allows someone with little or no programming experience to interact with the system.

The production rule of an expert system consists of an "if" part stating the condition (or the situation) and a "then" part stating the conclusion (or the action). It may also include a confidence factor, uncertainty, or probability estimates. An example of a production rule used in MYCIN is given next:

```
IF
```

1. The infection that requires therapy is meningitis, and
2. The patient has evidence of serious skin or tissue infection, and,
3. Organisms are not seen on the stain of the culture, and
4. The type of the infection is bacterial,

```
THEN
```

```
Evidence exists that the organism that might be causing the
infection is staphylococcus-coag-pos with degree of
confidence 0.75.
```

Translated into clausal form, the rule might look like,

```
EQUAL(complaint, meningitis), SERIOUSINF(xcf),
NOTSEEN(organism,culture stain), TYPEOFINFECTION(bacterial)
   → CAUSE(scp, 0.75)
```

where the degree of confidence is included as an argument of the conclusion atom CAUSE.

The user interface provides the translation of internally stored rules into ordinary language, which is very important for human understanding. No less important is the knowledge acquisition component, which must be able to interactively solicit rules from human experts. This process is often dull and time-consuming, and the extracted rules must also be verified by the human expert, posing another problem. In fact, the success of an expert system very much depends on the friendliness of its user interface, and the sophistication of its knowledge acquisition component.

In contrast, the reasoning part of an expert system is sometimes quite straightforward. It has been said that expert systems (as well as logic programming using a language such as PROLOG) is capable of *focused reasoning*, where the reasoning process is known (although a search for the solution, perhaps by backtracking, is still necessary). In contrast, a theorem prover based on predicate calculus is capable of *unfocused reasoning,* where the reasoning process is less well understood. Both will be needed in general problem solving. However, for solving specific problems, expert systems and logic programming offer great promise.

The knowledge base of a production system generally contains the following:

1. Database of facts.

    1.1. Known facts (or clauses of the form $\rightarrow$ C).

    1.2. New facts (goals or recently occurred events).

2. Rules.

    2.1. General axioms of inference $(A_1, ..., A_n \rightarrow B_1, ..., B_m)$.

    2.2. Special rules to simplify expressions (such as the demodulators to handle equality of two expressions: EQUALITY(expression-1,expression-2).

    2.3. Domain-dependent inference rules $(A_1, ..., A_n \rightarrow B_1, ..., B_m)$, or rules with arbitrary right-hand parts.

A general theorem prover normally does not have domain-dependent inference rules (2.3), nor does it distinguish known facts (1.1) from new facts (1.2).

The database of known facts (1.1) is sometimes called the context database, or the long-term memory. The database of new facts (1.2) is sometimes called the active database, or the set-of-support, or the short-term memory.

When an event occurs, this new fact is inserted into the new-facts database, prompting the expert system into action. The expert system uses rules to deduce other facts. It is also capable of moving data from the new-facts database (short-term memory) into the known-facts database (long-term memory) and vice versa.

For example, an expert system is asked to search for bridges in an image. This is posed as a query

```
(find bridge)
```

in the new-facts database. In the known-facts database, there are facts about locations of river segments. The expert system could use domain-dependent rules to search for possible bridges *along the river segments.* Notice some rule must invoke image processing routines to identify bridges in restricted regions of the image. Once found, the new facts about bridges can be included into the known-facts database, thus completing the processing.

III.5 PLANNING AND ACTION

Planning, theorem proving, mechanical inference, and state-space problem solving are closed related. In Figure III.5(a), an *agent* (a robot, a human being, a computer process, an organization) interacts with the external world. The agent can engage in information gathering activities to acquire knowledge about the external world. The agent can also perform actions which have effects on the external world.

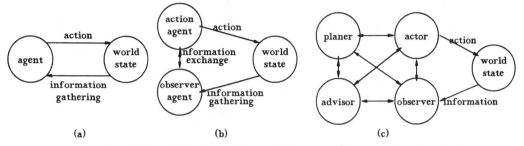

Figure III.5 (a) The agent and the world; (b) actor and observer; (c) distributed model of the agent, with actor, observer, planner, and advisor.

Usually, we take the simplifying assumption that the world is representable by a certain *world state*. An agent's action may change the world state. The agent engages in information gathering activities to acquire knowledge about the world state, which affects the agent's own state.

Clearly, this idealized view is an oversimplification of the real world situation. In the real world, external forces not controllable by the agent may also affect the world—that is, change the world state. We will discuss the implications of such perturbances later. For the moment, we concentrate on the idealized situation.

The role of the agent can be differentiated into the *actor role,* which performs the action, and the *observer role,* which performs information-gathering activities. This is emphasized in Figure III.5(b), which shows two agent modules, corresponding to the two roles of the (undifferentiated) agent. The actor and the observer can also exchange information.

Figure III.5(c) illustrates an even more complicated model of the agent, with modules such as actor, observer, planner, and advisor. The function of the planner is to plan for a course of action, based on the information about the world state gathered by the observer. The advisors criticize the action plan. They could, in computer implementations, be various expert systems.

Planning, therefore, involves *inference.* The usual problem posed to the planner is: Given an initial world state, how does one plan for a course of action to arrive at a final world state? Formulated this way, planning is regarded as a form of state-space problem solving.

As an example, we have the classical puzzle of the farmer. The farmer, the wolf, the goat, and the cabbage are initially all at the south bank of the river. There is a boat, capable of carrying the farmer and one other object. The goal for the farmer is to safely ferry all objects across the river to the north bank. The constraint of the problem is that the goat and the cabbage, or the wolf and the goat, cannot be left alone together.

To make a plan for solving this puzzle, we can approach the problem using the state-space representation. The world state can be represented by

```
                    state(x,y,z,v)
                  where x is farmer's position,
                        y is wolf's position,
                        z is goat's position,
                        v is cabbage's position.
```

Since each variable can take on only two values (either north or south), there are altogether 16 world states. The initial state is (S,S,S,S) and the final state, or the goal state, is (N,N,N,N).

We can represent a *ferry action* by a movement rule of the form

```
                        MOVE(wolf)
```

which indicates the farmer and the wolf will move from one bank to the opposite bank. The action rule is applicable only when the farmer and the object are at same side of the river. If the farmer moves alone from one bank to the opposite bank, the action rule is:

```
                         MOVE()
```

Therefore, the sequence of actions

```
                   MOVE(wolf),  MOVE()
```

will cause the following sequence of state transitions:

$$state\,(S,S,S,S) \xrightarrow[MOVE\,(wolf)]{} state\,(N,N,S,S) \xrightarrow[MOVE\,()]{} state\,(S,N,S,S)$$

The preceding state transitions will not be acceptable, because the state, state(N,N,S,S), means the goat and the cabbage will be left alone on the south bank, violating the constraint.

The representation, state(x,y,z,v), can be rewritten as a logical predicate:

```
                       STATE(x,y,z,v)
```

which is true if the farmer, the wolf, the goat, and the cabbage are at the positions x, y, z, and v, respectively. In other words, the predicate STATE(x,y,z,v) is a shorthand notation for the logical expression

$$POSITION\,(farmer,x) \wedge POSITION\,(wolf,y) \wedge POSITION\,(goat,z) \wedge POSITION\,(cabbage,v)$$

or equivalently,

$$EQ\,(POS\,(farmer),x) \wedge EQ\,(POS\,(wolf),y) \wedge EQ\,(POS\,(goat),z) \wedge EQ\,(POS\,(cabbage),v)$$

where POS(object) is a function mapping objects to their positions. When we use the abbreviated notation STATE(x,y,z,v), we must be careful with the position of the variables, because the first variable x now represents the position of the farmer, the second the position of the wolf, and so on.

The constraint can be expressed by a predicate ACC(x, y, z, v), indicating that STATE(x, y, z, v) is an acceptable state. Again, ACC(x, y, z, v) is a shorthand notation for

$$ACC(POS(farmer), POS(wolf), POS(goat), POS(cabbage)) \wedge$$
$$EQ(POS(farmer), x) \wedge EQ(POS(wolf), y) \wedge EQ(POS(goat), z) \wedge$$
$$EQ(POS(cabbage), v)$$

ACC(x, y, z, v) is true if the wolf and goat are either at the opposite bank or they are not alone, and the goat and cabbage are either at the opposite bank or they are not alone. This statement can be expressed by a rule:

R1. $((EQ(x,z) \wedge (EQ(y,z)) \vee OPP(y,z)) \wedge$
$((EQ(x,z) \wedge EQ(z,v)) \vee OPP(z,v)) \rightarrow ACC(x,y,z,v)$

In the foregoing, the predicate OPP(y, z) means y and z are opposite. Therefore, OPP(N, S) and OPP(S, N) are true.

Rule R1 can be expressed by four clauses using the canonical representation:

$R1.1. \quad EQ(x,z), EQ(y,z), EQ(z,v) \rightarrow ACC(x,y,z,v)$

$R1.2. \quad EQ(x,z), EQ(y,z), OPP(z,v) \rightarrow ACC(x,y,z,v)$

$R1.3. \quad EQ(x,z), EQ(z,v), OPP(y,z) \rightarrow ACC(x,y,z,v)$

$R1.4. \quad OPP(z,v), OPP(y,z) \quad \rightarrow ACC(x,y,z,v)$

Now we consider the acceptable actions. An action is acceptable, if it brings a state to another acceptable state. We have the following rule:

$R2. \quad STATE(u,u,z,v) \wedge OPP(u,w) \wedge ACC(w,w,z,v) \rightarrow STATE(w,w,z,v)$

[action: MOVE(wolf)]

This rule says if present state is state(u, u, z, v), the opposite bank is w, and state(w, w, z, v) is acceptable, then we can execute the action MOVE(wolf) to bring the world state to state(w, w, z, v). Three other rules can now be stated.

$R3. \quad STATE(u,y,u,v) \wedge OPP(u,w) \wedge ACC(w,y,w,v) \rightarrow STATE(w,y,w,v)$

[action: MOVE(goat)]

$R4. \quad STATE(u,y,z,u) \wedge OPP(u,w) \wedge ACC(w,y,z,w) \rightarrow STATE(w,y,z,w)$

[action: MOVE(cabbage)]

$R5. \quad STATE(u,y,z,v) \wedge OPP(u,w) \wedge ACC(w,y,z,v) \rightarrow STATE(w,y,z,v)$

[action: MOVE( )]

The specification of the system is now complete. We can use a theorem prover to deduce STATE(N, N, N, N) from the initial state, STATE(S, S, S, S), stated as

$$F1. \quad \rightarrow STATE(S,S,S,S)$$

We use the rules R1.1 through R1.4, and R2 through R5. In making the inference, we will obtain, as a side effect, a sequence of actions, or MOVE commands. This is our plan, which can be executed by the farmer in a real situation.

The foregoing example illustrates how a planner can use a theorem prover (or a production system, and so on) to prove that a sequence of actions can bring the system from world state $S1$ to world state $S2$. The actor can then perform this sequence of actions. After the system reaches the new state, the observer can make new observations, the planner makes new plans, and the actor performs an action sequence, and so on. This strategy can be illustrated by the following program skeleton:

```
while(no-sudden-world-state-change)
    begin
        observe(world-state1);
        plan(world-state1, world-state2, actions);
        act(actions);
    end
```

When the world state is subject to unpredictable external forces, the agent cannot always expect to complete the cycle of observe, plan, and action. When the world state suddenly changes, the agent must react quickly. In living organisms, this is done by reflex actions, which can be expressed by the following program skeleton:

```
On (sudden-world-state-change)
    begin
        quick-observe(world-state);
        reflex-action(world-state, reflex-table);
    end

while(no-sudden-world-state-change)
    begin
        observe(world-state1);
        plan(world-state1, world-state2, actions);
        act(actions);
    end
```

A complex system (multi-robot system, automated factory, office system, human body) usually consists of many interacting agents, which exchange information and reinforce or inhibit one another. The agents may play different roles, such as observer (information gatherer), actor, planner, communicator, filter, information source, information sink, information manager, scheduler, crisis handler, advisor, and so on. The study of these general, complex, distributed information systems will set new directions in advanced information system design as well as pictorial information system design.

R E F E R E N C E S

[BALLARD82] BALLARD, D. H., and C. M. BROWN, *Computer Vision*, Englewood Cliffs, New Jersey, Prentice-Hall, Inc., 1982.

[WOS84] WOS, L., R. OVERBEEK, E. LUSK, and J. BOYLE, *Automated Reasoning: Introduction and Applications*, Englewood Cliffs, New Jersey, Prentice-Hall, Inc., 1984.

Index

C

Cafforie, 104
Castleman, 7, 22, 24, 31, 333, 347
Chain coding, 26
Chang, 43, 49, 77, 122, 189, 231, 271,
    306, 321, 345
Chien, 122, 216
Clarisse, 306
Classifier, 33
    adaptive algorithm, 36
    linear, 35
    minimum distance, 37
    nearest neighbor, 38
    threshold logic realization, 36
Clausal form syntax, 349
Clause, 348
Clique finding algorithm, 162
Clustering, 308, 314
Cognitive aspects in visual information
    processing, 297
Color cube, 12
Computer-aided design (CAD) systems,
    3
Computer-integrated manufacturing
    (CIM) systems, 4
Constructive solid geometry (CSG), 138
Contour following, 47
    graph searching, 50
    tracing, 49
Cosine transform, 92

D

D-map set, 178
Data compression, 82
    binary picture coding, 109
    block truncation coding, 97
    color picture coding, 107
    Laplasian pyramid method, 97
    one-dimensional CCITT coding, 115
    picture sequenced, 103
    predictive coding, 83, 86
    synthetic high coding, 95
    system diagram, 83
    transform coding, 92

two-dimensional CCITT coding, 117
vector quantization (VQ), 100
Decision boundary, 34
    linearly separable, 35
Delp, 84, 97
Dematerialization, 185, 193, 306, 318
DENDRAL, 356
Dietterich, 224
DIMAP system, 173, 189
Discriminant function, 34
    linear, 35
Disparity, 14
DPCM, 83, 86
Dyer, 131

E

Edge detection, 43
    crack edge, 43
    Hough transform, 50
    relaxation method, 43
    resolution pyramid, 38
Entity-relationship (E-R) database, 293
Euclidean distance, 28
Expert system, 356

F

Feature extractor, 33
Feature vector, 33
Fifth generation computer systems, 3
Filter design, 329
Finzer, 273
Fishman, 227
Focused reasoning, 357
Form definition and manipulation
    language, 276
Form specification, 308
Formal specificaton of icon systems, 305
Fourier transform, 17, 325
Frame buffer, 14
Frame, 147
    object-oriented database, 152
    slot, 148

Freeman, 25, 124
Fu, 175, 306

G

Gaussian-Markov model, 84, 89
Glinert, 273
Global operation, 22
GRAIN query language, 202, 204, 206
Graph labeling, 165
  stochastic algorithm, 168
Graph matching, 156
  2D string matching, 239
  algorithms, 162
  attributed graphs, 163
  backtracking, 159
  matching cost, 161
  nonexact matching, 163
  partial graph matching, 160
  query processing, 157
  subgraph matching problem, 158
Gray level transform, 343

H

Hadamard transform, 327
Hayes, 224
Healy, 97
Herot, 295
HI-VISUAL, 287
Histogram, 43, 342
Histogram matching, 343
Hoffman code, 132
Huang, 103, 109
Hue, 13
Hypercube encoding, 124
  generalized, 124
  hierarchical, 128
  PIM-directed method, 130
Hypergraph, 153
  3D object, 154
  attributed, 153

I

Ichikawa, 287
Icon, 56, 122, 130, 228, 235, 254
  complex icon, 318
  definition, 31, 33, 264, 295
  elementary icon, 317
  icon algebra, 311
  icon communication, 278
  icon design, 278
  icon purity, 317
  icon system, 302, 305
  iconic indexing, 235, 254
  iconic languages, 281
  iconic sentence, 302
Image fidelity, 84
Image frame, 14, 186
  staging, 190
Image models (picture models), 84
Image plane, 16, 190
Image store, 188
Image understanding systems, 4
Indexing, 212
  definition, 220
  iconic indexing, 235, 254
  picture index, 217
Inference, 350
  using production systems, 355
  using semantic networks, 353
  using theorem proving, 351
INGRES, 296
Integrated optical density (IOD), 342
Intensity, 12
Interpolated reconstruction, 23

J

Jacob, 272
Jain, 106

K

Kawaguchi, 134
King, 227
Klinger, 122